NON-BULLSHIT
INNOVATION

www.**penguin**.co.uk

NON-BULLSHIT
INNOVATION

Radical Ideas
from the World's
Smartest Minds

DAVID ROWAN

BANTAM PRESS

TRANSWORLD PUBLISHERS
61–63 Uxbridge Road, London W5 5SA
www.penguin.co.uk

Transworld is part of the Penguin Random House group of companies
whose addresses can be found at global.penguinrandomhouse.com

First published in Great Britain in 2019 by Bantam Press
an imprint of Transworld Publishers

A CIP catalogue record for this book is available from the British Library.

ISBNs 9781787631182 (cased)
9781787631199 (tpb)

Typeset in 12/14.75 pt Dante MT Std
by Integra Software Services Pvt. Ltd, Pondicherry

Printed and bound in Great Britain by Clays Ltd, Elcograf S.p.A.

Penguin Random House is committed to a sustainable future for our
business, our readers and our planet. This book is made
from Forest Stewardship Council® certified paper.

1 3 5 7 9 10 8 6 4 2

For Sarah

CONTENTS

Introduction
How my despair at the 'innovation industry'
prompted a global quest   I

1 **Embrace Unmet Needs**
   A corporation re-educates Peru   17

2 **Empower Your Team**
   Lessons from the world's least powerful CEO   43

3 **Hire Pirates**
   Hackers take over the Pentagon   61

4 **Turn Products into Services**
   The bank that performs surgery   80

5 **Enable Moonshots**
   How monkey-training empowers Google's boldest bets   103

6 **Incubate Tomorrow's Business**
   How a swipe beat a match   126

7 **Prototype and Measure**
   An oil nation recalibrates its future   148

8 **Become a Platform**
   A civil servant erases his nation's borders   168

9 **Find Your Blind Spots**
   A software giant reimagines manufacturing   187

10 **Mine the Data**
   China's postmen build a retail search engine   206

11 **Engineer Serendipity**
   What Burning Man gives Silicon Valley   222

12 **Reframe Your Value**
   The airline that rewards walking the dog   243

13 **Build an Ecosystem**
   The phone giant kept alive by 460 startups   262

14 **Leverage Emerging Tech**
   Interactive saucepans and blockchain phones   285

15 **Stretch the Business Model**
   Counter-intuitive paths to profit   309

16 **Exploit a Crisis**
   India's bed-linen king embraces transparency   331

Last Word
Reflecting on an innovation quest   346
Acknowledgements   355
Index   361

INTRODUCTION

How my despair at the 'innovation industry'
prompted a global quest

I finally hit the limit of my tolerance for corporate innovation's spuriously sophisticated bullshit at the opening networking party for 'Innova-Con' – the annual convention of the International Association of Innovation Professionals (IAOIP). It's late February 2018 and I'm at a drinks reception in a room above Washington DC's International Spy Museum, being handed a red cocktail napkin on which a set of interlinked circles has just been hastily drawn. Above the hubbub Brett Trusko, the association's clean-cut president and CEO, is on a mission to convince me that innovation can be reduced to a repeatable formula. He's labelled the three overlapping circles on the napkin 'Social Science', 'Hard Science' and 'Business', and as a small crowd gathers Trusko proceeds to explain that the drawing represents the scientific formula for innovation.

'We're talking about the intersection between social science, ethnography, that kinda stuff,' he says with conviction, warming to the delegates' attention. 'There's hard science, which is engineering, math, et cetera; and business. This in the middle' – he places his pen's nib on the segment where they overlap – 'is where innovation science exists. And this is where we've got a problem – because in universities, all three are siloed.'

Trusko, a genial man in his mid-fifties with the targeted charm of a door-to-door brush salesman, warns me that such silos are blocking innovation. 'How many times does an engineer sit in his office, and a businessperson comes in and says, "Hey, we should build a bridge between New York and London, it will be awesome!" The engineer says this person is stupid. Then the engineer comes and says, "I just invented the greatest laptop ever, twice as fast as

anything that exists now, and it only costs $80,000 to manufacture."
The businessperson says, "What?!"' That is where Trusko's association fits in. Through its webinars, its certification programme, its
online iBoK (Innovation Body of Knowledge) and 'transformation-
leader' events such as Innova-Con, the IAOIP sees itself as breaking
down those walls, empowering the change-makers, and pushing
the world forward using the magical formula on the napkin.

Over two days, I will learn all about the supposed 'science' of
innovation and the many ways Trusko has positioned his organization as the home of 'innovation thought leadership'. Trusko, a
former accountant, business consultant and data scientist based in
Sugar Land, Texas, came to the innovation business when he took
over the *International Journal of Innovation Science* almost a decade
ago. He had been watching TV one evening when he saw three
commercials from companies that were all claiming to be innovators; one was for Dole, a fruit company, which made him wonder
how the hell fruit could be innovative unless they were growing
purple bananas. 'I thought, we have to professionalize this,' he
recalls. There are more people with 'innovation' in their job titles
than accountants, he says, yet too often they're unaware of the science that could bring them repeatable results. Only last week he
was in Saudi Arabia and Abu Dhabi, where three companies in three
days asked him to conduct workshops for their chief innovation officers and explain to them what innovation actually *is*. 'I had four
hours to tell them it's about culture, strategy, training, having the
right people. I said, "I'm going to orient you to what's going on in
your organization." I call it giving them an "invitation to innovate".'

Demand for Trusko's services is booming. After four years, the
IAOIP, registered as a non-profit, has 1,600 members in eighty-five
countries, with Trusko boldly forecasting 10,000 by 2020, and 20,000
by 2023. Members can take courses to 'gain skills in the science of
innovation', working towards professional qualifications such
as a Certified Manager of Innovation ($400 to pass) or a Certified
Chief Innovation Officer ($1,150). They pay just $110 for the *Global*

Innovation Science Handbook and a subscription to the *International Journal of Innovation Science*, whose combined retail value is normally $550. They can also access the newly launched IAOIP Academy, a 'learning management system' offering online courses, and they can buy places on immersion tours of Silicon Valley. And, as mentioned, there are the webinars – this month's is titled 'How to Identify Blockers and Amplifiers for Innovation'. Trusko, meanwhile, is also building a speakers' bureau and working on a book, provisionally titled 'Sex Wasn't Invented in Silicon Valley'.

As I look around the party, I notice one gentleman wearing a Bluetooth hands-free phone earpiece as he socializes. A friendly lady with a southern accent hands me a beer bottle, and I try to twist off the resistant cap. 'Be innovative! Put the cap on the edge of the table and hit it,' advises Jon Monett, a retired CIA technical operations specialist and US Air Force veteran who has just lectured at the Spy Museum about 'innovating on the fly'. When Monett retired, he started a security and intelligence advisory company and established a non-profit called Quality of Life Plus at Cal Poly in San Luis Obispo, California, to 'foster innovations that improve the quality of life of those injured in the line of duty'. Our conversation turns to tools and strategies for innovating, and I learn about TIPS – the theory of inventive problem-solving, based on a Soviet analytics and forecasting tool.

Brett's wife Kirsten Trusko, who runs her own advisory firm (her business card promises 'Deeds not Words'), joins our group and tells me that most corporate innovators 'have arrows in their back and don't survive'. That's why the association is developing practical tools to support the innovators, and is working with the International Organization for Standardization to develop ISO 279, the global standard of innovation management. Kirsten introduces me to John Wolverton, a retired US Air Force commander now with Sandia National Laboratories, who earlier today led a certification exam review session for Innova-Con delegates on the subject of innovation tools and methodologies.

Wolverton, tall, long-haired, and with a booming voice, typifies the hunger for stimulating ideas and yet the jaded expectation of their unscientific misapplication that I encounter repeatedly at the conference. He has, for instance, some very strong views on why most corporate innovators get killed. 'Have you read *The 48 Laws of Power* [by Robert Greene]?' he asks me. 'What's the first law? "Never outshine the master". Every time I succeed as an innovator, it's when I have a boss who is much smarter than me. Law number three? Conceal your intentions if you want to survive.' As I put down my beer and grab my notebook, Wolverton shares some of what he's learned as an innovator and innovation trainer in an intense ten-minute booklist-filled, anecdote-packed, hard-to-interrupt stream of observations:

'My mentor, [the management consultant and author] Robert Fritz, said: "Reality is an acquired taste." The biggest challenge I see time and again going into an organization: people cannot deal with reality . . . When Dr John Gorrie invented air-conditioning, the icemakers almost destroyed the guy. Because he was taking business from them. So often you have organizational icemakers blocking change . . . Einstein working in a patent office found forty invention principles, seventy-six tools, and I could teach you how to use them to consistently create innovation. The problem is, nobody studies this material, and they throw away the tools and listen to the last person who speaks . . . If someone says it's stupid, it's probably a good idea. Almost every innovation is stupid . . .' And so on.

Wolverton's conviction that innovation can be taught as a repeatable scientific process proves to be a reliable scene-setter for the next day's full-schedule conference in the city centre's Booz Allen Hamilton Innovation Center. It's an appropriate venue for the innovation professionals' meeting: the building contains both a Sandbox – 'an open-source innovation space and catalyst for ideas open to creators, thinkers and doers' – and a Solutions Studio, which 'connects the dots' across Booz Allen 'to accelerate solution delivery'. I've entered, I'm reminded, the realm of inno-babble. There are touchscreens, virtual-reality headsets, interactive whiteboards and plenty of Post-it Notes – the corporate world's preferred contemporary signals of transformative change-making.

The conference features stage sessions on idea management, innovation metrics, blockchain-driven innovation, creating an innovation ecosystem, and building innovation spaces. Speakers have come to share innovation strategies from Atlanta Airport, universities, consulting firms – even the military-industrial complex. Captain Steven Lauver gives an intriguing talk about a technology accelerator called AFWERX that he runs for the US Air Force. It brings in startups to work on national security challenges, and Lauver calls it 'an innovation programme to make us more lethal, capable and effective as a force'. And if he meets bureaucratic resistance to change? 'A general, sometimes a president, can help remove some of these systems barriers,' he says without a pause.

During a networking break, I meet Magnus Penker, who describes himself on LinkedIn as 'an internationally renowned thought leader' and who runs a Stockholm-based consultancy called Innovati°n360 ('The Home of Innovation'). He gives me a copy of his book *How to Assess and Measure Business Innovation*, the first of a dense five-volume series called *The Complete Guide to Business Innovation*, and explains that he, too, believes innovation can be reduced to a science. Penker has studied leadership approaches inside 6,000 companies, he explains, measuring everything from openness to clarity of vision. 'I'm called in to advise all sorts of companies from the Pentagon to unicorns,' he tells me. 'We post ninety-two questions to the whole organization, and compare and contrast the results with data from those 6,000 companies.' His website calls this methodology both InnoSurvey® and also InnoSurvey™, the superscript symbols presumably meant to warn rival innovation scientists to stay away from Penker's intellectual property.

By six p.m. on day one of the two-day event, my notebook resembles a traveller's phrasebook of foreign idioms: I've been taught about MVVs (mission, vision, values), designathons, bootcamps and a-ha moments; reinforcing value propositions and focusing on asks not tasks; failing fast and implementing that in my horizons. One speaker suggests moving the office furniture every night to force staff to interact differently; another talks mystifyingly of a playbook being a toolkit which helps move the needle forward. The blockchain presentation in particular contains jargon so esoteric that I have to confess I may not have fully understood its insights into 'transactionalization', 'abstractification' and 'self-healing swarm behaviour'. And the data points, the scientifically measured (if typically unsourced) data points. I learn that radical innovators 'have 51 per cent stronger capabilities in decision-making than incremental improvers'. That '72 per cent of people have creative insights in the shower'. That '95 per cent of all new product development initiatives fail to meet return on investment'.

But I can't get it out of my head that corporate innovation, that process of renewing a business to create future value in the face of changing realities, seems just too quirkily organic, too messily human, to be reduced to a scientific formula. The cover stars that sell copies of *WIRED* – the Musks, the Jobses, the Björks – never approach innovation from a formulaic perspective. They're difficult, complex, troublemaking creatures who somehow inspire followers to execute on bold, radical visions within specific cultural contexts. And their formulae are certainly not simplistically repeatable, otherwise Nokia might still be challenging the likes of Apple as an in-demand maker of smartphones.

I put my concerns during a networking break to Abram Walton, deputy editor of the *International Journal of Innovation Science*, chief operating officer of the association, and a thoughtful man who straddles the intellectual and commercial silos: a tenured professor of management at the Florida Institute of Technology while still in his late thirties, he's also been a Walmart store manager and a fireman. Surely, I say, the corporate delegates in the room can't all be scientists? 'The professional innovator is a translator,' he says. 'Cross-pollinating is what innovators do. The methodology of how you say this has market value, that's the science piece.' I'm still not clear. Walton explains that his own innovation company, which he runs in addition to his various day jobs, consults for clients such as NASA and General Electric, all of them engineered for the industrial age rather than for what's coming. They're paralysed by political inertia, organizational dysfunction, dislocated structures. 'So they call my team in to be a translator between all their teams. Because industries don't disrupt themselves from within. The science is pretty clear now. If you follow these techniques, then this is what could happen. It's like building a house.'

I catch Trusko as he comes off stage. His talk, to around eighty people, listed 'the greatest inventions of all time' – fire, wheel, nails, optical lenses, that sort of thing – as well as 'the most innovative people', from Ben Franklin to Charles Babbage. 'And how many of these were in Silicon Valley?' he asked, before making the point (interrupted only by his cellphone ringing) that true innovation doesn't happen in tech clusters that build apps for rich people. Hence his book title. 'Although when I give that talk in the Middle East,' he tells me, 'I have to change it from "sex" to "the wheel" not being invented in Silicon Valley.'

As a kid, Trusko wanted to be a doctor and applied to medical school, before being sidetracked by business classes and accountancy. But that's been for the best, he says. 'If I'd been a physician, I could have helped one person at a time. Maybe now I can help thousands. The problems of today's world are becoming so complicated, it can't just be some guy in an R&D [research and development] department trying to solve them.' His mission, he says, is to bring innovation to the world by making available more certified professionals. If you're building a team, he explains, you need to hire a Lionel Messi first – a star performer who will inspire fellow players. Trusko's job is to train more Messis.

'Steve Jobs said, make your dent on the universe,' he reflects. 'I hope one day someone will collect their Nobel Prize for solving climate change, and they learned things from us.'

As I leave, he gives me a sticker depicting a skull and crossbones, the IAOIP logo and the words 'Pirates wanted'. I say gently that Innova-Con doesn't seem particularly subversive to me. 'It's that other Steve Jobs quote, "Don't join the navy, become a pirate",' Trusko says. 'Let's figure out the rules on our own terms.'

The International Association of Innovation Professionals, I later discover, faces substantial competition. There's an International Society for Professional Innovation Management, formed in Norway in 1983; a Global Innovation Institute, run out of Grand Rapids in Michigan; and also a Global Innovation Management Institute, based in Cambridge, Massachusetts. If you're a corporate innovator in search of professional development courses, certification, internationally recognized standards, tools, publications, applied research and networking opportunities, well, these are golden times indeed.

Corporate innovation – let's define it as 'fresh approaches that deliver new value to an organization and its customers' – has never been so urgently sought. And that's largely because of the unavoidable demands of technology, which tends to show little respect for existing revenue streams or legacy processes. From retail to real estate, leadership teams are scrambling to transform, digitize, upend business models and generally avoid obliteration as technologies from computer processing to genomic sequencing advance at an exponential pace. Gordon Moore, the Intel co-founder, became famous for his 1965 observation in *Electronics* magazine that the number of transistors on a computer chip seemed to double every year. What became Moore's Law – adjusted to a doubling every eighteen to twenty-four months – defined the falling costs of computer processing and storage, which still continues; but a similar exponential curve is also slashing the price of solar-energy generation, genetic discovery, nanotechnology, digital fabrication and much more.

This matters, because exponential curves, by their nature, eventually turn something that was scarce and expensive into something commodified and cost-immaterial. A utility company that operates gas-fired power stations finds itself out-competed over time by a neighbourhood grid whose members share energy generated by cheap solar panels. Conventional health insurance becomes irrelevant in an era when every patient's DNA can be accessed to provide personalized treatments. Internal-combustion-engine cars become economically unviable when falling battery costs, and advancing machine learning, make autonomous electric vehicles an obvious customer preference.

For incumbent businesses, the dangers are manifold. Barriers to market entry are falling in almost every sector, as startups take advantage of benefits such as 'cloud and crowd' – the ease of using low-cost cloud computing and of raising capital through crowdfunding. Technology adoption curves in a networked world are also getting shorter: the telephone took around fifty years to reach 50 million users, the iPod four years, and Pokémon Go just nineteen days. And decision-making has moved from hierarchical organizations to consumers, empowered as never before by social media.

The lifespan of large corporations as a result is shortening. Richard N. Foster, a former McKinsey director who described a theory of 'creative destruction', calculated that the average tenure of an S&P 500 company in the US fell from sixty-one years in 1958 to eighteen years by 2012. A similar UK study by Rita Gunther McGrath found that, of the hundred companies in the FTSE 100 in 1984, only twenty-four were still there in 2012. Trusted brands, heritage, supply-chain advantage and vast advertising budgets all counted for nothing when these companies were too slow to react. Even the disrupted incumbents' digitally native replacements are worried. Facebook's employee handbook states bluntly: 'If we don't create the thing that kills Facebook, something else will.'

As editor-in-chief for eight years of the UK edition of *WIRED*, the magazine about how emerging technologies are changing the world, I would regularly meet corporate executives from banks and insurers and industrial-legacy companies who assured me that they 'got it' and were 'doing' innovation. They had read Clayton Christensen's 1997 bestseller *The Innovator's Dilemma*, and they could talk about disruptive technologies introducing simplicity, convenience and affordability in markets where high costs and complication are the norm. Some of them could even quote Jack Welch's observation that 'If the rate of change on the outside exceeds the rate of change on the inside, the end is near.'

Invariably I'd ask these executives to share any concrete outcomes from their innovation projects that were starting to transform the business or its thinking. And the typical response was that it was too early in the process to define actual results, but all the fundamentals were in place. Their chief innovation officer, or their startup incubator, or their innovation lab, would be their agent of transformation, supported by hackathons, ideas portals, startup investments and pilgrimages to Silicon Valley. And would I speak about startups at their company offsite to inspire the team?

I'd often instinctively think of the Looney Tunes cartoons in which Road Runner chases Wile E. Coyote off a cliff and he keeps running – until he looks down, realizes that he has not been on solid ground for a while, and then gravity belatedly and painfully returns him to reality.

Too often what is celebrated as innovation inside these large organizations is in fact 'innovation theatre' – a box-ticking, public-relations-led, self-reassuring alternative to radical changes in mindset and culture, just as 'security theatre' at the airport does little to increase actual security but does annoy passengers as per the protocol. I despair even at the fashionable new corporate job titles: the 'innovation catalysts', 'innovation sherpas', 'chief disruptive growth operators' and 'digital prophets'. At times, parody seems the most lucid response. Above my desk I keep a cutting from *The Onion*, reporting during the South by Southwest (SXSW) interactive-technology conference (frequented by the big corporates) that the word 'innovate' was being mentioned 'at a rate of 8.2 times per second, and at that pace we can estimate it will be uttered approximately 24 million times before the festival ends'. The phrase 'potential game-changer' had also been heard 230,000 times, *The Onion* continued, but there had been zero uses of the phrases 'investment model', 'practical business strategy' or 'economic realities'.

Still, I suspected that there was some genuinely exciting non-bullshit innovation out there somewhere, delivering real results inside successful legacy organizations. I just needed to find it, and to understand the conditions that enabled it. So I decided to embark upon a global quest to uncover compelling yet impactful approaches to transformation. Because I was still not convinced that innovation is as simple as a scientific formula.

My journey began with a visit to meet one of the most accomplished European tech entrepreneurs of the past decade, a man who took a fast-declining incumbent industry and somehow persuaded it to save itself by killing its current business model. Back in 2006, Daniel Ek, the CEO and co-founder of Spotify, was repeatedly rebuffed when he told the record labels that they should stop selling expensive plastic discs at huge margins, and instead give away their music for frictionless digital streaming. Eventually Ek persuaded almost all the main labels to work with Spotify – which ended its first day as a public company, in April 2018, valued at $26.5 billion.

On the wall above Ek's desk in his Stockholm office is a Fender Stratocaster and a George Bernard Shaw quotation: 'The reasonable man adapts himself to the world. The unreasonable one persists in trying to adapt the world to himself. Therefore all progress depends on the unreasonable man.' I ask him what his extraordinary and resilient journey has taught him about genuine innovation.

'So many companies talk about innovation, and they try to put processes in place,' Ek says. 'I don't think that works. I don't think any innovation happens at a desk – by someone structuring a creative brainstorm. Innovation is serendipity. It happens when people get totally new influences or ideas that come totally from the sidelines. It almost never happens with someone who's been staring at a problem for long enough.' You need team diversity, he suggests – not just of gender or ethnicity, but of thinking, of income levels, of educational backgrounds.

There's a reason, Ek adds, why the most successful startups are built around notions that come from the sidelines. 'Take Airbnb – built by people with no experience of the hotel business, no understanding of how it even works. Or me: I didn't know anything about the music industry; that's what made me successful. I didn't understand why things were the way they were. Instead of saying, "Oh, labels will never change," I just came at the problem from "This is how I think the world ought to be". You need to be the unreasonable man in some circumstances. That's how innovation happens.'

There certainly seems to be something in the notion of hybrid thinking. In 1959, the US Department of Defense agency that became DARPA (the Defense Advanced Research Projects Agency) was determined that a new ballistic missile defence system should be designed in the most creative way possible. Isaac Asimov was commissioned to write an essay on creativity, which began with a question: 'How do people get new ideas?' The theory of evolution by natural selection, Asimov noted, had been independently arrived at by Charles Darwin and Alfred Wallace at around the same time. Both had travelled extensively as they observed how plants and animals varied according to their surroundings, but both had also failed to find an explanation until they happened to read Thomas Malthus's *An Essay on the Principle of Population.* 'What is needed is not only people with a good background in a particular field,' Asimov concluded, 'but also people capable of making a connection between item 1 and item 2 which might not ordinarily seem connected . . . The ability to make a cross-connection is the rare characteristic that must be found. It is only afterward that a new idea seems reasonable.'

Asimov also noted that the greatest new ideas have tended to come from people who were working on something else, and thus were free to experiment without the burden of responsibility. These people 'weren't paid to have great ideas, but were paid to be teachers or patent clerks or petty officials, or were not paid at all. The great ideas came as side issues.' Which, if true, does not bode well for innovation professionals as a species.

Intrigued by the notion of the small, hybrid, empowered team as the gateway to transformative thinking, I searched for an example of a legacy corporation that has somehow built an internal startup experiencing extraordinary growth. If my quest for non-bullshit corporate innovation were to succeed, I sensed, I'd need to validate my premise by proving that such outlier examples exist.

It's in India that I found such an example – inside the media conglomerate 21st Century Fox, whose assets range from movie studios to TV networks. In 2015, its Mumbai-based Star India subsidiary launched a streaming-video service called Hotstar that, by summer 2018, had 150 million monthly active users, had had its mobile app downloaded more than 350 million times, and had established a new record of 10.3 million concurrent viewers watching an Indian Premier League cricket match. Viewers can watch without paying to subscribe, and 90 per cent of consumption is via mobile phones – thus directly challenging Star India's broadcast-based business model. So in August 2018 I travelled to Jaipur, in India's Rajasthan state, to meet Hotstar executives at a company offsite.

The first thing I discover is that, for all its corporate heritage, Hotstar is run independently with the culture of a fast-growth technology startup, with full permission to cannibalize the parent company's existing revenue streams. 'There was no fear of us disrupting the existing business,' CEO Ajit Mohan, formerly a consultant with McKinsey and Arthur D. Little, tells me. 'We saw expanding access to smartphone and internet consumption in India, and we thought, let's chase this even at the expense of broadcast television and blow up the current business.' So it's offering free advertising-supported programming in multiple languages as well as subscription packages.

Second, Hotstar sees itself as a technology company first, rather than an entertainment company. It tracks more than 2 billion data points a day to personalize the user experience, and is investing heavily in artificial intelligence. Of 330 staff, a hundred work on product and engineering, and hiring world-class tech talent is a priority. 'Our goal is to attract the top 1 per cent and inspire them to do the best work of their lives,' explains Varun Narang, in charge of product and technology, whose most important daily meeting concerns potential new hires. 'Then everything is a hot knife through butter.'

And third, it is importing execution strategies and cultural norms from digitally native companies such as Amazon, where Narang spent two years. 'Jeff Bezos's fundamental belief is that small teams of the right people can do amazing things and move really fast,' he says. Bezos famously instituted a 'two-pizza rule': that every internal Amazon team should be small enough that it can be fed by two pizzas. At Hotstar, technology and product teams organize themselves in 'pods' of fewer than ten people, who set their own targets and metrics, and iterate their strategies as they prototype, test, learn and optimize.

'It boils down to hiring smart people who want to work on difficult, interesting problems that affect millions of people and be stimulated each day,' Narang says. 'And they want to work in bullshit-free environments. Most companies are so mired in politics, and we want to minimize that.' Plus, he says, life is too short not to have fun at work. 'Put all those factors together, and magic happens.' It's a formula that Hotstar will be exporting around the world, adds Ajit Mohan, who has since been hired to run Facebook in India.

I'm intrigued that innovation hacks from companies such as Amazon are being imported into other organizations as a shortcut towards shifting a culture. I discover something similar happening even at London's Natural History Museum – the original dinosaur institution, literally and metaphorically, which opened its doors in

1881 in South Kensington and has lately had to confront declining visitor numbers and uncertain government funding. I learn from one of the museum's more recently appointed trustees, Simon Patterson, a managing director at the technology investors Silver Lake Partners, that the museum's leadership has committed to turning a legacy academic organization into a modern digital business. Silver Lake is the firm that led a majority purchase of Skype from eBay at a $2.75 billion valuation in 2009 – and twenty months later sold Skype to Microsoft for $8.5 billion. Could such a turn-around mindset help transform a 900-person Victorian institution staffed mainly by scientists?

Sure enough, as the museum slowly digitizes its vast collection and finds new ways to engage with consumers via smartphones, it is hiring outsiders to challenge its legacy thinking. Piers Jones, appointed as chief digital and product officer in 2016, previously worked at Amazon Video and before that at the *Guardian*'s digital business. He and his team have brought in a goal-setting tool from Google called 'objectives and key results', hired 'user experience' teams as at the *Guardian*, replicated Amazon and Facebook hiring processes for technology roles, and emphasized a 'product mindset' that challenges existing museum thinking.

It's early in the museum's innovation journey, but there are already symbolic changes happening. As one example, teams now adopt an Amazon process at the start of planning a new project. It's known as the 'working backward' process, and it's intended to align every stakeholder in creating an agreed customer experience. It starts with participants collaborating on writing a detailed press release that's due to be issued at the very end of the project. 'So we've written our press release for 2020, describing what we'd like the public-facing museum experience to look like,' Jones explains. 'Everyone writes a paragraph of the press release, which includes some of the metrics we expect to hit, some quotes from a customer on what they're enjoying, and an internal quote from the director of the museum on what we've achieved. It helps build collaborative, empowered teams focused on agreed objectives, with an agreed business case behind it.'

What, though, of the organizations that have already achieved measurable results by applying innovation approaches that the rest of us can learn from? What about the lessons from China's extraordinary entrepreneurial blossoming as ubiquitous mobile phones have built new markets; from the European industrial-legacy companies that have against all odds become digital-first; from even national governments that have rethought the very nature of the modern nation state?

It was time to delve deeper and hit the road in search of nonbullshit strategies that really deliver.

I

EMBRACE UNMET NEEDS

A corporation re-educates Peru

Do fish sleep?

An animated classroom of seven-year-olds, sitting in well-ordered circles of six, has just been set a challenge to find out. In neat blue jackets over clean white T-shirts, the children excitedly open their HP laptops and start working together in their groups to see what the internet has to say. It's just another morning of blended learning at Innova Cercado school on Sánchez Pinillos Avenue in central Lima, located between the Universitario football stadium and the National Museum of Peruvian Culture. Pupils seem to waste no time in finding the correct answer (yes, fish sleep, but in a daydreaming, open-eyed way), but that doesn't stress the teacher: she can always use her phone to choose from another 26,000 lessons in the school's cloud database.

This generously equipped 6,000-square-metre school, built from scratch on the site of an old convent just three years ago, is home to 1,100 students from a bars-on-windows, economically insecure neighbourhood that could euphemistically be described as 'in transition'. Yet in a nation that's consistently near-bottom of the Organisation for Economic Co-operation and Development's PISA educational attainment rankings, Innova Cercado parents have committed typically between 15 and 25 per cent of their income to their children's education here. Bright vinyl awnings hanging over the airy courtyard suggest some of the values they have bought into: 'Group learning', says one, in English; 'Design thinking', another. A vision statement dominating the modern staff-room wall goes further: 'Lograr que los niños del Perú tengan acceso a una educación de estándares internacionales,' it says – 'ensuring that Peru's children have access to a world-class education.'

That aspiration isn't hype. Innova Cercado is part of a fast-growing chain of forty-nine low-cost, high-quality private schools in Peru called 'Innova Schools', created with the San Francisco design agency IDEO in consultation with educationists from Harvard and Berkeley. IDEO rethought: the full curriculum for ages four to eighteen; the teacher-training course; the buildings; the use of technology to complement classroom activities; in fact the entire system of schooling, all with the goal of providing a scalable international-quality education at an affordable price. At an average monthly fee of $130 it's a profitable business, but it's also delivering academically: in national maths and communications tests, Innova pupils are scoring double the national average. But what's even more remarkable about Innova is its ownership structure. This is a school network built and owned by Intercorp, a banks-to-supermarkets conglomerate that accounts for almost 4 per cent of Peru's gross domestic product.

Why would a 78,000-person, $8-billion-revenue corporation want to run a chain of schools? The answer starts with the failure of government. Peru has gone through fifteen education ministers in fifteen years, four of them in the past two years alone. None has confronted the poor standards of public and private education in a way that has significantly boosted results. So when Intercorp's president and CEO Carlos Rodríguez-Pastor worried how his business would attract the qualified talent it needed to keep expanding – not to mention the aspirational middle-class customers it needed to keep buying its products and services – he made a radical decision. If government was not meeting Peru's needs, Intercorp would itself build the education system that the country lacked.

Intercorp would begin educating children at kindergarten level, and would even build the university that prepared them for the job market. It would serve the rising middle class more effectively and efficiently than the existing state and private schools, offering better value, and in a scalable way. But this was no philanthropic gesture. The schools would be a profitable business unit of Intercorp. Otherwise how would their future be assured?

'Peru won't be a sustainable country long-term if we don't improve the access gap to good education,' Jorge Yzusqui explains as we walk past children running on to Innova Cercado's AstroTurf sports pitch. 'You can't live in a country where access to good education is for just 5 to 7 per cent.'

Peru, a country of 32 million people, has 9 million students, a quarter of them attending 12,000 private schools. Fees for the best schools average around $1,000 a month, but overall results are poor. Yzusqui, who has two children of his own and two adopted Ukrainian orphans, had long wanted to do something to fix the disparity. He took matters into his own hands in 2005 when, after a twenty-year career in logistics, he quit his job, at the age of forty-five, and used his savings to start San Felipe Neri, a small 100-pupil school in Los Olivos, north Lima. His goal was simple: he wanted to show that it was possible to provide affordable quality education for the emerging middle class while generating profit.

By 2009, he had three schools. One day Carlos Rodríguez-Pastor arrived with five executives for a tour. A week later he invited Yzusqui to lunch and said that he wanted to invest. 'I didn't understand why a bank, insurance and retail business wanted to invest in education,' Yzusqui, a commanding presence with greying hair, in grey jeans, black puffer jacket and soft fabric shoes, recalls. But CRP – the name by which Rodríguez-Pastor is known inside his company – explained that Intercorp's future depended on education. 'He asked how many schools I wanted. I thought, and said fifty. He said, "Why not a hundred?"'

Yzusqui, now fifty-eight, became a minority shareholder in what was renamed Innova Schools, and Intercorp hired IDEO to scale up the project. If it were going to provide international-quality education at an affordable price in scores more locations, Innova would need to rethink its approach: Peru faced a shortage of trained teachers, for a start, and land prices were rising fast. Under Sandy Speicher, who runs its education practice from San Francisco, IDEO assembled system designers, interaction designers, ethnographers, architects, educators, communication designers, business designers and more; the design team embedded in Lima and interviewed hundreds of parents and observed them in their homes.

IDEO specializes not only in physical products (a mouse for Apple; a toothpaste tube for Procter & Gamble) but in organizational design (alternative economic opportunities for Iceland after the banking crisis; new approaches to education for the Kellogg Foundation). It became famous for 'design thinking'. This is an approach to solving problems that seeks to understand how people will use a product or service by observing and empathizing with them. A cross-disciplinary team typically studies how people behave, and then brainstorms ways to address their key human needs. Prototypes are then tested with an open mind, before a product is finally launched.

After visiting exceptional schools around the world and studying how other industries thought about scale, Speicher's team saw an opportunity in 'blended learning' – designing hands-on classroom experiences alongside optimized online learning. A central digital lesson bank would support teachers and let them (and parents) monitor pupils' work online; classrooms would be designed around flexibility, with furniture on wheels and spaces easily reconfigurable. The team produced financial calculations and put together a twenty-year plan, involving opening six or seven new schools a year. On average it costs $6 million to open a school, initially with 350 pupils but going up to 1,500. The chain is also expanding internationally, and in 2018 opened a school in Cuautitlán Izcalli, in Mexico. That year the business also hit profitability.

'We're working for our country, making a profit, and improving education,' Yzusqui says as we walk past a playground that is about to fill with desks as a flexible outdoor lunch area. At $130 a month, he says, fees are only $200 more a year than the government invests in high-school students, but the students here have far better outcomes. Plus high-potential pupils from families earning less than $600 a month can have three-quarters of their fees paid by the Perú Champs foundation, a non-profit set up by Intercorp. By 2023, he says, there will be 100 schools reaching 100,000 students. 'Our main problem is finding enough teachers, of a high enough quality,' he explains. 'So we're also creating our own teacher-training academy.'

Six kilometres further south in Lima, in Intercorp's eccentrically shaped Interbank Tower, Andrea Portugal in the Innova Schools open-plan back office is building that academy. Every year, she explains, a fifth of Innova teachers leave their jobs; with the new school openings, that leaves an annual shortfall of 1,000 teachers. Portugal's team is working with experts from Berkeley and Harvard; and to optimize efficiency, they have studied clinical practice inside training hospitals to understand how mentorship can spread knowledge quickly. The academy, due to open in spring 2019, will also teach social and emotional skills over a five-year course. This, too, is a business: most student teachers will pay around $200 a month. Still, on graduating they will have the chance to work at Innova.

Yet Intercorp isn't stopping there. Of Peru's 300,000 annual school-leavers, only half are working or studying a year later. This bothers Jorge Yzusqui. 'They're called "ninis" – ni trabajo, ni estudios,' he tells me – 'neither working nor studying'. 'We have getting on for 2 million ninis, and every year is adding 150,000 more. This is a bomb for our country.'

So Intercorp is developing a six-month course to prepare school-leavers for university tests. Again, this is a for-profit venture: students can pay their way by taking a part-time entry-level job in an Intercorp company, which helps the company fill low-skill roles. And then there are the universities themselves. Not satisfied with the existing quality of technical education, Intercorp decided to build its own version of MIT. Five years ago it created Universidad

Tecnológica del Perú (UTP), which now teaches 60,000 students job-market-based technical skills in five buildings in central Lima, four more on the city's outskirts, and two more in the provinces.

Jonathan Golergant, UTP's academic director, walks Yzusqui and me through rooms packed with 3D printers, mobile radio masts, shipping navigation simulators and Kuka industrial robots. Courses, he explains, are typically designed with input from Intercorp companies: the Intercorp packaging business San Miguel Industrias, for instance, couldn't find enough workers proficient in injection processes, so UTP developed a course taught by the company's production manager. More than 90 per cent of graduates are in work two months after graduation, earning an average of $700 a month, rising a year later to $1,000, which is three or four times what they invested each month in tuition. Many of them are hired by Intercorp for strategic roles (which has proved an effective way to find talented app developers). 'We want to be the engine that transforms the lives of thousands of students across Peru,' Golergant says. 'We have the highest employability rate for universities in Peru. And we're linking our programmes to the needs of the labour market.'

In a corridor near the cafeteria, a giant mural displays one of the university's key messages: 'Desaprende para aprender' (Unlearn to learn). 'Unlearning is so difficult, but you need to do it every day,' insists Yzusqui, who's on the university's board. I ask him if it isn't a little strange for a banking conglomerate to be building an education arm in such a contrarian way. 'The purpose of Intercorp is to make Peru the best place for young families in Latin America,' he replies firmly. 'We *need* to provide education. It's about values – how can we do this while developing our business and also solving important problems?'

In a gated street in the high-crime residential Lima neighbourhood of La Victoria, two dozen product designers, ethnographers, architects, economists, molecular biologists, industrial designers, philosophers and entrepreneurs are working from a conjoined pair of houses on what they call 'human-centred innovation'. This is La Victoria Lab, an informal hacker space created with IDEO to bring together interdisciplinary teams to solve business problems across Intercorp's portfolio. It's a space packed with Post-it Notes, whiteboards, graffiti wall art and posters imploring agile behaviour. 'Think big, start small, move fast' shouts one, inspired by the Mayo Clinic, based in Rochester, Minnesota. 'Tunking is an act of love' says another. Maria Paula Loayza, an industrial designer in the lab, explains that 'tunking' is an in-house term for giving harsh direct feedback with a lot of love. 'It's a cultural thing in Peru – people find it hard to give honest feedback,' she explains. 'The word gives them permission.'

Working on a laptop on an upstairs sofa, a researcher from Innova Schools is thinking through ways to attract vulnerable families to apply for places. Downstairs, activity centres on the kitchen, which Loayza describes as 'the heart of the family'. The family metaphor is deliberate: team members embed themselves in the daily lives of neighbouring Peruvian families to understand their needs and aspirations. Their target rising-middle-class families live in neighbourhoods like La Victoria. Four other Intercorp companies have set up nearby houses for prototyping their own future business lines.

'At La Victoria Lab we do three things,' explains Hernán Carranza, the lab's thirty-nine-year-old CEO and founder. 'We transform Intercorp's thirty-four companies and help them face the future; we create the next Intercorp; and we celebrate.' An example of 'celebration' was a two-day ideas festival the lab organized ten days before my visit, with 2,500 staff from the corporation plus thirteen speakers mainly from China, to explore how Chinese businesses are scaling so fast. Speed, scale and bold ideas are central to executing the mission Intercorp formally aligned itself behind in March 2018: to make Peru the best country in the region in which to raise a family.

It seems genuinely meant, and is partly a response to Peru's particular late-twentieth-century history of domestic terrorism. 'I grew up during a war, with so many bombs going off every week in the streets, on the beach, that you got used to it,' Carranza recalls. 'You'd have no power for days, every window on your block was smashed, and it was too dangerous to go to the movie theatre.' The Shining Path guerrilla movement was active until the early years of this century, and its local power bases made Intercorp's expansion of its retail business in the provinces a high-risk investment. So the corporation became comfortable with unusual degrees of risk. Linked to that, Carranza says, most of Intercorp's top leaders are driven by a nationalistic determination to make Peru a better country for their children.

Yet unlike some of its neighbours, Peru lacks talent trained overseas with a growth mindset and technical skills. So Carlos Rodríguez-Pastor made it a priority to retain and nurture gifted individuals whenever he discovered them. When Carranza told the company he was leaving for university in 2009 after five years' service, he was surprised to receive a personal phone call from CRP asking if there was anything that could persuade him to stay. Carranza thought it was a colleague playing a prank on him and slammed the phone down, muttering a curse. CRP called back and patiently explained that he was indeed the group CEO, and offered to fund Carranza's studies if he would consider returning afterwards. 'He's done that with fifty people,' Carranza tells me. 'For him then to imagine me today as an agent of change is a skill few people have.'

A few days after receiving CRP's call, Carranza went to see him. He suggested the corporation launch a group-wide innovation centre. CRP invited Carranza to build such a centre once he had returned from his studies at New York University. When Carranza moved back to Peru in 2013, he took up the challenge and launched La Victoria Lab. IDEO was brought back to help: it sent two representatives to work for a year with Carranza. CRP suggested locating the lab on floor 20 of Interbank Tower, one level above his own office, to signal that innovation was to be taken seriously, but Carranza fought back. He didn't need to signal importance or power, he told the boss, only freedom to experiment away from the legacy business. Much more on-message to move as a family into a nearby house.

It took two years for the lab to build credibility within the corporation. 'Nobody wanted to work with us,' Carranza says. That started changing after the lab offered to educate Intercorp's various companies on creating new digital apps and services. It invited them to send staff on a five-month 'digital accelerator' programme where they would learn to create online products that could potentially put today's company out of business. The lab calls these new digital products 'beacons', as they're intended to show the way to the rest of the organization.

In the first eighteen months of its digital programme, the lab helped launch fifty-three beacons across the group. The first was developed with Intercorp's national pharmacy chain, Inkafarma: it took fifteen people, and a budget of $450,000, to build digital products such as a pharmacy app. The lab then launched an incubator programme to support multiple beacons at the same time. As it became more efficient, it took its costs per beacon down to $60,000 with just five people involved. Group businesses such as Interbank, the department store Oechsle, and Innova Schools have sent teams to the lab, where they have learned to embrace its rituals such as 'tequila moments'– when teams collectively drink tequila shots if someone screws up, in order to make failure seem less daunting.

Before a beacon is agreed, the lab team makes company representatives screen it on a consistent set of criteria. Does it address an unmet user need? If a competitor launched it, would they curse? And does the organization need to change in order for the product to succeed? Because there's no point turning up unless you're prepared aggressively to learn how to do new things and unlearn old things. 'Ultimately a beacon is a Trojan horse to introduce new behaviour in the rest of the corporation,' explains Eduardo Marisca, a philosopher and web developer who has worked at the lab for almost five years. 'The teams that build the beacons are more important than the products, as they move on to do other things.'

Beacons need an initial commitment from the associated organization, with internal sponsors and budget agreed from the start. Then small teams work to validate the idea before an 'alpha' prototype is tested with users. Based on feedback, a 'beta' working version is tested further, before the product is launched more broadly.

La Victoria Lab has stolen Amazon's heuristic of the 'two-pizza team': no project should involve more people than can be fed by two pizzas. Teams have operational autonomy. And they're given strictly limited budgets: the six-figure cheques have been cut to just $25,000 as a starting point. 'We need to think like startups as we're burdened by having too much money,' Marisca reasons. 'So we identify our burn rates, our runway [remaining months of funding] and other milestones before additional budgeting is allowed. This is not how chief financial officers have traditionally accounted.'

The battle for digital transformation, meanwhile, is accelerating. Early in 2019, CRP invited five senior representatives of his financial services, retail, education and healthcare businesses to attend a series of long-term planning 'camps' in a beach house to work out what Intercorp should be by 2024. He set conditions to ensure the conversations were not dominated by senior male managers: each group must include at least one emerging leader under thirty and at least one woman.

Marisca defines the goal of digitization with a phrase he learned from Tom Loosemore, formerly of the UK government's Digital Service: 'applying the culture, practices, business models and technologies of the internet era to people's raised expectations'. And that comes down to delivery. Just starting to do things that signal change.

'Although we want to stop using the word "digital" at all when we mean transformation,' Maria Paula Loayza says. 'This is really about continuous transformation and adaptability.'

A few streets away in another unmarked residential house, Interbank is building three finance-tech startups to compete head-on with its core banking business. This is La Casita – 'the little house' – and the location is designed to give the new teams independence from the parent bank and its burden of compliance, but also to ensure they move quickly. One of them, Tunki, is a twenty-four-person digital-payments platform whose success would hit the profits of the parent company's credit-card business; another, Cima, uses data to offer loans to businesses. The third, Mercury, is an e-commerce marketplace that, when I visit, is due to go live within the next twenty-four hours. Each startup is tightly budgeted and recruits talent independently of the parent bank, combining insiders who understand the culture of Interbank with outsiders whose skill sets (such as user-experience designers) are not native.

In 2014, the year La Victoria Lab began, Interbank also launched its own finance-innovation lab called LaBentana, a play on the word for 'window'. Barely a quarter of the population had a bank account, and Interbank saw a big growth opportunity in building new digital business lines. CRP's brief was to 'bring in the Martians' – outsiders who ask the questions bankers don't ask. There are now fourteen 'LaBentaneros' working on floor 11 of the bank tower, a hybrid young team of anthropologists, human-centred designers, developers, and no actual bankers. Projects that show promise graduate to La Casita to be tested and iterated, pending a public launch.

It took a couple of years for the LaBentana team to win the core bank's trust. 'The first time I asked for money I had to go ten times for ten weeks in a row to the investment committee,' recalls Ale Corrochano, who runs the lab. 'They asked for business plans – but how can you do that for early-stage prototypes?' Eventually she learned that respect came from delivering early iterations of products – 'minimum viable products' – on shoestring budgets. Today the lab insists that the bank provides a sponsor for each new project, as well as two employees empowered to make decisions who live in the lab for up to six months.

And now Intercorp is ready to move beyond rethinking education and finance. Next on its list is healthcare. Around 30 per cent of Peruvians have no health insurance, and yet Intercorp, which owns the 2,300-branch pharmacy chain Inkafarma, knows their needs in great detail. So, in conjunction with Inkafarma, it's building what it intends to be the largest chain of low-cost private health clinics in Peru. Yet again, the conglomerate is stepping in where government has failed.

Its first Aviva clinic, in Lima's Los Olivos neighbourhood, is due to launch in early 2019; there are plans for ten to twelve more in Lima over the next eight years plus a few more in other provinces of Peru. Each clinic is expected to provide 40,000 consultations in its first year, growing to 100,000, with a mission to offer 'quality and accessible healthcare services for Peru's emerging middle class'. Patients will pay a modest fee per visit or join a local insurance scheme; the clinics will be modular buildings with separate entrances offering treatment (Arriva Cura) and healthy-lifestyle approaches to disease prevention (Arriva Cuida). Aviva is developing digital apps too, such as a pregnancy companion, as well as a digital coach for doctors.

And, as Aviva's CEO Jorge O'Hara explains, this is again a for-profit initiative which also meets Intercorp's wider goals. 'If you don't invest where government isn't fixing things, ten years down the road things will stall,' he says. 'If people are constantly sick and missing workdays, growth will slow. And you can't fulfil Intercorp's mission with terrible healthcare.'

And after solving healthcare? Oscar Malaspina, who I meet at La Victoria Lab, gives me some clues. In 2021, he explains, it will be 200 years since Peru declared its independence, yet since then the rural indigenous populations have not shared fairly in the gradual growth in living standards. Poverty has fallen by two-thirds since 2004, but there remains a huge urban–rural gap in per capita income. To mark the bicentenary, Malaspina's project intends to help them catch up – by bringing internet connectivity to the mostly offline countryside.

His team of six is just five months into the project, called Laika, and it doesn't yet have a CEO or a budget. All Malaspina knows is that whichever technical solution is arrived at will need both to solve a national problem and encompass a profitable business model. 'Laika is a country-changing project,' he says, 'so why do we have to wait for Google or Elon Musk to do it? Let's get it done.' They've started by visiting China, Kenya and Mexico – and avoiding getting caught up in the hype. 'Our job is to remain honest to ourselves, and not get seduced by the bullshit of innovation.'

My interview with CRP is not going entirely as expected. For a start, most of the questions are coming from him. What other companies have I encountered on my journey that he can learn from? Where should he visit to see effective education? Are there books I would recommend for the floor-to-ceiling wall shelves in front of us? Alongside a Ralph Waldo Emerson quote (a Spanish translation of 'Many times the reading of a book has made the future of a man') are hundreds of books with titles such as *The Startup Way, Blockchain Revolution, Double Your Profits In Six Months or Less* and *The Leader Phrase Book*. 'All these authors have been here to talk to us,' CRP explains. An Elon Musk biography sits by a whiteboard on which handwritten bullet-points about Intercorp culture have been left from a previous meeting: 'Flat . . . Meritocracy . . . Shared value . . . Human-centred design . . . Growth mindset . . .'

We're on floor 19 of a strangely curved and tilting twenty-storey tower by Austrian architect Hans Hollein, a heliport above us and a ten-lane highway intersection below. CRP is an unusual billionaire. Almost white-haired, in grey jeans and a blue North Face cardigan over a white open-neck shirt, he rarely gives interviews but radiates an unusual degree of curiosity. 'You can't learn if you're talking,' he says when I point this out. 'I'm very curious about lots of things, yet I get frustrated when obvious things don't get done. Especially things that traditionally we believe the public sector should take care of.'

When CRP started building his business, he was frustrated by the defeatist, disappointed mindset he kept encountering. 'Inflation was high, terrorism was everywhere,' he recalls. 'One phrase I'd always hear which drove me crazy was "Yes, but" – "Sí, pero". "Yes, the economy's growing, *but* there's a recession round the corner." I told my team we needed to change the O to the U – to "¡Sí, Perú!"' He had the advantage, he understood, of an outsider with relatively little to unlearn.

His father, Carlos Rodríguez-Pastor Mendoza, had run Peru's central bank in the late 1960s but was forced to flee the country in 1969 after a military dictatorship overthrew the ruling government. He settled in California and his wife and six children joined him. Carlos Junior, the oldest, was nine. He remembers his father having to start afresh, taking a junior banking job at Wells Fargo but never complaining. 'When you've been uprooted and lost whatever you've had, you're no longer frightened of change,' he reflects. 'It made me realize that any problems I might have were really very small. Everything is kinda temporary.'

Rodríguez-Pastor Mendoza returned to Peru to become economics minister in the 1980s, but a few days after he had left office in 1984 he survived an assassination attempt while at home. 'He, my mother and my sister were in the house, and he called me to give me instructions on what to do in case they didn't survive,' CRP recalls. 'Having been on the other end of that call, anything I've done ever since is Disneyland.' It was another reminder for CRP of how broken his country was.

He attended public schools and then Berkeley and Dartmouth, before going to work on Wall Street and managing a hedge fund. In 1990, he and his father bought the Peruvian operations of Bank of

America, then the smallest bank in the country. In its first year, with a staff of forty-two, it made a profit of just $80,000. Four years later, they put together a consortium to buy a state-owned bank, Interbank, and formed the Intercorp group. But within months Rodríguez-Pastor Mendoza died. 'I was faced with the dilemma, as the Clash song goes: should I stay or should I go? I decided to stay. I was a hedge-fund guy; I said the day I leave it will be on my terms.'

As the bank grew (it's now the fourth-largest in Peru, and the second-largest retail bank), Intercorp built a cinema group, launched a hotel business and bought a chain of supermarkets. They were making up strategy as they went along, CRP says, but the goal was consistent: to focus on businesses related to the emerging middle class, as that was the country's economic growth engine. 'We said early on that our real purpose is to be the private-sector group that's going to boost this country's economic prospects and have an impact,' he tells me.

Social purpose had always guided Intercorp's strategic thinking. It launched an award in 2007 for 'the teacher who leaves a footprint', giving away a car and an apartment to the best teacher in each of the country's twenty-five regions. Three years later its supermarket business, Supermercados Peruanos, launched a programme called Perú Pasión to train local farmers and small suppliers in commercial and tech skills to promote rural development. CRP began studying Singapore and South Korea to understand how they had emerged from poverty in barely two generations. His conclusion: the most important factor was their emphasis on quality education.

Why, he thought, couldn't Peru become a developed nation in his lifetime by investing in world-class schools? And if these schools could raise Peru from the bottom of the OECD league tables, why not boost national self-esteem even further by crossing borders and exporting the strategy across Latin America?

He made a series of undercover school visits in the guise of a prospective parent. He was shocked by what he found. Not only were the public schools poor and unambitious for their pupils, but that lack of purpose extended to the commercially driven fee-paying sector. CRP found schools misleadingly including spelling variations of Harvard or Princeton in their names; there was even a Bill Gates School unaffiliated to the Microsoft founder but displaying the company's logo.

'There was an a-ha moment for us,' he recalls of his tour. 'In one school where I pretended to be the father of kids who wanted to attend, this lady was getting restless with my questions. She said, "Are you from the tax authorities?" I said no. "The ministry of education?" No. "Well, why are you asking so many questions? I'd like you to go. I'm the principal *and* the owner." I said if I could ask her one last question, then I'd leave. I asked her why she'd decided to start a school. Her answer was, "Because it's more profitable than running a Chinese restaurant." You've got to be kidding me! The future of your country? There's no commitment here. We said no, we gotta get involved.'

The Innova project began with four priorities: fees had to be affordable; the model must scale to hundreds of schools; it would be guided by academic excellence; and it must be profitable. 'If I'm not profitable, how can I sustain it? Our group owns 51 per cent of Innova. Guess who owns the other 49 per cent? Our private-equity fund. These are the guys with the sharp elbows – some have a heart, but oftentimes it's hard to find. Why? To keep us honest.'

It was also important to keep asking questions. What of the locals who couldn't afford fees? That led to the scholarship programme, now helping 2,000 children. Could Innova also support the public schools? It's now designing a $50 digital curriculum intended to complement standard public-school lessons. Yet at its core, Intercorp's involvement is inherently self-interested. 'If the country is more prosperous, we'll do well,' CRP says. 'It's a virtuous circle. We could wait for someone else to do it and go along for the ride, but it's a lot more interesting if you design the road.'

So far, Intercorp has invested around $600 million in education – an extraordinary commitment. Yet this is still a giant profit-seeking conglomerate, with none of the accountability of elected politicians. I tactfully put it to CRP that, in schooling, healthcare and more, he is privatizing what should be some of the key responsibilities of government. 'Yeah, I hear the argument,' he replies. 'What's the alternative? There are 8 million K-to-12 kids in Peru. We have 37,000. The impact we will have if we do things well is that others will want to copy us, and there will be Innova alums in government, raising the bar for everybody.'

He lives in a country that still has 20 per cent poverty, he says, and he just happens to be among the lucky ones who won the lottery. His face takes on an impassioned glare. 'What if the big guy is actually doing good and improving the life of its customers?' he asks, raising his voice. 'We have so many examples of bad governance. Why can't we focus on the good?'

Some of the most impressive tech startup founders I've met have succeeded by avoiding short-term gains in favour of focusing all their efforts on meeting consumers' genuinely unmet needs. Among hundreds of commodified messaging apps, for instance, WhatsApp broke through by understanding what users actually wanted: simple, frictionless messaging that just worked, whatever their device.

When I spent a couple of days with the WhatsApp founders in late 2013, in an unmarked Mountain View office, I was struck by a fading handwritten note pinned years earlier to Jan Koum's desk signed by his co-founder Brian Acton: 'No ads! No games! No gimmicks!' In a market saturated with mobile messaging apps, this relentless user focus had allowed WhatsApp to overtake Tencent's WeChat, Facebook Messenger, Snapchat, LINE, Kik Interactive, KakaoTalk and more – and all with a staff of just fifty. 'We have a simple strategy,' Koum told me, the first magazine journalist to have been given deep access to the company.

'Our goal is to get out of the way. We take a similar approach to Google in search. Remember the portals that came before? Google wanted people to leave their site as soon as possible because they'd done a good job. We want you to talk without being interrupted by ads. We're not sitting here with a bunch of consultants figuring out how to squeeze the last penny out of our users.'

They were instead obsessed with service reliability and simplicity of use. They had ensured the service 'just worked' across seven platforms, from Android to Symbian. A whiteboard in the office listed WhatsApp's 99.92456 per cent uptime that year – with 600 servers ensuring smooth delivery of up to 250,000 messages per second and a billion images a day. Brian Acton had learned the lesson when he worked on Yahoo! Shopping, where there was a constant internal debate about putting more ads and logos on to the pages. 'What did this have to do with the user?' he recalled. 'It left a very bad taste in my mouth. A service model to me is a pure model – the customer is the user.'

When Koum and Acton added new features, it was only after intense discussion and user-focused experimentation, and a conviction that execution would simplify rather than bloat the service. On Koum's desk was a pair of walkie-talkies that he had been using to understand better how to simplify voice-messaging. For the recently rolled-out push-to-talk voice-messaging, it took a single tap to record and send a voice message; to play it, a phone would automatically switch from speaker-mode to soft volume when its proximity sensor detected that it was being held near an ear.

So devoted, indeed, were Koum and Acton to putting user needs first that they reacted with disgust when I suggested that some day they might be tempted to sell to a bigger company. 'We've made such an important promise to our users that to have someone come along and buy us seems awfully unethical,' Acton told me bluntly. 'It goes against my personal integrity.' So when two months later, in February 2014, Facebook acquired WhatsApp for $19 billion,

I could only reflect soulfully that integrity tends to find its own price, even if that price reaches $19 billion . . .

I noticed the same obsessive user focus in Drew Houston of Dropbox, the cloud-backup and file-sharing startup that for all its technical complexity aspired to serve users as a 'magic folder'. When we met in January 2012 at the DLD conference in Munich, Houston explained his mission to 'solve a really important problem – to build a fabric that ties together all your devices, services and apps'. His mother, he said, had her music in iTunes and wanted to listen on her Android phone, but the devices would not communicate. That's where Dropbox came in. His team had even had to hack Apple's operating system to show the Dropbox icon in the Finder, as part of their mission to keep the experience really simple – 'even though everything that goes on under the surface is pretty complicated'. Dropbox went public in March 2018 at an $8 billion valuation.

Yet it's not only tech startups that can benefit from embracing unmet user needs. In Australia, the National Roads and Motorists' Association (NRMA) has been repairing motorcars by the roadside since 1920. But as cars became more reliable, and the internal combustion engine started to give way to electric drives, Australia's largest member organization faced an existential crisis. Membership was falling; the accounts started showing losses. How would this much-loved national brand stay relevant into its second century?

In January 2016 the NRMA took a radical decision to put an internet and pay-TV executive in charge. Rohan Lund had been chief operating officer at Foxtel and Seven West Media, and he'd run the Yahoo!7 web portal. He knew he had to act decisively if he was going to overcome internal resistance to change. In his first month, twenty-seven out of thirty-four top managers left; interviews with fifty staff before he joined had convinced him that those in customer-facing roles had ideas but were frustrated by management's antiquated approach. 'The [management] attitude was, "We've got an innovation department with a head of innovation, and we do lots of venture startups, so everything should be OK,'" Lund recalls. By contrast, he defined true disruption as 'satisfying an unmet customer need'.

Innovation, Lund told his team, can never be something a company does on the side in the hope of striking it lucky. It can only come from understanding the causes of disruption and the needs not being met during the transition. He identified some key headwinds facing the NRMA: electrification of cars; manufacturers controlling vehicle data; insurers competing to offer roadside assistance; ride-sharing; autonomous transport; new transportation technologies. It couldn't reject these new realities. Instead, it would have to redefine its role to empower its members in new ways.

Rather than see the rise of electric vehicles as a threat, Lund's NRMA began rolling out Australia's biggest fast-charge network, offering free roadside charging to members. Rather than bemoaning how software was diminishing its roadside engineers' power, his teams started installing data-capturing devices in members' cars to offer remote servicing and advance fault prediction. Rather than fear autonomous car networks, the NRMA developed an autonomous shuttle bus of its own, initially for staff at its Sydney headquarters. The overall strategy, codenamed 'Light On The Hill', realigned the organization's customer-facing business so that it centred no longer simply on the vehicle but also on transport and tourism more generally. There would now be three aspects to the business: the car, the journey and the destination. 'It's so we're the ones disrupting ourselves,' Lund explains, 'creating relevance before someone else does.'

The first part of the strategic rethink involved 'the car'. In front of the NRMA's head office in Sydney's Olympic Park stands an elegant blue-and-white Veefil electric-vehicle (EV) fast-charging point, resembling a human-sized inverted safety razor, bearing the words 'NRMA – Born to keep you moving'. It charges a car's batteries to around 80 per cent capacity in thirty minutes, and is the first of forty to be installed in New South Wales and Australian Capital

Territory under a A\$10 million investment. But the man responsible for the charging network, Bernhard Conoplia, is no energy scientist or environmentalist. Until 2017 he was head of strategy at Foxtel, and was at BSkyB before that.

'EV take-up in Australia is horribly behind the rest of the world, yet we have a natural abundance of energy,' Conoplia tells me when we meet. 'Fifty-nine per cent of customers tell us the absence of publicly accessible charging stations or range anxiety is a significant concern. So we decided to change the infrastructure.'

It costs A\$150,000 to install each charger. But the investment is not simply a warm gesture. The network will eventually meet 5 to 10 per cent of Australia's charging needs, at which stage Conoplia sees all sorts of commercial opportunities. NRMA could sell charging points to commercial destinations, or offer units for home charging. Perhaps members with EVs will sell excess energy back to the grid through the NRMA's infrastructure. 'It opens up things,' he says. 'That makes us much more future-proof.'

The NRMA is not giving up on its core business, of course. Its patrols still take 1.7 million calls a year, and in 2017 they resolved 62,575 lockouts, 16,531 flat tyres and 303,193 flat batteries. Yet it's rethinking how front-line staff work to make them more responsive to changing customer needs. More than a hundred of them now drive new custom-built 'mobile response units' (MRUs) that carry extra batteries and turn into tow trucks at the touch of a button. 'I got my MRU six weeks ago, and when I tell a member we can tow them straight away it's the last thing they expect,' says Tony Tamine, a patrolman for twenty-two years, who I meet outside the office by his yellow-and-blue van. 'Going the extra mile for members makes all the difference.'

It's these customer experiences that define the NRMA as among the country's most trusted brands. And yet, on average, members break down just once every three years. So the company is looking to increase these touchpoints by offering car servicing, branded batteries, insurance and car loans. And, naturally, it's another outsider who is behind the expansion: Melanie Kansil, responsible for roadside assistance, was formerly running strategy and investment at Nine Entertainment.

The NRMA is also moving beyond cars. 'We keep people moving; that was our original purpose,' Lund says. 'We just got a bit lost.' It bought a commuter-and-tourist ferry business, Manly Fast Ferry, which cuts a seventy-minute car journey from Sydney Harbour to the northern beaches to fourteen minutes. It was the start of a wider new ambition for the association: to become Australia's largest transport and tourism service. This links to the second aspect of the 'Light On The Hill' strategy, 'the journey', and also the third aspect, 'the destination'. The NRMA has always represented the interests of car drivers; why not meet their needs by providing consistently high-quality places for them to drive to? So it's bought forty-two holiday parks and now controls the Travelodge hotel chain, with the goal of being the country's biggest operator of leisure destinations.

Lund has also taken a bold entrepreneurial leap in rethinking what membership means. The NRMA is now offering a A\$5-a-month membership called NRMA Blue that doesn't include roadside assistance at all. Instead, Blue offers discounts on fuel, insurance, travel and entertainment across 3,000 products from thirty-five partners – such as five cents off a litre of fuel, significant discounts on visitor attractions, accommodation and transport services, and a free two-month Spotify Premium trial. The goal is to use data to build a more personalized relationship with customers and to turn membership into a marketplace. Suddenly a tired car-repair business has become a highly competitive commerce business, touching customers' lives every week.

The results speak for themselves. After a steady fifteen-year membership decline, the NRMA has now grown membership by 5 per cent in the last two years, to 2.6 million; but it now reaches 5 million customers if the accommodation, car rental and travel businesses are included. From a period of financial uncertainty, it made A$129.3 million profit before tax in 2018, up 17 per cent year-on-year. And customer satisfaction, measured by Net Promoter Score, is at historic highs.

'In the next few years we won't be a small company,' Rohan Lund says. 'We're now a transport tourism company, probably Australia's largest within two to three years.' By building its digital future internally, and becoming a diversified data business, there's a far greater chance that the NRMA will be around for the next hundred years.

Plus, Lund says, 'We're having a lot of fun.'

Action Points

True innovators scent opportunity when emerging technologies, or changing economic circumstances, generate new customer needs that the market has yet to meet. Moore's Law slashed the cost of digital storage, just as the exponential growth in smartphones allowed universal cross-device messaging; yet it took breakout startups such as Dropbox, Spotify and WhatsApp to understand that the true unmet consumer need was simplicity of use and reliability.

Incumbent businesses can similarly build a protective moat around themselves by moving more quickly than rivals in identifying and fulfilling evolving needs. The new leadership of Australia's National Roads and Motorists' Association determined that drivers would increasingly value electric charging stations, trusted accommodation options and negotiated membership deals as roadside engine repairs became a less pressing need; rising member numbers and revenues suggest these needs were genuine. Intercorp, similarly, saw that a rising middle class in Peru lacked quality provision of low-cost education, healthcare and connectivity, and acted boldly to meet these needs with a range of profit-seeking new business units.

Understanding such changing customer needs can require established businesses to 'learn to unlearn', as Intercorp's Innova Schools teach. Here are some actionable takeaways:

1. How do you understand genuine customer needs that are not currently being met? Nothing beats living with the customer. Intercorp's La Victoria Lab, building on IDEO's playbook, conducts truly immersive research: shadowing customers, observing them at home, even embedding teams in their neighbourhoods. That's why anthropologists, psychologists, designers and storytellers are core members of the lab's team.

2. These hybrid teams need autonomy and independence from the core organization. Carlos Rodríguez-Pastor calls it 'bringing in the Martians': people who think in challenging ways and retain an outsider's curiosity. At La Victoria Lab, I encountered a friend from New York, Tricia Wang, who describes herself as a 'global tech ethnologist' and was starting a secondment in Lima. At the NRMA, Rohan Lund challenged the dominant culture by bringing in executives from TV and consumer-web businesses.

3. Independence for these teams is reinforced by locating them away from the executive suite but near enough to be top of mind. CRP compares his company's prototyping labs to candles that must be located just the right distance away from his tower: 'If you get too close you get burned; if you get too far you can't see.'

4. A clearly articulated company mission ensures consistency across the business in driving impactful change, and motivates the talent. Intercorp declared its mission to make Peru the best place in Latin America to raise a family. The NRMA redefined its role from fixing cars to keeping Australia moving. Everything else follows from the mission.

5. La Victoria Lab's 'beacons' offer a model for iterating new business lines and digitizing existing lines. First, work out how to compete digitally with the existing businesses. For instance, La Victoria Lab built a mobile-delivery app for prescriptions that competed directly with the Inkafarma stores. Second, think afresh about the tech you must invest in to deliver, say, real-time updates on fuel pricing. The NRMA's app couldn't simply be built on top of existing databases. And third, stretch your mindset. Intercorp started as a bank-and-retail business that was not in the habit of hiring user-experience designers or agile tech people.

6. Be prepared to fight some internal battles. It took Rohan Lund six months to convince directors that he could deliver on his mission of renewal. 'The former board felt it was almost offensive what I was trying to do,' he recalls. But he used small signals of progress to gain their confidence.

7. Listen to your front-line teams. At the NRMA, Melanie Kansil attends face-to-face lunchtime communications sessions twice a month, listens in on customer-service calls, and rides along with patrols at least once a month. Small meetings, she says, are better than big ones as 'you hear what they're say-ing'. Staff can vent their concerns – and also feed back what customers are asking for. The NRMA has found that ensuring gender diversity in senior management and at board level has made the busi-ness better at understanding the human skills that customers appreciate.

8.   Stay focused. As WhatsApp found, 'No ads! No games! No gimmicks!' was what customers actu-ally wanted.

2

EMPOWER YOUR TEAM

Lessons from the world's least powerful CEO

Along Brook's Mews, a steep service lane located behind Claridge's in Mayfair, only a small gantry crane jutting from board-covered scaffolding suggests that this five-star £1,200-a-night central London hotel might currently have the builders in. Entering the hotel through a revolving metal gate, I'm made to put on boots, eye protectors and a hard hat as Jim Mackey, a tall sixty-six-year-old with a wispy white beard and red face, leads me past mud-spattered walls and a screen monitoring structural movement towards a dusty great hole in the floor. 'This is the project they said was impossible,' he says proudly as we slowly descend a ladder through the void. 'I prefer to use the word challenging.'

Just above us, past the animated kitchen and the laundry room where tablecloths are busily being starched, the backstage drama of one of London's most famous hotels suddenly gives way through swing doors to the serenity of Oswald Milne's art deco lobby. Chopin drifts in from a grand piano in the mirror-lined foyer as a doorman offers to hold an elderly lady's chihuahua. The guests on the ground floor, enjoying finger sandwiches and scones under the Chihuly chandelier sculpture, seem serenely unaware that the 1854 hotel, a favourite of the Queen, Winston Churchill, Katharine Hepburn and countless other international royals and celebrities, is today also one of the capital's most ambitious construction sites.

Mackey, who is wearing a stripy black-and-white cotton top and site-worn jeans, doesn't like to call himself an engineer – growing up in Donegal, Ireland, he never completed his formal education. But over a career in London that spans almost half a century he's earned a reputation for delivering some of the city's toughest construction challenges, among them the demolition of a complex suspended-floor tower at 122 Leadenhall Street from the bottom upwards so that it could be replaced by the City skyscraper known as the Cheesegrater, and the removal of the roof from Liverpool Street railway station while it remained safely open to passengers, so that the Bishopsgate development could be built.

So when the Maybourne Hotel Group, which owns Claridge's and the equally lavish Connaught and Berkeley, decided in 2007 that it wanted to extend the hotel two storeys downwards, its main shareholder, Paddy McKillen, naturally approached Mackey's company, McGee Group, to build a basement. There were just two catches, McKillen explained to them. First, the hotel must remain fully open, with guests languorously unaware that McGee was tunnelling, digging and pumping out an ever-growing void beneath the reception floor. McKillen knew that the Savoy hotel was risking the loyalty of high-paying regulars by closing in December 2007 for a £100-million, sixteen-month refurbishment (which turned out to be a three-year closure that rose in cost to £220 million). He wasn't going to run such a risk here. Second, the only access point for contractors through which to remove debris or bring in equipment and concrete would be a single two-metre-square window by the mews at the back of the building.

It was, Mackey concluded, a beautiful dream that was impossible to enact. The 2008 property crash put the idea on hold, but in 2015 McKillen came back to McGee with a £35 million contract to create a plan for five basement floors. These would accommodate two swimming pools, restaurants, a spa, retail space and offices, and would rehouse the mechanical, electrical and air-handling plant currently occupying space upstairs, allowing for forty new rooms and six-star suites. He left McGee to work out how to design and build the 6,000 square metres of new underground floorspace, just as long as hotel guests didn't notice.

'The phrase that best describes me is, I believe there's nothing that can't be done,' says Mackey, who resembles a genial if slightly sceptical trawlerman. He knew that a series of leading building and engineering firms had for years rejected McKillen's commission as naive and unfeasible. But Mackey, who had been drawn out of retirement for this project, knew some people he thought might be able to help. He'd previously worked with an unusual team of structural and geotechnical engineers whose excitement about a project seemed to grow according to its technical complexity. They were part of a 15,000-person London-based global consulting and engineering firm called Arup, which is employee-owned and takes on the world's toughest construction challenges. 'I knew that if anybody could deliver the actual engineering, it would be Arup,' Mackey says. 'When I introduced them to the scheme, their response was that it was crazy, and that I should be held in a friendly [psychiatric] institution. And then there was a real enthusiasm to get on with it.'

Arup, founded in 1946 by Anglo-Danish engineer-philosopher Ove Arup, is the understated talent hive that actualized Sydney Opera House, Apple Park in Cupertino, Beijing's CCTV headquarters and the Øresund Bridge between Denmark and Sweden. Its expertise helped deliver the Shard and the Millennium Bridge in London, Hong Kong's International Finance Centre and New York's Second Avenue Subway. Yet for a £1.5-billion-revenue company with ninety offices in thirty-five countries, Arup is highly unusual in not telling its staff what to do. 'I'm quite powerless,' deputy chairman Tristram Carfrae tells me with a shrug in his Fitzrovia office. 'People here make their own decisions and are accountable only to themselves and each other.' And that's deliberate: Arup actively seeks to foster autonomy and curiosity among staff so that they choose the projects that excite them.

Jim Mackey invited Dinesh Patel, a thirty-eight-year Arup veteran he had previously enjoyed working with, to visit the hotel and see if his geotechnical and structural colleagues might collaborate with the McGee team to design the basement. 'It was called the unbuildable basement,' recalls Patel, a geotechnical expert whose obsessions include tunnels and jacked boxes. 'The client had tried for many years to find the right people for the project, and all said it was impossible. But at Arup we like to be challenged, to get our best brains to solve a problem. For us, it's not about protecting our arses when we take on a project. It's about testing the boundaries of people's capabilities.'

Patel, too, had war stories from hugely stressful London commissions such as the Cheesegrater; the 230-metre Heron Tower, the City of London's tallest building; a world-class gallery for the Victoria & Albert Museum; and the super-expensive residential development at One Hyde Park in Knightsbridge. 'They're all challenging projects, but nothing compared with this,' he says. 'The sleepless night is that normally, when you're doing a basement like this, you'd knock down and start again. You wouldn't get the Donald Trumps or Hillary Clintons in residence upstairs.'

Mackey thought there might be a way to suspend the hotel on a series of newly constructed columns with deep shafts and foundations built below each of the sixty-one columns that supported the existing 1920s art deco wing. Patel brought in some Arup colleagues to give their views and conduct early feasibility studies in December 2015. Immediately they were hooked. Yes, this was an impossible project that they wanted to take on. They found old copies of *The Builder* magazine from 1928, which discussed the problems the original construction team faced from soft soil in the first metre under the hotel. If this soil became wet, it would resemble toothpaste and the entire structure would become unstable. The Arup-McGee team solved that challenge using a method called vacuum dewatering – applying suction to the ground to remove water as if from a sponge.

They then confronted a second, more uncertain challenge. The hotel sits atop a century-old 50-metre-by-25-metre concrete raft that is a metre thick and reinforced with around 75 tonnes of steel. Would the raft be strong enough to withstand the pressures of building a five-floor basement? 'You can't have a foundation that goes "snap", especially with an occupied building,' says Sarah Glover, Arup's project manager at Claridge's. 'It was chicken and egg – the only way to know where the steel was in the concrete was to break through the raft. But if you break through the raft, you're destroying the structure that's holding up the hotel.' Her team removed part of the raft for lab testing, and the design team used numerical modelling to understand how ductile it was, and how much it could be bent by any ground movements caused by the works before it was likely to break.

The raft, according to Arup's calculation, was indeed strong enough to bear the construction pressures. Another small victory. But then came the biggest challenge of all. The hotel was being held up by sixty-one steel columns that were sitting on the existing raft; how could these columns be safely extended downwards to secure the new basement storeys, as well as the existing eight floors of the occupied hotel?

At Claridge's, the Arup team of highly experienced engineers worked in a small group alongside Jim Mackey to think creatively. What technological intervention could possibly allow the hotel to stay open and meet the constraints of that two-metre-square entry point? They found a solution that was brilliant in its simplicity. Why not hire a team of Irish miners to hand-dig tunnels 30 metres deep through the upper mud and the lower stiff clays under the hotel? The shafts, under the sixty-one existing columns, could then be lined with steel and at depth be filled with concrete to form the new foundation that would support the hotel. Fifteen miners and two pit bosses were hired, mostly from Donegal, and they systematically hand-excavated 1,800 metres of deep shafts and 400 metres of tunnels in just seventeen months, working day and night. 'That's five hundred truckloads, literally with a shovel,' Mackey says.

He leads me into the first basement level, now completed, where builders in fluorescent safety jackets are moving quickly, carrying construction equipment. It's an extraordinary achievement: a large, concrete-finished open space – it could be a subterranean metro-train platform – waiting for fit-out. Hydraulic jacks have been built into the columns to guard against any concrete shrinkage, and Mackey points out where a swimming pool will eventually sit between two columns. 'This entire building now is floating on hydraulic oil,' he tells me above some drilling noise. 'When we've finished, for £35 million we'll have created what I hear is £120 million of new real estate for the client. Unfortunately I didn't know that when I priced the job . . .'

Dinesh Patel, who is inspecting nearby flooring, looks pleased with progress. 'We're taking technologies from a completely different industry to apply here,' he says. 'Our competitors use "innovation" to mean they'll do a design up to a certain point and the detail becomes someone else's problem. But for a project like this, you have to collaborate as a team. Even if it ends up involving a mining technique, with everything having to come through a small hole in the wall.'

Mackey surveys the scene with evident pride. In January 2019 his team handed over the five basement floors and associated service link tunnels for fitting out, right on schedule. They had removed 3,000 truckloads of waste through the single window, each truck holding 10 cubic metres and around 20 tonnes. And all without disturbing the residents – although word reached some of the regulars that there was something extraordinary happening downstairs as they slept. 'We've had billionaire guests and rock stars wanting to come down here,' he says. 'They've been amazed to see what's been happening in such a constrained environment while they're enjoying their luxury dinner or five-star suites overhead.'

For Patel, it's further proof of what happens when you give good people tough challenges and then leave them alone. 'We're not afraid to take on jobs like this,' he says. 'There were huge risks involved. But Arup's biggest asset is our people. They're the intellectual real estate of the firm.'

*

'When I joined the board,' Tristram Carfrae says in his book-cluttered office, 'an ex-chairman said to me, "Congratulations, but don't think it means anything. If you're lucky, people will listen a bit more carefully when you say something." The truth is, junior staff know more than senior staff.'

Arup typically works on 18,000 projects a year for 6,700 clients. But its biggest project, Carfrae says, is the organization itself: how it recruits and motivates the best people, and then lets them choose how to collaborate – and get excited about impossible projects – without any central direction.

On 9 July 1970, Ove Arup spoke to a partners meeting in Winchester, Hampshire, about the company's values and purpose. His presentation became known as the 'Key Speech', and all new recruits are now asked to read it. The organization, Arup said, must be 'human and friendly in spite of being large and efficient. Where every member is treated not only as a link in a chain of command, not only as a wheel in a bureaucratic machine, but as a human being whose happiness is the concern of all, who is treated not only as a means but as an end.'

The main way to attract world-class talent, Arup supposed, would not be salary as much as 'the opportunity to do interesting and rewarding work, where [the employee] can use his [sic] creative ability, be fully extended, can grow and be given responsibility. If he finds after a while that he is frustrated by red tape or by having someone breathing down his neck, someone for whom he has scant respect, if he has little influence on decisions which affect his work and which he may not agree with, then he will pack up and go. And so he should. It is up to us, therefore, to create an organization which will allow gifted individuals to unfold. The authority [to make decisions] should also be spread downwards as far as possible.'

Five decades later, those values (if not their gender-biased expression) remain intact, and the world's greatest engineers choose to make their careers here. Carfrae came straight from Cambridge

University in 1981; he's worked on such iconic projects as the Beijing 2008 Olympics Aquatic Centre and Singapore's Marina Bay double-helix bridge. 'Arup functions best when there's no controlling mind or strategy,' he says. 'The business is owned in trust for the benefit of the staff, so there's no "them" and "us". That's worked really well so far: we've made a profit in every year, and nobody's invested in us.

'But,' he reflects, 'does our approach begin to fail if the world changes faster than we can? Are we still fit for purpose in a digital age?'

These are important questions, and Arup knows that it faces getting left behind in the talent race unless it fundamentally adjusts to a new generation's attitudes, assumptions and speed of adaptation. 'We have people joining us now who have greater knowledge and skills than people who have been here for thirty-five years,' Carfrae tells me. 'There's a potential dislocation: if you talk about block-chain, about machine learning, most of the leaders today won't know what it is. No,' he says, 'we're useless. We're internally focused. We're introverts who have become comfortable with each other, but not really comfortable in the real world. That has to change.'

Carfrae had dinner the previous night with his co-deputy chairman, who has been at Arup for some forty-five years. They were debating why digital natives, who solve problems through their networks and self-educate on YouTube, would want to join a stratified, inward-looking company that lauds the expertise of its most experienced staff. As in many professional partnerships, Arup staff typically join at the bottom and slowly rise as they're assumed to accumulate knowledge. But why would talented graduates wait a decade before being given significant responsibility when they could jump instead into a startup?

'We're the opposite of a startup,' says Carfrae. 'Today, we're really precious about "us", but Arup needs to become more porous, more networked, connected to other good people. People should come and go from Arup, not stay for life.'

His conclusion: Arup needs to think harder about keeping its people happy. To that end, the firm has been quizzing some of the younger staff on what 'maximum fulfilment' would mean to them. They value the independence to be creative that Ove Arup originally celebrated, and they aspire to find their own multidisciplinary ways to solve problems. But how that will work in practice as technology evolves will involve constant experimentation. 'In our building across the road, we've wired up desks with sensors, measuring things like CO_2 in the air and temperature, customizing the workspace to people's preferences, activating lighting according to what people are doing,' Carfrae says. 'We want to know how people are feeling. We're experimenting.'

Arup has survived seven decades of real-estate cycles and economic downturns that have obliterated many of its competitors. It's been consistently profitable, won the industry's top awards, and quite literally changed the face of the planet. It's built a rare reputation in construction for offering talented people a values-driven career, with work that is both challenging and fulfilling. And yet, as Tristram Carfrae understands, that is no guarantee that it will stay relevant tomorrow. 'We have to turn our organization inside out,' he says. 'I want to break through this idea that we know everything. That's the challenge.'

Jonathan Dower spent ten months leading the team of ten world-class games developers and designers working on *Smash Land*. The mobile game – 'You collect characters and battle against other players in something that resembles a pinball machine,' as Dower describes it – had been released for early testing in Canada, Australia and New Zealand, and was much loved inside the company. Yet, despite the team's constant iterations, it was failing to engage players as hoped. Dower, a quietly spoken artist from New Zealand, turned his chair round in his Helsinki office and gently asked his teammates to tell him honestly if they still had faith in the game. 'I was feeling it in the team, after we'd tried so many things to make it work,' he recalls. 'The meta-game just wasn't good enough, and all our fixes were turning it into a Frankenstein mess.'

The team decided to go for a sauna on Helsinki's Saunasaari 'sauna island', and during their conversation they realized they were getting far more excited about ideas for other games. 'That's when we decided to kill the game, as we weren't hitting something amazing,' Dower says. He emailed the whole company to formalize the decision. 'And we didn't consult Ilkka, as he wasn't in the country that day.'

That may sound odd given that Ilkka – Ilkka Paananen – is Dower's boss. But not being consulted before staff take a major business decision is just how Paananen wants it. As chief executive and co-founder of Supercell, one of Europe's most successful start-ups and certainly its highest-valued games company, Paananen is obsessive about empowering his 280 staff to take decisions autonomously – even if that means they kill a potentially profitable game just before launch without even talking to him.

'I aspire to be the world's least powerful CEO,' Paananen told me over lunch at Google's Zeitgeist festival near London in 2017. 'It's all about returning power to the teams, the cells, the people who develop the games. My job is simply to create an environment where we hire the best possible people and then let them decide how they'll have the biggest impact. And then from that point I have to get out of the way.'

The strategy has worked beyond his investors' dreams. In 2016, when the then six-year-old company had just four games on the market, the Chinese company Tencent spent $8.6 billion to buy a majority stake at a valuation of $10.2 billion. That year, its free-to-play games made $2.3 billion revenue and $1 billion profit, mostly through in-game purchases. The games – *Clash of Clans*, *Boom Beach*, *Hay Day*, *Clash Royale* and, since December 2018, *Brawl Stars* – are played each day by more than 100 million people, who typically log in eight or nine times for an average of six minutes. And that success, Paananen says, comes down to the radical autonomy that the company vests in the small teams, or 'cells', that collectively make up the 'super-cell' after which the business is named. It's a deliberate inversion of the traditional hierarchy that so frustrated Paananen at his previous games company.

'Decisions can come from anyone,' explains Dower when I belatedly follow up Paananen's invitation to visit the office, a former Nokia research centre, on a warm end-of-Finnish-summer Monday in September 2018. 'But if everyone removes their ego, those decisions happen by themselves.' Cells need to justify their decisions, of course – that's what the all-hands Friday-afternoon meeting is for. Some weeks, bottles of champagne are opened to toast momentous decisions, such as those acknowledging that a game such as *Smash Land* has failed. The bottles (branded 'The Learnings') include a blank label on which lessons learned are meant to be written. Because it's the lessons from the failure that are being toasted, not the failure itself, explains Dower, the tattooed, bearded, five-year Supercell games lead. He's wearing jeans, a black-and-white Lou Reed T-shirt and no shoes. Shoes, I discover awkwardly, must be left at the door here. I've flown in wearing comfortable but threadbare socks.

'Failing sucks,' Dower continues. 'I remember being very shaky and nervous when I presented to the meeting, and was close to crying so I almost couldn't drink the champagne. I showed graphs of where we were and where we wanted to be, and got big claps from colleagues as we toasted the learnings. The level of trust that's needed for a company to work this way is enormous.'

Members of Dower's team quickly found alternative cells to join. He became games lead on *Clash Royale* for two-and-a-half years; now he's part of a four-person cell working on a new game. 'There's no overarching scheme,' he says, 'just a bunch of people freestyling with the common goal of trying to get the best games out there.' The Supercell website used to include the slogan 'The best people make the best games'. At some point 'people' was replaced by 'teams'.

A wall of Polaroid staff portraits indicates that cell size varies from four people (recruitment) to seventeen (*Clash* and *Clash Royale*). The newest game, *Brawl Stars*, has thirteen people; admin, too, is a cell, at twelve members. In some Polaroid groupings there are gaps where one member has decided to join another cell. Diversity is important: staff from thirty-two countries work at HQ in Helsinki's Ruoholahti district, where English is the lingua franca; about eighty more work in San Francisco, Tokyo, Shanghai and Seoul, and there's a single music composer in Copenhagen.

The best work, Paananen believes, comes from small teams in which every member is passionate about their contribution. They have full control over their product roadmap; the boss merely asks questions occasionally, without imposing his own answers as 'that would destroy the culture'. Transparency matters, too. The entire company is invited to play a new game and give feedback before it's launched in beta. The game team also tells the wider company its targets for retention, user engagement and monetization; if it doesn't reach the targets, there's no room for excuses. As Paananen said at the Google Zeitgeist event, 'Org charts and processes don't translate into great games. We realized games are an art form, not a science.' And that means allowing teams to fail – because 'if there aren't many failures, we haven't been trying hard enough to do innovative things'.

Supercell isn't the only games company to empower its talent in bold ways. Valve, the multibillion-dollar Washington State company behind the Steam distribution platform and hit games such as *Half-Life*, aspires to be 'Flatland', where hierarchy doesn't exist. 'We don't have any management, and nobody "reports to" anybody else,' its 2012 *Handbook for New Employees* explains. 'We do have a founder/president, but even he isn't your manager. This company is yours to steer – toward opportunities and away from risks. You have the power to green-light projects. You have the power to ship products. There's no red tape stopping you from figuring out for yourself what our customers want, and then giving it to them.'

Desks at Valve have wheels attached, not merely as a symbolic reminder that staff should always be considering where they could move to be more valuable, but also as literal wheels that let them move their desk with them: 'Employees vote on projects with their feet (or desk wheels).' Financial compensation is partly determined by peer reviews; and there are no actual job descriptions. 'You were hired,' the handbook advises, 'to constantly be looking around for the most valuable work you could be doing. At the end of a project, you may end up well outside what you thought was your core area of expertise.'

Although Supercell doesn't encourage staff to unplug their computers and unilaterally move to another team – it prefers group discussions first – there are certainly parallels. 'It takes new staff two weeks to realize they have complete freedom on how to make decisions,' says Timur Haussila, a seven-year Supercell veteran who worked with Paananen before that at his last company, Digital Chocolate. 'You can set the direction of the game, the timelines, the deadlines, whether we're working with external partners. Of course, Ilkka is very powerful, but not in a way that involves micromanaging the teams. His power is asking good questions and connecting the right people. And then knowing when to step back. He trusts the team.'

Haussila, bearded and with hair in a bun, is a former game lead for *Hay Day* and *Boom Beach* who's now part of a seven-person team working on a new game. 'We don't stop to celebrate the past,' he says. 'Hundreds of millions of downloads for our games are nice numbers, but what motivates us is to create new features and new games.' The numbers, though, are pretty mindblowing. Near the office door is a vast display screen showing real-time user log-ins across the planet. 'It's called the world domination map,' says Alexander Patouchas, a member of the recruitment team. Clusters of bright lights shine red for *Clash of Clans* log-ins, orange for *Clash Royale*, green for *Hay Day* and blue for *Boom Beach*, their intensity following the path of daylight.

Much of Supercell's success clearly stems from the exceptionally defined culture that Paananen has created. And culture clearly creates winners in startup industries far beyond gaming. 'The stronger the culture, the less corporate process a company needs,' Brian Chesky, Airbnb's co-founder, wrote to his entire team in October 2013 in a letter that he titled 'Don't fuck up the culture'. 'When the culture is strong, you can trust everyone to do the right thing. People can be independent and autonomous. They can be entrepreneurial. And if we have a company that is entrepreneurial in spirit, we will be able to take our next "(wo) man on the Moon" leap. In organizations (or even in a society) where culture is weak, you need an abundance of heavy, precise rules and processes.'

Certainly game design requires a particular creativity-led approach. 'You don't want people on a car production line freestyling, as you want to be sure the brakes work,' Jonathan Dower says. 'But as soon as you get creative, you have to freestyle more, be open to more ideas. And there are more creative elements to so many types of industry now. Some of our thinking may be transferable.'

I ask Dower what's the main risk facing Supercell. 'Gravity,' he says. 'The bigger we get, the higher the risk that gravity will pull us to a more traditional style. Maybe the biggest risk is if we stop challenging and questioning ourselves. Because it's so easy to go with the flow and put processes in place.'

'We did the tunnels for CERN, and used drones to take internal video photography of the crack patterns, which we fed to algorithms we developed to determine whether the cracks are growing. In the past, somebody had to get up on scaffolding and examine every square centimetre to see if a crack was growing. *That's* innovation.'

Chris Luebkeman – wearing a bow tie, with a blue pen in his white shirt pocket – is explaining how Arup helps its people stay ahead of the trends that will affect their work. A software company such as Autodesk (see chapter 9), he explains, centralizes its experimentation and research; Arup, by contrast, decentralizes that function to give its 15,000 staff 'a deep sense of empowerment and autonomy'.

As Arup's 'global foresight, research and innovation' lead, travelling more than half the time but paying taxes in California, Luebkeman's role is to make sure they have the tools and knowledge to pursue their curiosity and do their best work. His remit is to enable 'fluidity, trust and curiosity': making sure people across the company are aware of what's driving change outside the business and fertilizing ideas among themselves, knowing that their line managers won't get in their way. This is, he explains, the opposite to the 'ivory tower' approach to corporate innovation. There's no CEO or CTO or CMO prioritizing the research that matters.

Luebkeman's decentralized team of thirty-five (half full-time) works with the Arup business units to inform discussions with clients but also their own curiosity. The Foresight team has a few tools available. It takes enquiries from across the company and feeds them to an internal network of fifty 'Inspire Scouts', employees in every region who send back case studies. Their observations contribute to an Inspire browser-based database open to the wider company. It publishes decks of 'Drivers for Change' cards, designed to prompt discussion about social, technological or political trends that may impact client work. How, for instance, will extended lifespans affect the Hong Kong subway? What will hydrogen fuel cells mean for Europe's road networks? How will future retail trends bear upon Procter & Gamble? Arup invites staff to workshops on emerging themes such as blockchain, robotics and machine learning.

And if staff have ideas for research of any kind, they can easily apply online for an Arup grant. All they need to do is explain how their new skills will benefit the firm and their colleagues; decisions are made both locally and centrally, depending on the scope of impact.

But none of this will matter unless Arup, like Supercell, keeps finding ways to attract the most gifted, most motivated professional problem-solvers and then lets them achieve their best work together. And that will depend on not acting like a normal business. 'The best value we can give clients is engaging multidisciplinary teams of people who are committed to Arup,' Dinesh Patel reflects as we leave Claridge's. 'At least we haven't got shareholders to think about – the destiny of the firm really does belong to the people who work here.'

Action Points

The best talent seeks workplaces which offer the opportunity to do the best work, and to grow in the process. Daniel Pink's 2009 book *Drive*, which evaluated behavioural studies of employee motivation, concluded that salary and status are far less effective motivators than autonomy (the freedom to work in self-directed ways), mastery (the opportunity to improve skills) and purpose (the wish to be part of something meaningful). For any kind of business that's in a race for talent, the success of Supercell and Arup offer some translatable lessons.

1. Hire great people, then get out of their way. Even the military has questioned the value of hierarchical decision-making in an era when the enemy may be decentralized. For many industries, empowering staff and setting clear expectations of their responsibilities can deliver strong results.

2. As well as giving staff freedom to act autonomously, minimize any internal barriers – such as formal approval processes or non-vital meetings – that might slow them down. Bureaucracy is the enemy of speed and creativity.

3. Bring staff at all levels into the company's conversation. This requires a high level of transparency. At Supercell, all employees receive a daily email with key performance numbers. Ilkka Paananen recalls a new employee who told him, 'I think I got the wrong email, I just got all the revenue data on our games this morning.'

4. Eliminate the fear of failure. If staff feel they can't take risks, they won't do exceptional work. But it's also important to stop and absorb the lessons from failures. Even if that means toasting those lessons with champagne.

5. A healthy, creative working culture relies on trust. 'If executives think that people who don't meet expectations should be let go, it means the team's not trusted by the company and the team can't trust the company,' says Timur Haussila. 'Without the trust, you can't take risks.'

6. Design a foresight function for the company. It helps the leadership team and staff understand where they think their market is going, and how they see their product and processes fitting into this evolution. Chris Luebkeman suggests scheduling two days a year: one to understand the issues, and one to react, followed by a year of planned action. 'That corporate deep breath puts oxygen into your brain,' Luebkeman says. 'It's about being mindful, responsible leaders.'

3.

HIRE PIRATES

Hackers take over the Pentagon

When Alex Romero was a sergeant in the US Marines fifteen years ago, he noticed something alarming as he was maintaining some secure fire-control missile systems. If lights were flashed towards a missile controller in a certain sequence, he discovered, its trajectory could be altered. An electro-optical specialist with a computer security background, Romero knew that a vulnerability like that could compromise the effectiveness of the weapons system. Yet when he tried to relay his concerns up his chain of command, he was told bluntly: 'This is not your realm.'

A few years later, running information security for the media division of the US Department of Defense, Romero felt similar disappointment after approaching bosses with what seemed to him a common-sense idea. Digital businesses from Alibaba to Zendesk were offering cash rewards, or 'bug bounties', to outsiders who privately pointed out software vulnerabilities that could then be fixed. Why not invite 'ethical' hackers to test the security of his agency's public-facing websites, to minimize the chances of, say, an ISIS beheading video being uploaded to Defense.gov? He was told, to his frustration, that that would not be possible. 'The US government didn't have a legal mechanism for people who knew of vulnerabilities in our systems to share them with us,' Romero, wearing a *Star Wars* T-shirt, recalls in a uniform-filled Pentagon dining hall. 'They'd risk prosecution under the Computer Fraud and Abuse Act.'

So Romero was deeply suspicious when some people in T-shirts and jeans approached him at work a few months later to help run a bug-bounty project they were calling 'Hack the Pentagon'. He hadn't heard of their unit, Defense Digital Service (DDS), which at the time didn't even have a website. Convinced he was being 'socially engineered' – psychologically manipulated to divulge secret information – he asked them to come back with a letter from their commanding officer. The next day they did indeed return with a letter – signed by the US Secretary of Defense. Defense Digital Service was not only real, it had become the first part of the federal government authorized at the highest level to invite pre-vetted hackers to penetrate its networks. Romero was in.

Hack the Pentagon launched at midnight on 18 April 2016, targeting five public-facing websites: Defense.gov, DoDLive, DVIDS, myAFN and DIMOC.mil. The first vulnerability was identified within thirteen minutes; six hours later the number had grown to 200. Of more than 1,400 hackers registered to take part, over 250 submitted a vulnerability report, and 138 bugs were found to be 'legitimate, unique and eligible for a bounty', earning their finders a total of $75,000. 'We know that state-sponsored actors and black-hat hackers want to challenge and exploit our networks,' the then Defense Secretary, Ash Carter, said afterwards. 'What we didn't fully appreciate before this pilot was how many white-hat hackers there are who want to make a difference, who want to help keep our people and our nation safer.' The pilot saved the department at least $1 million, Carter said, yet cost just $150,000 to run.

But that was just the start. Lisa Wiswell, who'd led the project, was determined to leverage the pilot's success. Wiswell was respected inside the Department of Defense: she'd come to the Pentagon from DARPA, the advanced research establishment, and had helped write the department's 2015 cyber-warfare strategy. So she distributed a robust report, which included policy recommendations, widely across government and invited every chief information security officer to a government-only industry day. 'We told them, "Here's the language to use, here's the way to legally do this,"' she says, sitting among the uniforms alongside Alex Romero. 'We want the practices that have worked in other highly regulated organizations to work in government. It's a hell of a lot less expensive to discover these things before they're live in the environment.'

Other military bug bounties followed, managed for the DoD by companies including one called HackerOne. Hack the Army, in December 2016, identified 118 vulnerabilities and paid out $100,000; Hack the Air Force brought in 207 valid reports and paid bounties of $130,000. 'We made some promises,' Wiswell recalls. 'We wouldn't go against anything mission critical, only public-facing sites that if they go down we can survive.' She was careful to keep public affairs well briefed, and to work closely with the Department of Justice to minimize legal risks.

There's no question the vulnerability programme earned its stripes. It revealed that hackers could access a heating system inside an actual server room, and that computers thought to be discoverable only on the internal network were in fact leaking to the open public internet; and, more fundamentally, that a bureaucracy that had repeatedly shut down bug-bounty proposals could be persuaded that it didn't always know best. Congress is now writing laws to have other agencies implement their own bug-bounty programmes, similar to the DoD's – and to consult with DDS in the process. 'Because the bad guys are already there!' Romero says. 'They're not waiting for permission. We're simply levelling the playing field.'

Wiswell has now ended her tour of duty, and is training to be a teacher. 'I'm going to have those kids compete for bug bounties,' she says with a smile. Romero, meanwhile, has moved full-time to Defense Digital Service to see how far he can push the idea. 'We're now trying to increase the complexity of what we go after,' he tells me. He won't spell it out, but the more complex systems owned by the DoD range from missiles to satellites. And even a lumbering bureaucracy has grasped that it needs to leverage tech in new ways to keep them secure.

'How crazy that a bunch of nerds can show up and do in months what nobody had been able to do in years. Just out of sheer will.'

Chris Lynch, director and founder of Defense Digital Service, swears constantly, keeps sunglasses over his forehead while indoors, wears yellow sneakers and a *Star Wars* T-shirt that exposes the mathematical Golden Ratio tattoo on his left arm, and doesn't give a damn who he pisses off. 'My slogan,' he tells me, 'is "May the bridges you burn light the way".'

Defense Digital Service, according to its Twitter biography, is 'a team of nerds on a tour of duty at the Pentagon to improve technology within the DoD'. It's made up of forty engineers, designers, project managers and bureaucracy hackers typically seconded from places such as Netflix, IDEO, Dropbox and Palantir, even technical talent hand-picked from the armed forces themselves. And it's proudly piratical in culture: its official website states that Lynch's job title is 'Fearless leader', and whereas Pentagon office-door signs are supposed to display a boss's name, the sign outside room 3A268 simply states 'Rebel Alliance'.

'Here's what I sell.' Lynch, forty-three, is sitting across a table from me deep inside a Pentagon dining hall, surrounded by hundreds of men and women wearing camouflage. 'You're going to come to a place with the most amazing mission in the world – 3 million people, on its best day a small country, on a bad day a big city. The mission builds bridges, cities, tanks, fighter jets; it puts satellites up into space and runs GPS to stop us driving into lakes. It's a mission that takes you into some of the most hostile parts of the world, and over time has become one of the most incredibly technical missions that exists. And yet there are no technical people. They have left the building. The system produces the results it's supposed to produce – it can send 100,000 young men and women anywhere in the world at a moment's notice – but it's not there for us. And the mission *requires* us now.' Lynch is quickly into his stride. 'It's hard,' he adds. 'It's the worst fucking job I've had in my life. Some days I want to curl up in a ball and cry. But occasionally you get a high that will be with you for the rest of your life. And you will die knowing something that you did mattered.'

DDS was born from the disaster of HealthCare.gov, the website launched in October 2013 to allow enrolment in President Obama's Affordable Care Act. The site crashed within two hours; just six people managed to register on day one. It ultimately took $1.7 billion to fix a project initially budgeted at $93.7 million, and only then after emergency help was called in from the tech community. Mikey Dickerson, then a Google engineer, was part of a geek rescue team drafted by the Obama White House; in August 2014 he was made head of a new United States Digital Service (USDS), with a brief to bring in digital talent for short periods to spread smart technology across federal agencies.

Lynch, a college dropout and serial entrepreneur, had just been offered $1.5 million from a prolific investor called Brad Feld to fund a health-records startup when he accepted a forty-five-day tour of duty at USDS. He and three other engineers jumped straight in to solve a heart-wrenching problem: 20,000 veterans' service health records had gone missing while being transferred from the DoD to the Department of Veterans Affairs, and one in twenty healthcare requests by retired veterans was being denied at the moment when illness could make treatment urgent.

It turned out that the system only recognized PDF files, and for years doctors had no idea that the JPEGs they were scanning into the system were systematically being discarded during the transfer. 'So you have cancer because you served in the Kuwait oil fields, and you need chemotherapy, but they can't find your medical records and deny you the benefits,' Lynch says. 'But don't worry, you can appeal, and over the next ten years they'll find your documents. You'll *die*.'

The team of engineers went to work. They correctly processed the 20,000 documents that had been lost; they cut the time needed to transfer records from three months to one day; they saw to it that system updates would happen every two weeks rather than every eighteen months; and they helped ensure the veterans could get access to the treatment to which they were entitled.

'Essentially, over forty-five days we wrote file-format converters, and now 5 per cent of the time somebody *won't* die,' Lynch says. 'Where else do you have that? That's amazing.'

On his last day, Lynch took a call from Todd Park, Obama's chief technology officer. Why not build a version of USDS specifically for the Department of Defense? He turned up for the interview to find he was up against other candidates, including a man in a suit who was sweating as he studied his large printed-out PowerPoint presentation. Lynch, in his standard hoodie, T-shirt and jeans, had no presentation. Instead, he offered a simple idea: 'What if we started with a SWAT team of nerds and we worked on the biggest, most important problems? And when we got a result, we'd move on to the next thing?'

He got the job, starting in November 2015 – and told Brad Feld to keep the $1.5 million. 'This was the biggest fucking detour of my life,' he tells me. 'It was not awesome, and caused a whole bunch of problems. But I knew that this would matter.'

Lynch came to work in the world's largest office building, with its 28km of corridors and armed uniformed guards; his previous workplace had been a coffee shop. He had no office, no staff, no computer and no support base in a bureaucracy that he knew didn't want him there. It was, he says, the loneliest experience of his life. He began to work out of his apartment kitchen, pulled in some people from USDS, and persuaded an administrative assistant he'd run into, called Reina Staley, to be his chief of staff. Staley's father was a veteran; she understood the mission immediately. With Staley on board, they found an available Pentagon room, ordered all furniture and wall partitions removed, bought MacBooks and commercial Wi-Fi, and sat on upturned waste bins.

A few months in, they found that even the building's security was broken. When Lynch booked in a guest on the new visitors' badge system, he noticed that he could pull up every previous visitor to the Pentagon. As he was emailing to alert the head of the Pentagon's internal security force, a colleague discovered that he could access every visitor's social security number too. Lynch quickly phoned the head of security and told him he needed immediately to take down the visitors' portal – which had just passed a year-long security-inspection process. 'It's all pretend!' Lynch says. 'In two hours we did more to test it than a bunch of bureaucrats did in one year.'

As DDS continued to recruit, its nascent SWAT team of nerds did indeed find some significant problems to solve in the incumbent machine.

First, there was the DoD's disastrously delayed and over-budget project to modernize the software that controls Global Positioning System satellites. This next-generation 'operational control system' is intended to offer greater accuracy and allow more than twice as many GPS satellites to operate as today – improvements that will benefit not only the military, but everyone who navigates using a digital map. The DoD's head of acquisitions made the call to Lynch's team. 'It was supposed to cost $700 million over five years, and we got involved in year seven, with years of work still to complete,' recalls Paul Tagliamonte, a DDS software engineer who attaches himself to whichever crisis seems most urgent. 'The contractor had close to a thousand software developers on it every day, but they were developing it in a very archaic way.' The system comprised more than twenty major software components; each took around three weeks to install and test manually in a satellite system.

Tagliamonte recalls how some colleagues took aside thirty of the contractor's developers and encouraged them to use a more agile approach to code-writing known as 'DevOps' (a combination of 'development' and 'operations'). They also taught them how to deploy the software components automatically, slashing the three-week manual-build time to around fifteen minutes.

But a hostile system was fighting back. As soon as the DDS coders left, the contractor disbanded the internal team that had been trained. 'We showed up again,' Lynch says, 'and had somebody there for two weeks this time. We leave; they disband them again. Fuck. So we decided we're going to *live* there – to have two people from DDS there every day for six months.'

It worked. 'We had a quarterly review, with engineers from the company, the Secretary of the Air Force, the Space Commander, the CEO of the vendor, and they fucking built ground-control software for controlling satellites in outer space in the actual meeting! Nerds built software!' The little pirate team had shown the bosses that its approach could deliver results quickly and cheaply; its reputation was burnished. The vendor, not to be overshadowed, hired a film crew to document its own achievements, and issued a press release pointing out that it had built software for the government using DevOps. 'It only took six months of punching them in the face,' Lynch remarks. DevOps is now being written into standard DoD procurement contracts.

The team has occasionally flown into battle zones, to find front-line forces encumbered with computers running outdated Microsoft Excel while the enemy uses the latest encrypted Telegram groups and consumer drones carrying explosives. In one undisclosed foreign location, they worked with technically adept US soldiers to develop drone-jamming tools. The DoD had spent $700 million on contractors trying to solve the problem, according to DDS; by coding, testing and iterating with in-the-field soldiers, they created a working prototype, portable and easily upgradable, in four weeks for less than $100,000. The soldiers they worked with were not authorized to download software to their government-issued computers, so as a workaround they'd built their own PCs from off-the-shelf parts. Lynch got permission from the then head of Army Cyber Command, General Paul Nakasone, to take some of these technically gifted serving soldiers out of uniform for a few months to work at DDS, writing code as members of the Rebel Alliance.

They worked their magic in Afghanistan too. NATO advisers who were training local officials to build democratic institutions there were having to document every conversation on a broken

DoD tool called ANET (short for 'advisor network'). 'It would take four hours to write up a report, though they couldn't go to the bathroom because if the screensaver went into effect they lost everything,' Tagliamonte says. In four trips to Afghanistan over fifteen weeks, DDS worked with the people who'd be filing the reports to rebuild ANET from scratch as a friction-free user experience. They then made the ANET code publicly available on GitHub, an open-software repository, so that it could be used by other agencies and NATO partners. 'Our only innovation,' Tagliamonte concludes, 'is we execute.'

DDS's office is more *Star Wars* fan convention than Pentagon. It has wrangled its own Wi-Fi network, its own non-military-approved MacBooks and Chromebooks, and an anti-hierarchical open-plan office design. There are wall posters you'd find at Facebook ('Move Fast and Break Things') and startups ('Get Shit Done') but mostly posters relating to *Star Wars* ('The Empire Wants You'). The conference room is called 'Yoda', the speaker-phone 'Death Star', and a large flag celebrates the Rebel Alliance (a knowing gift from the Secretary of the Air Force). Mischief is everywhere: a meeting-room wall advertises a fake Fisher Price 'Soul Crushing Meeting' toy ('Now your kids can suffer just like you'). Whiteboard-painted walls list buzzword-bingo clichés to avoid ('Dashboards . . . 3D-printing . . . AI . . .'). One wall has a drawing of an umbrella in a storm of what certainly doesn't look like rain.

'That,' Lynch tells me, 'is intended to represent me as this team's shit umbrella.' 'Shit umbrella' is how he defines his role to his staff. 'We hire great technical people to do technical things. Sometimes they run into barriers. That's when we escalate. We believe in early and often escalation. It's fine to have [the bureaucracy] not like us sometimes. We have our DoD validators, but some of them think we're assholes. That's a perfectly acceptable solution.'

The *Star Wars* theme intentionally promotes cultural opposition to bureaucratic friction. 'What I love about *Star Wars* is you can have a very small, highly competent group show up and do something that matters,' Lynch says. 'It's just having the courage to do it.'

The team's structure is flat, and everyone gets to choose the project on which they spend 80 per cent of their time (the rest they give to other people's projects). 'We're driven by impact,' says Reina Staley. 'What can we do in the shortest time that can impact the most people? I don't care if a particular project would save you $100 billion – that's just a number.'

One high-impact project that obsessed the team was the flawed paper-based system, pre-dating the internet, that processes all new military enlistments – around 250,000 a year across five services. Even its name is dysfunctional: the Military Entrance Processing Command Integrated Resource System, better known as MIRS. At a processing station recruits are given an envelope printed with their social security number, which over the day they'll fill with paperwork covering medical tests, their oath of allegiance, emergency contacts, their service contract, their pay grade, any enlistment bonus, and more. By the time a soldier reaches boot camp, the package might be sixty pages thick: yet for all the vital data it contains, data that will one day determine their veterans' benefits, it's the only copy until the information is manually entered into a series of HR databases. Sheets may blow away as a soldier stands to attention; envelopes get left in bathrooms; data-entry clerks make mistakes. The interface resembles early Netscape Navigator; a software update made the mouse behave erratically, so mouse-based navigation was disabled.

A DDS observer followed one new joiner for nine hours, and in hour nine the recruit was told, 'Actually, we noticed that the tattoo on your neck is too high up and doesn't meet our service requirements, so you can't enlist.' 'It's all siloed chambers and paper processes, where commanders have adapted their requirements to the shortcomings of this system,' says Patrick Stoddart, director of Army Digital Service, part of DDS.

The bureaucracy running MIRS did not want some Silicon Valley techies telling them what to do. Only when a routine audit found a range of technical faults did the commanders in control of MIRS, under duress, reach out. Stoddart sent a team to the command's base north of Chicago, and they began by coding a way to transfer two forms – the service contract and emergency contacts – across networks. It took three weeks to write the code, then seven months for the leadership to deploy it. 'That was our first exposure to how complex the bureaucratic process is,' says Stoddart, a twenty-five-year-old college dropout and two-time startup founder. He spent the next few months wrangling the project from the command, and hiring a contractor to help build it. An earlier attempt to modernize MIRS had cost hundreds of millions of dollars before Congress called a halt; DDS estimates that its solution will cost only around several million, more or less the equivalent of what it will save in data-input person-hours each month.

'We're effective because we do a few things right,' Stoddart tells me. 'We've stayed small and nimble, because we want the best people. We're empowered as a team – you're trusted to do whatever you think is best. And we're not trying to solve every problem at once. We're not an "innovation group". We're just trying to fix the problems that we see.'

DDS has learned a few shortcuts of its own along the way. One is to have 'bureaucracy hackers' on the team: lawyers who work alongside its developers, designers and product managers to help them cut through red tape. Sharon Woods works inside DDS as general counsel, with Will Gamble as deputy general counsel; they see themselves as problem-solvers who use their legal knowledge to help teams achieve their goals. With MIRS, for instance, the bureaucracy refused to let recruits enrol using electronic signatures; Woods drafted a definitive legal memo that led to digital signatures being written into wider departmental policy. 'Often, laws are misquoted or misapplied to block a proposal,' Woods says.

'But the barrier is often cultural rather than legal. We can find a way to get the job done.'

'I was a terrible child,' Lynch confesses as we drive from the Pentagon to a Washington DC dinner with his team leadership. 'I did a lot of hacking when I was young. It was inevitable over time that I'd get caught breaking into the school system.'

But when the FBI began investigating the bomb he'd planted at school at the age of seventeen, matters became a little more serious. Led in handcuffs from Kings High School, north of Cincinnati, Lynch spent five days in the Warren County Juvenile Detention Center; he was also expelled, and banned from public schools in Ohio. To be fair, the bomb had failed to detonate; and it wasn't actually dynamite wired together, as the girl who found it had claimed, simply a couple of smoke bombs left in a metal box under a fountain. But a friend had called in a bomb threat from a payphone in a local fast-food restaurant, and the janitor had recognized that student's voice.

It was October 1992, and Lynch, bored, had simply wanted to get out of school. He'd never had much respect for the school authorities. He'd previously broken into lockers and left inkjet-printed notes encouraging pupils to drive in at times designed to cause major traffic snarl-ups.

Not surprisingly, his conviction was an issue when he submitted the 136-page SF86 form to apply for clearance to work in the White House at USDS. 'It's "Have you been arrested, have you been arrested for explosives?"' he says. 'I actually have an answer that's "yes" to both of those questions, which I'd say is rare in the Pentagon. This woman from HR in the White House calls me. "So, Mr Lynch, I see you've put yes to being arrested for explosives. Do you mind telling me your story real quick?" I gave her the basic story. I swear to God, she said, "Do you feel remorse?" I said, "Yeah, and I'm not going to do it again." I was seventeen! Everybody did something really stupid when they were seventeen.'

Lynch grew up in Ohio in an entrepreneurial middle-class household, dreaming of working with Steve Jobs. He remembers being inspired by the phrase Jobs used at a 1983 company offsite to encourage his team to maintain its rebellious, independent spirit: 'It's better to be a pirate than join the navy' (after which a skull and crossbones was flown above the building where the Apple Macintosh team worked). I ask Lynch what he was rebelling against. 'I was the youngest of three, with an older sister and brother,' he replies. 'I think both my parents being entrepreneurs contributed – they had businesses that failed, businesses that did OK. I'd been on computers since I was seven. I started hacking to cheat in video games. That's one of my interview questions now – did you cheat as a kid in video games? It's a way to find people who work around a system.'

He didn't complete college, worked at a games company, then dropped out of that. He found his way to Microsoft in Redmond to work on web-based business software, then helped rebuild and sell an indebted software company called Daptiv. He launched a successful games startup, and a services company.

Lynch consciously imported the pirate mindset into DDS culture. 'You have to be irreverent to the system,' he insists. To arrange a meeting with senior DoD figures, for instance, you're meant to approach gatekeepers in their office who will then schedule a meeting weeks later according to your seniority. Lynch's team will simply turn up. 'It's super uncomfortable,' he says. 'When we showed up to meet the DoD leadership, for the first three weeks they thought I was there from IT to repair their laptops. And now the Defense Secretary and his senior staff put our people on stage with him. You can't just be eccentric and iconoclastic – you have to deliver.'

I ask him how he'll avoid going native as DDS becomes more embedded. 'Leave,' he responds. 'You can't stay. This group could die at some point, building relationships, trying to be too nice, giving in too many times. Change is not comfortable. It's easier to form the relationship and avoid the friction that comes with change. But you have to embrace the fights.'

Lynch is now preparing for his biggest fight yet. DDS is leading the development of a massive cloud-computing contract for the entire Department of Defense, which among other benefits will allow far greater technical automation. The Joint Enterprise Defense Infrastructure contract (JEDI, in another *Star Wars* nod) is reported to be worth $10 billion, and will go to a single contractor. It's unheard of for a small group like DDS to set the course for the entire department, which employs 20,000 people in acquisition and sustainment alone. Traditional military contractors and their lobbyists have been furiously attacking the likelihood that the contract will go to a tech company such as Amazon. A draft JEDI proposal in spring 2018 received more than a thousand mostly critical comments from forty-six vendors, two trade associations and three federal agencies. Lynch simply calls JEDI the 'arc reactor' (the fictional power source in the *Iron Man* movies) that will keep the department alive.

DDS is also racing to build insurgencies in other parts of the military by training serving personnel in its own particular way of getting shit done. Internally, the programmes are collectively nicknamed Jyn Erso, after Felicity Jones's character in *Rogue One: A Star Wars Story* who helps the Rebel Alliance try to steal the Empire's Death Star superweapon. The front-line counter-drone hack was a Jyn Erso initiative; so was a coding school for Army Cyber Command that cut a twelve-month training course down to twelve effective weeks. A third is building tools to detect anomalous activity on defence networks; four out of the six people on this team are on active military duty, working in civilian clothes in a Pentagon office. DDS is working to create an environment where officers are now protected from the bureaucracy, able to get their hands dirty and put their technical skills to use in productive ways.

Nicole Camarillo, who runs talent and special operations for Army Cyber Command, was instrumental in launching the Jyn

Erso pilot programme. Her goal: to identify, recruit, train, develop, deploy and retain the military's top technical talent. Concerned that gifted technologists within the army were being frustrated, she held candid one-on-one discussions – a cultural challenge in itself – with hundreds of them in military bases such as Georgia's Fort Gordon. 'Sometimes it's the most junior person in a team who has the best technical solution to the problem and will save lives,' Camarillo says. 'We're trying to embed a flat organizational culture, which is so contrary to what makes the military successful. It's about encouraging trust among a unit, providing psychological safety so people can speak up without fear of being punished. Because ultimately the military will need to bend if we're to solve today's more technical problems.'

DDS is currently establishing its first satellite office near the Fort Gordon base, home of the army's new Cyber Command HQ. Lynch describes it as 'a halfway house – a way to inject the DDS mindset elsewhere'. Its code name is Tatooine, after the remote desert planet that Luke Skywalker called home. Projects will be led by army staff who have graduated from Jyn Erso programmes. I ask one soldier attached to Tatooine what can be achieved now that wasn't possible back in the original unit. 'Buy a computer in less than a year,' is the soldier's reply. 'I'm not kidding. To do work that has value for the national security mission, I've had to fight tooth and nail to get the right equipment, as the powers-that-be thought it was better for me to run an obstacle course.' The soldier was sceptical when first approached to join Jyn Erso, having been burned in earlier 'innovation' activities, but was quickly convinced by the autonomy to make technical decisions and the mentorship provided. 'We've used common open-source industry-standard technologies – something that would never have been allowed before.'

Back at Rebel Alliance headquarters, there's a DDS office debate underway about which hacker film they should screen for the next movie night: *Sneakers*, *Hackers* or *WarGames*? On a wall, a scribbled list of current projects – Move.mil, the services' dysfunctional relocation portal; the Tatooine buildout; JEDI – suggests that after three years DDS is increasingly being taken seriously by the military establishment. The then Defense Secretary James Mattis signed a directive to all military departments demanding they cooperate with DDS; Lynch calls it his 'get-out-of-jail card'. Alphabet's executive chairman Eric Schmidt, who chairs the Department of Defense's Innovation Board, told Congress's House Armed Services Committee in April 2018 that DDS was so successful that it should be expanded to 300 people. And day-to-day it's being approached to advise on DoD procurement contracts, on rescuing departmental websites that have gone down, and on writing open-source policy into other branches of government.

I ask Tim Van Name, Lynch's deputy, what he sees as the biggest threat to DDS's survival. He cites a favourite quote from a former colleague. 'Bureaucracies hate two things,' he states. 'The way things are, and change. As we become bigger, we're a bigger threat.' Does he believe the group will outlive Lynch? 'That's a very good question,' he says after a reflective pause. 'There's an ethos that surrounds Chris, and relationships Chris has. The person who replaces him is a critical decision for the organization. But we'll manage that. I think we'll be OK.'

I put the same question to Lynch. 'We've built out an institutional concept of what DDS culture means, and how teams are run,' he replies. 'Change requires being a little bold: just showing up in people's offices and sitting there, or in a negotiation having the confidence to say something difficult and letting the moment fester. The framework is now so well institutionalized – it's like Fight Club. Every new recruit knows there's a DDS way. And the DDS way is you don't wait.'

He sits back in an Aeron chair. 'But what if it's OK that it didn't last for ever?' he asks. 'What if I gave you the authority to come here for six months, and the thing you worked on saved 10,000 lives, and the next day they shut DDS down because our approach was now embedded in the wider department? Was that worth it? I believe so. Because if it takes us years to build something that protects the young men and women who risk their lives, we've lost. We *must* hack the bureaucracy. Nobody is coming to save us.'

Action Points

It's not just 3-million-strong organizations with $700 billion budgets that can profit from the lessons Defense Digital Service has taught the US Department of Defense. Any large, slow-moving company could benefit from empowering a small, tech-savvy team with a measure of autonomy and the latitude to decide what to work on. To paraphrase Steve Jobs: it's better to hire pirates if that upgrades the efficiency of the navy.

I encountered an amazingly energized team spirit during my time in the Pentagon embedded with the 'Rebel Alliance' that is DDS. It's a team that has no time for 'innovation': as Chris Lynch says, 'Innovation isn't something you can simply "buy". It's a culture shift. Take ten steps back, and actually address the problem. Everything you see in our team has been born out of necessity.'

Here are some key components of the DDS approach that are transferable:

1. Hire the best people and give them autonomy. If a team is emotionally charged behind a problem, they are more likely to deliver results.

2. Leaders need to provide air cover to the people challenging norms and rules. 'Inevitably we run into barriers, whether processes, people or fund-

ing, so having a champion at the top is incredibly important,' says Reina Staley. The DDS's ultimate protection is its 'letter of mark' – a memo from the Secretary of Defense that demands cooperation from other units. It also makes sure its lawyers are on side and understand the project teams' needs.

3. When there's a fire, use it. The rules don't apply in a crisis, which offers an opportunity to build new norms. 'There are two states of being in government,' one DDS staffer says. 'Rock-hard solid matter, where nothing you do will ever change anything, and the plasma state when a crisis is on the front page of the *New York Times* and it doesn't matter what rules previously applied. We take advantage of the plasma state whenever we see it.'

4. A strong mythology amplifies the impact of a small team. DDS thrives in part because of its storytelling. 'Some big folklore pieces have made us successful,' says Tim Van Name. 'We tell everybody who joins the story of Hack the Pentagon and the big fights it took. We want them to think, "Stop talking about the problem; go figure out a solution."'

5. Ship! DDS is strict about launching products in the promised time-scale. 'This building thinks in five or ten years and it's easy to get sucked in,' says Staley. 'We're focused on what we can do right now.' Lynch adds: 'We don't make PowerPoint presentations, because they're stupid.'

6. Build with users, not for them. By prototyping and iterating the drone-disabling tool alongside front-

line soldiers, the DDS project team ensured it was fit for purpose – and responsive to their needs.

7. Focus on small wins, then iterate quickly. There was never a master plan to bring in serving military personnel to work on the Jyn Erso projects. It was simply a pragmatic expansion of an approach after the success of the initial counter-drone project.

4

TURN PRODUCTS INTO SERVICES

The bank that performs surgery

Rain cascades over Helsinki's Pikku Huopalahti neighbourhood this dark late-November afternoon, but inside the bright, design-led Pohjola Hospital, on a tiny street named Puutarhurinkuja, Nina Vesaniemi is enthusiastically greeting nurses and physiotherapists as she strides past two wheelchairs parked by the second-floor stairwell. 'Today we've performed surgeries on, let's see, knees, pelvis, shoulders, a fractured ankle, and a knee arthroscopy,' Vesaniemi says as she reads from a schedule pinned to the surgical-floor wall. 'We'll do 3,500 surgeries this year, up to twenty-eight a day, mostly on knees, shoulders and wrists,' she adds proudly. 'With six operating theatres, and five of them in use now, we can schedule a surgery within one to five days of the patient being referred.'

Vesaniemi, a former head nurse here, now manages this hospital and helped plan four new sister hospitals in Finland, in cities from Turku to Tampere. This five-storey building, a renovated office block, is now an LED-enhanced clinical take on a boutique hotel: iPad check-ins, art-filled walls, a Technogym-packed fitness centre, magazine racks and coffee machines at the customer's disposal. But the goal is not to encourage lingering: Vesaniemi's priority, and that of her ten full-time and two part-time surgeons, is to treat patients as quickly as possible so that they can be efficiently mended and back at work. There are two key performance indicators that matter here: how quickly a patient can be treated and successfully discharged; and customer satisfaction.

Our brisk end-of-shift tour starts on the fourth floor, where Vesaniemi explains that modular furniture allows each clean, soundproofed white room to be quickly repurposed as consulting spaces, treatment rooms or offices. We walk past two MRI machines that typically take fifty scans a day, a dental clinic, overnight rooms for recovering surgery patients, an orthopaedics centre that's open till ten p.m., physiotherapists working out with patients in the gym, and a 'digital kiosk' that uses a Microsoft Kinect motion sensor to train patients wearing interactive 'smart' arm casts in rehabilitation stretching exercises.

There's only one clue to indicate that this is not a conventional hospital: a small protruding wall sign, displayed by the insurance payment office. It's the orange-and-white logo of OP, Finland's biggest banking group – for this is a hospital built and run by a bank.

And no, it's not a misguided experiment by a brash, overfunded finance-tech startup seeking to differentiate. OP is a revered century-old Finnish institution. It goes back to 1902, when it was founded as Osuuskassojen Keskuslainarahasto ('The Central Lending Fund of the Cooperative Credit Societies Limited Company', to give it its full due). Finland's second-biggest insurance company, Pohjola, which the bank acquired in 2005, is even older: it began operations as Palovakuutus-Osakeyhtiö Pohjola ('The Fire Insurance Company') in 1891. Today, the OP Financial Group serves almost 5 million customers including 1.9 million 'owner customers', in a nation of 5.5 million people. But they are also its owners: as a cooperative, OP is mission-driven to invest locally 'to promote the sustainable prosperity, security and wellbeing of our owner-members', thus enhancing national prosperity.

So when the internet, smartphones, peer-to-peer loan-making startups, cryptocurrencies, blockchains, artificial intelligence, autonomous networked cars and all the other technology-led determinants of behaviour change gradually convinced the bank's leadership that maybe its century-old business model was not future-proof, they went into radical-survival mode. If traditional banking revenue might not be a long-term certainty for OP, they wondered, what new businesses could they launch that would replace the mortgages, business loans and all the other profit centres relied upon by an institution made ever less competitive by its high fixed costs, legacy computing systems and regulatory constraints? How could OP retain its social and economic mission while launching profitable and sustainable new business lines that respond to customers' changing needs?

Building on its daring move into medical surgery, in 2016 the board decided to make a €2 billion investment in rebuilding OP over five years as a new kind of 'digitalized' bank. It would launch design-led apps for smartphones, obviously, and would generally find ways to become more institutionally attuned to new customer expectations. But in internal discussions, senior management suggested approaches that would go radically further. What if the growth of autonomous car networks causes personal car ownership to collapse in the next decades? OP should explore ways to invest in 'mobility-as-a-service'. What if wealth management increasingly relies more on algorithmic decisions than on personal in-bank advisers? OP should invest heavily in machine learning to embed 'financial intelligence' in all its future products. And what if its declared mission to promote its customer-members' 'prosperity, wellbeing and security' no longer means making loans to buy tractors, processing storekeepers' payments, or selling annual travel insurance? OP should maintain their wellbeing in a more direct way: by operating yet more hyper-efficient hospitals that repair their injuries and get them back to work as quickly as possible, with a health insurance business attached. It's invested €125 million to build the first five hospitals, with plans to extend treatments to cover trauma and accident, and eventually chronic care and acute illness.

'It's down to the disruption of banking which is coming,' explains Samuli Saarni, the ponytailed and dark-suited head until recently of OP's healthcare business, Pohjola Terveys, when we meet for coffee at Helsinki's Finlandia Hall auditorium. As a bank, he explains, there are two ways to respond: you can automate your processes, and you can cut costs. But that risks losing customers to Google,

Apple and other digital-first competitors. 'We've chosen the other path – we want to stay with the customer. They don't need a bank, they need services. They don't need mortgages, they need accommodation. They don't want to borrow money to buy a car, they want mobility. We sold health insurance; people don't need health insurance, they need health. And in the future people will still need health. So our goal is to create digital services to get people to stay healthy and' – he smiles – 'away from us.'

The first hospital, specializing in orthopaedics, opened in Helsinki in 2013; over the next five years there followed others in Tampere, Turku, Oulu and Kuopio. 'Most of our customers will live less than two hours from our comprehensive offering of health services,' OP's executive chairman Reijo Karhinen pledged at the time. Moreover, he added, the goal would not be simply to maximize profits: 'The decision to expand the health and wellbeing business fits our basic mission, as our focus is on promoting the prosperity and wellbeing of our customers.'

To Samuli Saarni, it's also about repositioning the bank's business model around new types of digital services built on top of its core values. 'The fundamental value of a cooperative is not to make profit but to produce services for your owners,' he explains. 'You don't need a cooperative bank any more, so we have to produce other value around being a cooperative.' So the bank doesn't simply want to sell customers health insurance. It wants to help them stay healthy as part of a wider set of integrated services.

And this, Saarni states, is just the start. 'In healthcare, we haven't seen the revolution yet,' he tells me. 'In terms of digital services, we can start with genetics and personalized medicine. Then we can offer remote monitoring and automatic care of chronic diseases such as diabetes. And with that comes behaviour change: no one wants to go to a physician, just as they don't want to go to a physical bank. You'll go online. People will stop visiting the doctor, so the back office will change. I hear some hospitals in England' – he widens his eyes melodramatically at this point – 'still have paper records!'

Crucially, a radical, patient-focused approach also makes economic sense for a bank that provides both insurance and the healthcare itself. In Finland, employers (or their insurers) are liable for sickness pay each day an employee is off sick. That creates a financial incentive to get people back to work as soon as possible, which is why the Pohjola hospitals are optimized to treat patients quickly and efficiently. This system avoids the conflicts of interest inherent in American healthcare, where health providers tend to bill insurers for expensive treatments such as MRI scans or surgery that may not be strictly necessary. 'That's the traditional business model,' Saarni explains, 'whereas our business model is built on not doing unnecessary scans, lab tests, operations that make a profit.' He smiles. 'A cooperative has no interest in doing unnecessary things to people. Just the right things.'

The starting point for Pohjola Terveys was to find ways to align the incentives of health provider and insurance company. So it built them as one single company – which, Saarni points out, cuts unnecessary spending and ensures that patients receive what's clinically best for them, even if that means prescribing rehab over more expensive treatments.

The strategy appears to be delivering: Pohjola Terveys says its 'hospital service' approach is returning patients to work in almost half the time of other hospitals. 'It's quite fun to measure,' Saarni says. 'Half of our insured patients are still being treated by someone else, so we have a randomized control group. And it seems we can get twenty days' less sickness absence per patient, saving €2,000 per patient episode. We also follow the Net Promoter Score' – a measure of customer loyalty, which ranges from negative 100 to positive 100 – 'and it's fairly constant for us above [positive] 95, and about 96 in surgery. So it seems to work.'

Saarni's business card describes him simply as 'Senior VP for Health and Wellbeing', but that glides over his nuanced qualifications for this new kind of banking job. He has a philosophy PhD in healthcare ethics, and a second PhD in health-outcome measurement, but started his clinical career as a psychiatrist. 'I'm a physician by training,' he tells me. 'I believe it's best if you stay as far as possible from a physician. We can be dangerous. There's a saying in India – a hungry physician is more dangerous than a hungry tiger.'

As a psychiatrist and a philosopher, Saarni thinks a lot about the bigger context. And what matters now, he says, is to keep his bank relevant and true to its core beliefs – in other words, its cooperative values. 'If customers stay with you, they will stay with banking. That's the only way to stay in business.'

Even if that means providing services that are not very bank-like at all. 'It doesn't feel like I'm working for a bank,' Nina Vesaniemi reflects as she finishes our tour of Pohjola Hospital. 'In Finland, we don't see it as a bank performing surgery. It's an insurance company that's owned by a bank that's performing surgery. It's *healthcare*.'

OP's member-owned structure may shelter the bank from some of the coldest winds buffeting stock-market-listed companies, but its bold approach to transformation offers lessons for any business confronting tough new digital realities. Faced with fundamental threats to its revenue models, OP's management returned to first principles. They sought to identify the bank's core market differentiators, the defining factors that built a century of customer loyalty and trust – in OP's case, its cooperative mission, customer-service ethos and declared purpose of promoting members' 'sustainable prosperity, security and wellbeing'. They then sought to build new kinds of growth businesses on top of these core strengths. If OP's revenues from mortgage interest, auto finance, retail payments, agricultural machinery loans, foreign currency conversions, life insurance, portfolio management and so many other twentieth-century forms of value creation would no longer sustain a twenty-first-century bank, it would simply have to reframe its value around new products and services. And so OP's leadership team began to reframe the bank's value for personal customers in four key areas: health and wellbeing; mobility; home-related services; and financial planning.

In autumn 2015, the bank's then CEO launched a strategic review by asking an existential question. What will banks and financial service providers be needed for in the future? Will they in fact be needed at all?

Tom Dahlström, OP's forty-seven-year-old chief strategy officer, recalls how the journey began as he carries his lunch tray to a long communal restaurant bench in the OP Financial Group's corporate headquarters, in the Vallila district of north-east Helsinki. 'We'd done a bit of research on how, for millennials, banking could be replaced by other things,' he explains. 'Banking has forgotten its basic role. International payment systems, for instance, make no sense today. We knew the financial system was facing fundamental change. It needs to be blown up.'

And so his team set about blowing up the existing business. 'This isn't narrow product innovation, where someone might copy what we're doing,' Dahlström says. 'Our approach is comprehensive: we were a successful universal bank, with one-third of the Finnish market, covering all areas of banking from savings to financing. We weren't defined by being a bank – that was simply the task we were working on; instead, we were defined by working for our owner-customers. We're strong financially, with good corporate DNA, a good brand, tech capabilities, design insights – so, we thought, what are the more basic needs or value chains that we might be involved in? What are the fundamental problems our customers want us to solve, after health and wellbeing?'

The acquisition of the Pohjola insurance company in 2005 had already cemented the case for a healthcare business. But the 2015 strategic review went much further. 'We started thinking about mobility,' Dahlström says. Ten per cent of OP's earnings come from helping people buy and insure cars. But cars are getting smarter, producing data at scale. 'Tesla trusts data so much that it can offer its own insurance. Where does that leave us? So we're now offering cars-as-a-service, starting with electric cars that you can rent through our app by the minute.'

What else would OP's drivers need? Electric charging points for their battery-powered cars, for sure, so the bank partnered with an energy company to build a national network of charging points. It's also building a car-sharing model, and working with business customers to improve the efficiency of their car fleets. On top of that it's talking to housing corporations about offering 'mobility-as-a-service', or MaaS – the notion that the private car could give way to app-style services that conveniently integrate multiple forms of transportation.

Dahlström pauses to eat a mouthful of salad. 'Then we thought about retail. We're big in payments, but merchant services are very traditional. What does the small merchant need?' Talking to them revealed the hurdles that they faced in operating their online stores. So OP developed new payment and cashier services, and gave them access to stock-management, customer-relationship-management and logistics software. It bought Payment Highway, which offers mobile payments; it built chatbots for the merchants to use; it even developed a way to help concert organizers take non-cash payments at a gig. This small-business service is called OP Kassa, and it's currently being piloted with a few hundred customers.

The bank also considered how it could better serve other small-business customers. Obviously it could help them register a company and fulfil their legal, tax and salary obligations. But why not go further and help them through the entire journey: giving them access to a free academy of entrepreneurship, teaching them how to market their brand, offering guidance on selling internationally or recruiting talent? Now that *would* be a valued service.

Next on the list was housing. 'We're in home insurance and mortgages and real-estate agencies,' Dahlström says. 'And our pension fund invests in real estate, so we have wider sector knowledge. But, we thought, where can we add value? So now we're also working on intelligent homes to help older people stay independent for longer. We want to make the home safer – which connects to the health and wellbeing part.' Even more radically, OP is examining what it calls 'home-as-a-service' – a bold reinterpretation of home ownership itself. Let's say an OP customer finds an apartment for sale on the open market but can't afford the price. The bank might then buy it with its own real-estate investment fund, and make it available for the customer to live in 'as a service', at slightly above market rent, perhaps enabling some form of shared ownership. 'We want housing to be an attractive possibility,' Dahlström tells me. It sounds a brilliant solution to the unaffordable cost of first-time home ownership, while also giving the investment fund a secure long-term way to generate cash returns.

Like many Finnish businesses, OP is still processing the lessons of Nokia's sudden fall from global feature-phone domination to irrelevance in the iPhone era. 'Nokia taught us that if you give people a false sense of security, an arrogance that everything you're building is world-class – and it isn't – that's very dangerous. We can be the best in the world at some things – but we have to be modest and hardworking. And yes, we can lose everything. We can be dead in ten years.' Dahlström pauses. 'I don't believe that's likely for OP, but we do have to reinvent ourselves. There's a lot of false self-satisfaction in the financial industry. Humility is something our nation is fairly good at. Maybe too good at.'

And so OP, with its 12,000 staff, now plans to keep disrupting itself. 'We don't really define ourselves as a bank,' Dahlström says, and its long-term goal isn't to be a bank. 'That's not enough for us. There is so much room to innovate. So in health, we don't want to do what other people have done. It's about generating value to customers and society and solving problems in ways other people *haven't* done. It's about disrupting the health and wellbeing industry.'

To understand how a century-old bank transforms itself into an operating-theatre business, a car-by-the-minute business, a serviced-landlord business, even an elderly-care business, we need to unpack its unusually multilayered, cross-fertilizing, interdisciplinary processes. It knows that its future will rely on bringing artificial-intelligence research, service design and lean-startup methodologies into the bank. It also understands that it will need to partner with startups, make seed-stage investments in some, and acquire growth-stage companies. And it will have to bring all these disciplines together, out of their silos, to prototype potential future businesses through design sprints, agile-scrum management and live customer research. In other words, OP is driven by a general imperative to *execute*.

At the core of OP's transformation process is a 150-person unit simply called New Businesses – the bank's very own startup factory. I meet Masa Peura, a former media executive who runs the unit, in a meeting room at the bank's sculptural head office in Vallila. Even the building, a 2015 concrete-and-glass-enclosed campus by JKMM Architects, is intended to convey the bank's values. The ever-present Finnish granite was chosen to emanate durability and permanence; the glass walls are designed to make the inside visible to outside observers, signalling the bank's openness and transparency while reminding workers in turn never to forget the outside world.

Peura meets me on the corporate strategy floor, which has living green walls, collaborative breakout spaces, smaller quiet spaces and other architectural devices intended to promote fresh thinking. For an incumbent, he explains, it's not enough to digitize only the existing services. New services are critical – services that engage with 'the important moments of people's everyday lives', from keeping customers healthy to future-proofing their journey to work. And that means doing things a traditional bank would never do, such as build a tolerance for initiatives that may fail fast.

'We started more than thirty projects and killed half of them, from wealth management to a freelancer bank – just killed them,' Peura says. 'We gave these projects a little seed investment, then a bit more when they showed progress. We considered whether we should go into the telco business as a virtual operator; the business logic wasn't strong enough. Should we go into digital education? That was very off-the-wall – we killed it quickly.'

It's what Peura calls 'innovation in a really practical way'. He explains: 'Our role is to be open to changes happening abroad, but in a way that implements stuff. Our challenge is to create a new, entrepreneurial culture – an "experiment" culture that's not very characteristic in the traditional banking industry.'

That requires hiring staff from startup backgrounds and giving them space to experiment within a research department known as OP Lab, whose budget runs into the double-digit millions of euros. Kristian Luoma, who runs OP Lab, calls it the company's 'innovation platform'. Its real task is to bring the bank close to startups that it can learn from or partner with. So it invites startups to collaborate on programmes involving smart health, smart mobility, smart commerce and smart living. It co-hosts startup accelerators in Silicon Valley (with Plug and Play) and in London (with Accenture). And it uses a scouting network to source talent. Of 500 tech startups the network identified in 2017, OP signed collaboration agreements with a handful including EDlooper (context-based driving insurance), Raye7 (ride-sharing), Buddy Healthcare (post-surgery patient training) and Tomorrow Labs (blockchain-based real-estate transactions). It's an effective way to discover what's potentially around the corner.

'Honestly, startup–corporate collaboration is super-hard,' says Luoma, whose own startup journey to OP from Nokia includes a mobile game and a social-commerce app ('a mixture of Foursquare and Instagram') that ultimately failed ('but I learned a lot'). 'All too often I see companies approaching startups because it's the right thing to do, because it's a trend,' he says. 'So they go on innovation safaris, looking at the startups through safety bars, then they go away.' So why is OP bothering? 'We're engaging to learn,' he tells me. 'This is the fastest way to execute. We may then acquire the company, license the tech, or build it ourselves.'

The lab has closely adopted the teachings of the American writer Eric Ries, whose bestselling books *The Lean Startup* and *The Startup Way* popularized a company-building methodology based on iterative product launches in combination with feedback loops that measure customers' actual needs. He suggested that teams launch 'minimum viable products' as low-cost experiments, while constantly monitoring feedback using metrics known as key performance indicators (such as percentages of customer referrals or conversion from free to paid). They can then use the lessons from this 'validated learning' to alter the products quickly and repeatedly, based on what the market actually wants. 'Eric Ries and OP Lab think alike,' Masa Peura says. 'This is the Startup Way. Ideas here are validated, adopted and scaled. Go-to-market speed is important.'

The team has launched forty new services in the past year alone, Peura tells me – each code-named after a beer brand until it is ready for public announcement. It's just rebuilt its Pivo personal finance app, which has 700,000 registrations, through which it's introduced peer-to-peer payments. It's released a mobile cashier app for small businesses, enabled payments in its mobility services, turned Block-fest into Finland's first fully cashless music festival, helped new founders with their billings through its OP Kevytyrittäjä 'light entrepreneur' service, and switched on e-commerce payment for web stores. It's built a chatbot-based ordering service for the pizza chain Kotipizza, started experimenting with co-working spaces in the northern city of Oulu, and made minority investments in start-ups such as Shipfunk, which provides e-commerce logistics, and R3, a distributed-ledger platform. 'It's evolution,' Peura reflects. 'When we started two years ago, OP Lab was like a startup in a corporate setting. Now we have a viable portfolio.'

OP's approach to mobility services exemplifies how fast, and how radically, it has been executing. 'We realized we had a big business with car owners, accounting for one-tenth of the profits of the OP Group, with car loans and insurance,' Peura says. 'So we decided we needed to understand the changes in mobility and be able to build new services and add value in a new way.' The New Businesses team brainstormed and began working on minimum viable products – a car rental service, code-named (in OP's beer-brand tradition) 'Black Cab Stout'; a car-sharing service, called 'Corona'.

First, they needed outside talent to refine their thinking. Sonja Heikkilä had become an unusual media phenomenon in Finland in 2014 for the grand vision published in her Master's thesis at Aalto University: 'Mobility-as-a-Service – A Proposal for Action by Public Administration, Case Study: Helsinki'. This popularized the concept of MaaS. In November 2015, the OP team sought out Heikkilä at Helsinki's Slush startup festival. They needed her to help them build.

'A few years ago, we started thinking, how is mobility changing?' she recalls. 'Finns are very tied to car ownership, but we wanted to offer the freedom of mobility without needing to own a car. The needs of users are changing, moving from ownership to "usership". Plus, digitalization and connected cars enable smart services. Your mobile phone allows a seamless user experience, a personalized service, greater efficiency. The first stage of MaaS is car-as-a-service, which means car sharing or car leasing. We wanted to bridge the gap between having and not having a car. So we started building.'

The team approached BMW to franchise its DriveNow car-sharing service. Within six months, OP had 150 BMWs and Minis in Helsinki, rentable by the minute; six months later the service had 15,000 registered users and it has expanded to three cities. They worked with Tesla, Nissan and other manufacturers to launch a car-leasing business for electric cars called OP Kulku, which offers all-inclusive monthly bills that cover insurance, repair, home delivery, even car washes, over two- to four-year contracts. They partnered with Europcar to launch a flexible monthly leasing business, OP Kausiauto; and with the Nordic energy company Fortum to build a hundred electric car charging stations in Finland – including charging points connected to OP's high-street branches.

Currently the team is working on a companion app for car owners that offers everything from booking and paying for parking to sourcing the best-priced fuel; and on a mobility-as-a-service app called OP Matka, which finds the optimal journey route, lets you book and pay for trips using multimodal transport including buses, DriveNow cars and taxis, and sends receipts directly to your company every month.

If the services-led approach is transforming OP's car-related business lines, it's no less central to its plans for its real-estate businesses. OP owns Finland's biggest chain of traditional real-estate brokers, handling 12,500 home transactions each year from 170 branches. It calculates that it's Finland's biggest provider of home loans, and has 700 people working in property management. But the internet has a habit of shaking up profitable old-school sectors such as real estate. What if an online home aggregator makes OP's agencies irrelevant, or new kinds of peer-to-peer loans shrink its mortgage business? As technology-led startups upgrade customer expectations in what's becoming known as the 'proptech' (property technology) boom, what right does OP have to exist in the sector at all?

That's the task Jarkko Kyttänen is tackling, as OP's head of home services. Kyttänen joined in February 2017 after eighteen years at Sanoma, a media company, and with five people in his core team, and fifteen more outside OP, he is building what he calls the 'OP home ecosystem' – an audacious attempt to transform how Finns buy, rent and use their home. 'We're focusing on, first, how can we innovate when you're moving home, whether buying or renting?' he says. 'Then, when you are living somewhere, what services can we bring you, and how can we use smart data?'

His team's first product, launched in early 2017, was an online tool to give home-buyers transparency on market prices and likely future price trends. As Kyttänen explains, the service 'is taking power from the brokers and empowering the consumer'. It has brought together a consortium of banks to digitize home transactions using blockchain, thus speeding transactions and automating stamp-duty collection. It has vetted 160 startups to partner with three, one disrupting real-estate management, another operating smart homes, and a third digitizing the rental market. But OP is also thinking bigger: about its potential role, alongside the big tech companies, in creating an 'intelligent' sensor-enabled home for its customers.

Its biggest bet, being worked on now, is what Kyttänen calls 'home-as-a-service' – just as Tom Dahlström explained it to me: OP purchasing your apartment for you as a service minimizes your risk and affords some upside of ownership. 'We're also thinking about a marketplace for home-related services,' Kyttänen says. 'Who can you trust to repair the roof? We bring transparency and ratings. We already have 1,500 suppliers offering services.'

How big could its emergent housing 'ecosystem' be for OP? 'Hundreds of millions of euros in revenue,' Kyttänen estimates. 'The real-estate market in Finland is already one billion euros a year. And it's very analogue. You can already see there's money there.'

It's not just multibillion-euro banks that stand to benefit from moving into services. In the wealthy London neighbourhood of Mayfair – the Monopoly board's most expensive square – a cosy, cluttered bookshop that has traded on Curzon Street since August 1936 has found a delightfully counter-intuitive way to thrive in challenging times.

The Heywood Hill bookshop, a neighbourhood fixture nestled between Geo. F. Trumper, selling gentlemen 'all manner of toilet requisites', and Pastor Real Estate, listing a small two-bedroom Curzon Street attic for £2.5 million, has faced some troubled years. Not even a 2011 Royal Warrant for purveying books to the Queen could disguise a stark truth: up against Amazon and other discount retailers, a rented shop selling new and old books here could not make a viable business. No matter that John le Carré boosted the shop's fame by setting a scene here in his 1974 spy novel *Tinker Tailor Soldier Spy*; nor that the novelist and socialite Nancy Mitford worked here for £3 10s a week from 1942 to 1945, as the blue plaque above the door celebrates. Passing trade continues to decline, and a looming rent review is causing anxiety. When Nicky Dunne took over the business that's owned by his father-in-law, the 12th Duke of Devonshire (Mitford's nephew), in 2011, he knew something had to change.

'I started on the shop floor thinking, "Is there any future for a bookshop? Why would you come to a bookshop?" Amazon was doing very well, Waterstones not that well, and the e-book had reared its head.' Dunne, an outsider to the literary world having worked as a political consultant, then made an astute observation. 'Sitting here behind the desk, where Nancy Mitford used to sit, talking to customers, I realized that we had an unbelievable group of people coming through the door – international, affluent, English-speaking, leaders of businesses, people at the top of their field and across the culture. It made for an interesting day. I thought, "There's something here. What could we do that would be useful to them?"'

Dunne, now forty-eight, saw Heywood Hill as 'a pilot fish on the literary culture' – swimming around with the sharks, but too small to compete either with the discounters or the established antiquarian dealers. But then it struck him. If Heywood Hill's expertise in selling books was no longer viable, why not reframe its expertise around *recommending* books? Why not turn a retail business into a curation service, using the knowledge of its specialist booksellers to create bespoke libraries for discerning customers, while also promoting a personalized book-subscription offering? 'Rather than your coming here to choose your next book, we'll choose one for you based on what you tell us about your taste,' Dunne explains, in his crisp, educated English tones. 'It becomes the most personalized book subscription there is. Not an algorithm, but a *human* rhythm, as we call it.'

The idea, ironically, was partly prompted by his casual reading in the shop of Karl Marx. In *Das Kapital*, Marx observed that mechanization would turn nineteenth-century workers into the system's 'conscious linkages'. This was a new phrase to Dunne, but it made him reflect that human beings make conscious linkages rather than algorithmic and mechanistic ones. 'You don't want to just read about Burke, you might want a bit of Wodehouse in your life too.' And so A Year In Books, the Heywood Hill subscription service, was born.

For £950, you can sign up for the Anglophile Subscription, receiving four elegantly packaged boxes of British books over the year, tailored to your particular reading tastes. If you'd prefer a personally selected monthly hardback, £390 will buy you a reading consultation followed by twelve gift-wrapped books sent with a Cressida Bell illustrated bookmark. There are five full-time booksellers working on the subscription service from the shop's downstairs room: each of them reads between 100 and 200 books a year, and in their monthly huddle they hand-pick what they consider an exceptional book to suit a particular subscriber's reading taste. 'And what's nice about this service,' Dunne tells me, 'is it's really taken off.'

The fact that it took three months before Dunne had time to see me suggests that things are indeed looking up. When I finally get an appointment, he won't reveal how many subscribers there are, only that 'it's in the low to mid thousands, paying on average £265 each, in advance – which is transformative for cashflow'. In the company's published annual accounts, advance sums for A Year In Books subscriptions were listed at £350,763 for 2017 and growing fast year-on-year.

This is the opposite of Amazon's book-recommendation algorithm. 'The booksellers are absolutely to a woman passionate and deep readers,' Dunne explains. 'Their room downstairs is like a Booker jury room every day of the week. They're thinking, "What did David Rowan have last month? I might get him this William

Shaw book; has anyone read it?" They do this all day long, and then books get shipped out to seventy-five countries.'

And then there is the bespoke library service. Dunne had the idea after seeing his wife's grandfather, Andrew Cavendish, the 11th Duke of Devonshire, building a library on Ireland when in his eighties. Dunne then met the Hong Kong businessman David Tang, who created an endurance-themed library for his wife after she had taken up marathon running, and declared it to be the best present he ever gave her. So the bookshop began experimenting, taking on projects such as a 3,000-book library on the history of modernism for a wealthy client's Swiss mountain chalet. Dunne and his team are too discreet to discuss their clients, but I learn from elsewhere that the budget was approaching £500,000.

'The Swiss library was a proof of concept for us,' Dunne recalls. 'We've created two more libraries for that client in Los Angeles since then, as presents for other people. Since then we've put libraries on aeroplanes, cruise ships, hotels; this month we're completing three or four libraries, one on rowing as a present for someone who rowed for Harvard and Cambridge, another on the history of capitalism for a fund manager, mostly the people who have moved the markets. The common denominator is that these clients really love books.'

A separate libraries team spends time getting to know the client, listening, understanding their interests. The team draws up an initial proposal, which often gets tweaked, along with various budget options. The entry point is £10,000, but that can go up to seven figures. The team then goes out to source the books. Unlike traditional book-dealing, there's very little financial risk as they buy only books that have been pre-agreed.

Dunne's entrepreneurial energy has shown that redefining a retail business as a service business can have transformative impact. Heywood Hill is still a small business, but it's one with a renewed confidence. 'We like to think we're the biggest little bookshop in the world, a cross between Black Books and Downton Abbey,' he says with a smile. 'I even wrote a mission statement – people here go cross-eyed when I say that phrase – that we sell good books, old and new, to readers and collectors worldwide in innovative ways. And we're getting some creative energy into this space – that's what I love.'

I ask him how business is. 'Right now I feel the most optimistic I've ever felt about it,' he replies jauntily. 'It's looking very positive indeed. No one's getting rich here, but we are growing, creating jobs, and the business is on a firm financial footing, and it wasn't before. I'm feeling quite pleased about all of that.'

Dunne has to go, as he has another customer to visit – a client, naturally, who values books; Heywood Hill refuses to work with those who don't. As he leaves, oblivious to the two heavily armed policemen standing among the hedge-funders at the Curzon Street entrance to Shepherd Market, he extends a handshake and graciously suggests that Heywood Hill could send out this book with its subscriptions. 'But only if the ladies like it,' he cautions. 'I often make suggestions to them, but they have to love it. Church and state and all that . . .'

So what practical tools does an organization need to make a successful service-led transformation? The OP experience suggests that it requires not only intense management focus and a hybrid talent pool, but also a deep understanding of service design and design thinking, as well as strong technical expertise.

At OP, the design mission is led by Tuomas Manninen. Another Nokia refugee, Manninen, head of design and customer experience, leads eighty-five 'designers and design-thinking professionals' in Oulu and Helsinki. 'We would be the biggest design agency in Finland if we were independent,' he tells me. 'We may employ 10 per cent of all service-design people in Finland, but we're responsible for 50 per cent of all money invested nationally in service design.'

The team's main role is to prototype new products, using agile and experimental working methods. 'When we have an idea, we create a hypothesis and then test it on the market quickly,' Manninen explains. For instance, the team thought there was demand for Airbnb insurance. So they prototyped it, to see if there was a real need, by creating a Facebook ad in the Stockholm area, where there are lots of Airbnb properties. 'We asked people to leave their email address if they wanted to be the first to get the product. Yet the ad got hardly any response – which made us realize that there was no customer need, so we dropped the project. We then interviewed Airbnb hosts in Stockholm, and realized that it demanded too much effort. At that stage, we saw that there was a similar insurance service in Norway, but we discovered that it was not selling. Isn't a Facebook campaign cheaper and faster than launching a full product?'

Designers are embedded across the company's business units, each allocated to a 'tribe' to ensure effective inter-departmental communication. But every project begins with the customer. Before the bank launched its Personal Finance Manager app, Manninen's team hosted five workshops with customers on under-standing trends and drivers, on creating a vision, on strategic opportunities. After prototyping the resulting ideas, they then conducted fifteen interviews per concept, followed by written questionnaires. 'We found that financial wellbeing was being under-served, and that behavioural psychology was more critical than demographics,' Manninen tells me. 'So we began to think of consumers in terms of whether they were a hedonist, an optimizer, a dreamer, a hassler . . .'

His team is now thinking about the next stages of OP's housing services, now that 'low-cost sensors are bringing connected "Inter-net of Things" devices into the home. Can we combine health and housing and use the data the home collects for diagnostics? It's busi-ness design rather than business development. We're looking from the outside in. We've found that you get transformative learning by doing, so we have three-day design sprints to create products. It beats doing hundred-slide PowerPoints.'

But design skills alone won't allow OP's new service businesses to reach scale. Executives know it also needs deep technical knowledge. That's why the company is investing heavily in artificial intelligence and data science, in a twenty-person team under Meeri Haataja, the head of AI and analytics. 'I'm building enablers,' she says. 'We're putting financial intelligence into products and services using service design; we now have the capability to build AI. The focus of the next year is how to scale, using personal and contextual data, predictive analytics and recommendations, and building conversational user interfaces. We should be disrupting most of the processes in this company by then.'

One example becomes apparent on the day I visit: OP is launching its AI-based 'smart cast' to help rehabilitate trauma patients. Just six weeks earlier Haataja had invited Suunto, the wearables manufacturer, to discuss what could be done with its motion sensors. 'We'd talked to our physiotherapists and wanted to see if we could use sensors to gather real-time data on activity of an arm or leg in a cast. We're now starting a pilot. As Google's CEO says, AI is the new UI [user interface]. Health is an amazing opportunity.'

'Tech, for us, is an enabler,' Tom Dahlström remarks as he and I walk through OP's headquarters building, past the staff medical centre, gym, hairdresser, massage and physiotherapy room, multiple restaurants, and a fundraising display by an invited charity, Helsinki Mission. 'But design is also very important, as are customer insights and human interaction. It comes down to inspiring trust. Think about your best customer experiences – they're generally not with a computer.'

Dahlström has worked here for seventeen years. An economics PhD, he knows every aspect of the business: he was an assistant to the CEO, writing speeches and advising him on projects; he then became responsible for market intelligence; then head of strategy, and chief strategy officer on the executive board; and he held various roles responsible for IT, HR, security, investment processes, M&A and customer insight. 'If you're a progressive thinker, it doesn't matter if your background is as a bank,' he avers. 'We make more than €100 million a year based on people owning their cars, and now we're building business models based on people *not* owning cars. We're disrupting ourselves! But this will happen anyway.' It helps, too, that cutting individual car ownership fits neatly into OP's sustainability goals.

For, as Samuli Saarni sees it, the ultimate determinant of OP's success, even its long-term survival, will not be any particular business line but its wider social mission. 'I like the fit of corporate and individual values. When you have a patient in front of you who is ill, you don't think about money. You want an organization that supports you. If at work you can live by your internalized values, you really enjoy it. Management becomes quite easy, actually.'

Anyway, he reflects, illness isn't likely to disappear. 'Our hospital employees aren't worried for their jobs. But bank employees – they do get worried, they're risk averse. Disruption in banking is not here yet – traditional banking and insurance are still doing very well. But while they're still really profitable, we want to stay ahead of transformation. Because the transformation journey of OP is just beginning.'

Action Points

OP has a few natural advantages – owned by its members, it avoids the short-term pressures facing stock-market-listed companies; and the board was committed enough to change that it approved that €2 billion transformation budget. But I see wider lessons from OP's digital repositioning that other organizations can learn from:

1. Identify your core purpose and values, stripped back from current revenue models. It's these

inherent identifiers that will define your future purpose. What are your strengths?

2. Monitor customers' changing needs. They may differ from your own assumptions. What are the fundamental problems customers are looking to solve?

3. Define threats to current revenue lines and consider how new services could replace them. What services would customers pay for?

4. Design experiences, services and systems that will enhance customers' trust in you.

5. Study how emerging technologies, such as artificial intelligence or blockchain, could enable new revenue models.

6. Prototype new products and services, using agile and experimental working methods. Study agile development methods and measure customers' responses to early iterations before investing more.

7. Seed your own internal investments and prepare for many of them to fail.

8. Diversify your culture by working with outsiders: startups, academics, potential partner businesses.

5.

ENABLE MOONSHOTS

How monkey-training empowers Google's boldest bets

It was a risky decision to let Kathy Hannun lead the audacious mission to turn seawater into carbon-neutral liquid fuel. For a start, at just twenty-seven, Hannun was among the youngest employees when she joined Sergey Brin's secretive 'moonshot factory', Google[x] (since renamed X), in Mountain View, California, in 2012. She'd been hired as a junior marketer and hadn't even expected to get that job, having run late for her Google Hangout interview from a Hawaiian surf vacation, sand and seawater still in her hair. She was also 'timid', to use her word, and from rural New Hampshire, where tech 'wasn't a thing and all the adults had jobs like teacher or doctor. I didn't know anyone who invented new technologies. So it felt absurd that I was leading this project.'

But Hannun's gift for maths and science had taken her to Stanford to study civil engineering and computing, and she had long been obsessed with renewable energy. In June 2013 she attended a dinner party hosted by her boss Astro Teller, who in turn answers to Brin ('In the Batcave I'm Lucius Fox to Sergey's Bruce Wayne,' Teller explains). Hannun grew excited when conversation turned to an intriguing paper in the journal *Energy & Environmental Science*. The 2012 publication, by a team at Xerox's Palo Alto Research Center (PARC), was titled 'CO$_2$ extraction from seawater using bipolar membrane electrodialysis'. It described a novel and highly efficient way to extract carbon dissolved in the sea as carbon dioxide gas. If that carbon dioxide could be combined with hydrogen, it could create a carbon-neutral fuel such as methanol that might power ships or cars or factories while cutting greenhouse-gas emissions.

'That piqued my interest,' recalls Hannun, by then a project manager in X's Rapid Evaluation division, which vets new project proposals. She suggested to the executive then running the division, Rich DeVaul, 'Why don't you let me move this forward?' DeVaul was always looking for radically ambitious technology-based proposals that in all likelihood were going to fail. As he told the crowd from the stage at FutureCon in Washington DC in March 2018, while wearing a green Mohawk and a kilt, 'Sometimes I feel the rest of Silicon Valley is working on the problems of, well, assisted living for millennials. "Can I have an app that will get me my laundry done?" We need to work on some bigger challenges too. Problems like healthcare, for billions of people. Energy. For a long time we've been doing energy wrong.'

DeVaul's own energies were to end his career at X suddenly in October 2018, after the *New York Times* accused him of sexually harassing a female job applicant. But back in 2013 he agreed to Hannun's suggestion, and gave her a limited budget to begin investigations. As she explains, 'The deal was, I'd keep running with it till there was a reason not to.' It was a mission that fell squarely in the sweet spot of X, the division within Alphabet that seeks to turn bold research projects into new businesses that could potentially have the impact of another Google. An X project must address a huge problem with a radical solution that uses breakthrough technologies. It must aim for at least a tenfold improvement to the current way of doing something – or, as they say in X, 'Ten X rather than 10 per cent'. And it must be a 'moonshot' that moves from invention to an actual business launch, with the goal of some day making the world 'a radically better place'.

In August 2013, Hannun invited the PARC research lead, Matthew Eisaman, to present his work at X. 'He came off as being so thoughtful,' she recalls, 'and he didn't gloss over the challenges and the risks involved. I knew I could learn a lot by working with him.' She asked him to run some costings to see if the approach could potentially be commercially viable and was encouraged by the estimates. So she put together a small team involving Eisaman and three of his colleagues at PARC, plus another X staffer, and set about testing the science. By now the project had a code name: Foghorn.

To gain approval for an X project, a team must agree up front to a set of 'kill metrics' – criteria that determine whether an otherwise promising project should be ended. Kill metrics help identify the riskiest parts of a project from the start, before the team is too emotionally invested. The Foghorn team committed to producing fuel no more expensively than $5 per US gallon equivalent within five years. And then they proceeded to prove the science.

The Foghorn team faced two fundamental challenges: would the science work, and would it prove cost-effective? The team's theoretical models suggested that, if Eisaman's ideas worked in practice, they might eventually generate fuel at a price equivalent to $5 to $10 per US gallon, when the price of petrol at the pump was approaching $4 per gallon. But it was a big 'if'. 'At the beginning it was clear you could make methanol from seawater, just at an astronomically high price,' Hannun says. 'We had to continually improve the technology, always bringing down the cost to where we had any hope to commercialize. At first it went from $1,000 a gallon to $70 to $30. Of course, as you get to the harder problems, progress started to slow.'

Progress was nevertheless exciting. The team built a working prototype that extracted carbon dioxide from seawater, looked into making hydrogen using clean electricity, and showed that they could be combined to create a liquid fuel. Hannun was gaining confidence as a team leader – she prompted spontaneous applause in one otherwise all-male Rapid Evaluation meeting when she called out a male colleague who kept interrupting her – and her team kept notching up significant wins. By June 2015 they had found a possible way to use electricity to produce hydrogen from desalinated or purified water at scale (known as solid oxide electrolyser cell technology) that might work alongside Eisaman's electrodialysis approach to obtaining carbon dioxide. They visited desalination plants to see if co-locating their extraction tech could cut costs. They met electrolysis researchers in Copenhagen to learn how to optimize efficiency. All the while they kept revising downwards the projected price per gallon equivalent: by the end of 2015 it was already as low as $12 or even $10. The five-year goal was in sight.

And then, in February 2016, Kathy Hannun abruptly killed the project. Her decision earned cash bonuses for her entire team.

'It just became increasingly clear that the complexity and challenge were rapidly expanding to a point where the $5 projected cost seemed unrealistic,' she explains. 'It was hard, as we'd put a lot into the project, but I realized I didn't want to waste people's time working on something that wouldn't come to fruition. I framed it first as a question to Matt [Eisaman]: once we were on the same page, it wasn't that hard to tell the team.'

Hannun's kill metric had been set after an extended period when oil had been roughly $100 a barrel. By the start of 2016 it was down to $30.12, which made gas at the pump a whole lot cheaper than Foghorn's original projections. But it would be too simple to blame oil-price volatility for the death of this moonshot. 'It wasn't really about the cost of oil,' Hannun admits, 'more that, in order to solve the remaining problems, we'd need to solve renewable hydrogen – how would you make hydrogen using electrolysis in a cost-effective way? We'd need to invest pretty heavily in that technology.' A billion dollars was being suggested, plus years of further research. And all with no certainty of success. 'The dream slipped away slowly, one fact after the other. We had a quarterly check-in with X's leadership and proposed that we not continue with Foghorn but instead publish our findings in a scientific journal. I think Astro was surprised – but he was happy that there was intellectual honesty.'

When I meet Astro Teller, he makes clear – as do many of the truly bold innovators I visit for this book – that he really doesn't want to talk about 'innovation'. 'That word is so overused, I'm not sure

we're going to have a meaningful conversation,' he says warily in
X's brightly lit warehouse-like building. He's wearing a black pin-
stripe hoodie over a grey T-shirt displaying a yellow X logo, jeans
and inline skates, and sports a ponytail and goatee. Teller is famous
at X for mostly being on skates. 'But I'd be happy to talk about what
it takes to cause change in an organization, the different muscles
you need to develop,' he tells me.

Teller's business card describes his job title as 'Captain of Moonshots'. He's forty-eight, has a PhD in artificial intelligence, ran an
AI-powered hedge fund called Cerebellum Capital, has published
three books, gave a TEDx talk with his second wife about truth,
love and divorce, and sold a body-monitoring wearables business to
Jawbone. His grandfathers were Edward Teller ('father of the
hydrogen bomb') and Gérard Debreu, a Noble Prize-winning
mathematician. Disappointingly, his actual name is Eric (Astro was
a school nickname based on his AstroTurf-like hair, and clearly it
stuck). When I first met him, at Google's Zeitgeist event in 2013, he
gave me such a memorably cogent diagnosis of bold startup entrepreneurship as actual madness that I've referenced it ever since:
'Really great entrepreneurs have this very special mix of unstop-
pable optimism and scathing paranoia,' he told me then. 'If you
don't have a ton of optimism, you're not going to make it, you won't
be able to stay sane and you won't be able to evangelize to everyone
else. And if you aren't constantly paranoid about what can go
wrong and put plans in place, then you're going to get bitten along
the way.' Distorted perceptions of reality plus clinical paranoia:
entrepreneurialism as mental illness. Brutally perceptive.

Teller was recruited by Sebastian Thrun, the über-smart
Stanford AI and robotics professor hired by Google to work on
self-driving cars. His job, as Teller sees it, is 'to hand new, Google-
scale businesses back to Alphabet. And it's OK if we don't succeed
all the time, as long as we do it often enough that the basket of
value we produce is much larger than the amount of money that
we've spent.'

Though X won't reveal its budget or headcount, its successful 'graduate' projects have certainly substantially boosted that basket of value. Waymo, the autonomous-car company, has developed IP that may potentially value the business in the hundreds of billions of dollars. Google Brain, building machine-learning tools, was spun back into Google, where its research has boosted revenues in search, advertising and YouTube. X has built a network of strato-sphere-level balloons to deliver internet connectivity, spun off as a business called Loon; a cybersecurity company, Chronicle; a life-sciences spin-off, Verily; and a drone-delivery project, Wing, that's currently testing at speeds of 120km/h in Australia. It's also quietly investigated space elevators, jetpacks, cold fusion, magnetic-levitation hoverboards, floating solar farms and cargo blimps. This is not your typical corporate R&D unit.

Sergey Brin, the Google co-founder, walks past our meeting room while speaking intensely to a colleague, and looks in to see if Teller is free before walking on. I ask how much autonomy Brin and his co-founder Larry Page allow him, and Teller laughs. 'They spend a lot of time in the building, and they give me lots of advice, which we sometimes take, but X is not wired to just pick up and carry their thoughts and do it their way. They're smart enough to know that that approach wouldn't scale. I don't believe that top-down management is a recipe for innovation or anything close to it. In a very real sense, Larry and Sergey are our customers. They're also our funders, but they're actually quite good at not overly con-straining how the factory functions.'

Teller's role is to empower a team of what he calls 'card-counters rather than gamblers'. His job is to foster a culture that allows anyone to suggest a project, no matter how off-the-wall, and that then evaluates these ideas in unbiased ways in order to turn the best efficiently into commercial applications. He doesn't want to be the filter; it's far more scientific to rely on dispassionate meth-odologies to assess proposals 'and then throw them into the waste bin for the right reasons. If you want to make flying cars, good for you; but anyone here with an *idée fixe* ends up leaving in tears.'

That means encouraging staff to propose audacious missions and get passionately behind them, but also to be cool-headed enough to know when to quit. 'Being passionately dispassionate is one of our contradictory goals,' Teller says. 'Responsibly irresponsible is another: we want to go fast, unbound by any rules, but we also need to follow laws, and build a safety culture. As card-counters we need to be honest about those tensions, in looking for ways to have the odds lean in our favour.'

Managing team psychology, and neutralizing human biases, are key to systematizing innovation at X. Teller shares a few lessons learned since X launched in 2010. First, how to ensure that team members don't self-censor in order to avoid peer judgement of their more outlandish ideas. This, Teller says, comes down to creating a team ethos of 'psychological safety'. He mentions one staffer, Emily Ma, who came to him a few months ago embarrassed that her last three ideas had been rejected. 'I said, "OK, Emily, I understand, that's painful. But how painful was it? Did your manager yell at you?" She said no. "Are your peers still positive about you?" She said yeah. "Do you feel it impeded your promotion prospects?" No.' He advised her that the best way to learn to ski is to go faster, even if that means falling down a few times. 'She responded by saying, "Yes, you're right." That's psychological safety. When someone kills their project in a brave and thoughtful way, they'd better get a promotion' – or, in Hannun's case, a cash bonus – 'because if they don't, no one's going to end their own project ever again.'

Teams have learned the importance of confronting the toughest part of a problem first. Teller talks of it as the 'monkey-first' approach. Imagine you're having to teach a monkey to recite Shakespeare while standing at a pedestal. How would you allocate your time and money? The temptation in most organizations, with shareholders or bosses demanding early evidence of progress, is to start with the pedestal – but that's the wrong choice, as it creates a false sense of progress. The right choice is to start with the hardest part: training the monkey. 'I'll tell people, "Either your project has an Achilles heel or it doesn't; and if it does, would you like to find out about it now or three years and $20 million from now?" Right there I've made it a little bit more urgent for you to work on the hardest part of the problem.' The notion of 'monkey first' has become so totemic within X that staffers often insert monkey icons in their internal slide decks to signal to colleagues which is the toughest challenge in a project.

Second, the factory needs to be systematic in how it filters projects for rejection. 'We choose not to continue with projects for all kinds of reasons,' Teller says. 'Very occasionally it breaks a law of physics. Or it's just immoral, at best a zero-sum game that may hurt people. There are then the techno-economics: there's a big difference between making 5 per cent profit and losing 5 per cent. You won't change the world with things that lose money, as they shrink, they don't grow. Sometimes it's a portfolio thing. Would we now start another cybersecurity moonshot? That would be kinda odd: we just graduated one. In some cases we already have a couple of bets in a space; we'd consider another one if just the right idea came up, but that's less exciting than getting into a new space. Satisfying these three circles – a huge problem for the world, a radical proposed solution, a science-fiction product or service that would solve that huge problem – turns out to be shockingly hard. We have to look at hundreds every year just to get a handful to go forward.'

Another key lesson is the value of learning from failures, and of building those experiences into institutional memory. 'We do post-mortems on a lot of things. We write down a lot. I know we stopped doing lighter-than-air variable-buoyancy cargo ships three years ago and why, but a lot of people here don't. When we fail two years in at a project's techno-economics stage, people start to say maybe we could have stopped after eighteen months – that learning gets baked into the process.'

X's greatest public failure has been Google Glass, a pair of smart spectacles incorporating a heads-up computer display. It was unveiled in 2012–13 with a twelve-page spread in *Vogue*, a Diane von Fürstenberg catwalk at New York Fashion Week, Glass-using sky-divers dropping into Google's San Francisco developers' conference, and media coverage of Glass-wearing celebrities ranging from Beyoncé to Prince Charles. The hype for a consumer product whose utility had been barely proven was ill-advised; the fact that Brin pushed hard for public testing among 'Glass Explorers' (who bought pre-release models for $1,500) added to frustrations within X. The project was closed in 2015 amid highly negative press coverage: the *New York Times* called Glass 'the Edsel of Silicon Valley'.

'We did one thing right and one thing wrong,' Teller tells me. 'We were right to go out early with a learning platform. We talked to the Explorers in that way: we made this thing, we think it's the future of how people will interact with the digital world, help us figure out what it's for. That was totally right. The part where we told people it was a product when it wasn't yet – that was an enormous mistake.' Unrealistic expectations had been raised, and tensions grew within X as to whether Glass should ever have been pitched as a consumer product. It's now being revived as a hands-free device to help workers assemble machinery or service large appliances.

One weakness of human beings is their bias against imagining what could go wrong with work that excites them. At X, it's called 'launch fever'. The worst possible scenario is that a whole team ends up with a blind spot about the warts a project could have. 'But if you get them in a room, and tell them to imagine they've had that launch, and it's been an abysmal failure, and they feel like throwing up they're so upset, we can't even look at each other walking down the hall . . . Here's a piece of paper, you've got two minutes to write down now why this was such an abysmal failure. Go. And people are immediately sixteen again, scribbling to please the teacher. You take them to a different place. It feels awkward the first few hundred times, but eventually you're teaching people to have a moment of dispassion when that's hard.'

Another heuristic: Teller asks teams for a list of the twenty things needed to make a project successful. 'I guarantee that if you ask how they ordered the list, they'll look at you like an idiot and say the thing at the top is the most important. I'll say, "Oh. Call me crazy, but what if we make the list again but we put on top the thing that would teach us the most?" And there's virtually nothing in common with the old list. This is why we do things in learning order rather than importance order.'

At the entrance to the building is an exhibition space of early product prototypes: taped plastic frames for Google Glass, torn Loon balloon parts, dented drone bodies. Many exhibits in the jewel cases are notably dirty and damaged. That's another deliberate signal that innovation here is not about shiny, neat narratives. 'Other companies might celebrate the making, but we celebrate the process of learning,' Teller explains. 'So we display the beaten-up, dirty, mangled thing that was where you did the learning. I can say "Fail fast blah blah blah", I can say "moonshot" or "innovation" till the cows come home, and it won't make any difference. But these small, visceral things, these signals, that's what people respond to.' That's why he spends his time trying to ensure the emotional paths of least resistance are aligned with the mission. It also, Teller says, extends to closing down people's flawed ideas with hugs and high fives, 'because it's 110 per cent emotional if you're trying to do something unusual and counter-intuitive'.

I observe that Teller seems to be leveraging psychology more than engineering – as if he's the mind doctor of Alphabet. He grins. 'From Captain of Moonshots to the Mind Doctor – that sounds like a cool X-Men thing. Hmm, I like that.'

A Waymo autonomous car stops politely as I cross Mayfield Avenue towards the moonshot factory's inconspicuous entrance. Inside the factory, Project Wing drones dangle proudly from the ceiling in progressively more polished iterations. From the high-ceilinged atrium I can make out an upstairs room, through a secure glass door, where Kuka robot arms are being trained to grasp objects in the 'arm farm', a machine-learning collaboration between X and Google Brain. A wall sign states 'Warning: robots in motion'. I'm led past the 'Failure Analysis Lab' and the 'Design Kitchen', a fabrication lab with 3D printers, laser-cutters and other tools for rapid prototyping.

X, 3km from the main Googleplex, has been home to moonshots only since 2015. In earlier lives, 100 Mayfield Avenue served as the Peninsula Curling Rink, a Hewlett-Packard service centre, and a then fashionably carpeted shopping mall, Mayfield Mall. The engineers working on Loon balloons sit where Singer's Sewing Center once stood. It's a small reminder that any era's hot technology will soon fade into insignificance.

Today, it's a building deliberately redesigned for impermanence. Plywood walls are affixed to steel beams over concrete floors, but it takes only the unscrewing of a few flanges for a wall to be popped off and relocated. Meeting rooms can be enlarged or combined as projects evolve, the architecture creating a constant work-in-progress ethos that feels disarmingly temporary.

'The design of the building is intentional – having the café in the middle, and only one café, even though everyone complains about the lines, that's to provoke unplanned conversations while you're standing in line.' Obi Felten, a charmingly assertive German-born Google marketing veteran, was brought into X in 2012 to help Teller systematize its mad-scientist chaos. Her job title is Head of Getting Moonshots Ready for Contact with the Real World (quite seriously), and she thinks a great deal about what will optimize X's chances of graduating viable businesses. 'At the start it was a Wild West, with no processes at all,' she tells me. 'People would waste a lot of resources on the wrong problems. We had super-talented people quietly working on projects for two years and then we'd find out. That happens much less now.'

She's also focused on boosting staff diversity. 'Not just more women, but cognitive diversity. In the beginning it was mostly engineers and scientists. Now it's a whole load of disciplines, from hardware to software to machine learning, and a real variety of backgrounds. I have a woman in my team who's an engineer, but has in her past been a concert pianist, a wildland firefighter, a first-aid responder in a national park, and an artist who interned at Autodesk; and she also happens to be a woman and a lesbian.' Cognitive diversity, having people from very different backgrounds collide, is key for Felten. 'When you have a scientist who only needs things to work once, so she can publish a paper, working with an engineer, who has to make something work over and over again – that creates friction but it propels the project forward.'

A culture that has ex-US Navy Seals working alongside fashion designers, and theoretical physicists alongside an Oscar-winning FX specialist, helped, for instance, make Project Wing a lot more relevant. Its drones' first intended-use case was to deliver defibrillators to heart-attack victims. Engineers focused on making drone and defibrillator work; but user-experience researchers discovered that bystanders took so long to work out how to use the defibrillators that in the meantime an ambulance would arrive. The engineers were thinking about how to make the tech work; the researchers thought about why. Teams are also kept deliberately small, but with access to a wider pool of in-house experts in fields such as mechanical engineering, design and public policy.

Most of what X has learned about processes has been the result of experimentation. One important lesson has been the value of staggering resource allocation. At the Rapid Evaluation stage, budgets are tiny and projects are often not allocated even one full-time staffer. This stage is mostly about understanding if a moonshot is even possible, building very early-stage prototypes and exploring what the main risks are. Promising projects move to the 'foundry' stage, when Felten gets closely involved. At this stage a small team assesses the moonshot's risks and likely costs as prototypes are tested, and managers check in more often. Budgets and headcount are increased as milestones are met. The next stage is to become an independent X project such as Makani, which uses kites to harness wind energy, with quarterly progress meetings and increasing supervision.

Staff can choose what they work on. 'There's a pretty frictionless internal market,' Felten says. 'All the jobs are posted, and if an engineer wants to switch to a new role, they don't even need to tell their manager. Though it's nice if they do . . . That enables people to take slightly bigger risks – you're not going to lose your job if an X project goes bust.'

Felten thinks a great deal about enabling constructive forms of disagreement. She wants to make it safe for people to articulate unpopular viewpoints. 'In meetings, it's making sure people who dissent feel space to speak up. Some companies have a head of innovation, and nothing changes for the rank and file, so people get penalized for thinking differently – that doesn't work.' Promotions are also used not simply to reward successful projects. 'When Glass wasn't doing super well, we wanted to check that an engineer who was doing great work on the optics got promoted, but maybe not someone working on the business strategy.'

When Larry Page was an engineering undergraduate at the University of Michigan, he joined a student leadership-training programme called LeaderShape, which promoted 'a healthy disregard for the impossible'. This thinking helped frame the way he and Sergey Brin have run Google ever since. 'I feel like there are all these opportunities in the world to use technology to make people's lives better,' he told *WIRED*'s Steven Levy in 2013. 'At Google we're attacking maybe 0.1 per cent of that space. That means there's 99 per cent virgin territory. If you're not doing some things that are crazy, then you're doing the wrong things.'

He also expressed frustration towards short-term thinking in business. 'I worry that something has gone seriously wrong with the way we run companies,' he said. 'If you read the media coverage of our company, or of the technology industry in general, it's always about the competition. The stories are written as if they are covering a sporting event. That's why most companies decay slowly over time. They tend to do approximately what they did before, with a few minor changes. But incremental improvement is guaranteed to be obsolete over time. So a big part of my job is to get people focused on things that are not just incremental.'

The 10X approach is Google's answer. Digitizing every streetscape, building cars that drive themselves, acquiring a research team hoping to enable artificial general intelligence . . . None of these missions is incremental, all risk the humiliation of failure, yet all could potentially benefit billions of people.

In 2009, Page and Brin decided to create a management role – a Director of the Other – to develop fresh ideas outside Google's core businesses. The next year, Google X was launched under Thrun, who had been leading the autonomous-car project. It wasn't the first corporate R&D lab to think big. Bell Labs, a 1925 spin-out company then owned by the American Telephone & Telegraph Company and Western Electric, invented the transistor, the laser and the Unix operating system, winning eight Nobel Prizes and three Turing Awards along the way. Xerox's PARC lab created the graphical user interface and the laser printer. Lockheed Martin's secretive Advanced Development Programs, better known as Skunk Works, used small autonomous teams to work on breakthroughs such as the U-2 spy plane in the late 1950s and America's first fighter jet.

Clarence 'Kelly' Johnson, the aeronautical and systems engineer who ran Skunk Works from inception in 1943 to 1975, developed fourteen rules to build intelligent constraints into all its projects. These included:

- The Skunk Works manager must be delegated practically complete control of his programme in all aspects. He should report to a division president or higher.

- Strong but small project offices must be provided.

- The number of people having any connection with the project must be restricted in an almost vicious manner. Use a small number of good people (10 per cent to 25 per cent compared to the so-called normal systems).

- There must be a minimum number of reports required, but important work must be recorded thoroughly.

- There must be a monthly cost review covering not only what has been spent and committed but also projected costs to the conclusion of the programme.

- Access by outsiders to the project and its personnel must be strictly controlled by appropriate security measures.

- Because only a few people will be used in engineering and most other areas, ways must be provided to reward good performance by pay not based on the number of personnel supervised.

When I first met Teller in 2013, I was curious to understand if he thought such a Skunk Works approach, and in particular a willingness to learn from failure, could be absorbed in more conventional corporate organizations. 'The only time you have no excuse *not* to do it is in a corporate structure,' he replied. 'You just need to place a huge number of bets. It's how good hedge funds work.' If most bets fail, that's fine, so long as you still have others that could hit the moon. Playing it safe inside a corporation is unarguably the wrong thing to do. It's harder, he admitted, for a smaller, less-well-resourced business to take big risks. But that's what has differentiated Silicon Valley startups over Europe's. 'There is a culture of creative destruction in Silicon Valley, and a pride in placing the best, not the safest bet; and there is no shame in failure. In fact, if there is shame to be picked up in Silicon Valley, it's for wasting your life trying to hit singles and doubles.'

Why isn't there a European Google or Facebook or Microsoft? Because of a cultural willingness to play it safe, Teller argued, and to favour small incremental improvements in order to avoid the humiliation of failure. I replied that I could imagine European corporate executives responding that it's fine for this guy with his crazy job title to talk about moonshots, but that's a Silicon Valley fantasy that ignores their short-term needs to keep shareholders happy. 'They're right, and that's part of the problem,' he answered. 'They need to reset expectations with shareholders. This is one of the things that Larry and Sergey have done brilliantly and unwaveringly: they told their shareholders from day one that there will be two classes of shares – you don't get to vote, we do, so we're going to control the company. And if you're not in this for the long haul, you're better off putting your money somewhere else. And the stock price is doing just fine.'

Teller often presents on innovation at conferences to mid-career executives, giving them two choices: you can deliver a million dollars' bottom line to your company this year guaranteed, or you get a one-in-a-hundred chance of delivering a billion dollars of value. 'Nobody raises their hand for choice A; everybody raises their hand for choice B. I say, "OK, congratulations, you've all passed the math test, choice B on an expected utility basis is worth ten times as much. How many of you believe that your manager, your boss or your board would let you choose choice B?" Not a single hand in the room goes up. And then I say, you don't need a lecture on innovation, you need to quit your job.

'You can lecture till the cows come home about innovation, but if the people at the top don't have the stomach for a real risk, nothing is going to happen. And that's why Google is successful. Larry and Sergey just innately aren't interested in going slow. They're not interested in playing it safe. And that permeates the whole organization.'

I was at TED in Vancouver in February 2016 when Teller gave a main-stage talk on 'the unexpected benefit of celebrating failure'.

The previous year, he told the audience, X had killed a project in automated vertical farming, even though it met X's requirements of combining a huge problem that affected millions of people with a radical solution and a breakthrough technology 'that could actually be built'. The team working on the project in Mountain View made progress on automated harvesting and efficient lighting, and the approach used ten times less water and a hundred times less land than conventional farming. But it couldn't get staple crops like grains and rice to grow this way, so it killed the project. The 'variable-buoyancy cargo ships that are lighter than air', powered by helium cells, were killed too, even though the technology was promising – because it would have cost $200 million to design and build the first one.

Finding a major flaw doesn't necessarily doom a project. Sometimes it helps a team correct course by shifting their perspective. A team studying ways to capture wind energy at scale found that wind turbines were limited by the amount of steel that could be assembled; so it instead experimented with offshore kites that capture wind energy that's sent back to earth via their tethers. The Loon team, working on stratosphere-level balloons to deliver internet connectivity, initially planned to build a ring of balloons around the world to act as floating cell-phone towers. But the huge cost and manufacturing challenges led in 2016 to a new approach: instead, small groups of balloons were made to dance in the winds over regions where internet access was most needed.

Asking the right questions at X is almost more important than coming up with answers. It's what the staff call 'falling in love with the problem, not the solution'. Not having a fixed answer is celebrated. 'Ignorance, laziness and impatience are actually hidden superpowers,' André Prager of the Wing project wrote on the X blog. 'Full acceptance of your present limitations makes you fearless, curious and genuinely humble. It enables you to identify gaps early and to fill them efficiently.' The Wing team knew that to scale up their drone tests they would need to pack them flat for transit.

But they didn't know how to do so without compromising their aerodynamic shape. The answer they discovered was ingenious: they brought in origami specialists, who, alongside packaging designers, aerodynamicists, mechanical engineers, material specialists, user-experience researchers and cardboard manufacturers, created a pattern that allowed the bodies to be folded flat.

This philosophy makes recruitment a challenge. Amazingly talented engineers won't cut it at X if they have developed habitual ways of working. 'If you have fixed ideas, all of your insides will be screaming at you to teach us that we're stupid so we can be as normal and smart as you are,' Teller says. 'After two years, you'll either leave or go native.'

Obi Felten, meanwhile, aims to tether the entire organization to real-world concerns. 'When I first met Astro and he told me about Loon, my response was: Wow, is it legal? Have you talked to any governments about this? What about privacy? Do you have a business plan? Are you going to collaborate with mobile-phone companies or compete with them? He looked at me and said, "Um, we're working on making the balloons fly and connecting phones to talk to the balloons . . . Will you come and help us?"'

Hence Felten's implausibly long job title. She challenges teams about safety and legal risks, about partnership possibilities and business models. 'If you can't build a meaningful business, there's no way these projects will ever scale,' she says. 'Internet access is an example. If you can make it a profitable business for the telcos, Loon will make it big. If we solve self-driving, a whole lot of people will make money, and we'll make some of it. If you want real impact, it has to be self-sustaining.'

When Ruth Porat was appointed Alphabet's chief financial officer in 2015, there were reports that she planned to bring new commercial rigour to X. I ask Teller if this scrutiny has caused him to curtail his less market-focused projects. He locks eyes with me. 'The way I talk to Larry, Sergey and Ruth is exactly what I told you – I've got this black box, but you know how much money you've put in and you know about at least six things that have come out the other side. Come up with estimates of what that's worth. Is this bucket of things that we've produced bigger than the money and the hurdle rate? If it is, give me more; if not, give me less.'

I ask, finally, what's the single most important lesson that decision-makers reading this book can learn from Teller's moon-shot factory. He pauses. Any company that aspires to build an effective 'futures' team, he says, must grant it genuine independence from the core business. Otherwise it will take the comfortable path whenever challenges get tough. 'Without guaranteeing it full autonomy, every single business will start their X-lite thing and will then crush it and make it impotent as soon as it scares them or they have a bad quarter.' The only company outside Google to demonstrate such boldness, he says, is the Spanish telco Telefónica, which has a unit in Barcelona called Alpha working on health and energy challenges. Even if its projects make Telefónica's leaders uncomfortable, they can't intervene. That, Teller says, is a necessary condition for success.

'You can be Steve Jobs and go into the next building and raise the pirate flag. But almost nobody is Steve Jobs. For most people, you need some legal and practical pirate flag handed to you. The leader of that organization needs not to be normal. If you want it to be very engineering driven, maybe hire an engineer. If you want a culture engineer, hire an Astro. We've made some progress on systematizing innovation. We're constantly trying to reinvent our factory as we're running it. Which definitely makes it harder.' X is, he declares, 'the worst moonshot factory in the world. Apart from all the other ones.'

Kathy Hannun didn't let the closure of Foghorn kill her spirit. After she disbanded the team, she published a blog post on X's website sharing a few lessons learned while turning seawater into fuel. First, by setting kill metrics at the very start, her team had later been able to make an unbiased decision about their prospects of success. 'You haven't invested a ton of capital and there isn't a big emotional investment to cloud your judgment,' she wrote. 'These criteria essentially help you fight human nature.'

Second, the process had forced them to consult experts from the outset in order to make informed cost estimates. 'Although you might expect a team at a place like X to spend a majority of our efforts on technology, half of our work was in modelling cost estimates. Seeking out this reality check early saved us a huge amount of time and money.'

And finally, even idealistic moonshot factories need a healthy culture of relentless scepticism. 'Sometimes it seems as if Silicon Valley can characterize unyielding belief as a kind of innovation pixie dust: if you "think happy thoughts" and never give up, wondrous things will happen,' Hannun continued. 'There's no denying that an inspirational vision is essential to achieving something great: it lets you convene the most talented people and align them toward a shared goal. But it'll only be characterized as "visionary" when it's proven correct in retrospect.'

Alongside her work on seawater-derived fuels, she had also been investigating how geothermal energy might provide homes at scale with renewable heating, cooling and hot water. The project, called Dandelion, recently graduated from X and was spun off, with Hannun as CEO, as a Brooklyn-based business, Dandelion Energy, initially targeting the northeastern United States. In March 2018, Hannun raised $4.5 million in a venture capital round led by New Enterprise Associates. The day after the deal closed, she gave birth.

'When Foghorn wound down, I could spend more and more time on Dandelion,' she says. 'But unlike Foghorn, the deeper we get into Dandelion, the better an idea it seems. It's a good counter-example of what happens when you deeply investigate an opportunity.'

I ask what wider lessons she has taken from her time in the moonshot factory. 'At X there's always an emphasis on trying things in the real world, and learning from doing,' she replies. 'We do that even more so at Dandelion: we have to sell things to exist. We've also adopted X's "solve the hard problems first" mentality: we've done so much early work on developing drills, which have to dig hundreds of feet deep, even though that's so expensive.' To serve densely populated suburban markets such as Long Island, Dandelion realized it would need a smaller, faster drill. 'We started on that early on. I hope we'll be thankful we did.'

And what advice would she give to other corporate executives, based on her own journey? 'It's a complicated question,' she says. 'Google is a very innovative company, but also a big publicly listed company. The incentive structure and the permissions culture have a big impact on empowering or motivating people to do things in better ways. In a big company, often the incentive is *not* to take risks, not to be noticed, to politically increase your strength but maybe not with a direct tie to results for the company. That's the opposite of what you need if you're to change and be innovative. And a lot of people don't feel that it's their job to think of new opportunities for the company.' Hannun felt that the turning point for her was when Rich DeVaul and others gave her permission and empowered her. 'That was so explicit. It's pretty important to make the employee give their all to something.'

Action Points

You don't need the resources and talent of a Bell Labs or a Lockheed Martin Skunk Works to incubate product lines and businesses with the potential to add huge bottom-line value. There are lessons from Google's moonshot factory that can be more widely applied to solve two universal corporate problems: first, to challenge the legacy company mindset and processes in ways that can enable fresh thinking; and second, to create a space to develop high-risk long-term projects unrelated to today's core business. X has learned many lessons the hard way:

1. It's more important to refine the questions, rather than concentrate on the likely answers. A relentless focus on questions can allow unexpected answers to emerge.

2. You need processes that help prioritize the allocation of talent and financial resources. At X, the 'kill metrics' agreed right at the start ensure that teams' emotional attachment to their project does not get in the way of a rational decision at later stages about whether it's likely to succeed.

3. Ensure autonomy from HQ. A separate building, and discrete culture, are a must. And if one of the parent company bosses gets involved in the lab's day-to-day activities, that boss needs to be unusual enough to ignore parent-company pressures.

4. Psychological safety is vital. Make it safe for staff members to propose taking bold risks that may fail. This might mean giving bonuses if they fail in intellectually honest ways.

5. Recruit a diverse team made up of people with varying backgrounds, perspectives, skill sets and cognitive styles. Having a group of people who think the same way won't get you there. X actively seeks out people who think in challenging ways.

6. Motivate teams to work on the toughest ('monkey-first') problems at the beginning, however difficult they are.

7. Celebrate the lessons learned from failure (rather than failure itself). X has an annual 'Day of the

Dead' during which staff are encouraged to share their feelings about personal and professional disappointments. 'If the idea of "failing fast" feels counter-cultural,' Obi Felten says, 'try reframing it as "learning fast".'

8. When projects fail, X asks staff to write post-mortems and present them at company all-hands meetings. It also rewards team members who work effectively on these failed projects – which signals to other staff that they should not shy away from bold risks.

9. Partnerships are important in creating significant new business lines. X has worked with Novartis on smart contact lenses, with Telefónica on Loon, and with auto companies on Waymo's cars. 'We don't have expertise to take products to market in a range of industries, so we partner with people that do,' Felten says.

10. Moonshot factories can't rely on manuals: pro-cesses need to keep adapting. 'These are not recipes, just a bunch of ingredients,' says Felten. 'We're constantly changing our processes to make the next meal better.' And that means an organiza-tion's biggest challenge for its new-product unit may be to keep improving the internal processes that enable the greatest impact.

6.

INCUBATE TOMORROW'S BUSINESS

How a swipe beat a match

Whitney Wolfe wasn't even supposed to be working on the Match-Box app when she proposed heading back to her college campus to promote it in an outrageously direct way to the hottest kids on campus. She'd been hired to build partnerships for Cardify, a fairly conventional customer loyalty app, but frankly she was bored trying to sign up Los Angeles coffee shops and nail salons. MatchBox's potential as a location-based 'flirting game' seemed to hold so much more potential. So she took a leaf from Mark Zuckerberg's book. 'I told the team that if we take this MatchBox project to a university, I really think we could get some traction,' she recalls. Nobody objected, so she returned with some girlfriends to her alma mater, Southern Methodist University in Dallas, and talked her way into a bunch of Monday-night sorority dinners.

Wolfe, then twenty-two, had been part of what she calls the 'smart, popular, good-looking' crowd of girls at SMU, where she'd been active in the Kappa Kappa Gamma sorority, and, in her words, could sell ice to Eskimos. So she began by grabbing a chair at the dinners, stood on it, and shouted for everyone's attention.

'I'd tell the girls there that all these cute guys were looking for them on this app which they needed to download, and the sorority house that did the most downloads would get $10,000,' she says, energized, with a big grin on her face. 'I'd then run over to the boys' fraternity houses, taking all the girls with me, while they were in the middle of *their* dinner. I'd say, "Guys, every gorgeous girl on campus has just downloaded this app, and they're literally

126

on it right now, looking for you. You have to download this app."
And then we'd do the same in the bars while wearing branded
T-shirts.'

By next morning, some 400 of the most socially influential and
attractive students on campus were searching, chatting, flirting
and matching through the new app. Within days it had been
downloaded hundreds more times. Wolfe, the ambitious and
entrepreneurial daughter of a Salt Lake City real-estate broker and
housewife, had hit on the perfect way to build virality among a
carefully defined demographic that conventional marketing had
failed to engage (when MatchBox spent $500 testing mobile ads, it
was downloaded by mostly middle-aged men – disaster!). But not
even Wolfe guessed then that MatchBox, born out of a hackathon
at a startup-building company called Hatch Labs, would soon
become the most successful dating app in history, generating a
million in-person encounters a week across 190 countries, and be
valued in the billions of dollars. Maybe it helped that the Hatch
Labs team designed MatchBox as an addictive game which
involved swiping profile photos right to indicate attraction and
left for quiet rejection – and that, for the App Store launch in
August 2012, they decided to give it a more knowing, mischievous
name: Tinder.

Hatch Labs, a small, barely managed team of twenty-somethings,
certainly produced some duds as they quickly prototyped, tested
and iterated a bunch of mobile apps. It turns out that the world
wasn't clamouring for BroDown ('Challenge people around the
globe to see who can do the most consecutive push-ups') or the
embarrassing-videos app Crowdfail ('Our videos will make you
wet your pants . . . and if that happens, take a photo and send it
over'). Yet some of the products thrown against the wall stuck, at
least for a time. Blu Trumpet helped app publishers find new audiences and was acquired by a games company (although it became
less web-famous than its developer Ian Ha's side project, Shitter,
which for $35 plus postage would deliver four toilet rolls printed

with your Twitter feed). Blush, a wine-discovery app, raised funding from outside investors. Cardify seemed promising, though Apple was concerned by how the app stored credit-card numbers and delayed its App Store approval.

But it was Tinder that quickly built scale – 1.6 billion swipes a day! 20 billion matches! – touched the wider culture and mortally wounded the business model of so many incumbent dating websites. Tinder alone made Hatch Labs, by the time it closed in 2013, the most commercially successful digital-business incubator funded by a corporate. For in truth Tinder was not quite the scrappy, hungry tech startup sometimes portrayed by its marketing team. As part of Hatch Labs, it was in fact majority-owned by the multi-billion-dollar corporation which for years has dominated the online dating industry. Barry Diller's IAC/InterActiveCorp, owner of dating brands including Match, OkCupid, PlentyOfFish and Meetic, even provided office space to the team that was delightedly eating their lunch.

'We were incubated in IAC's office, on computers they'd bought, even sitting near the Match.com team,' Wolfe remembers. 'It felt like I was working for a startup, but I had the safety net of a big corporation. You could email someone with a request and they'd make sure it happened. You had this almost parental safety net, but also got to play in the backyard for a few hours a day.'

All of which raises some perplexing questions. How could a publicly listed corporation as aggressive as IAC have risked the profitability of its market-leading dating businesses by backing their more agile mobile competitor? What allowed Diller's corporate incubator to build genuine future-facing value through Hatch Labs when so many similar attempts fail? And what was it about the team culture at Tinder that allowed the app to break through as a textbook model of disruptive innovation?

This story begins with a Mumbai-born entrepreneur who emigrated to the US aged four with his parents and sister and grew up in Houston, Texas, then Orange County, California. Dinesh Moorjani was always an over-achiever: a chemical-engineering degree at Northwestern University was followed by consulting roles with Arthur D. Little and Mainspring, an MBA at Harvard Business School, and time at Goldman Sachs to learn about investment management. Moorjani built digital media and hardware businesses at Samsung Electronics North America, managed cross-border teams in the Samsung chairman's office, and helped launch an Indian art marketplace and an online travel startup. He then had a more ambitious startup idea: he wanted to launch a local online directory. That got him talking to the team at an IAC company, Citysearch, who made him an offer. Why didn't he come to work for them instead as VP of strategy and mergers and acquisitions?

It was early 2007, and a new device called the iPhone had just been announced at the Macworld convention. Moorjani knew that it represented a huge opportunity, and shortly before it went on sale in June he changed roles to launch IAC's mobile group. IAC owned or had spun off brands including Ticketmaster, Expedia, TripAdvisor, Vimeo and Ask Jeeves as well as the dating websites; Moorjani was soon helping them make the transition to mobile and, according to IAC, his team oversaw more than 40 million app downloads and a doubling of mobile revenue each year. His remit covered everything from initial product development and ideation to marketing and business development. Barry Diller was a man who respected those sorts of numbers.

Diller, who built up IAC, is often described in the press as a 'media mogul' or 'e-commerce czar'. The clichés are unusually apt: after starting in the mailroom of the William Morris Agency, Diller, an opinionated and sometimes fiery character, led Paramount Pictures over a golden decade, ran 20th Century Fox and co-founded Fox Broadcasting, built up the USA Broadcasting group of TV channels, brought together travel, dating and internet companies under IAC, and became a multibillionaire in the process. Diller, famously tough and outspoken, relished a deal. So when

Moorjani told him in spring 2010 that he planned to leave and build his own bootstrapped startup studio for launching mobile apps, Diller saw an opportunity.

'I recall sitting in Barry's office,' Moorjani says, 'and I told him I'm going to wrap up my current role so I could start a new tech lab. I wanted to build startups for a new wireless generation, and I wanted to have multiple shots at goal. I already had commitments from seed investors and I'd identified my initial hires. To his credit, Barry asked if that was something I would build with IAC. I said nicely that that sounded like a terrible idea. I said we'd risk getting the operating model, governance and incentives wrong. "I'm an entrepreneur," I remember thinking, "and I want to build a company."'

The next morning, Moorjani was attending the quarterly executive meeting at IAC when Jack Welch, the former General Electric CEO who was an IAC adviser, put him on the spot. 'There were maybe twenty-five people round the table, and Jack said he'd heard I was going to start this incubator thing. Barry must have told him. I said I was thinking about it. He said it was a good idea and I should pursue it.'

Moorjani wasn't sure he wanted to build his startup inside a big public company. From his observations, corporations tended to stifle innovation, decision-making was too slow, and he worried about a culture clash. Still, after five months of negotiations with IAC executives and lawyers, Moorjani was persuaded that IAC's scale, marketing prowess and distribution channels could give his studio an edge. They agreed that it would be established as an independent for-profit Delaware company, but with IAC investing $6 million in return for 70 per cent of the equity, three of the five board seats, and the option to be the first investor in any companies spun out. Moorjani also brought in Xtreme Labs, a Toronto-based mobile developer, as a minority investor (with 13 per cent and a board seat) in exchange for its insights and resources. On 21 October 2010 he finally opened Hatch Labs, renting office space from IAC on the fifth floor of its Frank Gehry-designed New York building.

As CEO, Moorjani set about hiring 'natural entrepreneurs' for what he called his 'technology innovation sandbox'. Engineers, designers and product managers would earn a generous salary (typically $160,000 for a product manager) and receive equity in Hatch Labs as well as in their own projects. This diversified their risk, gave them a stake in their specific business, and incentivized them financially to help the lab as a whole. He had been frustrated by Samsung's hierarchical, almost militaristic culture and was determined to build a collaborative problem-solving ethos at Hatch Labs. He spoke of it as 'a family', with prospective hires invited to social events and hackathons to ensure they would fit in, and an expectation that team members would test and help improve other teams' products.

In February 2012, Moorjani held an internal forty-eight-hour hackathon in which he paired his first employee, a talented engineer named Joe Muñoz, with a new West Coast hire named Sean Rad, brought in to develop Cardify. Muñoz was known as the lab's 'hacker in residence', problem-solving across projects; Rad, an LA-born Jewish-Persian-American whose immigrant parents had made money in a consumer electronics business, was a college dropout who had built a failed messaging app called Orgoo and a more successful startup called Adly, which connects brands with celebrities. Muñoz had already worked on a digital representation of Facebook users' interests, known as an interest graph, which he was planning to use to match people to local services; Moorjani encouraged him to work on social discovery instead, as a more scalable opportunity.

The result, MatchBox, was awarded first prize in the hackathon. But the priority was Cardify, which Rad and Muñoz continued to refine. They boosted the team, hiring a front-end engineer, Jonathan Badeen, and a designer, Chris Gulczynski. Although Hatch Labs now had space in IAC's West Hollywood building on Sunset Boulevard, the Cardify team often worked out of the personal office of Rad's best friend Justin Mateen, a party organizer he'd attended the University of Southern California with. 'He's like my twin,' Rad later told *Rolling Stone*. 'I mean, he's one month older than me, Persian Jewish, parents are friends, same community, we went to the same college, people say we look alike – it's funny.'

In the spring of 2012, Mateen introduced Rad to Wolfe, a friend of his sister Alexa, and she was taken on as a contractor to boost sales. By May 2012, Cardify was ready for launch and Rad convincingly pitched it at the TechCrunch Disrupt NYC startup contest. But the delayed App Store approval left the team in limbo, and that's when Moorjani switched them to MatchBox. Within twenty-three days they had a version ready for internal testing, although it didn't yet incorporate swiping. His only concern was the name. It sounded, well, masculine. Plus, their investor already owned the similar-sounding Match.com. That would be storing up potential trouble.

According to Jonathan Badeen, they landed on Tinder one day when they were crossing Sunset Boulevard while reading out fire-related words from the thesaurus. 'We knew a lot of people might mistake it for "tender", which we thought was nice since we often think of "love me tender".' But still the brand overlap wasn't entirely resolved: once two users mutually swipe right, they're connected inside the app with the celebratory message 'It's a Match!'

On 2 August, Tinder quietly launched in the App Store, bringing hookup culture mainstream. Moorjani moved his family to Los Angeles; Rad hired his friend Mateen as Tinder's chief marketing officer; and Wolfe was formally brought in as VP of marketing. That made Mateen Wolfe's line manager, which would become a little awkward a few months later when they began a tempestuous romantic relationship. But for the moment, as the downloads rocketed, Tinder was an InterActiveCorp success story that, perversely, IAC seemed to know very little about.

On stage at the South by Southwest conference in Austin, Texas, in March 2012, Barry Diller described Hatch Labs as 'a hothouse in the company [which] keeps the juice going'. But in practice it was a very arm's-length relationship. When Tinder moved into IAC's Sunset Boulevard offices – also occupied by the Match team – there was barely any communication between the two divisions for the first six months, according to Moorjani. Eventually they were even located on the same floor. 'We were walled off as a separate entity, renting space in IAC's building, operating autonomously other than sharing a coffee machine and a back office,' he recalls. 'Once we started taking off, the Match folks got curious and asked, "What's going on here?" They started reaching out to us through the IAC network to get to know us. We were open, but we didn't need Match for anything at the time.'

When Moorjani first told IAC about Tinder, he says, he was gently discouraged from launching in the dating space. 'Early on, the sort of facial expressions I read were, "Why are you doing this?" But to their credit, they didn't use their investor role to intervene. I'm not sure they were excited about us doing something that could become a threat to Match, but it was unclear if they thought we could succeed, so it may not have mattered to them.'

This laissez-faire approach by IAC proved key to its successful incubation of Tinder. The incumbent company faced the classic innovator's dilemma, with a new technology – the smartphone – about to slash the web-based dating brands' income. It used Hatch Labs to build a disruptive mobile business from within, one that soon eclipsed the revenues of the original Match.com business. And it succeeded by simply leaving the Hatch Labs founders alone, avoiding the temptation to crush Tinder as it was a competitor. Although this lack of intervention may have owed more to luck than to strategy. 'We were lucky enough – smart enough, I wouldn't say so much – that we left it alone to the founders,' Diller said at Business Insider's Ignition conference in December 2014. This parental detachment, Diller suggested, was what had allowed the team 'to create this incredible virality. Since then it's just skyrocketed.' By then Tinder had been downloaded more than 40 million times, with more than a billion swipes a day.

When I ask Moorjani what lessons he believes other organizations can learn from his experience running the incubator that hatched a unicorn, he replies a little wearily that he's approached all the time to advise companies that want to replicate the Hatch Labs model. It comes down to finding an experienced entrepreneurial leader who can attract talent, he tells them. 'First, you need someone who can start companies, be very disciplined about killing off those that are not succeeding, and equally disciplined about working inside a big public company,' he says.

Second, he continues, it's important for the corporate to give up control to some extent. 'You can't be involved in the operations, and board governance should be very limited. The overall value of Tinder as a standalone company would have been higher if they'd ceded control and let VCs invest. But no CEO is going to want to hear that.'

Third, the incentive structure needs to be flexible enough to allow market compensation for employees who create a commercial success. 'The people at Hatch Labs will make more than the leaders of the company in the year of an exit. Are you as a culture comfortable paying top performers tens or hundreds of millions of dollars if they create commensurate market value with those big entities?' Corporate CEOs tend not to like to see their staff making nine-figure salaries.

Fourth, the operating model demands a highly disciplined leadership that can not only act fast to kill projects that are failing but double down on successes. And finally, fifth, something that's less tangible: you need to be able to create a special spark among the team. 'I spent 40 per cent of my time recruiting,' Moorjani tells me. 'The DNA of a special startup team is very hard to create, but if you don't know how to recruit to get people to unlock value in the way they interact with each other, forget it. Great people, if they don't get along and love working together, will destroy that company.'

I ask if he'd advise other businesses to launch a corporate incubator or accelerator. That, he responds, depends on the company's history, heritage, culture and willingness to adopt his advice above. And in general? 'It's generally a terrible idea to use an accelerator as the starting point for an innovation strategy,' he says.

Hatch Labs closed in early 2013. It had achieved its goal of building more than ten businesses, had stretched its initial capital from eighteen months' funding to two years, and had built a future cash cow: Tinder's paid features brought IAC around $800 million in revenue in 2018, while also contributing the majority of the Match Group's market capitalization. Moorjani decided against building a successor inside IAC, as he wanted to construct a wider investor base and create more independence for his future company-building projects. In 2016 he became managing director at Comcast Ventures, the Sky-to-Xfinity conglomerate's independently operating venture capital arm, after working for a global private-equity firm and taking numerous advisory and board roles, including at companies he co-founded.

The Hatch Labs chapter in the short history of corporate-startup incubation may have ended, but the sex scandals, betrayals, power struggles, lawsuits and money fights that came out of it had barely begun.

You can buy a £500 signed first-team player shirt, or for £120 an unsigned one personalized with your name, at the Emirates Stadium in Holloway, north London. Hywel Sloman is proudest of the framed shirt on his office wall signed by the legendary centre-back Tony Adams, who in twenty-two years at Arsenal Football Club captained the team to four League titles and victory in three FA Cups, two Football League Cups, a UEFA Cup Winners' Cup and two FA Community Shields.

As operations director at Arsenal, Sloman, team-loyal, enthusiastic and chatty, has risen from IT director to a role he clearly relishes: ensuring that all parts of the business are optimized to fund the best possible performance on the pitch. But as the digital transformation *Weltanschauung* has persuaded companies ranging from airlines to waste managers that they need to think more like start-ups, his responsibilities now extend to something not normally associated with a 132-year-old football club: the Arsenal Innovation Lab. For ten weeks from January 2018, six tech startups whittled down from 250 were provided with workspace in the press photographers' room, offered mentorship by Arsenal executives, and given access to 200 million fans. It's yet another example of how incumbent businesses are looking to partner with early-stage technology companies to deliver the magical elixir known as innovation.

For Sloman, it's a no-brainer. Arsenal's £424 million turnover is split roughly equally between match-day income, broadcast rights and commercial revenue. The board restricts ticket-price rises, and TV rights income offers no competitive advantage against other Premier League clubs, so any boost in funds available for player acquisition, wages, transfer fees, training and scouting needs to come from commercial growth. As player costs rise, Manchester United, with revenue £157 million a year higher than Arsenal's, has an inevitable advantage. It's startups, Sloman believes, that can teach the club new ways to maximize income from retail, stadium tours and match-day catering.

'The fundamentals of this business are eleven guys kicking a football around twice a week, but with these quite substantial support organizations generating revenue to allow us to spend as much as we can on those eleven guys,' he says. 'So how do we bring new ideas into this business? How do we change the culture of the organization? We're quite good at saying no to ideas because they come from elsewhere.'

Still, Arsenal does have certain natural advantages. Sloman once gave a talk at an event run by Microsoft, which at the time had 118,000 employees, a $61 billion turnover and 14 million Facebook and Twitter followers; Arsenal had 600 staff, a £400 million turnover – and 50 million followers. 'Of all the organizations you've spoken to for your book, I suspect that the big Silicon Valley firms are the only bigger brands than us,' he says. 'We have a similar-sized retail business to [British clothing chain] Ted Baker, which has 370 stores; we've got three, but for two hours, twenty-six times a year, we do traffic in our stores that Ted Baker could only dream of.'

Arsenal has a historic reputation for innovation in football. Herbert Chapman, manager from 1925 to 1934, pushed to install floodlights to enable evening games, and successfully lobbied to have the local Underground station, Gillespie Road, renamed Arsenal in an early example of sports brand-building. But those were yesterday's achievements, and Sloman wants some new ones. His answer has been to partner with a consultancy named L Marks to source startups that could solve challenges such as improving the matchday experience or upgrading the retail operation. A shortlist of twenty-two startups pitched in the stadium to executives including the CEO; the six selected included an AI chatbot, a mobile payments company and an augmented-reality business.

I can't see how the startups – such as I Like That, enabling click-to-buy on third-party websites, or WoraPay, delivering food to stadium seats – could have impacted the business in any significant way. Could this simply be PR, or the 'innovation theatre' that falsely reassures executives that their initiatives are building the future? Financially, certainly, there's been no measurable impact on Arsenal, Sloman admits. 'But mindset? Definitely. The startup culture has energized people with the idea that we can do things differently and at pace, and fostered collaborative working. The programme has opened conversations with some of the brightest people in the London tech scene.' And staff are now proposing new ideas. 'We solved more problems in those ten weeks than we could have imagined.'

L Marks has been running what it calls 'commercialization programmes' since 2014 to bring together startups and established businesses. It started with a pilot programme for the UK retailer John Lewis, and now includes clients such as British Airways' parent IAG, BMW, Lloyd's of London and frozen-food retailer Iceland. 'We're about integrating technologies developed by early-stage companies that will solve real business challenges,' explains chief executive Daniel Saunders, formerly chief of staff to Israel's trade mission in the UK. His twenty-eight staff, mostly in London, scout for startups that might align with their clients' businesses and organize pitch days followed by ten- to twelve-week programmes based typically at corporate HQ. It has seven 'missions' live when I visit his Islington office; it also invests in selected startups – thirty-five so far.

A commercialization programme doesn't need to deal only with early-stage tech companies. The Bridge, a Tel Aviv-based programme for Coca-Cola, Mercedes-Benz and Turner Broadcasting, connects the corporates with companies that have typically raised $2 to $8 million and have decent revenue. Over seven months, the startups learn storytelling, negotiation training, business development and other commercial skills, and are matched with specific executives within the sponsoring companies. Ten or eleven startups in a class are flown to the sponsors' corporate HQs in the US and Germany and over three days have an average of fifty meetings with the goal of building commercial relationships.

In his Rothschild Boulevard office in Tel Aviv, Gabby Czertok, the general manager, shares an example. Cimagine, an Israeli augmented-reality startup, had developed a way to show on an iPad how furniture would look in a room. A Coca-Cola executive from Brazil was excited: he was responsible for 20 million vending machines and coolers, and it typically took up to five visits by any one regional salesperson to position his or her quota correctly. Could AR make it simpler to put the machines in the right place? 'We did a ninety-day test, and took that down to one visit by a salesperson,' Czertok says. 'Multiply that by 60,000 salespeople around the world, and you've got your return on investment.' Coca-Cola deployed the tool in thirty countries before Cimagine was bought by Snapchat.

It's become fashionable for corporates from Airbus to Yandex to launch 'incubators' or 'accelerators' which typically give funding and workspace to startups in the hope of transforming, or at least influencing, the parent company. They take a range of approaches. Founders Factory in London, born out of the Founders Forum entrepreneur event series, builds thirteen new startups a year, and invests in thirty-five that already exist, for clients such as L'Oréal and easyJet. Techstars, Plug and Play and other specialist firms work with corporates to build internal incubators (offering startups services such as workspace and mentorship) or accelerators (providing a structured programme over three to six months). The goal is typically to let the corporate outsource R&D, learn about trends, invest in and sometimes acquire the talent, or more pragmatically to signal that they 'get innovation'. Daimler and Disney have them; so do Technogym and Target. And yet I've still to find a case study of a corporate using the model to create substantial additional value, on a par with IAC's experience with Tinder, or to radically alter its business model. Too often they resemble innovation theatre: showcases for the corporates' wish to seem future-ready, without actually challenging the status quo.

Jeremy Basset has experienced the challenges from both sides. In 2010 he joined Unilever's New Business Unit, which aimed to build five €100 million businesses by 2015 that would help define the future of the $160 billion Anglo-Dutch owner of 400 consumer brands. But none of the unit's couple of dozen launches took off, and in 2014 it was wound down. The unit, answering to Unilever's chief technology officer, had proved too detached from the core company, failing to ensure buy-in from the existing brand teams; it also had an overly generous budget that may have made its leadership see themselves as the gateway to fresh ideas, rather than their enabler.

Basset, an Australian who joined the century-old company's finance and marketing operation in 2003, decided to put those lessons to work. In 2014, with a tinier six-figure budget, he launched the

Unilever Foundry, designed 'to enable innovation through collab-oration'. Unlike the New Business Unit, it would only take briefs from the core business, and it required $50,000 from existing brand teams to help fund pilot projects that addressed their needs. This ensured they had skin in the game.

The Foundry would not take equity stakes in the startups it col-laborated with, but could make introductions to Unilever Ventures, the company's investment arm. Instead, it aimed to build commer-cial relationships that benefited both sides. It invited startups to pitch ways to solve challenges posted on its website, from new product ingredients to disruptive business models. The Foundry received 10,000 proposals that led to 200 pilot projects, half of which were scaled up. And there were significant success stories. Its Magnum ice-cream brand partnered with Olapic, an influencer-marketing platform, in which Unilever Ventures invested – a decision rewarded in 2016 when Olapic sold to Monotype for a reported $130 million. In Brazil, Unilever's detergent brand Omo partnered with subscription laundry service aLavaderia to create Omo Express, with the tagline 'The best way to do your laundry? Don't do it.' The company had wanted to go into laundry services for two years; this pilot proved a success from day one. 'Partnering takes all the risk out for the brands,' Basset says.

He now runs Co:Cubed, a six-person boutique innovation con-sultancy which works with twenty-three of the FTSE 100 companies, including Diageo and Burberry. It uses a database of 500,000 start-ups to deliver programmes, partnerships and hackathons for the corporates. I ask him what he's learned in Co:Cubed's first eighteen months. 'That corporates are terrible at building stuff and are bet-ter off partnering,' he tells me. 'You have to realize there are people reinventing your industry. You can't copy them. You need to re-engineer your organization around collaboration rather than building internal capabilities to do it yourself.'

When he started at Unilever, it took big factories and vast media budgets to build a brand; now any entrepreneur has the distribution power of Amazon or eBay, and can buy advertising for the same price through Google or Facebook. 'There are no more barriers to entry, and corporates have to realize that,' he says. 'So they have to work out what is their role in that ecosystem now.'

At Hatch Labs, Dinesh Moorjani formalized both a 'Hatch Value System' and an 'Operating Manifesto' for his teams to live by. The values ranged from 'Share everything' to 'Root for others'; the operating principles included 'Own up to mistakes and learn from them' and 'Recognize individual relationships can transcend institutions'.

Unfortunately for Hatch Labs, some individual relationships transcended the institution more perniciously than Moorjani could ever have predicted.

Whitney Wolfe's turbulent romantic entanglement with her line manager Justin Mateen ended bitterly with her departure from Tinder in April 2014. On 30 June she filed a lawsuit in the California state court against Tinder, the Match Group and its parent, IAC, claiming 'atrocious sexual harassment and sex discrimination'. Mateen and Rad, the lawsuit claimed, had 'subjected Ms Wolfe to a barrage of horrendously sexist, racist, and otherwise inappropriate comments, emails and text messages, including describing one person as a "liberal lying desperate slut" and others as "middle age Muslim pigs"'. Mateen repeatedly called her a 'whore' and a 'slut', the claim alleged, and threatened to remove her 'co-founder' title because having a young female co-founder 'makes the company seem like a joke' and 'devalues' it.

The writ, replete with screenshots of painfully personal text messages between Mateen and Wolfe during the worst of their relationship disputes, claimed that Tinder harboured the 'misogynist, alpha-male stereotype too often associated with technology start-ups' and sought substantial damages. It also went to some length to stress Wolfe's 'instrumental role in the founding of the company', claimed she suggested its name, and stated that 'in interviews and articles she was held out as a co-founder of Tinder'. The writ included a copy of a business card that announced Wolfe as 'Co-Founder / VP of Marketing'. Her claims, naturally, were disputed by the lawsuit's recipients.

The matter of whether Wolfe's contributions amounted to equal status as co-founder of Tinder would of course affect any financial settlement. There was clearly concern within the company about some claims reported in interviews with her: after *Harper's Bazaar* called Wolfe 'the woman who invented Tinder', for instance, Tinder's PR team demanded corrections. Tinder called the allegations in the lawsuit unfounded, but suspended Mateen, who later left the company. Rad, for his part, sent a memo to Tinder employees stating: 'We did not discriminate against Whitney because of her age or gender, and her complaint paints an inaccurate picture of my actions and what went on here. We take gender equality very seriously.'

The dispute was settled with no admission of wrongdoing, a reported seven-figure payout, and mutual non-disparagement clauses. Wolfe then founded another mobile-dating service, Bumble, aimed at empowering women, who get to message suitors first. It launched in December 2014, and claimed more than 100,000 downloads in its first month. Ever the college marketer, she devised another sorority-based promotional campaign to encourage early downloads – this time involving thongs. Again, she would stand on a chair at a sorority dinner and offer a cookie to women who downloaded Bumble; but if they texted ten friends to download it, they would be given underwear.

For all the amorous aspirations of swipe-led hookups, the Tinder project generated an unusual degree of hostility. Maybe it was simply a legacy of the culture that Hatch Labs incubated. In March 2018, the Match Group made the first move on Bumble by launching an aggressive lawsuit of its own. Wolfe (now Wolfe Herd, after marrying a Texas oil heir named Michael Herd) had 'copied Tinder's world-changing, card-swipe-based, mutual opt-in premise', the lawsuit claimed. 'Bumble sought to mimic Tinder's functionality, trade off of Tinder's name, brand, and general look and feel, meet user expectations that Tinder itself and its brand created, and build a business entirely on a Tinder-clone'. Match also claimed that early Bumble employees Chris Gulczynski and Sarah Mick, who had both worked at Tinder, stole 'confidential information related to proposed Tinder features'. These claims, too, were denied by Bumble.

Wolfe responded four days later with a curt rebuff, a notification delivered via full-page advertisements in the *New York Times* and *Dallas Morning News*. 'Dear Match Group,' the ads began. 'We swipe left on you. We swipe left on your multiple attempts to buy us, copy us, and, now, to intimidate us. We'll never be yours. No matter the price tag, we'll never compromise our values. We swipe left on your attempted scare tactics, and on these endless games. We swipe left on your assumption that a baseless lawsuit would intimidate us.' The next week Bumble filed a state-court lawsuit of its own against Match Group, alleging that it unsuccessfully tried to buy Bumble for $450 million in June 2017, but came back in early 2018 requesting sensitive business data in order to make a higher offer – only to use this information to prepare the Match Group lawsuit. Match Group sought to 'poison and devalue Bumble', the claim continued, and itself copied Bumble's keystone features. Nonsense, replied Match Group, which dismissed the claims as having 'no substance'.

Ah, the course of true love. But there was worse to come in the unravelling of the relationship between IAC and other Hatch Labs employees. Sean Rad and some of Tinder's other co-founders filed a separate lawsuit against IAC in August 2018, claiming at least $2 billion for what they alleged was a deliberate undervaluation of their equity. IAC used 'misleading and incomplete financial information' to value Tinder at $3 billion in 2017 – considerably less than its true value, they claimed – and by merging Tinder with Match Group it devalued their stock options. 'Through deception, bullying, and outright lies, IAC/Match stole billions of dollars from the Tinder employees,' the plaintiffs said in a press release. 'IAC/Match cooked the books to manufacture a fake lowball valuation of Tinder.' At the time of the writ, the Match Group share price was $59. In February 2016, it had been less than $10. The business was certainly thriving: in August 2018, the Match Group announced that Tinder had more than 3.7 million paid subscribers, up 81 per cent over the same quarter in 2017, and that it was on track to exceed $800 million in revenue in 2018.

The fifty-five-page-long lawsuit, filed in the New York Supreme Court, included some extraordinary further allegations. One involved Match Group CEO Greg Blatt, who it claimed 'groped and sexually harassed' Tinder's VP of communications and marketing, Rosette Pambakian, at a 2016 company party. Blatt, who had been vice chairman of Match Group's board of directors, resigned from the board shortly after the lawsuit was filed and subsequently left the company. Pambakian also left, but not before emailing staff that she had determined to 'shine a light on the terrible practices I have witnessed from Match, including covering up sexual misconduct by senior executives and depriving talented employees of hard-earned compensation'. I had been trying for five months through IAC's press office to reach Blatt, or any other senior IAC executive, to understand more about how the corporate side saw the team of upstarts. Now it became clear why no help was ever forthcoming.

IAC/Match Group responded to the lawsuit with a statement pointing out that since Tinder's inception it had paid out 'in excess of a billion dollars in equity compensation to Tinder's founders and employees'. Match Group and the plaintiffs, it said, 'went through a rigorous, contractually defined valuation process involving two independent global investment banks, and Mr Rad and his merry band of plaintiffs did not like the outcome'. Rad, it said, 'has a rich history of outlandish public statements, and this lawsuit contains just another series of them. We look forward to defending our position in court.' At the time of writing, the case is unresolved.

Rad hadn't helped his reputation within IAC by giving an interview to the London *Evening Standard* that was published two days before Tinder's parent company, the Match Group, was due to float on the New York Stock Exchange in November 2015. Regulators expect company executives to abstain from media comment during this 'quiet period'. Rad, who talks in the interview about his gold Audemars Piguet watch and $115,000 black Mercedes G-Class SUV, mentions that he has slept with only a modest twenty women. A 'supermodel, someone really, really famous' has been 'begging' him for sex, he adds, 'and I've been like, no'. He also offers thought leadership about 'hook-up culture', including the observation 'that feminism has led to it because now women are more independent and pursuing their desires'.

Rad, who had been demoted from his CEO role in November 2014, was fired in September 2017, a few weeks after Tinder had merged into IAC's Match Group. A month earlier, according to US securities filings, he exercised some of his stock options. The payment he received, for $94,413,552.06, would at least fund Rad's day-to-day needs until a judge could unpick what had become the dating industry's most dysfunctional soured relationship.

Action Points

It's always tough for an established, management-layered organization to move with the agility and risk appetite of an early-stage technology startup. So partnering with startups can be an effective way to adapt the core business to embrace fresh thinking and new commercial models. As we've seen, approaches to startups can include funding, co-locating, acquiring, partnering with or even building them. Whatever the decision, these are some common guidelines recommended by the practitioners:

1. Don't muzzle the talent, however threatening their activities are to today's business revenue. For all the

legal, sexual, regulatory and other problems that
came out of Tinder's creation, IAC got one thing
right: it allowed a bunch of pirates into the building,
gave them space to experiment, and didn't meddle
even when they challenged the business model of the
dominant cash cow, Match.com. This may have been
more out of corporate ignorance about what was
happening in the Hatch Labs office rather than actual
strategy, but look what it built. Though maybe try to
get the talent to avoid lawsuit-inducing behaviour.

2.   Give air cover to both internal advocates of change
     and the startup partners they're working with.
     'Figure out how you give people protection in your
     organization,' says Gabby Czertok, especially when
     they're challenging norms. Czertok, who spent
     time in 8200, the Israeli army's secret intelligence
     unit, sees parallels with effective innovation in the
     military. 'The heroes inside these organizations get
     protection at the highest levels,' he says.

3.   Engage or go home. Startup programmes need
     the support of senior executives inside the parent
     company, as well as access to junior staff with time
     to mentor the startups. If it sits in the IT team,
     nothing happens. That's why Arsenal ensured that
     the CEO was in the room for startup pitches. It's
     also a common mistake for the bigger company to
     see the startup as a supplier rather than as a long-
     term partner. 'Don't go through your standard
     procurement processes,' Daniel Saunders advises.
     'If you push something off for a couple of months,
     the startup can go bust.'

4.   Start with clear goals. 'You need to understand what you're looking for, and where tech can and won't help,' says Gabby Czertok. 'There's no silver bullet, no secret solutions.' Define quantifiable goals and the bite-sized steps needed to reach them.

5.   Kill the paperwork. Speed of decision-making and roll-out is of the essence. If an incubator housed within a large company is to succeed, it will need to be free of normal corporate regulations and attitudes. Pilot projects were horribly slow to launch in stores during the first JLab organized by L Marks for John Lewis, because of delayed local decision-making. That problem had to be solved for the second JLab.

6.   Don't be afraid to steal. Sometimes the core business can be improved simply by copying an idea being effectively used in an unrelated business. Arsenal's retail team needed to improve the in-store customer experience for fans queuing to buy their team shirts, and then queuing twice again to order personalized lettering and then to collect them. They borrowed the answer from a salad chain called Tossed, which lets customers use in-store tablets to customize and pay for their order. 'We turned a pain point into quite a fun experience,' Hywel Sloman says. 'That's not an idea that came from sport – it came from salads.'

7

PROTOTYPE AND MEASURE

An oil nation recalibrates its future

The wedding ceremony in September 2017 of Omar Sultan AlOlama and his bride Amal bin Shabib was a bizarrely futuristic affair. The groom, wearing the traditional white Emirati dishdasha robe and ghutra headdress, sat near his black-robed bride in a circular white booth in a tower in central Dubai and recited his vows before a Beam telepresence robot. Performing the Islamic sharia ceremony via remote video conference was a Dubai court lawyer, whose smiling face could be seen on the small head-height screen. Then, once the groom had signed the marriage contract, the notarized licence was brought to him by a second gliding automaton, this time a roaming Savioke autonomous delivery robot. And that formally concluded Dubai's first digital 'Mabrook Ma Dabart' ceremony (Arabic for 'Congratulations on your marriage') – one more indication that a once oil-dependent desert state is radically working to reinvent itself.

Sitting between bride and groom as an official witness, bringing an extra gravitas to the ceremony, was their boss, Sheikh Mohammed bin Rashid Al Maktoum, who is both ruler of Dubai as well as the United Arab Emirates' Prime Minister. Partly he was there to celebrate a beautiful partnership commitment between two young members of his staff. But the presence of media indicated that there was also something symbolic happening here. Sheikh Mohammed often talks about the importance of making the UAE's government 'smarter', and the robot-conducted wedding ceremony, in the new Services 1 centre in Emirates Towers, was an important signal. Designed to be a showcase one-stop shop giving citizens access to a hundred services from fourteen government bodies, the Services 1 centre incorporates touch-screens, robots, IBM's Watson artificial-intelligence technology, and a single human employee to offer seamless birth registration, housing-loan applications and passport renewals. It is, in the sheikh's vision, 'just the first of many centres and innovations to come. We will not stop, because our goal is to be the first in the world when it comes to government services by 2020.'

Before his wedding, AlOlama had been running the World Government Summit, a kind of Davos to promote better government, held annually in Dubai since 2013; bin Shabib had been the summit's head of content. It is an ambitious showcase: the 2018 summit attracted speakers such as Craig Venter and Malcolm Gladwell, with sessions including 'Mars: A Platform for Progress', 'Redesigning Longevity' and 'AI: The New Measurement of Happiness'. AlOlama had become obsessed with the ethical and practical considerations of AI: he'd risked speaking out in one internal meeting with the country's leadership to ask some difficult questions, in a country where one learns to obey rather than query. What, he asked, would happen to civil servants or foreign workers rendered redundant by AI? How would the Emirates manage any resulting social unrest? Was AI even at the stage when it could be significantly more productive than humans? 'Honestly speaking, the strategic thinking [around AI] was too rushed,' AlOlama recalls now. 'There wasn't any thought given to the social impact. I didn't mean to be rude, but I was really concerned.'

Sheikh Mohammed's advisers replied by calmly asking AlOlama what he would do differently. 'I gave my recommendations, got on an airplane to go on my honeymoon, and didn't give it much more thought,' he says. 'I'd come back a month later and it would be someone else's problem.'

Two days into their honeymoon, Sheikh Mohammed announced an ambitious national artificial-intelligence strategy as a 'mega enterprise [intended] to expedite and ensure more efficiency in government services at all levels'. 'I remember reading it and saying to my wife, "This is the wrong decision,"' AlOlama tells me. 'I said, "Whoever is working on this, God help them."' The next day his phone rang, telling him to take the next flight back from Japan. 'I explained that if I broke my honeymoon I'd come back single. But I have faith in the leadership, so I booked a flight back – without telling my wife.'

Then, at six p.m. Japan time, Sheikh Mohammed tweeted that he would be announcing a Cabinet reshuffle. 'I found that interesting, and felt maybe one of my colleagues was going to become a minister and that I might take his old position,' AlOlama recalls. 'My wife and I discussed a few likely names.' At around seven p.m., the sheikh tweeted that he was going to appoint a Minister for AI. 'I remember saying, "This guy has the toughest job in the entire Cabinet, as no one understands what he's working on, and no one sees the dangers." My wife said I should stop bothering her about AI – it wasn't something I'd be working on, and I should think positively. The very next tweet was *my* picture as the Minister for AI.'

At the age of twenty-seven, AlOlama had unexpectedly become the world's first Minister of State for Artificial Intelligence.

The UAE and, of the seven emirates, Dubai in particular have for some time displayed the gaucheness of a nouveau-riche, emotionally avoidant relative addicted to insecure superlatives: as if the world's tallest building, the largest man-made archipelago, the biggest shopping mall, the busiest international airport could disguise an absolute monarchy's anxiety that, stripped of its recent oil wealth, this forty-eight-year-old desert nation would struggle for validation beside its more established neighbours. The ecologically injudicious indoor ski slope, well-documented cases of human rights violations, alleged abuse of migrant workers, jailing of women who report rape, and sharia punishments such as stoning and flogging have hardly boosted the Emirates global brand as a beacon of Middle Eastern modernity.

Billboard portraits of the benevolent ruler are disconcertingly ubiquitous in this nation where the airport, bridges, highways, towers and other infrastructure are often named dutifully in the Al Maktoum family's honour. Still, Sheikh Mohammed does seem to have understood the urgency of preparing his country for the post-oil era. At a Cabinet meeting in 2010 he launched a strategy called UAE Vision 2021, demanding 'a shift to a diversified and knowledge-based economy' by the country's fiftieth anniversary, with key performance indicators (KPIs) to measure progress precisely. A national agenda would turn the UAE into 'one of the best countries in the world by 2021' in education, health, the economy, policing, housing, infrastructure and government services, united under a new 'culture for innovation'.

Four years later, Sheikh Mohammed launched the eponymous Mohammed bin Rashid Centre for Government Innovation to stimulate new thinking within government. There would be government innovation labs, a 'CEO of Innovation' post in every ministry and agency, a Year of Innovation and an Innovation Diploma in conjunction with the University of Cambridge. He even, in 2016, appointed a Minister of State for Happiness, and a Minister for Youth Affairs (aged just twenty-two).

I'd been intrigued for a while. Although the regime seemed unhealthily reliant on unrealized hype to sell its story – We'll commute in hyperloops! We'll soar in autonomous flying taxis! – it was also investing serious resources in understanding how emerging technologies, from genomics to 3D-printing, could build new non-oil economic value. Abu Dhabi's showcase 'zero carbon' desert city, Masdar, may have been widely derided as a 'ghost town' that failed to deliver on its arrogant promises; and yet the regime's space agency seemed to be making initial progress towards reaching – and by 2117, it hoped, settling – Mars. With much of the work conducted by a state body called, naturally enough, the Mohammed bin Rashid Space Centre.

More significantly, they were hungry to learn. When a delegation from the Prime Minister's office visited London shortly after his Cabinet reshuffle, they asked to meet me as the *WIRED* founding editor-in-chief for introductions to startups and investors they might collaborate with. I was impressed that they had already visited MIT, Singularity University in Silicon Valley, Stanford, Imperial College London and startup clusters from Berlin to Barcelona. I mentioned that a radical new Paris school, called 42, was training a generation of super-talented coders through a beautiful new form of teacherless peer learning; within three days the delegation had rearranged their agenda to be there. This seemed like genuine curiosity.

So I asked them for my own tour of the innovation nation they were building, starting with the Cabinet minister responsible for artificial intelligence.

It turns out that the Minister for AI doesn't spend his days figuring out how to save humanity from the rogue Terminator. 'That's science fiction,' Omar Sultan AlOlama – now, formally, His Excellency – explains with a smile when we meet high up the Emirates Office Tower. 'I'm not looking at general AI at the moment. Instead, I'm looking at short- and medium-term narrow-use cases of AI in government to enhance processes and services, and bringing in the best startups and brains from around the world to experiment with this technology.'

The AI minister's first job is to boost the efficiency of government services, as part of Sheikh Mohammed's declared intention 'to become the world's most prepared country for artificial intelligence'. The UAE government, which is obsessed with quantifying impact, has calculated that AI, together with blockchain technologies, could save it $3 billion, $100 million of that simply by eliminating paper. But the smart machine will also evaluate policies far more efficiently than human advisers. Before launching a new education strategy, the government plans to create a computer simulation to understand how it will affect schools in practice. And why not use

AI to give citizens control over how their personal data is used by diverse government agencies?

'We'll see services that are much more tailored to you,' explains the minister, an investment banker before he moved to policy-making. 'The bureaucratic systems that make you turn up at a particular place and time to get a test certificate – they'll all die out. Services will come to you. And AI will optimize our lives.' He goes on to offer examples: it will maximize traffic flow, and transform education – the AI will understand what you're good at, and studying will be more like playing a game on your iPhone. 'Or logistics: we have the busiest [international] airport on the planet, the seventh largest port, and roads that will be autonomous-transport-ready by 2025. Expect such synergy between them that the flow of traffic, of goods, of people, will be so smooth. We'll wonder how we lived a life of congestion.' The AI will eventually monitor citizens' bodies to keep them healthy, too. 'Through the smart toilet, by monitoring your breath, we'll be able to tell a lot about you. Even a tissue box will have sensors.'

There's certainly something appealing about a government that seeks to cut the friction in its interactions with citizens. It's hard to argue with a more personalized approach to healthcare or education or traffic management. And yet . . . is it healthy for a regime described by the BBC as 'authoritarian' to accumulate such granular data from its citizens? Aren't there risks, I tactfully ask the minister, in a government tracking individuals so precisely?

'This is an interesting discussion,' His Excellency replies patiently. 'Throughout history you've always trusted the government with everything. We understand that government will have access to our information, will have control over us . . . and you understand that what makes government is *us*, the people. You can always change the government's agenda – through the civil rights movement, the Arab Spring . . . So the risk of government having your data is much lower than the risk of the private sector having your data. You have no leverage over Uber or Google or Tesla; but you have leverage over government.'

Politeness prevents me from pushing the point – I am, after all, a guest being given a government-organized tour – but I reflect silently that this is a regime with a track record of monitoring its citizens to ensure obedience. According to Human Rights Watch, the government 'arbitrarily detains and forcibly disappears individuals who criticize authorities'; you can be jailed for long periods for such vaguely defined acts as 'undermining national unity' and 'insulting state symbols'. But I'm here to learn about the government's investment in artificial intelligence, so I listen.

'When it comes to government, there should be a lot more transparency,' the minister continues. 'We're also trying to include the citizen in selecting what data should be collected in the census.' He's meanwhile working to attract foreign AI talent to work with the regime in a gigantic 'controlled experiment', and ensuring that other ministries pick up the baton. The Minister of Infrastructure Development, for instance, has already calculated that using AI in a new highway project, the Kalba Ring Road, 'would contribute to a reduction of 54 per cent in project duration, 37 per cent in fuel consumption, 80 per cent in manpower dependence and 40 per cent in equipment and manpower'. Those precise measurements again.

If AI will be so important to the future running of the country, I ask, shouldn't it eventually replace the Minister for Artificial Intelligence himself? 'It should,' the minister replies with a smile. 'That will be my success. In the past, the minister was the all-knowing, all-seeing executive decision-maker who changes the future of our country. AI will serve as the adviser, bringing to the minister the decisions that need to be taken. The AI scans the requirements of the people, understanding what's happening globally, comes up with policy recommendations, and the minister looks and decides. Certainly you need ministers who are much more optimized.'

★

On the temperature-controlled ground floor of the Jumeirah Emirates Towers Boulevard, at the entrance to the Mohammed bin Rashid Centre for Government Innovation, a large digital screen is displaying the scientific formula for transformation:

$$V \times D \times C \times S > R = \text{Change}$$

In smaller letters, a key to this 'change equation' explains that V is 'a vision of the future', D 'dissatisfaction with the current situation', C 'capacity for change', S 'knowledge of the first steps to take' and R 'perceived cost of change or resistance to change'.

A Pepper robot greets visitors to the Emirates NBD 'bank of the future' next door; nearby, past a hairdresser's, a shoeshine stand and a dental clinic, younger Emiratis sit at laptops in the Youth Hub, a government-provided co-working space. On the corridor floor, a painted running track leads to the entrance to the Dubai Future Accelerators, where a state-backed nine-week programme connects technology startups from around the world to government organizations so that they can build a relationship and, ideally, develop products together. Sponsoring bodies have included the Dubai Police, the health authority and the Emirates airline. The airline has its own separate space, where a panel greeting visitors makes an unlikely promise: 'Tomorrow, bridges will fly 40,000 feet above the Earth.' More grounded are the challenges set by another nearby accelerator devoted to improving government itself. Announced as the first of its type in the world, its cohorts have, for instance, helped the Ministry of Justice resolve small claims in a single day instead of three months, and allowed the Cabinet to draft by-laws more quickly.

As he leads me into the government accelerator, Walid Tarabih, from the Prime Minister's office, explains that its role is to take a startup approach to enhancing services, linking entrepreneurs with government in an intensive programme. 'If we identify a problem area, we create a hundred-day challenge in the accelerator,' he says. 'There was an issue of unemployment among locals, for instance. By mapping the right people to the right location, the team found jobs for one thousand of them.' Speed of execution is key, he tells me. 'I learned from Sheikh Mohammed that the only scarce resource we have is time. He said you can postpone anything but happiness; and the role of the government is the happiness of its citizens.'

A temporary exhibition called 'Edge of Government' showcases projects from around the world that have inspired the team. 'What role could "human sensors" like barbers play to rethink government services?' asks one wall panel, depicting a UK project that trains barbers to spot potential suicide risks among customers. In this KPI-driven culture, there is naturally data to quantify the benefits: '53 per cent of men are more likely to discuss private issues, such as depression and other mental health issues, with their barbers.' Another exhibit asks: 'Can a porch rich with memories be recreated in a nursing facility?' This case study is a US nursing home designed to enhance its patients' memories by programming smells and sounds to recall the neighbourhoods they grew up in.

Tarabih leads me outside, where we walk inside a large white structure which he says is the world's first 3D-printed building (a heavily contested claim). Currently a space for meetings, tended by a suspicious security guard, it's a tangible prototype for a future where, by government decree, a quarter of all new buildings must be 3D-printed by 2030. Inaugurated by Sheikh Mohammed in May 2016, the white-painted curved structure is intended to serve as 'the office of the future'. It stands a short stroll from the under-construction Museum of the Future, an eccentric oval structure, partly 3D-printed, that's destined to join the Burj and the Atlantis hotel as a Dubai visual icon, financed by a new government tax called an 'Innovation Fee'.

'Future' is a word almost as popular as 'innovation' among government representatives. From what I can tell, the Dubai Future

Foundation, with forty-five staff, is the Prime Minister's anointed vehicle for delivering the palpable results of his grand vision. It's an independent yet widely representative arm of government. I arrange to meet its CEO, Khalfan Juma Belhoul, who seems to have a free hand in imagining how a nation can execute its most ambitious dreams.

And Belhoul certainly wants to provoke. Why, he asks, should we endure the stress of an airport terminal each time we want to take a flight? 'Why can't the whole of Dubai be the airline terminal?' he reflects aloud. 'Why do travellers need to sit in a physical terminal to check in?' In his fantasy vision, a car will collect you and your luggage from anywhere in the city, and after a quick backseat passport check you'll be driven straight to the plane. At least, I think it's a fantasy, until he adds that the Future Foundation is all about bringing outlandish visions to life. 'Ideas are great,' he says, 'but we focus on execution.'

The foundation sets challenges to promote the UAE's 'knowledge-based economy', provides funding, and corrals the multiple stakeholders. On space technology and exploration, for instance, where there is a declared intent to be 'among the top countries worldwide in the field', the foundation's think tank – naturally enough called the Mohammed bin Rashid Centre for Accelerated Research – has funded thirty-six projects for the Mohammed bin Rashid Space Settlement Challenge. Remarkably, it attracted more than 260 research proposals from 200 universities in fifty-five countries; those selected included 'The Sustainable Space Settlement: Stability Analysis of Lava Tubes' (Purdue University), 'Mushrooms on Mars: A Subsystem for Human Life Support' (Rutgers University), and 'Combustion of Indigenous Martian Chemicals for Planetary Mobility' (University of Liverpool).

'We're a restless nation,' Belhoul says. 'We want something better for our citizens, for the world. We're not happy with the status quo. We think we can do a lot of things better.' As he defines innovation, it's something non-existent that has a positive impact on humanity, while also bringing local benefits. 'Projects need an RoD effect' – that's 'Return on Dubai', a local impact-driven variant of return on investment – 'so we want to see how many jobs have been created, how many people in the UAE have joined the innovation side of the business. We're marking our territory using a long and complicated formula that measures a combination of long-term benefits and impact. Then we go with our gut and take risks.'

Dubai wants to become a living lab, defined by targets and measurable impact, that prototypes, tests and deploys transformative technologies. Already the foundation has signed 122 memoranda of understanding after meeting 5,000 startups for its accelerator challenges, persuading companies such as Virgin Hyperloop One and the blockchain company ConsenSys to move to the city.

I gently suggest to Belhoul that the UAE's enthusiasm for attracting foreign startups making hyperloops, jetpacks and flying taxis might be perceived as story-led public relations, with little concrete benefit for citizens. He's polite and patient in his response. 'We're a country less than fifty years old,' he says. 'We started by trading pearls. Once artificial pearls were out in the market, we shifted and found oil, with the blessings of God and our leadership. Now we're no longer an oil-dependent country. We've diversified and proved that we can create a Dubai that is a financial and touristic hub – so why can't we become an innovation hub? The urge is there. The fact that we've moved so quickly gives us the right to do something really innovative. What we need more in the region is belief from the private sector, investing in those innovative startups.'

For all its economic might, Belhoul insists, the UAE is attempting to adopt startup thinking. 'We're trying to be humble – this might not work, but we have to try. When we started, people laughed at the idea that we'd get government entities to be part of an accelerator. But we're lucky: the leaders are pushing the mandate. It's not just hype, it's tangible deliverables.'

His deputy CEO of projects, Abdulaziz AlJaziri, has some metrics at hand to validate Belhoul's claims: record citizens' approval of government strategy, statistics to demonstrate the economy's diversification, evidence of women's growing empowerment now that they control one-third of ministries. Plus, AlJaziri adds, government has become agile and quick to execute. 'During the World Government Summit, a lady approached the guy who runs the Knowledge and Human Development Authority, responsible for Dubai's private schools, and explained that she lives half in Dubai, half in Abu Dhabi, but her son can go to only one school. He looked at all the policies, and said, "What if we allowed a child to go to two different schools?" Now that kid does. But what if we push this further, he said, so that *every* student in the UAE could learn maths in one school, use a swimming pool in another, study art in a third? What if the full schooling system was disrupted? That's what we mean by ten X thinking. Look at something ten years ahead, outside the box, and try to deliver it today.'

It helps that the tower is itself a meeting point for the nation's power brokers. Seven ministers work from here; the Prime Minister is based here; most government entities are represented in the accelerators; and it's home to a new space called Area 2071, where public and private entities come together for creative problem-solving.

I reflect that at its core the government wants to be Amazon: a customer-first operation that keeps making incremental improvements by measuring how people are using it. I heard ministerial advisers discuss their department's 'one-click approach' to serving citizens, the need to 'redesign customer journeys', the centrality of real-time data analytics to make faster decisions. They study the country's bespoke Abu Dhabi Innovation Index to measure progress towards innovation. They proudly quote the UAE's rise in the Global Innovation Index from forty-first to thirty-fifth. They even have a special Cabinet department to hold them to account.

That department is run by Maryam Al Hammadi, assistant director-general for Government Performance & Excellence, based in the Prime Minister's office. Her job is to make sure every ministry and department knows how fast it is progressing. 'We have fifty-two national KPIs based on national and international criteria, and we measure everything from queuing time to happiness,' she explains. Federal entities compete for the Mohammed bin Rashid Government Excellence Award when they exceed their targets; and when they don't, they know who is watching.

'I'll show you the dashboard on Sheikh Mohammed's iPad,' she says. She scrolls down. It shows data-rich results for each of six nationally defined priorities, from healthcare to a 'cohesive society'. For each priority, the sheikh can see national KPIs, the current status, the 2021 target, customer satisfaction ratings, 'mystery shopper' findings, international benchmarks, areas of improvement. 'He can email ministers directly, asking for detailed reports,' she tells me. 'Or a meeting.'

The system is designed to create competition between government entities. Are they using robots yet? How are they leveraging tech to lower costs? And the relentless scrutiny means there is no slipping back to old thinking. 'Every six months, all the executive teams making ministers accountable for achieving targets – 500 employees – present to us and His Highness what they have achieved in the national agenda,' Al Hammadi says. 'We set milestones for them. We build scenarios for them to help prioritize highest-impact indicators. We don't leave them alone.'

I'm invited to a working lunch hosted by the government's Innovation Diploma Team. There are currently fifty-three ministerial employees working towards the diploma, a three-year part-time programme designed with the University of Cambridge and Britain's Nesta (formerly the National Endowment for Science, Technology and the Arts) to embed a culture of change across government. Two professors from Imperial College

Business School are leading a discussion; participants include many of the forty-five 'CEOs of Innovation', one in each ministry. There are conversations about how to make regulators more entrepreneurial; about the success of the recent UAE Innovation Month; about a recent UAE Hackathon (theme: 'Data for Happiness'); about how best to leverage a government fund called Afkari, which backs federal government employees' suggestions for becoming 'the most innovative country in the world'. A typical winning proposal involved repurposing sewage water to nurture public gardens.

There's no question that such initiatives are transforming the culture inside government. The ministers and senior government staff I meet are universally driven, engaged and impressive. But it's the nation's wider ambition to attract the best international startup, creative and tech talent that gives me pause. In my experience, free-thinking entrepreneurs tend to thrive in cultures that respect personal freedoms, including the ability to speak openly or to be openly gay. Where a controlling state that limits free expression seeks to build a thriving tech hub – I think of Russia's failed experiment with Moscow's Skolkovo Innovation Centre – the impact is generally limited. Can the Emirates buck the trend?

'If you'd have asked me two years ago, I'd have said of course not,' says Paul Bennett, chief creative officer of the San Francisco design agency IDEO, who has visited Dubai twenty-two times in the past year. 'Today I'd say absolutely yes. I went from scepticism to complete belief.' Scratch under the shiny 'flying cars' surface, he says, and a real ecosystem is embedding, an emerging creative culture, an uncynical commitment to taking an international lead. 'It has all the underpinnings of a really interesting creative culture – iconoclastic creativity, permission to play, a recognition of the opportunity in young people. And there's money behind it. The leadership know this is their moment. They don't want to mess it up.'

The sheikh's team approached Bennett with a classic IDEO challenge: how would he change the way a country is perceived? Bennett was asked how he would neuter the appeal of radicalism among young people in the Middle East; he responded by writing a children's book, *The Palm and the Redwood*, about two trees in a storm (think: ISIS) that responded by forming a forest in the desert.

Out of that project was born Palmwood, a joint venture between IDEO and the UAE government that's part project designer, part creativity enabler, part social laboratory. Based in Area 2071, Palmwood works with groups in and outside government to build what it calls 'generosity, curiosity and creativity' in fields from education to the creative economy. It's conducted workshops on improving society with children aged nine to fourteen; in one, Mthayel, aged thirteen, designed a home built from recycled materials, and Basma, fourteen, imagined a rocket that would colonize Saturn. 'She put 101 rooms in her rocket ship, fifty for men, fifty for ladies, and one for a comedian,' Bennett recalls. 'Because she said we'll need difficult conversations in the future and it's important we remember to laugh. That's how you fight radicalism – we need 30,000 of her.'

The government has committed to funding Palmwood for five years, and to sending its youngest and brightest ministerial talent on secondment. 'I'd love this country's main expertise in five years to be the way government behaves, with speed and agility,' Bennett says. 'They'll be a prototype society for other places in the Middle East.'

And yet the children's playful idealism, as well as the state's administrative professionalism, can't be fully celebrated without acknowledging some awkward political realities. The UAE's ambition to be a beacon to the world's creative and tech talent is unlikely to be fulfilled while the government remains so repressive of what it sees as dissent. Human rights groups have chronicled repeated accounts of torture and arbitrary detention of activists, foreign workers and tourists whose behaviour or social media posts have upset the regime. Amnesty International lists 'beatings, electric shocks and sleep deprivation' as among 'common' abuses in the UAE's jails. One recent example: in May 2018, Emirati citizen Ahmed Mansoor, a member of Human Rights Watch's Middle East and North Africa Advisory Committee, was jailed for ten years and fined a million dirhams (around $275,000) for 'defaming' and sharing 'false information' and 'rumours' about the UAE on social media.

The state's cybersecurity laws have also been used to target expats and locals who use Facebook or WhatsApp in ways the leadership disapproves of: in 2016, a foreigner was detained after sharing a Facebook link to an international charity's fundraising page, as the charity was not legally registered locally. An expat woman was deported and fined in 2016 for searching her husband's phone after she suspected him of adultery. When Matthew Hedges, a British PhD student on a research visit to Dubai, was jailed for life in November 2018 for what the state claimed was spying (strenuously denied by the British government), Western media coverage focused on his poor treatment and questioned the judicial process. After strong diplomatic protests and threats of a wider academic boycott, he was swiftly pardoned and released.

Some critics of the regime find it hard to reconcile its focus on future-centred innovation with today's lack of tolerance. After my trip, I met a local writer who had been arrested after falling foul of the government, and was forced to seek asylum abroad. 'The regime's emphasis on future technologies is to stop young people asking the harder questions,' the writer – whose identity I'm withholding – tells me. As foreign workers (who have no political rights) have families, their children will increasingly demand more say in how they are governed. This, the writer suggests, is what worries the rulers.

'The demographics are politically unsustainable,' he says. 'In the 1960s there were 300,000 Emiratis, now there are 10 million – of whom 90 per cent are non-citizens. By 2050 that will be 96 per cent.

And the next generation [of non-citizens] born in the UAE will have greater expectations. Is "innovation" distracting from this unsustainability by simply making things more efficient?'

Atraf Shehab, director of the Future Department in the Ministry of Cabinet Affairs and the Future, has heard all the innovation hype before. 'Have you met during your journey the go-getters and the wannabes and the pretenders?' He laughs. 'Because they won't stop texting me. I've seen a lot of crap, a lot of pirates who claim they can help you.'

Shehab has worked on future government strategy since 2005, and he's seen a lot of wrong-headed approaches. 'We learned that copying and pasting from other organizations doesn't work,' he says. 'We've had to customize and improve. We needed to transform a culture, and I didn't realize how difficult that would be. It took ten years to get everyone [in government] to jump on the bus. Not all were on board, some were suspicious. What helped was having a strong leader in each of those teams that pushed the work.'

So what else has he learned? First, scouting the world for best practice is not enough unless that knowledge is built into user-focused services. The team studied 'smart government' in Estonia (see chapter 8), Canada, Singapore and the UK, but only when the lessons were built into a useful consumer app called Dubai Now did the team start to see uptake. With the help of a Siri-like artificial intelligence called Rashid, the app lets residents access more than fifty government services, from renewing vehicle registration to finding the nearest ATM to paying the water bill. You can use the app to pay for parking, to buy your metro ticket and to find daily prayer times. It even monitors tremors to give earthquake notifications.

Second, the way to get multiple departments to buy into such a project is to nurture a healthy competition between them. Dubai Now required bodies ranging from the courts to the health authority to make their databases available. When one organization did, that was publicly recognized.

And third, a successful plan comes down to setting targets and measuring progress. The UAE Vision 2021 strategy determined, for instance, that 12 per cent of city trips should be by autonomous driverless systems, and that public transportation should account for 20 per cent of all journeys. Faced with such specific targets, each relevant body had to declare its own improvement plan. 'And now we're thinking beyond the next ten years to the next fifty years,' Shehab says. 'It gets hazy, so we're going to take it step by step.'

And step by step – through its KPI-setting and corporate partnerships and AI summer camps and international blockchain summits and World Economic Forum collaborations and additive-manufacturing promotion and university-course upgrading and global innovation tours – the leadership team is proving that, in government modernization at least, the UAE is becoming a role model to the region if not the world.

'The first requirement is that there's a dream,' Shehab says. 'Dare to dream. You need inspiration to sell a different concept that people will buy into. Second, make it relevant. Play with an ecosystem. You need to turn that vision into actual plans and a business model.

'Because the future is a business model. It's not just fancy thinking or identifying trends. Dubai has managed to diversify away from oil successfully. Now it's about showing where we can play in the long term.'

Action Points

If you're an unchallenged hereditary monarch with vast oil wealth, you can skip this part. If not, here are some lessons from the UAE's continuing transformation that will be relevant to a wide range of other organizations confronting change:

1. Start with the big vision, and then tell compelling stories around achieving it. Noah Raford, chief operating officer of the Dubai Future Foundation, talks about the foundation's role in creating 'immersive, rigorously imagined futures'. He quotes Victor Hugo: 'Dream no small dreams, for they have no power to stir the souls of men.'

2. The power of a tangible prototype can be profound. The UAE leadership is obsessed with creating visible symbols – a 3D-printed office building, an architecturally wondrous Museum of the Future – that stand as physical embodiments of the intended transition.

3. Firm central leadership can align divergent interests, ensuring a commitment to long-term change. The strictly hierarchical nature of the Emirates' leadership ensures that all government departments know what to prioritize. There is never any doubt about the boss's expectations.

4. Granular targets and key performance indicators allow progress to be monitored, challenges to be addressed early, and stakeholders to feel a need to compete with each other. Create a culture of measurement and target-setting.

5. Find your own points of difference. Dubai will never be Silicon Valley, but it can ensure that regulators are unusually startup-friendly in enabling emerging ('pre-legal') technologies such as autonomous vehicles and flying taxis. Regulatory flexibility has led the UAE to partner with

emerging businesses that have the potential to become huge.

6. Create an internal system for encouraging suggestions from your talent. 'We have multiple systems that let anyone propose ideas,' Atraf Shehab says. 'The power of ideas is very motivating – when people see their ideas become reality, it's the ultimate satisfaction for them.'

7. Never stop exploring what's happening elsewhere. The Prime Minister's office has teams that are constantly scouting, travelling, reading to see what they're missing.

8.

BECOME A PLATFORM

A civil servant erases his nation's borders

In a former paper factory on the outskirts of Tallinn, nestled between a furniture workshop and a hairdresser's, Kaspar Korjus, a slim, clean-cut, thirty-one-year-old civil servant, is explaining how he is turning his Baltic homeland, the Republic of Estonia, into an app store.

It's not that Estonia, a Switzerland-sized former Soviet northern European state of 1.3 million people, lacks physical presence: its 42,000 square kilometres and 2,222 islands, facing Helsinki and St Petersburg across the Gulf of Finland, have over the centuries attracted the attentions of conquering Danes, Swedes, Germans and particularly Russians. But now that we're all living digital lives, Korjus reasons, there's no need to constrain his nation's ambitions to its actual geographic borders. By offering identity cards to millions of foreigners who don't physically live here, and helping them to remotely build businesses registered here, he wants Estonia to be the world's first borderless nation.

'The nation state has been around for just a few hundred years out of the millions for which people have existed,' Korjus explains when we meet in Estonia's e-residency office on Tartu Road, a twenty-minute walk from Tallinn's airport (whose website declares that it 'will never be the largest in the world but it can be the cosiest'). 'Nations are a very recent concept. So it's inevitable that states will become borderless.' Countries will compete for global citizens' loyalty based on the quality and range of their services, he reckons; you might choose one nation for business, another for healthcare, a third for digital education or banking. If a particularly efficient nation can attract a global base of customers who don't actually live there, its entire economy can be transformed. 'Plus, I realized today, why would you need ever to conquer a neighbouring country if the wealth of that nation is not dependent on physical people there, but on how many people want to use its services?' Korjus asks, his clipped English words delivered in the bi-tonal, emotionless voice that to an Estonian signifies high excitement. He leaves the thought in mid-air.

Estonia's answer is to allow almost anyone in the world to apply online to become a digital resident – an 'e-resident' – for a €100 fee, a passport scan and an uploaded photograph. You can do it today, if you have twenty spare minutes. You don't actually need to visit Estonia to confirm your e-residency; simply turn up a few weeks later at a local embassy or accredited pick-up point to be fingerprinted and to collect a digital ID card, a card reader and your two PIN codes to access its national systems. E-residency doesn't earn you a passport, guaranteed entry or actual residency, and you still need to pay personal taxes in your home country. But if you're over eighteen and lack a criminal record, it does let you establish an Estonian company and trade globally from within the European internal market, and you can use commercial banking services, run your business remotely and access local public services. All of which is tremendous news for an economy until now largely dependent on oil shale, timber and industrial machinery. By 2025, according to Deloitte, the e-residency programme could generate €340 million in net direct financial revenue for Estonia, part of a €1.8 billion boost e-residency is forecast to bring to the national economy by then.

By October 2018, 45,000 people had registered as Estonian e-residents, predominantly from Finland, Russia, Ukraine, Germany and the US. In Korjus's office, past a blue-and-white neon sign warning that you are 'entering e-Estonia', weekly application numbers are scribbled on to the side of a desk: in week 44, Ukraine provided 169, India 83, Turkey 625, the UK 158. But Korjus, the project's managing director, has far bigger ambitions. Once there are 10 million, he says, his country should be able to abolish income tax entirely in favour of charging e-residents a subscription fee, just as Netflix does. After all, if 10 million people pay, say, €100 annually to subscribe to Estonia as a digital nation, that's a handy €1 billion in fees. 'We don't need to assume that taxation will stay,' he says in his nation's flat tones. 'It's only been here for a few hundred years anyway.'

This is the first time I've ever heard a government official making the case to abolish taxation. But Korjus doesn't talk like a typical civil servant: for one thing, he describes his nation in terms of an 'app store' with its own global customer base. 'I've never seen a more profitable opportunity for a nation than becoming borderless, having hundreds of times the number of customers for services you're already providing,' he says. Once Estonia has millions of e-residents, he suggests, private companies and even other governments will compete to offer them extra services, just as developers do today on Apple's App Store. Business customers based in São Paulo or Sofia might source their lawyers through the e-residency store, and stock exchanges around the world might use it to offer frictionless investment and shareholder voting. And, like Apple or Google, Estonia could charge a percentage of every transaction. Ching ching.

The prospect of issuing digital ID cards to non-citizens had been discussed in parliament for a while, but it was an entry to a 2014 contest organized by the Estonian Development Foundation – 'for ideas that would lead to economic advancement and a higher standard of living' – that put e-residency into the mainstream. Taavi Kotka, the country's then chief information officer, Siim Sikkut, the current CIO, and Ruth Annus, from the Ministry of the Interior, submitted a joint proposal entitled '10 million "e-Estonians" by 2025!' Their project would bring more foreign entrepreneurs, investors, scientists and educators into the national economy, they argued, and would boost Estonia's international competitiveness.

The proposal won the €24,000 award and Korjus, who had worked after university for a telco, TeliaSonera, was brought in on a government scholarship to develop the concept.

The project grew incrementally. An initial €300,000 budget was secured, mostly from Enterprise Estonia, part of the Ministry of Economic Affairs, and a small team leapt into action, helping develop the legal framework, finding partners and promoting the story. Banks were approached, regulators consulted. By 1 December 2014, Estonia was ready to welcome its first e-resident: the British journalist Edward Lucas, a friend of then president Toomas Hendrik Ilves. Not only could Lucas register a company remotely and digitally sign documents, but he could bank online, click to submit an Estonian tax return, even have his medical prescriptions digitally fulfilled.

It sounds a fun conversation starter to carry an e-residency card along with your airline loyalty cards; Angela Merkel and Emmanuel Macron have one, as does the Duke of York. I can't help but wonder if there's a genuine benefit to joining, however, so I ask Korjus to explain the point of e-residency. 'It depends where you're from,' he says in his steady monotone. 'If you're from outside the EU, you might want to be part of the EU business environment so you can invoice your customers as part of the European regulatory environment. If you're from an emerging market, such as India or Ukraine, and you're selling services or products globally, it lets you access PayPal and banking services, and to take dollar or yen payments. And if you're from within the EU, you may be a freelancer who wants to minimize your administration costs, issuing your contracts digitally, and remotely managing your business.'

So there could be benefits if I'm a writer from, say, a former European island state let down by incompetent political leadership? Korjus allows himself a brief smile. 'The online application takes twenty minutes, and you pick up your card at our London embassy,' he says. 'It will take one month to establish residency and a day to establish a company and a bank account.' Virtual-office services will provide the requisite local address, and startup banks such as Finland's Holvi are common options for opening an account. And my obligations as an e-resident? 'We haven't done that part yet,' he admits, almost apologetically. I'm reminded that Korjus's department is still an early-stage startup whose big ambitions remain mostly aspirational. 'You don't have rights or obligations. It's just digital identity today.'

Estonia has had intermittent trouble with its Russian neighbour ever since Yaroslav the Wise came and occupied its land back in 1030. Relations soured again when Ivan the Terrible invaded in 1558, and they didn't get any better after Russia grabbed the territory from Sweden in 1721. But it was the repressive Soviet occupation from 1944 that defined modern-day Estonian statecraft. When independence finally came in 1991, it brought with it a national determination to protect the nascent state from any future Russian intrusion. It also left an economically battered country whose new government lacked the resources it needed to rebuild.

'We had three choices,' recalls Linnar Viik, a technology adviser to the government in the 1990s, and now programme director at the Estonian e-Governance Academy. 'Stop providing some public services; continue to provide lousy public services; or radically redesign how you provide public services. So we challenged tradition and used technology to rethink public administration.' An early consensus emerged that Estonia would use digital tools where possible to operate all aspects of government: if Russia were to play dirty again, the state would at least be able to back up its data logs somewhere safe beyond its borders. It would also use the emerging internet protocols to hack together cheap but secure systems for running government departments. 'We were lucky that we regained independence at a time when we couldn't afford to buy a proper IT mainframe system,' Viik recalls. The state budget for IT was around $4 million, which wouldn't pay for the big IBM mainframe computers typically bought by governments. 'But with

$4 million you could buy 40,000 PCs and connect them over the old Soviet copper infrastructure with the only communication protocol that actually worked and was free – the internet.'

On the dark November afternoon when I visit Viik at his office in Rotermanni, near Tallinn's harbour, he has been receiving delegations from Japan, Ukraine and the Dominican Republic and has a conference call scheduled with the Cayman Islands. That's because Viik, fifty-three, a tall, welcoming, almost bald, university professor and entrepreneur, is considered a founding father of Estonia's digital transformation. He was central to the Tiigrihüpe (Tiger Leap) project that from 1996 set about installing computers and internet connections in all Estonian schools. He advised the Look@World foundation, which trained more than 100,000 Estonians to use the internet. And he helped his government become the first in the world to adopt web-based, paperless Cabinet meetings in which ministers need not be physically present.

It was an exciting national reboot, in which resource constraints offered the opportunity to think big. As the first ten-year Estonian passports were expiring in 2001, the government prepared to issue all citizens with a mandatory secure digital identity card. There are now 1.3 million active cards, connected in turn to more than 52,000 organizations through a distributed data exchange called X-Road. The government claims X-Road saves citizens and government 800 million hours a year, simplifying everything from property transfer to paying for parking and registering births. It operates on a 'once only' principle: once you supply information for one purpose, you shouldn't be troubled for it again by any other branch of government.

'We built digital ID cards for everybody,' Viik says. 'As the prime minister's adviser, I convinced banks not to build their digital authentication solutions with expensive equipment but to rely on government-issued infrastructure. I explained that this was the future. The banks said if the government was behind it, we can trust it. Then people in public administration started using it, so digital documents became legal. Over a decade, we created a shift in culture.'

Estonia made tax declarations digital in 2000, allowed online voting in 2005, and gave every patient their electronic medical record in 2008. Its determination to run every aspect of government through secure digital networks was only reinforced by a series of destructive cyber-attacks on government, media and financial websites in 2007, which the government blamed on the Kremlin. Today, the only government-related services that require a citizen's physical presence are marrying, divorcing and transacting real estate. As a principle, citizens own all information recorded about them, and every time it's accessed by a border guard, a doctor or any other state functionary, that action is recorded. It has built a free Wi-Fi network that covers most of the populated areas, and launched the world's first 'data embassy' for government data – a high-security set of backup servers in Luxembourg that are legally under Estonian jurisdiction. This is, quite literally, a nation in the cloud.

E-residency is built on this digital-first culture; my deputy editor at *WIRED*, Ben Hammersley, called Estonia 'the most advanced digital society in the world' when we sent him to become one of the early e-residents in 2015. And that's why other countries keep sending delegations to Viik's office to see what they can learn.

'I've been working for fifteen years with governments from around the world,' Viik tells me, 'and I strongly believe the next big disruption will be the nation state itself.' He mentions some African countries that lack the internal capacity to run efficient services, and suggests that they could delegate these services – customs, or air-traffic control – to other, better equipped countries on the continent. 'We need to start seeing the nation state as a platform,' he says – just as an app store is a platform on which developers anywhere can distribute their software. 'The only decision you'll have to make is whether your platform is on the equivalent of Android or iOS.'

Could it be that the nation state itself is an incumbent idea that's indeed ripe for radical disruption?

The nation defined by fixed territorial borders, after all, is an idea that makes less sense now that we're increasingly living digitally connected lives. The world is still run according to the 1648 Treaty of Westphalia, which established the principle of territorial state sovereignty, reinforced by a consensus after the First World War that there should be a right to national self-determination. And yet technology has changed the rules. How can this antiquated system remain relevant amid today's unconstrained transnational capital flows, decentralized information networks and peer-to-peer digital currencies? How can traditional governments adapt to a world where wars are waged by 'post-national' Islamist fighting forces, and supranational trillion-dollar tech companies decide where and whether they pay taxes?

National political authority, meanwhile, is being undermined by weakened international organizations, authoritarian state capture from Turkey to Venezuela, mass refugee migrations, and resurgent tribalism whether defined by race or regional cultures. Maybe the Estonians are on to something.

'There was, for much of the twentieth century, an authentic "fit" between politics, economy and information, all of which were organized at a national scale,' argues Rana Dasgupta, author of *After Nations*. 'National governments possessed actual powers to manage modern economic and ideological energies, and to turn them towards human – sometimes almost utopian – ends. But that era is over. After so many decades of globalization, economics and information have successfully grown beyond the authority of national governments. Today, the distribution of planetary wealth and resources is largely uncontested by any political mechanism.'

As Linnar Viik sees it, national identity will become just another elective aspect of personal identity, just as your passport does not affect your choice of identifying as Jewish or speaking Swahili. 'Loyalties change,' he reflects. 'I can be, in terms of my religious identity, part of any sort of nation. Your experience of your nation state may feel like being part of a church, but the underlying functions of the state – customs, border guards, tax, the kindergarten registration system, digital content in school – could be delegated to another nation state. It doesn't matter which app delivers your public transportation schedules.'

Whatever your geographic coordinates, you'll want to interact with a responsive, intuitive government that understands your needs and delivers its digital services to you automatically. It's the geopolitical evolution of a formative text that shaped early internet culture, 'A Declaration of the Independence of Cyberspace', written in 1996 by John Perry Barlow, a founder of the Electronic Frontier Foundation. 'Governments of the Industrial World, you weary giants of flesh and steel,' it began. 'I come from Cyberspace, the new home of Mind.' In sixteen paragraphs, to a large extent targeting American regulators, Barlow argues forcefully that our online identities fall beyond the scope of traditional government control. 'Cyberspace consists of transactions, relationships, and thought itself,' he writes. 'Ours is a world that is both everywhere and nowhere, but it is not where bodies live. You are not welcome among us . . . You have no sovereignty where we gather.'

Kaspar Korjus has a vision of the radically different ways in which government of the future might interact with his young son Ruufus. At birth, Ruufus received his personal ID number, which ensured that he will automatically receive his required childhood health checks and that his parents were allocated paid leave. At school, his work will be set and marked digitally. But it's as an adult that Ruufus's opportunities will be transformed. He might choose to run a company in Botswana as Africa's economy booms, pay personal taxes (or a subscription) to South Korea to use its health services, and build a pension through his subscriptions to Japan. Choosing nations for Ruufus will be as easy as choosing Facebook groups.

But first the e-residency team needs to promote the borderless nation to the world. The team had grown to fifteen people by

September 2018, backed by an €8 million three-year budget, and is now drumming up media interest, building partnerships and improving the 'product'. A private company in Seoul will now take fingerprints and issue ID cards to locals; if that arrangement works out, in 2019 the team plans to open thirty new local offices. It has a representative in Kiev working with the growing community of Ukrainian e-residents, and support partners in India. A trial version of an online 'community platform' is live, allowing e-residents and Estonian business owners to meet and exchange ideas, post and apply for job opportunities, rate and recommend services.

Still, as with many excitable startups whose investment pitches promise unrealistically exponential customer growth, the e-residency team has learned a difficult lesson in expectation management: its declared goal of 10 million e-residents by 2025 seems unlikely based on current take-up. Perhaps it has failed to present a compelling enough narrative to persuade significant numbers of the value of joining; maybe among the early 'digital nomads', journalists and traders who signed up, there are too few mainstream aspirational role models. At the end of 2017, the team said it now aimed for 150,200 e-residents and 20,000 new companies by the end of 2021. Still, the number of new e-residents has overtaken the number of babies born in Estonia: there were 11,096 applications for e-residency in the first ten months of 2017, compared to 10,269 births. Plus, each business the e-residents established will on average generate €70,000 for the Estonian economy, according to Deloitte. Korjus himself claims, in what sounds a rather unscientific calculation, that each euro invested by the Estonian state in the e-residency programme will return €100.

But he has another super-ambitious plan to optimize economic benefits to Estonia through the scheme. In a world where cryptocurrencies such as Bitcoin, Ethereum, Litecoin and countless others generate transactions valued in the billions of dollars, what's to stop Estonia issuing its own cryptocurrency and letting anyone invest in the country itself through a tradeable asset?

'The secure digital identities used by e-residents (as well as citizens and residents of Estonia) are now the ideal mechanism for securely trading crypto assets in a trusted and transparent digital environment,' Korjus suggested in a now famous blog post on Medium in August 2017. The cryptocurrency – or, more precisely, the tradeable part of it known as crypto 'tokens' – couldn't be counterfeited, and government supervision would ensure that they were not used for illegal purposes. 'This is why we are proposing the introduction of estcoins,' which, he suggested, could enable anyone to invest for the first time in a country 'as a digital nation'.

Government-backed estcoins, Korjus proposed, would be open to any e-residents to invest in through the crowdfunding mechanism used to launch so many cryptocurrencies and blockchain-based startups: an initial coin offering (ICO). He quoted the founder of Ethereum, Vitalik Buterin, in support: an ICO within the e-residency ecosystem, Buterin said, would incentivize investors to support the country's economic development in ways that central-bank interventions never could. Plus, if estcoins were issued in conjunction with a decentralized, secure database (a blockchain), 'then it would become easy and convenient to use them inside of smart contracts and other applications'. Estcoins could help fund Estonia's investments in emerging technologies such as artificial intelligence and could be used as a 'community-run' venture capital fund to invest in companies deemed to be working in the public good. 'And eventually,' Korjus argued, estcoins would function 'as a viable currency used globally'.

It was a tremendously audacious proposal coming from the representative of a government inside the euro zone. The blog post went viral. Naturally, the European Central Bank was quick to slap Korjus down. Its president, Mario Draghi, insisted that 'no member state can introduce its own currency: the currency of the eurozone is the euro'. Estonia's central bank also moved to distance itself: its governor, Ardo Hansson, stressed that the estcoin was not a government proposal and that the bank had not been consulted. It didn't help that a few weeks later Venezuelan president Nicolás Maduro announced his own state-backed cryptocurrency called the petro, intended to counter hyperinflation and circumvent US-led sanctions.

I met Korjus a few weeks after these knock-backs, at the end of November 2017, and he was still refining his thinking. 'I don't see much value in replacing euros,' he said, but he was still keen on an initial coin offering, with the state selling tokens as a bold alternative to taxation as a means of boosting national coffers. Here's one option he suggested: 'We issue a crypto coin, and through an initial coin offering people internationally can buy them.' E-residency would be part of compliance in validating investors' identity. Some e-residents would acquire the tokens as an investment, he said, 'believing the price will rise because Estonia with its digital services will become bigger'. Others would use them to spend within the ecosystem, for instance to pay taxes. The tokens could also be used to incentivize behaviour supported by the government: establishing companies, creating content, advising other businesses. But, Korjus admitted, the actual launch of a token was 'pretty far away'. So in the meantime he would be publishing a series of blog posts to develop his thinking.

The next month, in a December 2017 blog post, Korjus suggested three possible uses for estcoins. The 'community estcoin', issued through a national ICO, would incentivize activities that support e-residency. You'd earn estcoins by signing up a new e-resident, or spending time providing useful advice to other e-residents; and you could trade them on an open exchange. There would also be non-exchangeable 'identity estcoins' – blockchain-based tokens tied to your digital ID and used for activities such as digitally signing documents or enforcing smart contracts. If you broke the law, you could lose them. And finally there would be 'euro estcoins', pegged to the euro, which would 'combine some of the decentralized advantages of crypto with the stability and trust of fiat currency'.

Estonia's government has been testing blockchain technology for more than a decade, and has used blockchains since 2012 to store data relating to national health, the judiciary and national security. But it's still a huge leap for a government team in Europe to propose an actual cryptocurrency that would have utility beyond the official currency. So far, it seems that the idea is proving just too radical for the Estonian mainstream. 'We're not building a new currency,' the country's CIO, Siim Sikkut, told a newspaper firmly in June 2018.

Still, the debate has helpfully promoted Estonia as a blockchain- and cryptocurrency-friendly nation, and that's not a bad market to be in. According to Tallinn-based funding and trading platform Funderbeam, $2.8 billion was raised globally in initial coin offerings in 2017, up from $228 million in 2016. Korjus has been positioning the e-residency programme as supporting 'responsible' ICOs (as opposed to the many which will flame out after obtaining naive investors' money). 'Our aim is for Estonia to become the best option globally for trusted ICOs,' he wrote in his December blog post. 'We now have the opportunity to cut out the middlemen of central stock registries with a combination of blockchain, crypto tokens and secure digital identities.'

If the blockchain community were to hold its own version of the Cannes Lions advertising festival, estcoin would win a Gold award for Creative National Brand-Building. Even as a provocative idea alone, it fits neatly into a compelling narrative of a startup nation that's defining its own rulebook – while conveniently tapping into the opportunism of a well-capitalized blockchain startup boom. 'Estonia is now a blockchain nation,' declared the then president Toomas Hendrik Ilves in 2016. 'Through e-residency, Estonia is ready to support blockchain pioneers from anywhere in the world so they can build the future through our digital infrastructure, even without stepping foot in Estonia.'

And the pioneers are coming. Joyjit Bhowmick, from Bangladesh, used e-residency to launch Nobar, a Tallinn-registered business aiming to help international merchants accept crypto payments. Arseniy Zarechnev, a 'digital nomad' from Moscow, became an e-resident to set up Mothership, a cryptocurrency exchange. Renato P. dos Santos, a Brazilian physicist, remotely runs Sofia eConsulting, registered in Tartu, Estonia, to advise companies on ICOs. It doesn't hurt as a positive signal that a former Estonian prime minister, Taavi Rõivas, recently became chairman of Lympo, a local block-chain startup that uses tokens to reward exercise.

But there's a far more immediate set of problems that e-residency is solving for entrepreneurs. Amazon sellers from India are estab-lishing Estonian companies to take PayPal payments and trade in Europe. Freelance workers who sell their services digitally are using e-residency to simplify their tax reporting and administrative burden. Entrepreneurs and academics in the UK are registering Estonian companies to ensure they can trade without friction in the European market, or access funding, after Brexit. It helps that Estonia keeps topping the international tax competitiveness index for OECD countries: its low 20 per cent tax on corporate income is applied only when profits are distributed.

There's something else interesting happening in the background. Estonia has grown from its awkward position as the poorest of the euro zone's seventeen nations, when it joined in 2011, to being among its most entrepreneurially successful. In 2018, it became the country claiming the most billion-dollar 'unicorn' tech startups per capita, after ride-sharing company Taxify attracted $175 million in an investment round led by Daimler at a $1 billion valuation; this followed high reported valuations for Estonia-linked companies such as money-transfer service Transferwise and gambling-software firm Playtech. The multimillion-dollar investments keep coming: in 2018 alone, Pipedrive, which makes customer-relationship software, raised $60 million; Starship Technologies, which pro-duces delivery robots, attracted $25 million; and Veriff, which verifies online identity, raised $7.7 million from investors including the actor Ashton Kutcher and Transferwise co-founder Taavet

Hinrikus. And, of course, there's Skype, registered in Luxembourg but built in Estonia.

Hinrikus was the first employee at Skype, which launched in Tallinn in 2003 and remains Estonia's biggest tech success story. 'If you're talking about technology entrepreneurship in Estonia, you can't not talk about Skype,' he tells me. 'The happy incident that Skype was started in Tallinn, even by a Dane and a Swede [Janus Friis and Niklas Zennström], and sold to eBay for $3 billion two years after launch – that legitimized technology entrepreneurship as something real.' Hiring talent was hugely difficult at first, Hinrikus recalls: parents couldn't see why their child wouldn't prefer to join a bank. Skype's success shifted the mindset, trained a pool of talent who had experienced a fast-growth tech company, and created liquidity that enabled investment in new startups. 'You worked in Skype for three years and had enough savings to spend a year working on your idea,' he recalls. 'It was super-important for the ecosystem's development.'

Today's digital nation also draws on the constraints of the Soviet era. 'In a perverted way, life during the Soviet regime was some-what creative and entrepreneurial,' Hinrikus, thirty-seven, recalls. 'You weren't allowed a private company or to make money, but if you needed anything you'd build it yourself or repair what you had as nothing was available in the shops' – perfect for building a lean startup. Scarcity also meant that, despite strong scientific and math-ematical education, there was little technology infrastructure in place when independence was declared in 1991. The lack of legacy systems, Hinrikus says, meant the new country could embed a dig-ital culture from the start.

I ask Hinrikus, who lives in London, to what extent the 'border-less' aspect of e-Estonia reflects a genuine opportunity. He sees himself as the proof: Transferwise was born in January 2011 out of his need to convert his euro income from Skype into pounds to spend in London, alongside his friend Kristo Käärmann's need to convert his UK earnings from Deloitte to pay his euro mortgage back in Estonia. They came to a mutual arrangement which bypassed the banks' commissions – and built Transferwise to solve the problem at scale.

'If you look at the macro trend, it's really obvious that physical location matters less and less,' Hinrikus says. 'The financial system is not made for the way we work now.' Transferwise has capitalized on the demand it saw from customers working between countries to launch what it calls the Borderless account: a multi-currency bank account with a Mastercard debit card which stores money in more than forty currencies and converts them at a favourable exchange rate whenever needed. Already customers have deposited £2 billion in Borderless accounts. 'It's still early days,' he adds, 'but it's about using technology to make customers' lives simpler by providing the basic tools to live a borderless life.'

In the meantime, Estonia – 'the only truly digital society which actually has a state', in current president Kersti Kaljulaid's words – continues on its path towards being an app store to the world. 'We're building government as a service, available to other nations,' Kaspar Korjus explains. 'The goal is you don't feel the government, you don't need to declare taxes at all, we don't need to disturb entrepreneurs at all as we have all their information. Eventually your nation will realize it can't be good at everything, and will outsource everything else. The citizen gets better services and can choose where they want to be part of.' And, for those buying crypto tokens, there's the added financial commitment to the borderless nation as an engine of economic growth creation. 'Crypto tokenization will alter the nature of our world whether we act or not,' he says, 'so we must ensure we are taking a lead.'

Until then, Korjus just can't accept that a nation assigned to us at birth should stay with us for life. Why, he asks, should our identity and opportunities be determined by the random accident of geography that defines our passport? It's a question with intriguing social and political implications. What if pro-democracy activists in a repressive state could ally themselves with a friendlier liberal regime? Or if an entrepreneur in hyperinflationary Venezuela signed up to join a more stable economy? Or if a gay couple could choose in which national jurisdiction they wished to be recognized as married?

I ask Korjus to look fifty years ahead. 'There will be a range of communities you'll belong to,' he says. 'Just as today I belong to Google, to Amazon, to my street community organizing a festival – it will be like Facebook groups. You'll choose where you want to belong and who has the same values as you.' Still, he reflects, disruption can be frustratingly slow. 'I don't know if it's fifty or two hundred years away, but we won't have those borders any more. Twenty years ago in Estonia the technology was there to make this happen, but it's only now we're seeing it being used. It's true that we overestimate the short-term impact of technology and underestimate its long-term impact.'

Action Points

I think of e-Estonia as the plucky small-town startup that ignored the consensual rules of business to pitch to a global market. It's still too early to declare e-residency an outright success, but the numbers say one thing: it's delivering the beginnings of incremental revenue to the treasury, adding liquidity and talent to the business ecosystem, and promoting a 1.3-million-person country to the world more effectively than an expensive social-media marketing campaign. Here are a few lessons we can draw from the first four borderless years:

1. First, build the culture; the business model can come later. The benefits of e-residency were possible only because a generation of Estonians had

built and accepted a digital-first culture. By making every interaction with government digital by default, Estonia opened up opportunities unavailable to more powerful nations.

2. Tell a compelling story. It's hard to imagine e-residency appealing widely based simply on practical grounds such as automated taxation services or efficient accountancy. It was the future-facing narrative of a borderless nation open to global nomads and independent spirits that allowed the story to go viral.

3. Simplify the customer experience. The X-Road data exchange on which Estonia's digital governance is built is predicated on delivering security and efficiency while saving time for citizens and state employees. The 'once only' policy, which states that no single piece of information should be entered twice in the system, cuts through the frustration normally created by inefficient bureaucracies. Friction-free customer experiences build trust and loyalty. If your tax declaration can be fully automated, or your medical prescription will be available through your phone, you'll be a happier user of the service.

4. Constant small improvements eventually create magic. 'True innovation lies in making small things better for the customer every day,' Linnar Viik says. 'Small, nitty-gritty things, such as improving the databases to let you pay by phone for parking, or creating a company in less than a minute. Politicians think too much about the big narratives, and too little about the incremental work that needs to be done.'

5. But always learn from things that go wrong. Viik does not teach 'best practice' when he lectures visitors from other governments: it makes no sense when what has worked in one environment may fail in another. Instead, he argues that the only thing you can learn from are your own mistakes. 'I want to take our politicians away from their comfort zones, bullshitting about innovation,' he says, 'and instead make sure they have daily management meetings where they discuss what was the biggest failure of last week and what did we learn from it.'

6. Ask for forgiveness rather than permission. Kaspar Korjus knew that his estcoin proposal was going to be controversial. If he'd run it past the central bank and senior ministers before going public, he would have hit a wall. Better, he decided, to set the idea free and then pragmatically alter his position in light of the subsequent debate.

9.

FIND YOUR BLIND SPOTS

A software giant reimagines manufacturing

Above a calm San Francisco Bay, facing away from an unsuspect-ing city towards Alcatraz and Treasure Island, a black *Millennium Falcon* spaceship is executing a delicate figure-of-eight manoeuvre to elude the vengeful imperial enemy. Twisting and gyrating, the spacecraft races for its survival past asteroids, stars and black holes as it defies hostile fire. Only its effortless three-dimensional agility saves its crew – and perhaps civilization – from seemingly inevit-able obliteration at unimaginable speed.

Video of blurred stars racing on a digital screen behind the space-ship suggests that humanity was always going to survive this apocalyptic intergalactic conflict: the spaceship, a 30cm 3D-printed balsa model, is firmly affixed to a six-axis Kuka robot, which is being tracked by a Red professional video camera secured to a sec-ond floor-mounted robot two metres away. Black-and-yellow police tape separates the production crew from cables snaking towards the robots across the film-set floor. Wall-stapled black curtain-sheets block out the early-evening California sunshine.

This could be a Hollywood studio lot, but in fact I'm standing at the far end of an enclosed Pier 9 on San Francisco's Embarcadero. This pier is where a thirty-seven-year-old software company called Autodesk runs a 2,500-square-metre research lab and fabrication workshop to help it discover, and then prototype, the future. Today it's playing with industrial robots to learn how filmmakers might use them – if only the robots were simpler to program. Autodesk makes Maya, the visual effects and animation software favoured by count-less Oscar-winners, so it has a vested interest in understanding how its customers might want to use it to film with robots. Besides, if its tools can help filmmakers effortlessly program robots, imagine the wider industrial applications of a frictionless robotics operating system. What if future Autodesk software could effectively liberate robots to better serve their human overlords?

Erin Bradner, the Autodesk research scientist who runs the robotics lab, explains that the spaceship was hand-made for today's shoot by a collaborator at Industrial Light & Magic, the visual effects company founded by George Lucas to work on *Star Wars*. 'This is not a typical day in the robot lab,' she says with a grin as she watches the improvised shoot. The shoot is part of an experiment, she explains, to understand how Autodesk's existing software – it is a world leader in computer-aided design and 3D visual effects – could be adapted to make robots more easily controllable. The standard way to program the robots would be to move each arm manually and slowly, and record each step using a hand-held control called a teach pendant. Here, by contrast, the team has pre-programmed both arms with a version of Maya that automatically and instantly generates robot code simply from their start and end positions. The software, working from these two instructions, ensures that the robot moves smoothly and quickly along its six axes without the need for any human intervention. That saves huge amounts of time – and lets the software define the path that to a film camera seems most lifelike.

'Robots are typically programmed to do highly deterministic tasks in inflexible environments, but we want to unbolt them from the floor, metaphorically and physically, and get them to function on unstructured tasks in unstructured environments,' Bradner says, excitedly, as the robots dance in cinematic harmony. So what's actually an animation tool – Maya helps artists build a time-based sequence if shown a start and end drawing – is now able to give robots intuitive movements. In other words, the animation software has been hacked to solve a problem it was never designed for. The endgame, Bradner explains, is to transform how humans work with robots, not just for filming, but for manufacturing. 'Toyota has its robot whisperers – the revered gentlemen who come in to program the robots, so that the rest of the factory can pick up the mantle. But what if the rest of us could approach that domain with less expertise, less mysticism? What if we could create *real* robot–human collaboration?'

This matters to Autodesk, because Autodesk makes software for the people who make our physical world. Architects, engineers and the construction industry design, model and build with products such as AutoCAD and Revit; industrial manufacturers prototype and scale production with Fusion 360 and Autodesk Inventor; infrastructure providers rely on Civil 3D and InfraWorks. There are Autodesk products for digital prototyping and injection-moulding simulation; for home tinkerers and amateur makers; and, as we've seen, for movie rendering and visual effects. 'If you've ever driven a high-performance car, admired a towering skyscraper, used a smartphone, or watched a great film,' as the company brochure puts it, 'chances are you've experienced what millions of Autodesk customers are doing with our software.'

Yet this is a $30 billion company born in 1982 during the last great computing-platform transition, from mainframes to desktop PCs. It understands that the old rules won't keep it relevant during the current transition to cloud services, artificial intelligence and decentralized networks. So it has been aggressively searching for a sustainable and profitable role in this unpredictable future. It knows it must turn from a legacy business, selling software in boxes, to an agile enabler of emerging manufacturing processes. And that this may involve helping tomorrow's clients design nano-factories, write DNA, empower robots . . . or whatever else comes next.

Autodesk's answer to these challenges is to search relentlessly for its 'unknown unknowns' – to invest heavily and consistently in what Jeff Kowalski, its recently departed chief technology officer, calls 'discovering our blind spots'. Out of total revenues of $1.5 to $2 billion in recent years, it has typically dedicated $700 to $750 million to R&D. For Kowalski, those letters stand for 'risk and determinism': while most of the company pursues the deterministic goals of pleasing today's shareholders, the CTO's office funds longer-term, riskier experiments in machine learning, material and life sciences, digital manufacturing, artists' fellowships, and wherever else it identifies knowledge gaps. 'You and I don't have very different jobs,' Kowalski confides to me over a beer. 'We go out and explore and talk to people, and we start piecing things together. My team does the science, makes the prototypes, and brings further-out speculation to customers to explore. This company got really good at shipping known product with known resources – we've been around for ever. The problem is, what do you put at the front end of the machine *tomorrow*?'

That explains why I've come to Pier 9, where as well as the robotics lab Autodesk runs a reconfigurable micro-factory, an advanced fabrication lab, a 3D-print studio, Instructables training courses, resident artists' workspaces, and a hybrid pool of talent hired to push the boundaries of digital manufacturing. I'm given a leisurely tour by Mickey McManus, an accomplished and intellectually curious industrial designer who has ten patents and co-wrote the book *Trillions: Thriving in the Emerging Information Ecology*. Kowalski, CTO for twelve years from 2006, brought in McManus as an Autodesk Fellow, a part-time role designed to challenge the leadership with provocative ideas.

Which he certainly does. McManus talks quickly, thoughtfully, and with a stream of radical notions that take me a while to digest. As we walk past a giant metal-cutting water jet, a vast laser-cutter and an electronics lab, he explains the pier's new experimental, AI-dependent micro-factory. 'What if you flip the design of a factory so you don't know what it will build tomorrow? What if it just dreams overnight, learning in the cloud how to make a new product based on market demand, and then reformats itself in the morning to produce it?'

My eyes widen.

McManus shows me a row of robot arms that have taught themselves how to recognize and manipulate piles of bricks, and to build the TransAmerica Building out of LEGO by downloading assembly instructions from the cloud. We meet some of the pier's twelve resident artists, one working on 'sculptures dreamed by a computer studying classical sculpture', and another coding free-form string structures. 'Getting to observe how they use the tools gives us the "risk" part of R&D,' McManus says. 'You can't predict the future, but you can wander with people who are passionate, who fall down and then get up again.'

Today McManus is thinking a lot about how artificial intelligence will replace universities as we know them. 'The universities are set up to pump out people to do the same things for forty years,' he reflects as we walk. 'We'll have 10 billion people by 2050, three-quarters living in cities, yet those cities don't yet exist in the emerging world or those that do are crumbling. And our customers, who build the real world, can't find trained workers. So little of the knowledge they need makes it into those artisanally crafted things called degrees.' He has an answer: to reinvent education as a constant process of feedback-based learning. Artificial intelligence will monitor individual workers' skills and personalize their training, based on what they already know, so they can work effectively alongside the robots. He calls it generative learning, and believes that it will not only train workers for tomorrow's jobs, but will also challenge the self-doubt that keeps those workers from using Autodesk products. Because, after all, this is a profit-driven business.

'Ultimately I'm thinking about what it takes to get you from self-doubt to curious to curious doer,' he says. 'Because a new technology isn't going to slow down and wait for you to use it. And Autodesk needs people to swipe that credit card each month.'

Such abstractions suggest that this is an unusually future-obsessed software company. I first discovered that when I spent a week in 2012 at Singularity University, the Silicon Valley think-tank-for-the-future, where senior Autodesk executives were mentoring students founding 'exponential' startups, and delivering guest lectures on emerging design disciplines such as synthetic biology. I've also regularly encountered Autodesk teams at the annual TED conferences in Vancouver and Edinburgh, showcasing nascent 'maker' technologies such as self-assembling building materials, or hosting design-thinking workshops. Each time I thought their involvement was led more by curiosity than public relations.

But funding blue-sky investigations into AI teaching? How does a listed company explain *that* to its shareholders? At Autodesk's own 'university', a three-day series of workshops and presentations for 10,000 ticket-holders at the Venetian Hotel in Las Vegas, I get to ask the CEO. Andrew Anagnost has just come off stage at a side event for C-level executives, where he set out his core philosophy: 'You have to break something to make something.' His talk cited the Spanish conquistador Hernán Cortés, who, during the conquest of Mexico in 1519, ordered his troops to sink (some say burn) their ships so that they would have no option but to continue. He also mentioned Elon Musk's decision at SpaceX to bet the entire company on building a reusable rocket – which had to succeed for the company to survive. 'By declaring the irreversible event, you force people to respond,' Anagnost declared. As for Autodesk, that irreversible commitment, he explained, was to help customers reinvent manufacturing – while itself shifting from selling software to becoming an AI-led subscription company.

'It takes a lot of discipline to say we're going to do something none of our customers is asking for but we know they're going to need, and it's going to completely turn our revenue model upside down for a while,' Anagnost says to me offstage afterwards. 'But if we don't do it, we're extinct. That takes a lot of fortitude, and I can see why not many companies do that.'

Anagnost, a twenty-one-year company veteran who became CEO in June 2017, has enthusiastically embraced a McKinsey innovation strategy called the Three Horizons Model, introduced in the

1999 book *The Alchemy of Growth*. Simply put, Horizon 1 involves maintaining today's core business, Horizon 2 nurturing emerging businesses that could potentially become significant, and Horizon 3 conceiving new future businesses in a more speculative way. Continuous growth, according to the strategy, comes from engaging with H1, H2 and H3 simultaneously.

'Our key advantage is running multiple experiments, and having a mechanism for mainstreaming some of those experiments,' Anagnost explains. Pier 9's genesis was one of those experiments that initially failed. It was conceived both to allow staff to experiment with Autodesk tools to make things for themselves, and also to let the company's consumer group showcase 3D-printing and other technologies to the public. But that unit was broken up, and the company decided to use the space to experiment more with professional workflows, liberating it for filmmakers to play with robots. The film set is only one of the experiments currently underway there. A team on the pier is using virtual reality as a tool for programming robots; another is creating customizable production lines for small manufacturing runs, which they call 'configurable micro-factories'. These projects may go nowhere – or they may spur the development of an original, highly profitable new software product.

Jeff Kowalski, who joined Autodesk in 1993, seems to relish the tensions. He has an intense gaze and his mind moves simultaneously in divergent directions. One moment he is explaining with persuasive certainty that construction companies need to understand DNA, the next that skateboard parks are a proxy for car parks, or that CAD, Autodesk's lifeblood, is built on a lie ('The computer never assisted the designer, ever'). And if that riles the company's sales teams, then so be it. 'To get internal resistance is a reasonable signal that we're doing our job,' he says. 'There's always going to be tension but you need to be on the positive side of complacency. I'm really fond of the quote about the best way to predict the future being to create it.'

'Do I agree with everything that Jeff sees around the corner?' Anagnost says. 'No.' But he relishes how Kowalski's questioning approach creates organizational tensions that challenge status-quo thinking. That's why Autodesk is deliberately structured into three horizon-model silos: established businesses, in Horizon 1; businesses that are scaling fast, such as digital manufacturing, in H2; and, in H3, the speculative explorations sitting under the office of the CTO – known inside the company as OCTO (and sometimes inspiring octopus logos on staff business cards). 'If we're really stretching it, we put 10 per cent of the budget into H3; less than 5 per cent and we worry,' Anagnost tells me. 'You've got to make some outrageous bets, to look outside and play with wacky ideas. Jeff's a philosopher, and sometimes you need philosophers to bend your mind. If the company just had engineers, we'd be a great engineering company but we might not stay relevant.'

From time to time, an H3 exploration proves so promising that it's rapidly promoted to H2, where project teams look to take it to market. One hugely exciting current example is an emerging technology known as generative design. It's an idea borrowed from evolutionary biology. If nature can take a living object and then repeatedly iterate to make that object better suited to its environment, why shouldn't human designers explore every possible permutation of their project by letting computers in the cloud work with them? By applying machine-learning algorithms as a designer works, Autodesk software can turn whatever they're working on into a complex living system, suggesting endless iterations based on goals and constraints they have programmed in.

Generative design is already helping Autodesk customers achieve what had been impossible. Airbus has used it to imagine a 'bionic' aircraft partition that separates the passenger cabin from the galley. The 3D-printed result mimics the organic cellular structure found in living organisms (it was partly inspired by slime mould) and is structurally strong yet 45 per cent lighter than the existing design. If used in the world's A320 planes, Airbus estimates that the generative approach could save 465,000 tonnes of carbon dioxide each year – not to mention the fuel savings. General Motors is using generative design to reduce the weight of car parts: Autodesk's software suggested a seat-belt bracket that's 40 per cent lighter yet 20 per cent stronger than today's version, yet combines what had been eight components into a single part that can be 3D-printed (thus saving the cost of welding). And Under Armour has used it to create the lightweight UA Architech performance training shoe, inspired by tree roots: the resulting 3D-printed lattice midsole is flexible at the toes yet rigid at the heel.

The industrial applications of generative design are vast: it is already being used to design medical implants, skyscrapers and armchairs, in each case in response to constraints set by the designer (weight, size, cost, strength, style, materials and any number of other criteria). It has even been used to reimagine the layout of Autodesk's own workspace in Toronto's MaRS Discovery District. Staff were surveyed on how they preferred to work, and the response data was combined with hard constraints such as building dimensions and planning requirements. The software generated 10,000 potential floor plans, based on maximizing outside views, minimizing distractions and prioritizing personal relationships. Then an algorithm sorted through these configurations to select those that managed trade-offs and scored the highest among staff.

Autodesk has taken a lead in this new field, already incorporating generative design in commercial products such as Fusion 360 and Netfabb, online tools for creating and printing 3D objects. And yet its work in search of what Kowalski calls generative design's 'infinite expressibility' began only in 2014 as an H3 project called Dreamcatcher. Led by the computational science and design research teams answering to the CTO's office, it brought together experts in machine learning, mechanical engineering, mathematical optimization, material science, structural mechanics, user-experience research, software development and more, and was boosted by the acquisition of startups such as Within Technologies and NEi Software, specialists in 3D-printing and simulation software. It also built on another Autodesk research project called Design Graph, in which researchers fed the system millions of 3D models so it could understand the essence of, say, a chair or a gear or an aircraft wing. And then algorithms classified each element and component, identified how they inter-related, and learned what they did. The system could then suggest thousands of configurations according to constraints set by the designer – for a chair that's 52 per cent more Herman Miller, perhaps, or a titanium spinal implant that's 26 per cent lighter.

Which, if Kowalski is right, could keep a thirty-seven-year-old software startup relevant for a considerable while longer.

Autodesk never set out to be a market-dominating multibillion-dollar corporation. Initially it was just a loose collective of software programmers pursuing their own obsessions.

When Mike Riddle started writing computer-aided-design software in his spare time back in 1977, the 16-bit processor on his S-100 computer was so basic, and the 48K of available memory so limited, that he had to assemble the program in pieces while waiting for larger memory boards to become available. Riddle was a big believer in Moore's Law, though, which predicted the rate of growth in the industry as doubling every two years, so he knew more powerful microcomputers would eventually come along. And when in 1979 he was ready to release his software, called Interact, it didn't take long to find thirty customers – the first being the California oil company Atlantic Richfield, which used Interact to plan dives for offshore oil rigs.

Riddle was a hobbyist – he'd built his first computer out of rudimentary components while at junior high school in California – and also a man of fixed views. He hated lawyers, for instance, so when in 1981 he received an $8,000 offer to sell the rights to his software, which became AutoCAD, he insisted on conducting the negotiations himself. When his demand for $15,000 was rejected, he successfully insisted instead on selling a non-exclusive licence for $1 plus 10 per cent of all future revenues. The purchaser was John Walker, whose company Marinchip Systems had made the circuit board that Riddle used.

Later that year, Walker invited a group of programmer friends to his house in Mill Valley, California, to suggest they combine resources to market software they developed in their spare time. Eighteen co-founders put up $59,000 the next year to start a company called Marin Software Partners, before its name was changed to Autodesk. The company launched AutoCAD, now rewritten for the new IBM personal computer, at the COMDEX computing trade show in November 1982. It proved a sensation: it was awarded Best of Show, the booth was packed, and over the next year Autodesk sold more than 1,000 copies. A company that had grossed $15,000 in the 1983 tax year took more than $1 million in 1984.

Suddenly the collective had to grow up.

On 21 June 1983, Walker, as CEO, wrote urgently to shareholders warning that Autodesk may be out of business within sixty days – because of AutoCAD's unexpected success. 'Our company is in a very deep crisis,' he wrote. 'Each single segment of the company is overloaded to the point of collapse. We cannot return all the calls from people who desperately want to do business with us, no less plan a coherent advertising campaign. We do not have a customer support group. We have no business plan, even an informal one. We have no budgets for departments, and no way to coherently authorize expenditures or to hire people. The management has not been given a mandate to hire people with stock options . . . This is a prescription for disaster.'

He urged each of them to donate their time and skills – from coding to finishing the business plan – to help the company professionalize and meet the sudden demand. The call to action succeeded. By 1984, the newly structured business sold 10,000 units; the next year it sold 25,000. The value of Autodesk grew from around

$200,000 at the time of Walker's letter to $500 million four years later, and $1.4 billion by 1991.

And yet Walker then again felt the need to warn the company that it was complacent and failing to prepare for the future – a theme that continues to echo today. On 1 April 1991 he wrote a forty-four-page memo to senior management warning that 'most companies that attain great value then lose it do so by *failing* to adapt when technological progress or the market demand[s] they change'.

The memo was blunt. AutoCAD was expensive, was behind in development, was underestimating the fast-growing Microsoft Windows operating system, and was neglecting its dealers. 'When a company ceases to change at the rate demanded by the industry it exists within,' Walker wrote, 'it finds itself rapidly left behind. Before long, its customers discover products of competitors that better meet their needs. As market share slips, sales fall, and earnings decline, the management of the standstill company asks, "What's happening? We're still doing all the things we used to do."

'Autodesk possesses all the prerequisites to lead the next generation of the PC industry, yet it seems to have become stuck in the past, mired in bureaucracy, paralysed by unwarranted caution, and to have lost the edge of rapid and responsive product development and aggressive marketing and promotion on which the success of AutoCAD was founded.'

His recommendations included a company reorganization, a new pricing strategy, better Windows integration, direct customer support, and the prioritization of a new CAD product. The memo quickly leaked throughout the company. Walker was serious about investing in Autodesk's blind spots.

By then, AutoCAD was generating sales of more than $200 million a year. Nine months after the memo, Autodesk finally bought out Mike Riddle's royalty rights. Walker, who had originally turned down a $15,000 demand from Riddle as too expensive, now agreed to pay him $11,875,000.

*

Post-it Notes are being thrown scrappily on to flipchart easels by a dozen standing teams of Autodesk customers wielding marker pens. 'Never stand still' one reads. 'Contracts in blockchain' says another. Yet more speak of 'A Spotify of spare parts', 'Gaming tech for simulations', 'Startup mentality'.

It's Autodesk University's June leadership summit at Tobacco Dock in London, and Autodesk Fellow Tom Wujec, a four-time TED speaker and author, has taken an animated workshop on 'Managing the mindset of innovation' into brainstorming mode. Maurice Conti, for a few more days the director of strategic innovation in the chief technology officer's team, has just given a talk on 'How to innovate in a crazy world'. It was Conti whom Jeff Kowalski hired to set up and run the Applied Research Lab back in 2010. The pier opened three years later. 'A year ago, we were working with two artists from Paris who got it into their heads that they wanted to be tattooed on their leg by a big industrial robot,' Conti said in his talk. 'We thought: of course! So we explored how it could happen. And it got us researching real-time algorithms for safety. Real innovation can't just be some cool thing in the lab somewhere – if it doesn't make it out into the real world, it's not innovation.'

Afterwards, I ask Conti – who's about to join Telefónica's Barcelona-based 'moonshot factory', Alpha, as chief innovation officer – to drill down on the practicalities of his Autodesk role. 'The brief Jeff gave me was, "I need you to go look in our blind spots",' he tells me. 'So the group is entirely undirected, no one tells us what to do. From time to time, I'll tell the leadership, "Here's what we're working on and why." There's a lot of trust, little oversight, zero direction. Which is important if you're trying to break out. Creating a strategy will by definition fail.'

At first, Conti's lab was given a staff of four plus two contractors, and zero operational budget. For funding, they had to petition product managers in other parts of the company. 'It was a great discipline,' he says. 'If we couldn't sell what we were doing to the people we were asking money from, it probably wasn't going to work.' Typically cash would be diverted from product development or, more frequently, marketing. The marketing department saw the value of the stories that Conti's lab was generating, in addition to the value of potential future products. 'Our team of a hundred people in the office of the CTO gets about 50 per cent of the press that Autodesk as a whole gets,' he says. 'There's a dollar value associated with telling a great story.'

As the lab team grew, it started to define itself as Autodesk's 'special forces' unit: a small, high-performance, diverse team, designed for any mission, reporting to the top, and free to act as needed. Its brief: to determine whether an emerging technology is desirable (by Autodesk customers tomorrow), feasible (buildable inside an Autodesk product) and viable (potentially a business line). 'Diversity on the team is absolutely critical,' Conti says. 'Our team is 50 per cent female, which is hard in tech. Even their hobbies are diverse. No person on the team is a one-trick pony. We have mechanical engineers who can do machine learning, electrical engineers who understand robots.' And, because their work is not directed from the centre, the team manages to avoid much of the friction and office politics typically found in corporate settings.

And Conti's role? 'My general input is telling my team: "Don't fuck it up." The risk is, people start to pursue things that are irrelevant. So I have to make sure the company leadership is comfortable that we're not wasting time and money.' The team might run an internal science fair, where researchers have booths and colleagues drop by; or special guided tours for senior leadership. 'We did it two weeks ago, walked every senior executive through the pier, showed them what we were working on, got them to wear the virtual-reality goggles, explained our thinking. They don't see a single PowerPoint slide: if I'm talking about a robot, there's a robot next to us. Their senses come alive. They walk away energized, with an intimate understanding of the projects. It becomes part of their data set and RAM [data-storage memory] that they're going to touch on for the next six months.'

I ask Conti if he can quantify how his team has changed Autodesk. He pauses. 'We've had a tactical impact,' he says. 'We've written code that will end up in products, we've proven out certain trends and disproven others. But the biggest impact is internal culture. Showing people that it's OK to take risks, to prototype stuff. At first it was, "Those guys are weird, they work on cool stuff but are not relevant". And now, indirectly, pockets of teams around the company have adopted this behaviour.'

The magic of the pier, he says, does not lie in the machines and the tools; anyone can do that. 'It's the community that's been created around them. If I'm interested in a new technology, the pier staff will know the world-leading expert and connect us. That access is hugely valuable. And unlike Google's X, we're not closed. We had 20,000 visitors come through the pier last year.'

The San Francisco pier is part of a global network of Autodesk future-exploration spaces. The new Toronto office includes a research lab; a Boston studio focuses on architecture, construction and engineering; and in Birmingham, in the UK, there's an advanced-manufacturing facility.

Yet sometimes the company's commitment to its future-focused investments fails to live up to its compelling stories. For a while Autodesk ran a research group called Bio/Nano/Programmable Matter whose hugely ambitious goal was to develop software to fabricate living things at the nanoscale. In 2014, Andrew Hessel, an Autodesk Distinguished Researcher based at Pier 9, announced that the team had 3D-printed a virus, called synthetic Phi-X174 bacteriophage, for less than $1,000. The bacteriophage was designed to attack *E. coli* bacteria, but Hessel's bigger aim was to design synthetic viruses to fight cancer. The research group had already announced a partnership with a medical research company, Organovo, to design three-dimensional human tissue and perhaps entire bio-printed organs. Kowalski was so excited he told the media that synthetic biology could be a bigger opportunity for Autodesk than 3D-printing.

And yet the company seems to have rolled back on its grand ambitions. Hessel left the company in February 2018 when his role was terminated, and the team incorporated into a more commercial Life Sciences unit 'building a cloud platform for the next generation of biological design'. The unit's two projects were rather less radical: a visualization tool for molecular data, and software to code gene sequences. These were suspended when the group was dissolved in July 2018. 'It's a company that's willing to experiment fearlessly,' says Hessel now, still a declared supporter of his former employer, but running a new business, Humane Genomics, working on virus-based therapies to target cancer, initially in dogs. The company was generous in funding early research, he tells me, 'but a weakness was that the strategic approach to these explorations could be more coherent'. In other words, there wasn't always follow-through.

But then Anagnost and Kowalski currently face other priorities. Most urgently, they need to build a sustainable new business model as the software-licensing model dies. When Autodesk was founded, customers bought boxes containing software disks; today they want to access software online. So it is moving aggressively to a subscription model – customers access the software from Autodesk's servers. But it's experimenting around what exactly they're charged for. Their bill may be based on how complex their design jobs are, and how much computing time they consume. 'We don't sell software now,' Anagnost tells me. 'We sell outcomes. The cloud is turning all software companies into subscription companies, while machine learning is turning all subscription companies into consumption companies.'

So if a customer wants to create beautiful photorealistic 3D renderings, for instance, Autodesk might sell them 'cloud credits' that they spend according to how intricate their results are. 'The same for generative design: we don't care how complex your design is, we'll charge you based on the number of constraints. It's absolutely a whole new approach to software revenue. Will it open up an entirely new market for us? Absolutely. The value of generative design might not be what we charge every time you push that button; it might be in the fact that people using other software think, if I don't work with Autodesk I'll be left behind.'

The transition to consumption-based subscription has required some tough restructuring: staff numbers were cut from 9,200 to 7,200 in less than two years (though are now back up). But shareholders are starting to see results. Subscriptions were up a fifth to 3.72 million in the 2018 fiscal year, and annualized recurring revenue rose a quarter to $2.05 billion. The stock price also rose sharply in 2018.

But Anagnost knows the journey has barely begun. 'We're classically viewed as a design software company today,' he reflects. 'But we're going to be seen as a design-and-make company. It's either that or we don't exist. Period.' And that means investing in research that competitors might dismiss as wacky. 'Dassault Systèmes, who we compete with, thought we were literally bonkers with all the things we were doing in the cloud with 3D-printing. They said explicitly in numerous forums that their customers were not asking for that. I anticipate we're going to be eating their lunch over five to ten years. Because we've done the hard work. We've changed the company mindset.'

That company, until recently, was making almost all its revenue by licensing its most popular software package, AutoCAD. Today Autodesk is a cloud-centric subscription company, betting its diversified future on artificial intelligence, generative design, synthetic biology, self-programming robots, virtual-reality design and whatever next it discovers in its blind spots.

'To save your business you gotta break your business,' Anagnost says, banging an over-ornate Las Vegas hotel table. 'Stand up, tell a story about how you're eating your own young. Otherwise you won't make it. People have this idea of "I'll leave the core business alone, and just acquire a new business that will over time eat the core business". Sorry, the world is moving too fast. You've got to eat your own business, and you've got to do it now. Because if you don't have the courage, someone will do it to you.'

Action Points

Like many technology businesses born during an earlier platform shift, Autodesk has faced existential challenges as cloud computing and artificial intelligence have transformed customer expectations. It's far from the first tech business to invest in blue-sky research as a way to stay relevant: Microsoft's research unit has built labs from Bangalore to Cambridge in the UK; IBM has invested in an AI research lab at the Massachusetts Institute of Technology; even Facebook has launched a data-focused startup incubator in Paris. But Autodesk's commitment to free-form explorations is unusual both in its relatively generous budgets and central corporate backing. And it seems to be paying dividends.

1. How much of current revenue should you be prepared to invest in unconstrained investigations of emerging technologies? If technology touches on your business model, then the answer is probably much more than you are.

2. Your investigations of future potential business opportunities need to be ring-fenced from today's customer-facing business. Because determining what will or will not be market-ready in ten years is too high risk to be evaluated by today's income-generating decision-makers.

3. Powerful storytelling needs to be central to your future explorations. 'Story is the vehicle for us to

embrace risk in order to reduce it,' Jeff Kowalski says. 'It's the way we bring the future to the present.'

4. External investments and startup acquisitions can accelerate your internal team's explorations. The seed of Autodesk's success in commercializing generative design, according to Andrew Anagnost, was the $88.5 million acquisition of the London software house Within Technologies.

5. You need to prototype and experiment. But you also need a process that moves these experiments to teams that build products.

6. Challenge your assumptions by funding internal programmes for artists and industry experts (Autodesk calls them 'Fellows'). These are the people who will lead you to emergent behaviours.

7. And prepare to see all your current assumptions cast away as irrelevant. Jeff Kowalski likes to quote the late futurist Alvin Toffler: 'The illiterate of the 21st century are not going to be those who cannot read and write, but those who cannot learn, unlearn, and relearn.'

10

MINE THE DATA

China's postmen build a retail search engine

Lou Wener works damn hard. Five a.m. to ten p.m., seven days a week, including national holidays, as the forty-five-year-old shop-keeper confirms in a distracted manner from behind the cluttered counter of her general store in Zhejiang province, a couple of hours' drive west of Hangzhou city. In fact, she explains as she checks a customer's egg delivery for freshness, she and her husband don't close the shop, not even for Chinese New Year. 'Of course we stay open,' she says, smiling tolerantly as an elderly customer holding detergent looks on bemused at a Western journalist's presence. 'That's a very busy day for us.'

Lou grew up here in Xiabao, a Chinese village of around 1,000 people set among paddy fields and hectares of longjing tea, its out-skirts marked by roadside stalls selling locally grown melons and apples. She's run the store for twenty-one years and lives upstairs with her farmer husband, his father and their twenty-one-year-old son. 'When we first opened, business was good, as people didn't often go to town to buy things,' she tells me. 'But in recent years it's got much harder. It's [e-commerce website] Taobao. People started learning how to buy online around 2014 – their kids taught them. Then the smartphone arrived. They just stopped buying daily goods. We felt the pressure: it was only old people coming into the store. If we didn't change, we would be eliminated by the internet.'

Then, in July 2015, the local postman offered to turn Lou's simple store into a data-enabled, real-time-responsive, globally connected e-commerce hub of its own. With help from the postman, she plugged an electronic point-of-sale laser scanner, a till-receipt printer and a digital weighing scale into a new Asus laptop that sits between a router, a cash register and a landline towered over by Western and Chinese cigarette packs. Now whenever a customer pays for a Funkid Grapefruit Juice or Hazelive Soap, their purchase is tracked instantly on a central database. It is linked to both the shopkeeper and that particular customer, whose membership card is then credited with loyalty points that can be redeemed for a purchase of blueberry juice or rice wine.

A wall-mounted 42-inch Sanyo TV displays the WeChat group that Lou maintains for the store: a special offer on trainers if ten villagers will commit; prices for latex pillows and organic duck eggs that the postman can deliver to the store by next morning. WeChat lets her tell customers that their order has arrived. On hot days she'll even deliver to local homes.

There is a China Post logo on the shop awning above a red lantern, which sits alongside a red logo containing the web address 'ule.com'. These are clues to the ambitious retail experiment that has embraced this village store and is leveraging the power of data to transform the business prospects of China Post. Ule is a fast-growing national e-commerce network set up by China Post to build new revenue across rural China. The postal service is turning hundreds of thousands of village stores like Lou Wener's into hubs in a national retail-delivery network, linked together by a million postal workers. But it's also using the new digital tracking systems inside each store to learn exactly what customers are buying across the nation at any moment. In a very Chinese way, China Post is collecting vast amounts of customer-purchase data to understand shoppers' desires and needs in unprecedented detail – creating the world's largest real-time retail database.

Moore's Law continues to force down the cost of computer processing, storage, sensors and connectivity. And that has created an opportunity for traditional offline businesses to discover profitable ways to collect and sell data that they had hitherto ignored. It's happening to even the most heavy analogue businesses. Wanxiang, the biggest car-parts maker in China, founded in 1969, recently announced a $30 billion investment to build a 'city of the future' in Hangzhou, called Wanxiang Innova City. It will record the movements of autonomous cars and track other city services using blockchain and use that data to create new business revenues. That's one way to fight the commoditization of carburettors.

For years we've been hearing about the exponential growth of 'big data'. Now big legacy businesses are finding increasingly creative ways to leverage data science to build new income streams by mining data that was previously inaccessible.

So far the data flow is working out very nicely indeed for Lou Wener. On the floor of her store sit two half-opened boxes of yams that the postman brought today for her customers from a neighbouring province. They lie next to a large box of packed tea brought to the store by a local farmer to be sold on Lou's store website and collected for delivery by the same postman on his way back into town. These are what Lou calls her 'virtual SKUs', or stock-keeping units, which give her customers access to thousands more lines than can fit in her cluttered physical store: cotton shirts, denim jeans, dry beef jerky, flowerpots, adhesive tape, chopsticks, dragonfruit, socks, cooking oil, doormats . . . all brought in reliably by next-day China Post delivery.

In one month, Lou says, her website sold 800 pairs of shoes to this 1,000-person village. So far today, according to Ule's mobile app, she has taken forty orders, earning RMB 1,719 (£200) in revenue and RMB 116 (£13) in profit. Yesterday, seventy-one orders brought in RMB 3,295 and RMB 180 profit. Ule's point-of-sale device lets customers pay utility bills in the store and manage their Postal Bank accounts, further boosting Lou's income. A quarter of her turnover is now online, with a growing trade in outbound sales of local farmers' shredded bamboo, fungus and dried vegetables. There are so many products that she's had to rent a nearby warehouse to store them.

Because Lou's trading data is transparent within Ule's network, the Postal Bank has offered her an RMB 90,000 revolving credit line at a preferential interest rate. The offline, non-Ule store next door, meanwhile, 'isn't doing well', according to Lou; yet her revenue, she says, has doubled since she joined Ule. 'I was going to close down as business was so hard,' Lou tells me. 'Young people weren't coming, but now with mobile sharing they know there's a promotion on milk, and we can sell eighty boxes of milk in a day. Or they tell me what they want. I search on Ule for it and it comes in the next day. It may be a bit more expensive than Taobao, but you don't have to worry about fake products. I take care of everything. It's a long, hard day but I feel fulfilled. With the mobile, we're very busy. Before it was so boring that I wanted to cry.'

Samson Yeung won't relent in connecting China's village stores until he's reached saturation. 'A million stores would be a very good number to dominate the market,' he asserts as we drive along the winding hills that lead to the last remaining store in the village of Yaocun. It's 20km past the nearest small town. 'China has 700,000 villages, and we're planning to have one Ule store per village, plus twenty or thirty per city. Then we'll cover all China's rural areas and the best parts of the city.'

As Ule's chief operating officer, Yeung understands just how valuable all that data will be. 'Point-of-sale is just the beginning,' he explains. 'Being on the network makes each store a virtual Walmart: they can sell what they like, even if it's not in the shop, to turn themselves into internet businesses. Plus we're capturing every transaction that's made in the store, to help the shop owner. We know who they're selling to, at what time of day and in what weather. We work with owners to decide where to shelve products for maximum impact.'

Yeung's team is moving fast. In August 2016, when we tour the villages of Zhejiang province, there are 250,000 stores on the Ule system; by late December, that figure will rise to 330,000. At the start of 2019, it was up to 500,000. And because each store owner scans every product variation into the system, to identify every-thing from Coke to local cabbage, Ule tracks more than 3 million individual SKUs.

The Yaocun store is open even longer hours than Lou Wener's: from six a.m. to midnight, 365 days a year. This is a village of just 150 households, where flowers and wood have brought relative wealth: a 60-inch TV is visible through an open door in one house in the small market square. 'There used to be three stores in this village, but the other two have closed,' explains forty-seven-year-old shop owner Han Guo Min, who lives upstairs with his wife, mother and twenty-one-year-old son, who is also their delivery driver. After twenty years here, he joined Ule on 20 May 2015. 'It's increased the wealth of the village and given us better-quality SKUs,' Han says. 'Ule has meant a 25 per cent growth in revenue, with utilities payments and China Post insurance sales bringing more people into the store. The inventory is automated. Before, I had to memorise prices: if I wasn't in the store, we couldn't sell something.'

On an Android phone, Yeung scans the store's daily stats. It's four p.m. and Han has taken twenty-two orders worth RMB 1,500, resulting in an RMB 152 profit. His seven online orders, including rice wine and a pillow, amount to RMB 436. Store data is updated every five minutes.

That level of near-real-time data from stores across China opens doors that Western consumer-insight businesses such as Nielsen and dunnhumby can only dream of. By recording millions of daily purchases and linking them to individual customers via loyalty cards or phone payments, Ule is building an unprecedented bird's-eye view of what Chinese consumers are buying right now.

Let's say you're a beer firm wanting to optimize distribution when demand rises on an unusually hot April day. Ule knows where to send your trucks. Or imagine you're Chanel and you want to know which forty-four- to forty-eight-year-old women, in vil-lages two to three hours' commute from the nearest city, have today bought a Dior product. Ule's data can potentially identify them, perhaps allowing you to send a 20 per cent Chanel discount voucher to their phone.

And that's a holy grail that makes Tesco's Clubcard look quaintly Victorian.

'What would you do if you had all the retail data in the world?' Kerry Liu, founder of a Toronto analytics company called Rubikloud, is sitting across a Hangzhou conference table from me explaining how he's turning all this village-store data into power. 'First, there's retail optimization – you can change how large mass retailers connect with customers and influence them. Retailers need to build relationships with customers in the same way Netflix, Amazon Prime or Facebook treat their customer base, constantly tuning their parameters. Second, you can influence brand and product development – we did a pilot for a big pharmacy chain – and you can influence consumer spending, say, to encourage healthier foods. And third, you can shape new product launches.' He cites a razor manufacturer that wanted to launch a new product without cannibalizing existing sales. Rubikloud mined the retailer's database to draw up a list of what it considered the 25,000 most likely customers for the new razor. It then tested various pricing strategies using artificial intelligence that processed price data for male-grooming products scraped from other websites. The result, Liu says, was a 42 per cent rise in product spend.

Customer data, in the venture-capital-backed world of fast-growth tech businesses like the thirty-three-year-old Liu's, is invariably assumed to be an unquestioned good. I rarely hear entrepreneurs pause to consider the wider ethical questions about such vast personal-data accumulation. After all, they have financial targets to reach.

Rubikloud launched in April 2013 with a mission 'to index and predict the world's retail behaviour while turning data into revenue'. When Liu and I meet, its machine-learning PhDs and data scientists have processed $250 billion (£195 billion) in transactional data, which adds up to 500TB. Its first product, largely for the North American market, took point-of-sale data, inventory data, promotional data, customer loyalty data and more to help retailers predict the behaviour of individual customers at scale. And then Liu met Solina Chau of Horizons Ventures, the Hong Kong-based fund which manages the tech investments of Li Ka-shing, one of Asia's wealthiest men.

Horizons Ventures quickly led a seed investment round. But Chau had bigger plans for Rubikloud. Li's internet and media company, TOM Group, had embarked on a huge joint venture in 2010 with state-owned China Post to digitize commerce. The result was Ule, which roughly translates as 'happy post'. Ule and TOM Group both made an investment in Rubikloud. They also both invested in a Hong Kong-based finance-tech startup called WeLab, which uses mobile and offline analytics to determine whether a shopkeeper or a customer is a good credit risk for Ule to offer a loan. According to WeLab co-founder Simon Loong, a former banker, 64 per cent of rural Chinese have no access to banks, and store owners lack the credit history to borrow at an affordable rate. So his business evaluates them with data from credit bureaux and social apps, but also from their mobile devices, which they must use to apply for a loan.

'We've processed 5 million members, and haven't lost a case in fraud,' Loong explains when we meet in Hangzhou. Shop owners can take unsecured cash loans at 9 per cent APR and use them to buy stock from Ule; the postal bank provides the cash. And shop customers give WeLab's WeLend business access to a vast amount of mobile data for a loan decision within five minutes.

'We look for personality traits, level of responsibility, by collecting 800 data points,' Loong continues. 'The model of phone, your apps, how you interact with others, the structure of your social networks, how you fill in your address on the application form. Whether you use capital letters correlates with bankruptcy – we think that's education level. Even what time you apply for the loan affects credit performance: one a.m. to six a.m. applicants are more likely to be bad customers compared with eight a.m. to one p.m.'

Borrowers also give away their reliability simply by how they use their phones to communicate. 'We work with telcos to measure inbound call frequency, the longest gap and variability between calls, as very talkative customers are not good borrowers,' Loong explains. 'We even look at messaging, and connections between the phone numbers of poor credit users, as they influence each other.' Prospective customers are also asked to take a selfie, which is matched using face recognition to the police ID system.

And so a retail-data and logistics business is also building a data-led money-lending division to oil the wheels of commerce.

'What the hell is a Toronto-based data company doing in Hangzhou?' Rubikloud's Liu reflects. 'You can't ignore the world's largest consumer market. A cookie company we talked to missed their forecast by $50 million in ten major cities, because they underestimated local demand for other brands, got the pricing wrong and mis-targeted promotions. Today they need a Ule – competition is too high otherwise. It's very difficult to predict demand: one company lost $100 million this year because it had no visibility of demand. They need a more real-time system.' That comes down to knowing who the customers are, what they are buying, and where. 'Ultimately we want to sell real-time placement in the physical store,' Liu tells me. 'Nielsen, dunnhumby – they're up for disruption.'

'This is innovation from China. It's China IP. Internet companies are copying us.' Chen Qing, the fifty-two-year-old founding member and chairman of Ule, as well as China Post's general manager in the province, hits the table for emphasis as he explains how he's modernizing a 200-year-old enterprise that stretches from a postal savings bank into insurance. We're in China Post's Moganshan Road building in Hangzhou, being served a lunch that I notice warily includes snake soup (in fact, it tastes like bony white fish).

'Ule is a major weapon, a catalyst, for China Post renewal,' Chen continues. 'To change a culture, you need to use innovative tech and a market-driven mindset. Our parcel business has grown 450 per cent in this province because of Ule. Now I demand at least 100 per cent growth every year. I've been with China Post for twenty years. I've never failed. I won't fail this one.'

Zhejiang province was chosen as the test bed for Ule, Chen explains, because it's an established e-commerce hub: Alibaba is based in Hangzhou, as are more than a third of China's e-commerce sites, according to the *Hangzhou Daily*. And, Chen says, it's ready to roll out nationally – with central and regional government backing: 'The government is endorsing Ule, to back its rural policy, for instance, subsidizing the capital expenditure of each store to upgrade computers and encouraging farmers to list produce on Ule.

'Seventy per cent of the population is rural and there are lots of gaps: how do rural people get access to quality manufactured goods? How do farmers sell back to cities efficiently? Then there's information asymmetry. If you harvest when everyone else is, your price can collapse. China Post is the only entity in China that has complete coverage down to the last mile. So we want to use tech to solve those problems.'

Plus, of course, it's very good for business to reinvent China Post as the backbone of a national retail-commerce transport network built on its own data platform. The main China Post business gets a significant uplift, with boosts to the financial and logistics operations. Chen estimates that transactions on Ule will soon exceed RMB 200 billion. The farmers get more business, which creates more logistics volume for Ule and more cash on deposit for the postal bank. In 2015, the postal bank had RMB 150 billion in cash deposits. In 2016, it was 200 billion. Ule, Chen tells me, contributed half of that growth.

Today he is busy connecting half a million rural stores. 'After that, the next 500,000 will be urban,' he says. 'Imagine anyone in a city being able to order organic greens from farmers via Ule. We have cold storage – so we'll deliver to the neighbourhood shop in the city. And think of the benefit to the farmer.' In the city today, Chen explains, ginger is selling for RMB 6 per half a kilo, of which the farmer gets RMB 1.5. 'We will pay the farmer RMB 3 and then sell it on Ule for RMB 4.5. China Post provides the lending capital, Ule provides sales, and we all share the profit.'

There is the small matter of persuading postal workers to upgrade from bicycle to minivan. And also ensuring that the workers, rather than their employer, buy the vans. 'We're encouraging postmen to borrow money from the postal bank to buy their vans, as they can make extra income,' Chen tells me, enthusiastically. 'China Post outsources delivery to them, even as employees, and subsidizes their gas. But staff own the car. He'll take good care of his own car! They get extra income for delivering wholesale goods. No other postal service is doing this!' He grins. 'Changing people is disruptive. You need to change their brain.'

And if workers refuse to buy their own van?

'All staff are Communist Party members,' he replies solemnly. 'We have no unions here. They know what is in the best interests of China.' Then he smiles. 'Or – I can move them to another job.'

Ken Yeung, brother of Samson, later explains to me how Ule's particular model will solve China's 'rural problem' before scaling fast to the cities. 'It's how communism started. The revolution began with the farmers.' Yeung is the Hong Kong-based CEO of the TOM Group and an enthusiast of his time at Singularity University. He is walking past stacked boxes of Wahaha water, Victory Vitamin Water, El Sotillo wine, Funkid Grapefruit Juice, Red Tea and a thousand other SKUs of snacks, sauces and toiletries in a 550-square-metre former letter-sorting warehouse in Yuhang county that's about to be replaced by one five times the size. This is one of 400 China Post warehouses across China that work with Ule to stock village stores directly. Local specialities include lotus fruit, sausage and duck. Food authenticity is guaranteed by the China Post brand.

The TOM Group, which owns 42 per cent of Ule, 'is here to empower China Post', which owns 43.7 per cent. 'We put in people with a tech background and they run ground operations,' Yeung says. 'We were running eBay in China. We understand e-commerce. We're digitizing retail, just as Uber digitizes taxi drivers. We get feedback every day from hundreds of thousands of retailers. Postmen visit fifteen villages daily, so we can roll out fast, installing point-of-sale devices, training the store owners. They're like coaches, telling you how to use a new [software] release.'

The results are demonstrable. Gross merchandise value is rising threefold a year; politicians are coming to pay their respects. Shortly before my visit, Wang Yang, one of China's vice-premiers, visited JiuDu township in Sichuan with Lu Jiajin, Postal Savings Bank president.

'Alibaba is also trying to connect the last mile,' Yeung says. 'They thought they'd have 200,000 outlets after two years. They have just 17,000 after eighteen months. But Alibaba is a transaction company. Ule is a *data* company.'

A few steps from Zürich Oerlikon railway station in northern Switzerland, Guido Jouret is explaining how his 140,000-person industrial giant, which has been manufacturing heavy-steel devices since 1891, is now turning to data to build tomorrow's business models.

You've probably seen ABB's initials in photographs of its bright-orange factory robots, but robots are merely the friendly six-axis vanguard of ABB Group's ubiquitous marks on the modern urban landscape. If you're in the market for electrical transformers, circuit-breakers, solar-power inverters, or all sorts of other analogue building blocks of the world's engineering infrastructure, there's a very good chance that ABB will be your chosen supplier.

Yet a company that pioneered transformer technology in the 1890s, and began making circuit-breakers to protect generators in 1954, is being forced to re-examine its place in the value chain. And that's why Jouret, an internationally educated computer-science

PhD living between Silicon Valley and Switzerland, is busy helping ABB understand how it can add internet-era technologies to its heavy-machine product range in ways that deliver new revenue streams with a digital edge.

Jouret, comfortably mid-Atlantic in a navy-blue, open-collared cotton shirt, short greying beard and design-studio glasses, is ABB's chief digital officer. Having run Cisco's internet-of-things business unit, and taken Nokia into digital health, he knows all about using internet-linked sensors to connect, monitor, gather feedback and suggest actions. And that, for an ageing industrial giant, offers the promise not simply of selling more machines but of selling its clients intelligence gathered by sensors collecting data about their machines.

'If you operate a factory, what did the internet do for you? Not much,' Jouret tells me as we sit in the company's Oerlikon head-quarters. 'It didn't transform the world of manufacturing, gas, mining, logistics. But fast forward to today's cheap ubiquitous computing, and computing and connectivity are no longer a bar-rier. The volume of data from these industrial applications will potentially dwarf anything we've seen so far.'

By adding sensors to heavy machinery used by clients in the energy, industrial, transportation and infrastructure sectors, ABB has discovered that it can charge those clients for remote monitor-ing and optimizing uptime, reliability and productivity. So it's digitally enabling power transformers; networking robots and motors; and monitoring vibration and power consumption of off-shore platforms. Already it's connecting 70 million devices through a business unit called ABB Ability, which takes sensor data, analy-ses it with machine learning, and suggests a physical action for clients such as Shell Oil, BASF and BMW. And that's just the start.

'Consider the new channels of value this creates,' Jouret says. Monitoring a ship's diesel engine, for instance, provides data that an insurance company might want to buy. Putting fibre-optic lines into oil-well machinery helps operators predict when those wells will run dry. Connecting robots to its servers lets ABB sell clients the opportunity to download software 'upgrades' that offer new functionality. There are even benefits for ABB's own product designers: continuous feedback loops let them know which product features customers are using so they can better plan future revisions.

'We've gone from monitoring to optimization to continuous feedback about the product to convergence, and then finally to business-model innovation,' Jouret says. 'If I'm connected to this device I sold you, I can charge you for a robot based on how much the arm moves and how much it lifts. And you've just converted your capex [capital expenditure] into opex [operating expenditure], which makes it easier for companies looking to minimize capex to order another robot.'

Another option is to charge clients based on outcome. In the cement sector, where energy consumption is a substantial part of the costs, ABB is now charging for projects based on the energy or efficiency savings delivered by its monitoring systems. Working with a cement producer in India, for instance, ABB claims that its monitoring processes boosted productivity by 5 per cent, cut operating costs by more than 3 per cent, and delivered a 15 per cent boost in cement quality. Suddenly ABB isn't simply selling machines, which a customer will buy just once; instead it's now selling a regular service, which a customer will pay for repeatedly. Let's call it a new cement-production-as-a-service business.

Rami-Johan Jokela, ABB's head of digitalization, walks me to a nearby factory to show how remote monitoring is being built into its hardware. The Toro building is where ABB manufactures its generator circuit-breakers. These are large fuses, he explains, resembling doorless washing machines, which sit between generators inside power plants and step-up transformers to block short-circuits in milliseconds. ABB has 70 per cent of the global market. But now they are being built with embedded data-gathering sensors: control systems collect data on real-time metrics such as voltage, current, gas pressure and temperature, while also measuring the machine's electrical lifetime, mechanical lifetime and time-based lifetime. Customers can decide whether to give ABB access to the data to predict future maintenance needs and optimize efficiency.

Jokela, a twenty-two-year ABB veteran, explains that digitizing its hardware is a $20 billion opportunity for the company. 'In the past, customers liked to do everything by themselves, but now they see collaboration as important,' he says as we walk through a strangely peaceful 2,200-square-metre factory floor. 'So this becomes a data-monitoring business, with our domain experts monitoring these systems 24/7.' The company applies machine learning and data analytics to the information flow coming from the connected machines; customers receive visualizations showing how their systems are working, so they can plan maintenance that will extend their equipment's lifespan. ABB is also launching its own app store for ABB Ability, Jokela tells me – a 'marketplace' that lets customers buy extra functionality for their machines as they need it.

Still, recalibrating an industrial giant is hard. Jokela is on the road for 120 days a year, learning what customers want and keeping up with technology developments. With Guido Jouret, he's also working to change ABB's internal company culture. Partly, he says, they're achieving this by showcasing customer success stories; partly it's by building an ecosystem with outside partners, such as TaKaDu, an Israeli startup that uses data analytics and artificial intelligence to monitor leaky water pipes.

Jouret sees his own role as 'internal change agent', finding a balance between being engaged with and visible in today's core business while incubating, isolating and nurturing the data-centric new opportunity. He's built a 200-person team across the company who are educating, informing, prodding and goading the business units to change how they work – and how they think. It's not on the scale of China Post, which is turning a million postal workers into a new form of data-collection machine. Still, Jouret's modest team is meeting internal friction and resistance all the time. He understands the reasons. People aren't always comfortable with change.

'Because technology progress is more acute, more rapid and broader than anything we've ever seen,' he says. 'And now it's coming for the industrial sector.'

Action Points

Creative uses of data analytics are enabling all sorts of new commercial opportunities. A business that can access a reliable data stream and process it to enable better decision-making can generate remarkable new value. Take data from satellites, access to which is falling in price as venture-funded startups build constellations of nano-satellites scanning the Earth in real time. Orbital Insight, a California startup that's received $80 million in funding, uses satellite monitoring to count cars outside retail malls, among other things; it sells the data to investors as an advance indicator of rising or falling customer demand. An Israeli company, Windward, in which I've invested, uses satellites to track 200,000 ships on the oceans and spots unusual behavioural patterns; its clients include intelligence agencies and insurers.

But how does a traditionally analogue business effectively launch new data-led business lines? Once you've identified the data sources, here are some tips from executives who have been there:

1. Digitizing a non-digital business often requires a new structure, new leadership or a combination of both. At ABB, new business lines are incubated under the protection of separate executive teams. Guido Jouret explains that, in the early days, new

business lines need internal protection, away from the core company, in order to thrive. But once these new teams have shown some success, they are brought back into the core company and their roles are promoted evangelically. Think about the process as a series of phases to effect change, Jouret says – and be prepared for a high failure rate.

2. Don't make transformation one person's responsibility. ABB's approach has been to scatter 200 advocates for digitization throughout the company's business units – ideally people already trusted inside the organization.

3. Internal communications must be firm and consistent. 'Every communication coming out of HQ touches on our digital project,' Otto Preiss, Jouret's number two, explains. 'People see that it's here to stay.'

4. Offer budgetary incentives. Teams can resist business-model changes that hit short-term revenue targets. ABB makes available central funds to pay for new requirements such as cloud hosting; it also half-funds internal experiments from the centre.

5. Don't neglect the value of soft skills in nurturing change. Build informal networks, identify and promote champions of change, and focus on team-building to identify digital champions.

6. Fight any signs of a 'not invented here' culture. To succeed in digitizing a business, you will need to work with outside partners. Your future success lies in being part of a wider ecosystem.

II.

ENGINEER SERENDIPITY

What Burning Man gives Silicon Valley

Can a building's design help cure cancer? It's a question that obsessed architect David King for the seven years he was working on the Francis Crick Institute, a vast biomedical research centre by St Pancras Station in central London. The 'Crick', named after Sir Francis Crick, the British scientist who helped discover DNA's double-helix structure, is the largest and most ambitious bio-medical laboratory in Europe, an 83,000-square-metre home to biochemists, neuroscientists, immunologists, computational bio-logists and other specialists collectively targeting cancer, heart disease and genomic illness by breaking down metaphorical and physical walls between their scientific disciplines. Because if we're to uncover the biology underlying human health, the Crick's found-ers reasoned, and find new ways to diagnose, treat and prevent awful diseases, then researchers will have to collaborate in unpre-cedented ways. And so King, a motorbike-riding, complexity-loving architect whose previous projects included St Bartholomew's Hospital, the Royal London Hospital and Barclays' global head-quarters in Canary Wharf, set about creating a space that would actively promote conversations across disciplines.

You don't see many walls inside the brightly lit twelve-storey building, just a short walk from the British Library, Google's new European headquarters and fifty-seven other clinical and research organizations. King, a 'take-toys-apart-to-put-them-back-together' child whose fascination with functionality led him to a career among giant construction projects, leads me through a cavernous glass atrium, past interlinked corridors, open lab rooms, a 500-seat restaurant, and plenty of colourful, informal 'collaboration spaces' intended to promote serendipitous encounters. 'Collaboration is about talking to people who do things you don't do – say, a biologist having a conversation with a mathematician,' he explains as we stop at one such breakout space, by a door that doubles as a white-board. 'It's about learning how things happen in other fields. The whole building is designed to encourage people to interact.'

The Crick was a hybrid project from the start. Funded by the UK government's Medical Research Council, the charity Cancer Research UK, Wellcome Foundation and three London universi-ties, it was designed around the concept of 'discovery without boundaries'. There are no departments, unlike traditional research centres, and researchers have no tenure but are free to follow their instincts. There are no physical barriers between the 120 lab groups of around ten scientists, and teams from unrelated fields are located close to each other to encourage interdisciplinary discussions. Team leaders' offices are designed to be too small to hold large, closed meetings.

King, an admirer of Filippo Brunelleschi and Christopher Wren (for being both scholarly and practical), points out two wide atria that separate the building's four main sections. Lab blocks are grouped around a transverse atrium, and there are break areas and meeting spaces where the atria meet. A third of the floor area is missing on each level to create a double-height visual link to the floor above, and a continuous open staircase in the middle con-nects the eight above-ground storeys. This open, visually connected design makes it easy to run into colleagues, and to know what other teams are up to. Clear sightlines ensure that each of the build-ing's 'neighbourhoods' can be seen from all the other floors. 'A lot relies on openness and visual permeability,' King tells me, 'and on a notion of a central collaboration space that we thought of as a vil-lage green.' The stairs are deliberately easier to reach than the lifts, and wide enough to encourage lingering when scientists meet. The external floor-to-roof glass walls also create a feeling of transparency, as opposed to the closed, defensive nature of typical research labs. 'Here is science on display,' King states. 'And people inside the building don't feel cut off. They get daylight. It feels livelier.'

There's a persuasive rationale behind such an open, interconnected, collaboration-inducing building design. Siloed thinking won't solve cancer. From the start, the £650 million project's planning teams understood that the accelerating pace of genomic discovery, combined with emerging disciplines such as bioinformatics, synthetic biology, immunology, proteomics and machine learning, offered exciting opportunities to devise novel diagnostic and treatment approaches that tore open conventional research specialisms. A microfabrication engineer working with an epithelial stem-cell researcher and a data scientist would collectively confront problems in fresh ways; a mechanobiologist and a theoretical physicist might start a conversation that prompts an acclaimed peer-reviewed paper. Sir Paul Nurse, the Nobel Prize-winning geneticist who runs the Crick, says his mission is to 'encourage a sort of gentle anarchy' that ignores traditional science's fixed boundaries. Innovation, as Sir Paul sees it, happens when brilliant, divergent specialists' ideas collide.

It's a mindset with applications far beyond science. Workspace architecture that enables constructive collisions among divergent experts can deliver genuine innovation in fields from finance to manufacturing. The telecommunications industry offers perhaps the most persuasive case study. America's former monopoly telephone company, AT&T, through its Bell Labs research unit, gave us the transistor, the silicon solar cell, the laser, early communications satellites and the first cellular phone systems. Jon Gertner, who spent five years studying Bell Labs' innovation processes for his book *The Idea Factory*, credits the culture of creativity to Mervin Kelly, who between 1925 and 1959 rose from researcher to chairman of the board. Kelly firmly believed that workers' physical proximity was key, and put experts in theory, research and manufacturing on the same teams, under the same roof – in part to ensure clashes. He helped design a building in Murray Hill, New Jersey, that would encourage interaction through architectural devices such as enormously long hallways. 'Travelling the hall's length without encountering a number of acquaintances, problems, diversions and ideas was almost impossible,' Gertner writes. 'A physicist on his way to lunch in the cafeteria was like a magnet rolling past iron filings.'

Francis Crick himself understood the value of spontaneous conversations developed over an unhurried communal lunch. On 28 February 1953 he famously dashed into the Eagle pub in Cambridge, where colleagues would regularly drop by for his beer-and-sandwiches working lunches, and declared, 'We have found the secret of life!' – the double-helix identified with James Watson, Maurice Wilkins and Rosalind Franklin. Crick, Sir Paul Nurse explains, 'was an advocate of discussing scientific ideas over food and drink. He believed the best collaborative ideas arose during informal moments.'

That's why a ground-floor cafeteria to hold 500 people was central to the Crick Institute's design, complete with long tables to encourage researchers to sit together. But the local planning authority at Camden Council initially refused consent, insisting that staff instead patronize neighbourhood restaurants. Nurse deftly pointed out that the Eagle's communal lunch table had accelerated the discovery of the double-helix; councillors surely wouldn't want to delay any progress towards halting cancer? The council planners gave him his cafeteria.

The Crick opened in August 2016. Even the construction process had been multidisciplinary: David King's firm, HOK (Hellmuth, Obata + Kassabaum), had to bring in experts in fields such as acoustics (Cole Jarman), lighting (Pokorny Lichtarchitektur), shielding (Vitatech Electromagnetics), biological labs (Boswell Mitchell & Johnston), building maintenance (REEF Associates), cladding (Emmer Pfenninger) and architectural visualization (Glowfrog); it also worked with PLP Architecture and Arup (see chapter 2). Now that the 1,250 scientists and 250 support staff are in place, I ask King whether they are behaving as he expected. He's honest about the experiment not going entirely smoothly. 'When I came down here at the end of January 2017, I was surprised to find very few people in the collaboration spaces,' he says. 'But by the end of March, they were the most popular spaces in the building. It was quite a task to encourage people to think beyond how they'd done things in the past, to how they *could* do things.' Still, he's confident in his conclusion that closed doors are the enemy of collaboration: 'If you're going to persuade people to talk to each other, don't give them too many meeting rooms.'

The science is on King's side. As the Crick began to take shape, an emerging field of peer-reviewed research suggested that innovation, as measured in scientific discovery, is greatest when institutional buildings encourage unplanned encounters – especially among individuals working in unrelated disciplines.

This notion took root in the 1970s, when Thomas J. Allen, a professor at Massachusetts Institute of Technology (MIT) specializing in organizational psychology, described what became known as the 'Allen curve' – an exponential relationship between how often engineers communicated with each other and how far apart they sat. Engineers who sat two metres apart were four times more likely to talk regularly than those sitting 20 metres apart – a correlation that Allen later found holds true even in the age of text-messaging and voicemail. It may not sound surprising – why wouldn't you talk more with nearby colleagues? – but it's where that proximity leads that is interesting. Colleagues who work near each other not only produce more scientific papers than other joint authors, but higher-quality papers that are cited more often by subsequent researchers.

In 2010, Kyungjoon Lee, John Brownstein, Richard Mills and Isaac Kohane published a study in the journal *PLOS ONE* which analysed life-sciences research across three Harvard University campuses. Using the PubMed search engine, they examined 35,000 articles with at least one Harvard author across 2,000 journals (a total of 200,000 authors) published between 1999 and 2003. They then painstakingly mapped each author's location to the particular office they occupied in the specific year of publication, and measured the physical distance between co-authors. Their conclusion: the impact of a paper, based on the number of times it was subsequently cited, was positively correlated with how closely its authors sat. It's as if the benefits of global connectivity stood for nothing: face-to-face encounters tended to produce more significant research papers.

We still mythologize the 'Eureka!' moments of heroic individuals' breakthroughs, but in fact team collaboration has been on the rise since at least the 1950s. In science, in particular, it's increasingly producing the most influential work. Benjamin Jones, Stefan Wuchty and Brian Uzzi of Northwestern University, Illinois, analysed 19.9 million scientific papers published over five decades, and 2.1 million patents, to demonstrate that teams typically produce more highly cited research than individuals, an advantage that is increasing over time. For example, a team-authored paper in science and engineering was 6.3 times more likely than a solo-authored paper to receive at least 1,000 citations, they wrote in a 2007 *Science* paper. As scientific knowledge has proliferated, scholars seem to have been drawn towards ever-greater specialization, necessitating larger and more diverse teams to push forward the frontiers of discovery.

Does the cultural diversity of collaborators also make a difference? Richard Freeman and Wei Huang of Harvard University came up with an ingenious way to find out. They examined the ethnic identity of US-based authors in more than 2.5 million scientific papers from 1985 to 2008, a time when the frequency of English and European names among authors fell relative to the frequency of names from China and other developing countries. They found that authors of similar ethnicity were more likely to co-publish than overall numbers predicted; and yet ethnically similar writing teams tended to publish in lower-impact journals and with fewer citations. By contrast, greater ethnic diversity in a research team 'contributes to the quality of the scientific papers that the team produces'.

In other words, it's not the lone-genius Einsteins today who tend to publish the science that matters. It's the diverse, specialist teams whose members sit a serendipitous conversation away from one another.

Nicholas Negroponte, founder of MIT's cross-disciplinary Media Lab, and the original 1992 investor in a new magazine called *WIRED*, wrote a perceptive column in that publication in November 1995 that still holds true. 'Where do new ideas come from?' he asked. 'The answer is simple: differences. While there are many theories of creativity, the only tenet they all share is that creativity comes from unlikely juxtapositions. The best way to maximize differences is to mix ages, cultures, and disciplines.' That recipe had kept the Media Lab constantly creative: a faculty of 'artists, engineers and scientists who collaborate instead of compete', its inventions have included electronic ink as used in Kindle screens, LEGO Mindstorms, early wearable computers, and the *Guitar Hero* video game. And on my regular visits to some of the world's greatest research universities, it's the one I get most excited about.

Joi Ito, the lab's current director, presides over what he calls 'permissionless innovation'. 'As long as it's not illegal, we're happy,' he says. 'Although I don't run the lab. My role is somewhere between custodian and bouncer.' A successful entrepreneur and investor, who has served on boards including Sony and the *New York Times* but never achieved an undergraduate degree, Ito says that his most relevant qualification for running the lab may be an early career as a nightclub DJ. 'It comes down to culture,' he explains. 'If as a DJ you change the music based on seeing what people are wearing, you can get people on the dancefloor.' At the Media Lab, this means hiring and setting free people with diverse skills and backgrounds – even if they have unconventional qualifications. A 'director's fellows' programme Ito established to attract talent with 'less-than-traditional backgrounds' has welcomed a NASA astronaut, a former prisoner and a cyber-illusionist.

On a recent visit to the lab, a 15,000-square-metre playground on the corner of Ames and Amherst Streets in Cambridge, outside Boston, I spent time talking to Kevin Esvelt, who's working on editing the genes of malarial mosquitoes to save human lives; Canan Dagdeviren, who's making sensing devices to wear inside the body; Caleb Harper, who's rethinking agriculture by building 'food computers'; and Fadel Adib, who beams radio waves through walls to measure who is present, their body posture and heartbeat, even their emotional state. This proximity of brilliant and diverse specialists is what gives the Media Lab its genius. The risk is that they stay within their individual project groups and stop running into each other.

Steve Jobs understood this. In December 2000 he moved Pixar Animation Studios into a new 20,000-square-metre building in Emeryville, California, where an abandoned Del Monte canning factory had previously stood. It was initially planned as three buildings – one for the animators, another for the technical team, a third for the management – but Jobs overruled that and insisted on a single vast space with a large two-storey atrium at its core. 'We wanted to find a way to force people to come together, to create a lot of arbitrary collisions of people,' Jobs told the *New York Times*.

But how would he force all 550 employees to pass through the space and linger, prompting unexpected interactions between artists and software engineers? First, he decided to put the mailboxes there; then the meeting rooms and a cafeteria. Most compellingly, he planned for the only set of toilets to be located in the atrium (something that protests later forced him to compromise on). 'The atrium initially might seem like a waste of space,' Brad Bird, director of Pixar movies *The Incredibles* and *Ratatouille*, later said. 'But

Steve realized that when people run into each other, when they make eye contact, things happen.' And it worked. 'I've never seen a building that promoted collaboration and creativity as well as this one,' John Lasseter, Pixar's former chief creative officer, concluded. It's hard to quantify innovation's impact precisely, but twenty years after Jobs bought Pixar for $5 million, it was sold to Disney in 2006 for $7.4 billion.

Greg Brandeau was VP of technology at Pixar working closely with Jobs, who had previously hired him at his computer company NeXT. Since then he's spent ten years studying what it takes to transform organizations to create new value. True innovation leaders, Brandeau tells me when we meet at a Las Vegas software convention, see their role not as the visionaries but as the creators of an environment in which others can thrive. They look beyond short-term stock-market pressures to focus not on what the business should be doing, but what it potentially *could* be doing – a turn-of-the-century computer company, say, creating a new kind of MP3 player. But how do these ideas emerge?

From his research, which he wrote about in the book *Collective Genius: The Art and Practice of Leading Innovation*, Brandeau discovered some patterns. First, an effective innovation culture will foster 'creative abrasion' – an internal expectation of no-holds-barred discussions to generate new ideas. Second, there will be 'creative agility' – protocols to test and refine ideas through quick pursuit, reflection and adjustment. Echoing the experience of Google's 'moonshot factory' X (see chapter 5), Brandeau concludes: 'You can't fall in love with your ideas so much that you won't drop them for something else.' And third, there needs to be 'creative resolution' – the ability to take integrative decisions. 'The best companies we looked at somehow take idea A and idea B and come up with a whole new idea, C,' he says.

Plus, a little luck can help. Brandeau was in charge of computer operations when Pixar was making *Toy Story 2* in 1998. The open, collaborative nature of Pixar meant that staff generally had widespread access to the computer network. Unfortunately some-one in the company (who has not been publicly named) entered a rogue programming command, '/bin/rm -r -f *', on the computer drive that stored all the animation files. This command told the system to delete every file. Worse, it transpired that the backup tapes were not working properly. Most of the film had been deleted. 'We'd lost eighteen months of work,' Brandeau recalls.

Amid the panic that overtook the Emeryville HQ, Galyn Susman, the movie's supervising technical director, calmly men-tioned that she had a Silicon Graphics workstation back at her house. Susman had given birth to her son Eli a few weeks before and had taken a copy of the movie home to work on while on maternity leave; periodic updates, she explained, had been auto-matically downloaded through her ISDN telephone line. All eyes locked on Susman. A Volvo was sent to retrieve the computer, wrapped in blankets, that contained the only remaining copy of the almost-up-to-date animation. That healthy delivery saved the movie. 'I wrote my resignation letter, and took it in to Steve and Ed [Catmull],' Brandeau says. 'They'd asked people in the company if I'd screwed up through incompetence, or whether it would have happened anyway.' They then told him they wouldn't accept his resignation – 'but don't ever lose data again'.

The most persistent demonstration of the power of serendipitous encounters is an annual festival called Burning Man, which was, as so often happens in life, triggered by a love affair that went sour. Larry Harvey had taken his then girlfriend and her fourteen-year-old son to Baker Beach, in San Francisco, to celebrate the summer solstice. It was a supremely romantic moment: a boom box playing music around a fire, a couple of mannequins piled on to a couch and thrown sacrificially on the flames, a burning stick with which to write love declarations in the sand. Two years on, the relation-ship having collapsed, the solstice anniversary was a painful moment for Harvey. 'I had a heartbreak, I had a mid-life crisis, lasted unconscionably two years,' he said in a speech in Nevada fourteen years later. 'So I called up a friend and I said: "Let's . . . let's burn a man, Jerry."' And with his friend Jerry James, Harvey built a 2.4-metre-tall statue of a man out of scrap lumber, drove it to the beach with a group of friends, doused it in petrol, and burned it sacrificially as a crowd of around thirty-five gathered.

It was 22 June 1986, and Harvey, an artist, philosopher and landscape gardener, had launched what would become an annual celebration of personal experimentation and creative expression. Today, Burning Man is a week-long gathering in the Nevada desert where 70,000 people come together in late August to construct a temporary city of mutant vehicles, art installations, experimental living, intense participation and radical self-expression. Facebook's Mark Zuckerberg and Amazon's Jeff Bezos have attended; so have the founders of Tesla, Uber, Airbnb and Dropbox. After Google founders and regular 'Burners' Larry Page and Sergey Brin had spent a year looking for a CEO, they were finally swayed towards a then forty-six-year-old Berkeley PhD and former Sun Microsystems executive called Eric Schmidt. 'Eric was . . . the only one who went to Burning Man,' Brin told blogger Doc Searls. 'Which we thought was an important criterion.'

Black Rock City, the name of the temporary desert settlement, occupies a dusty 17-square-kilometre stretch of dry lava beds and alkali flats about 160km north of Reno. It's inhospitable, off-grid territory, a long and hot drive from the nearest town, so participants need to be self-reliant and bring all the food, water and supplies they will need. Burning Man is a non-cash economy where gifting is encouraged but the only items for sale are coffee and ice. Commercial activity is so frowned upon that even logos on vehicles are expected to be covered up.

The city is arranged in a clock-like pattern, with radial streets named after their position from two o'clock to ten o'clock, bisected by annular streets ranged alphabetically (Algorithm, Bender, Cylon, up to Leon). You might find your camp at four o'clock and

Leon; and it might be a theme camp, with six to 400 people, or a specialist camp for participants who support the art, the mutant cars, or Burning Man itself. There are rules for registering a theme camp, which give a flavour of Burning Man culture: they must be 'visually stimulating', 'neighbourly' and 'interactive', with events or activities open to the entire community. At the very centre of the circle is the Man, a huge wooden sculpture that is ritually burned on the Saturday night, a day before the burning of an ornate temple, packed with intensely emotional mementoes of Burners' losses, from parents to pets.

In 2004, Harvey defined the Ten Principles of Burning Man. They include Radical Inclusion ('Anyone may be a part of Burning Man'), Radical Self-Reliance ('Burning Man encourages the individual to discover, exercise and rely on his or her inner resources'), Radical Self-Expression (arising from 'the unique gifts of the individual') and Communal Effort ('Our community values creative cooperation and collaboration'). The anti-transactional culture was captured in the principles of Gifting and Decommodification; self-expression was moderated by the principles of Civic Responsibility and Leaving No Trace; and the authentic experience was defined by Participation and Immediacy. Beyond that, the lack of rules promotes an extraordinarily entrepreneurial spirit through which magic tends to happen.

That's why any organization in pursuit of creative thinking, serendipitous ideation or the open-minded exploration of new business models could gain a great deal from experiencing, or at least studying, what makes Black Rock City such a rich seam of invigorating ideas. It's hard to imagine the counter-intuitive collaborative economy of Airbnb, or the crowd-supported maker-led ideation of Kickstarter, without the influence of Burning Man. It forces you to think about group behaviour, about social interaction, about markets, in fresh ways.

As a self-regulating, judgement-free community of creative excess, Burning Man works remarkably effectively. I saw that while cycling through the playa (the sea-less 'beach') past uproariously decorated art cars, elaborate hand-made costumes alongside unembarrassed nakedness, spontaneous gifting, intensely choreographed LED-embedded fashion displays, unplanned collective dances, participatory art installations, constant welcoming music and unbridled human warmth – and barely a smartphone in sight. It's where Elon Musk and his cousin Lyndon Rive devised the idea for their solar-energy company SolarCity in 2004, and where volunteers turned a decommissioned Boeing 747 into a surreal giant 'art car' in 2018. It's at once a giant maker space, open-air art gallery, edge-pushing fashion show and social experiment, defined by a disregard of the status quo, rapid prototyping, and a spirit of optimistic self-reliance. And it performs a key role in the Bay Area's startup culture, reinforcing a mindset of experimentation, iterative problem-solving and counter-cultural norm-breaking. As Musk declared, Burning Man 'is Silicon Valley'.

In 2009, Fred Turner, a professor at Stanford University, published a paper in the journal *New Media & Society* on how 'Burning Man's bohemian ethos supports new forms of production emerging in Silicon Valley', particularly at Google. For one week each year, he argued, Black Rock City becomes a 'commons' for the otherwise super-capitalistic tech elite. Corporate tech engineers can come and celebrate 'the ideals of collaborative peer-production' in this cashless economy as they launch small technical projects for artistic purposes and build communities around those projects. And yet Burning Man actually serves to legitimate their day jobs creating wealth in high-tech firms, Turner suggests: the Utopian world they're building in the desert, in pursuit of self-realization and project engineering, in fact reassures them for the rest of the year that 'engineering can remake the world for the better'. 'I think Burning Man is to the contemporary tech world what the Protestant Church was to industrial manufacturers,' Turner later reflected. 'It models the kind of project-centered, team-oriented manufacturing practices that drive Silicon Valley and at the same time reconfigures them as a collective spiritual exercise.'

Examined up close, this evolving experiment is something of a flawed Utopia. The communitarian ethos is tarnished by private VIP camps whose members pay tens of thousands of dollars for private chefs, security guards and luxury bedroom suites. The dust storms and searing heat make for a tough physical environment. And the extreme behavioural tolerance may prove more challenging than conventional corporate leaders can accept: as I was spending three days at the organizers' Centre Camp while researching this book, the *Daily Mail* back home ran a censorious two-page exposé headlined 'Debauchery in the Desert' ('Wife-swapping. Orgy tents. Drugs on tap . . .'). The fact that I neglected to partake of any such distractions did not prevent one awkward moment: when I finally found a weak Wi-Fi signal to check in with home, I learned that an older relative, leafing through her *Daily Mail*, had raised concerns. 'Isn't that the technology conference,' she'd asked, 'that David's away attending?'

But as a way to study emergent leadership, idea generation, maker culture, team-building, product iteration, social collaboration, compelling storytelling, self-reliance, problem-solving and resilience in challenging the status quo, there's no training academy like Burning Man.

What lessons can be adopted by the corporate world? The rise of co-working spaces certainly signals an appetite among both corporates and insurgents for access to more diverse networks and influences. At Second Home, an east-London-based international co-working chain where I made an early personal investment, part of the sell is the hybrid culture that unites multinational businesses with early-stage tech companies. Volkswagen, Ernst & Young and Cushman & Wakefield are among the corporates to have taken space at Second Home's Spitalfields site, in a former carpet factory surrounded by curry houses; Cushman & Wakefield, the New York-listed commercial real-estate company, launched a property-focused startup accelerator there and met and invested in companies such as Unmortgage, which offers a part-ownership, part-rental way to live. Early-stage companies, too, benefit from connections made in the communal corridors and café: Bulb, a renewable-energy gas and electricity supplier, grew from two to a hundred employees in two years at Second Home, building a marketing campaign with co-tenants Blue State Digital, hiring talent through fellow occupants Congregation Partners, and developing its branding after Second Home made an introduction to design agency Ragged Edge.

Some corporates are launching their own co-working spaces in an attempt to feed in fresh ideas. Orange, the French telco, has a Paris space called Villa Bonne Nouvelle ('Good News House'), which it says promotes 'corpo-working', a cousin of co-working designed to teach how teams behave among startups. State Farm, Google, Sprint and SAP are among large companies operating co-working-like spaces open to staff and others in their communities. In Brooklyn, the MINI car company opened A/D/O, a combined co-working space, café, store and fabrication lab, aimed at learning from local designers. More ambitiously, in Grand Rapids, Michigan, non-competing businesses such as Steelcase (office furniture), Wolverine (footwear manufacturers), Mercy Health (healthcare) and Meijer (groceries) occupy a work area at 70 Ionia Avenue where they have dedicated space but also share conference rooms, kitchens and open workspaces. It's called GRid70 and is intended to prompt unexpected conversations that generate new business lines. According to a Steelcase executive, 'Our belief is that mixing creative teams from different industries will spawn "happy accidents" that inspire innovation, new products, and different ways of thinking.'

But the tech world's single most ambitious attempt to engineer serendipity at scale is currently taking place a ten-minute stretch-limo ride from the Las Vegas Strip. In the downtown area of Vegas, for years a neglected and low-income neighbourhood, a Burning Man regular named Tony Hsieh is, at the age of forty-five, spending

$350 million of his own money to turn this long-moribund part of town into 'a place of Inspiration, Entrepreneurial Energy, Creativity, Innovation, Upward Mobility, and Discovery, through the 3 C's of Collisions, Co-learning, and Connectedness'.

That's how the goal was first described on the website of the Downtown Project, Hsieh's bold Black Rock City-inspired experiment to revive the neighbourhood and attract entrepreneurial and creative talent through real-estate development ($200 million) and investment in tech startups, education and culture, and small businesses ($50 million each). Hsieh is the unconventional CEO of Zappos, an online shoe retailer he built up and sold to Amazon in 2009 for $1.2 billion. He's contradictory – a former party organizer who comes across as awkwardly shy – and occasionally divisive: a 2015 experiment in holacracy at Zappos, in which job titles and hierarchy were abandoned in favour of distributed decision-making, prompted resentment and mass staff departures.

I first visited Hsieh's experiment in May 2013, when it was just taking root. It was a boisterous day in the Zappos offices, a short drive away: staff were being encouraged to shave and dye their hair to raise funds for local charities, and when I visited Hsieh's workstation (decorated as if in a jungle, complete with hanging toy monkey) a spontaneous conga danced through the management floor. At his downtown apartment 5km away, in a building called the Ogden, locals were being encouraged to plant Post-its on to an 'idea wall' that asked 'What do you want in your downtown?' Scribbled answers included 'Dentist', 'Climbing gym', 'Dog park' and 'Unicorn store'.

As we sat on bar stools in the apartment, Hsieh explained his mission to me. 'We're investing in tech, manufacturing, fashion, arts, music, healthcare,' he said. 'If there's this whole ecosystem with people from all different backgrounds that in any other city would be in different parts of the city – if we're helping build a culture where there's a bias towards sharing and collaborating – then we'll see some pretty amazing innovations. That will put us on an exponential growth curve.'

It was a compelling vision. He talked about RoC – 'return on community' rather than on investment – and explained that he hoped to raise population density from 14.5 people per acre to 100. Through 'collisions, co-learning and connectedness', downtown Vegas would become 'the co-learning and co-working capital of the world'. Influenced by urban thinkers such as Edward Glaeser and Richard Florida, Hsieh was convinced that by encouraging social and entrepreneurial mixing – making a hundred Tesla cars available for hourly rental, programming a speaker series, creating hacker spaces and shared workspaces – he could build long-term economic growth.

He was funding businesses not simply on investment grounds, he explained, but because their owners cared about building a community. 'It's whether the entrepreneur running the bakery wants to do more than just bake bread, but to connect customers who have the same interests.' Though at times a little vague ('What matters is the connections between the people,' he said more than once), generally things sounded happily mission-driven.

For Hsieh, the Downtown Project is a natural development of his own interest in engineering creative social gatherings. When he was running parties, he would locate multiple bars to encourage guests to circulate and interact. At Zappos, he was obsessed with getting employees to run into each other as he built a company culture around fun, excellence in customer service and – as his 2010 book title put it – delivering happiness itself using 'profits, passion and purpose'. All new staff were famously offered $2,000 to quit halfway through their compulsory four-week customer service training in order to weed out those not fully committed.

The Downtown Project reflects the Zappos ethos, Hsieh explained. 'There's plenty of research that shows companies with strong company cultures outperform their peers financially. Culture is to a company as community is to a city. So I'm looking at what's the return on the ecosystem, the community.' If the city was the iPhone, he continued, his $350 million investment would build out the hardware, the operating system and a few killer apps. But the power of the ecosystem would be the platform.

I asked Hsieh how he thought the project would develop. 'If downtown Vegas can become a place of entrepreneurial energy, inspiration, accelerated learning and community, [when this was] a place voted least likely to succeed, then there's no excuse for any other community or city,' he said. He then urged me, unsuccessfully, to relocate *WIRED* there.

Five years on, how has the grand experiment panned out?

It's October 2018, and a 17-metre-tall, fire-breathing praying mantis, which Hsieh found among the art at Burning Man, towers over the Container Park's shipping-container stores and geodesic immersion dome. The nearby Heart Attack Grill ('Over 350lbs Eats Free') is still there. But some of the early spirit of experimentation seems to be missing. The Teslas are long gone, as is Factorli, an ambitious 2,300-square-metre manufacturing centre. I'd heard from friends who had worked for the project that the idealism had quickly dissipated amid opposition from locals who felt excluded, and questions over management. The VegasTechFund, set up to back local tech businesses, is now VTF Capital, focusing mainly on companies in commerce, with just 15 per cent of its portfolio companies based in Las Vegas.

As a real-estate investment, however, the Downtown Project appears to be thriving. It now owns and operates more than 700 residential units in the neighbourhood and is rapidly filling 231 new apartments and 1,400 square metres of retail development. The project is in the process of developing 18 hectares of land and owns businesses such as Gold Spike, a co-working space by day that becomes a giant party at night, plus hotels, restaurants and bars. Marketing material for the apartments explains that they will 'not only provide residents a place close to Downtown businesses, but also the opportunity to collide with others through their design and location'. It may be an opportunist nod to the Burning Man ethos, but Gifting and Decommodification this is not.

I ask the head of operations, Michael Downs, how I should understand the project today. 'I describe us as a hospitality company,' he replies. 'We own and operate bars and retail. We're a real-estate company. We're an investment company.' The project has been profitable for the last two years, he says, and he offers some numbers to confirm progress. The apartment portfolio is at 90 per cent occupancy, compared with 70 per cent five years ago; the new 231-apartment complex is at 45 per cent occupancy after just two months. Downs cites an economic-impact report prepared by outside consultants, Applied Analysis, which concluded that the construction has led to 1,743 job-years of employment and $272 million in output; and that the Downtown Project's 61 small-business investments should generate 393 job-years of work and $16.1 million in salaries.

And yet these balance-sheet numbers don't add up to a visionary new model of urban infrastructure built around creativity and innovation. On a balmy October evening walk through the neighbourhood, guided by a Downtown Project publicist, I want the celebrity-artist murals, the Lyft art park and the Airstream park where Hsieh now lives in a luxury trailer to add up to something magical. In truth, this is a real-estate development zone with some thriving bars and a few strolling families, but it lacks soul. Downs insists that the project still focuses on 'connectivity' – although when I press him for examples, he talks of locating parking spaces a short distance away from attractions so that people have to walk, and of using social media to promote a new bar by 'creating a tribe of people' who will share their experiences on Instagram. Capitalism, it seems, has once again commandeered the commons.

'Sure, there are things we could have done better,' Downs says when I mention some of the critiques I'd heard. 'There's always room for self-reflection. But it's a delicate balance. We're a private for-profit company, and there were some expectations out there that we were going to resolve the homeless issue. That's not a responsibility of our company.'

I remember that Hsieh had been frustratingly abstract during our conversation five years earlier. Downtown Vegas would, he said, be 'the most community-focused large city in the world', but he never quite explained what that meant. Still, I'd bought into his early idealism, and had been eager to return to see what sort of authentic community-building the Downtown Project had enabled. I find instead that capitalism has caught up with the grand experiment, and that the main goal now seems to be to optimize real-estate values. Indeed, on the day of my visit, the Downtown Project formally rebrands as DTP Companies, to 'align the company's name with how its business operates today'.

On my 2013 visit I'd been excited that the Downtown Project had declared its primary goal on its website as 'to help to create an environment that encourages serendipity . . . the opportunity to unexpectedly collide with people from different backgrounds. Serendipity encourages people to connect with each other, exchange ideas, and accelerates learning. This means that a community must remain accessible to people from all economic backgrounds.'

That paragraph is no longer on the website.

Action Points

Collisions, serendipitous clashes, unlikely juxtapositions – call them what you will, encounters with people who think differently are a powerful spur to fresh thinking. Architecture that enables such interactions is a proven driver of change. The rise in co-working spaces, even co-living projects, partly reflects corporate demand for access to the startup mindset. So what should you look for?

1. The value of a co-working space lies in its curation. The community manager is key: a role akin to a magazine editor, they define the culture, organize the space, filter the membership and oversee activities that bring members together. In choosing a location, look for a commitment to cultural activities and evidence that co-located business members have benefited each other.

2. A corporate co-working space needs committed executive sponsors with clearly articulated expectations. SAP's HanaHaus 'community workspace', in downtown Palo Alto, had the personal backing of SAP co-founder Hasso Plattner; Orange's Villa Bonne Nouvelle in Paris was supported by the HR leadership. It's not enough to provide snacks and a football table; the internal sponsors need to define how they hope staff members will use the space to interact with outsiders.

3. GRid70 was born after a group of CEOs in Grand Rapids, Michigan, decided they could collectively benefit from shared access to the same workspace. This concept is transferable. You may hesitate before considering co-locating your finance team with those from other businesses, even if non-competing; but for your design team, your new-product team, perhaps your marketing and strategy teams, there could be unforeseen benefits to open discussions in the office with colleagues representing different industries.

4. Even within a company, office reconfigurations can enable conversations that may spark new ideas. The Crick cost £650 million, but could you break down internal walls by investing in a few strategically placed sofas and a Nespresso machine?

12.

REFRAME YOUR VALUE

The airline that rewards walking the dog

Australia's national airline – the Flying Kangaroo, more formally known as Qantas – has been advertising for a full-time Scrum Master. It's also recruiting an Agile Project Manager, as well as an Iteration Manager. If these don't sound the sorts of jobs typically associated with flying 484-seater aeroplanes, the requirements of the roles will baffle cabin crews even more: these new hires will discuss 'spring retrospectives' and 'burndown charts' for 'backlog refinement and grooming' while building 'minimum viable products' using 'heartbeat reviews'.

If you thought airline jargon was all about doors-to-manual-and-cross-check, then come with me inside Qantas Loyalty's innovation space, a bright, exposed-ceiling, Post-it-Note-strewn collaboration hub that is reinventing the very notion of a modern airline. Just beyond Sydney International Airport's perimeter fence in an aviation suburb called Mascot, a mere priority-boarding-lane-length stroll from the airline's global headquarters, 150 staff in a converted warehouse are building all sorts of apps and digital experiences that seem to have little to do with flying. With job titles such as Mob Programmer, Continuous Deployment Lead and Process Engineer, they're using what software startups call agile methodologies to prototype new products fast, iterate based on feedback, and test, test, test before releasing them to the ultimate hero of this story – the loyal Qantas customer.

'We just had an internal Olympics here, with teams showcasing their work and competing by country,' Brian Funston, who runs the unit, is explaining as he walks past multicoloured balloons and flags floating over an improvised circular theatre in the centre of a clean open workspace. A pirate flag looks down from a wall as Funston, in a dark-grey T-shirt, jeans and sneakers, hikes past a table-tennis table, long white benches hosting intense discussions between web developers and designers, and endless walls covered with Post-its and annotated coloured cards. 'This is the showcase area, where developers present what they've built at the end of every two-week sprint,' Funston explains. A 'sprint', in agile-development terminology, is the time a team has to finish work so it can be reviewed. 'We call the showcase "QF1 day", after the number of the first Qantas flight. The presentations boost engagement and make people feel very motivated. It's about how you move the culture.'

The Qantas culture has moved an awful lot since the airline was founded in 1920 as the Queensland and Northern Territory Aerial Services, with two biplanes used for joy-riding and demonstration flights. But in recent years the business has hit turbulence caused by factors beyond its control: unpredictable rises in the price of aviation fuel, its main fixed running cost; the downward pressure on ticket prices brought about by low-cost competitors; and the general commodification of airlines as the internet transfers profit margins to promiscuous online aggregators such as Kayak or Skyscanner. Earlier this decade, heavy financial losses threatened the very future of the company.

Brian Funston's department is intended to solve that problem. It's called Qantas Loyalty Ventures, and its remit is to challenge airline economic realities using a bold and ingenious strategy: radically reframing where value lies in the business. If, Qantas figured, flying 51 million passengers each year on 312 hugely expensive aircraft is a complex, financially challenged, intensely competitive way to make money, then why not plot future growth around one particular aspect of the business where it has an unfair market advantage? Why not fundamentally reframe the airline's future value around a wholly owned unit undergoing extraordinary and consistent growth – the airline's loyalty programme?

Qantas Loyalty is a data-rich, emotionally engaging, high-margin frequent-flyer programme that, at 12.4 million members, embraces half of the Australian population. Members earned more than 120 billion points and redeemed 5 million flights in 2017, but flying represents just one aspect of the programme. They also earn points through endless daily activities beside travel: dry-cleaning their suits, ordering caffè lattes, furnishing the baby's nursery. And they can 'burn' points on goods and services that have nothing to do with flying, from playing golf to buying life insurance.

That has quietly made Qantas Loyalty a hugely profitable part of the overall business. In the 2018 financial year it returned A$372 million in underlying pre-tax earnings, at a remarkable 24.1 per cent profit margin – close to the earnings of the airline's entire international business, which produced A$399 million but at a tiny margin. By 2020, according to Bank of America, the loyalty division could be Qantas's biggest contributor to profit, as it continues to launch new non-aviation product lines to a brand-loyal audience it knows well and warmly communicates with. As Qantas's then international and freight boss Gareth Evans told the Aviation Festival in London, 'Why not go out and disrupt other industries? You have a right to play. If you've got a strong brand and consumer base, it is an avenue for growth.'

And that is why Brian Funston's team in the innovation warehouse is moving fast to develop, prototype and market-test new business lines designed to be launched on the loyalty platform. Their raw, iterative approach was popularized by the American entrepreneur Eric Ries, who advocated that 'lean startups' should grow by prototyping a low-cost, basic 'minimum viable product', learning from customer feedback, constantly improving the product, and 'pivoting' if the initial approach proves misdirected. Ries in turn was building on the work of software engineers who advocated what they called 'agile' development methods. Seventeen such engineers met in Snowbird, Utah, in February 2001 and published a Manifesto for Agile Software Development, which prioritizes flexibility, continuous improvement and speed. This work is often implemented through 'scrums', small teams that work in one- or two-week 'sprints' to deliver software.

Funston's department, Qantas Loyalty Ventures, includes Qantas Insurance, the loyalty-based insurance business; the finance arm, Qantas Money; and new business lines still to be launched. The open space was designed to encourage co-creation and experimentation; there are collaborative team-based work areas as well as spaces for individual focused work. A wall-board displays the team's manifesto:

> We . . .
> Trust our team
> Seek diversity in ideas and people
> Keep thinking bigger even if it's uncomfortable
> Choose to be positive (you might see us clapping)
> Move with speed.

Its ambition is captured in a reproduction Lunar Rover parked by the main entrance.

'We're as much a software business as anything else, and we try to think digital first,' Funston says. Projects are divided into two-week sprints, and teams hold daily 'standup' meetings to share progress on achieving sprint goals. Walls are crammed with story cards with new product ideas and progress updates. 'We actually had to bring in extra portable walls because we ran out of wall space,' Funston adds.

And staff are living the brand. The section of the 1,400-square-metre space devoted to enhancing the health insurance line is packed with standing desks and green wellness-ball chairs, intended to promote a healthier posture. In one corner lie a surfboard and a Sydney Half Marathon T-shirt; the chocolate machine has been replaced with one dispensing healthy snacks. Index cards and Post-its on a wall offer hints about ideas under investigation ('Yogaholics';

'Skin checks'). Around them are motivational slogans: 'Care beyond the air', 'Australia's most rewarding insurer'. One wall sign implores staff to 'Exercise your mind'. 'That one's an internal mental-health project, which fits our wellness agenda,' Funston says. 'We're concerned about anxiety, so we pioneered a wellness festival last year under the Qantas Insurance brand.'

A cascade of Post-its on one wall maps out planned improvements to the health insurance app. The notes contain measurements of page load times, customer satisfaction, and 'pain points' based on customer research. Another wall displays coloured index cards setting out the planning calendar for the next six months – a 'travel funnel' sprint, for instance, and 'Apple Wallet fulfilment'. 'We call this the roadmap,' Funston explains, unpicking some of the department's lingua franca. 'These initiatives within a sprint are the "epics", and once we've agreed on them we take the epics to another wall, the "scrum-of-scrum" wall. And you'll see a star here and there – that means we're putting a new initiative into the customer's hands.' It all sounds very organized, in a sticky-label kind of way.

'When you're standing at the wall looking at cards with colleagues, you're trying to solve problems together and build growth,' Funston says. But isn't it, I suggest, also about helping a century-old corporate think like a startup? 'We're a hybrid corporate and startup,' Funston interrupts. 'The combination is a big factor. They come together and dance.'

Qantas came under pressure to sell its loyalty programme in 2014, after the airline posted a record A$2.84 billion loss. Instead, CEO Alan Joyce made it a core aspect of a wider A$2 billion transformation project intended to make the group sustainably profitable. The project was geared not simply to cutting costs and centralizing processes, but also to investing in customer experiences and deepening staff engagement. The efforts have delivered: Qantas announced its highest-ever pre-tax profit of A$1.6 billion in 2018, alongside record levels of customer satisfaction and employee engagement. Profits at the loyalty business keep rising: in 2017, they were almost 30 per cent of total group profits, and Joyce was projecting them to rise to A$600 million in 2022. When the ratings agency Moody's upgraded Qantas's credit rating in May 2017, it said the strength of the loyalty programme was a major factor.

That's because Qantas Loyalty is a brilliantly reliable money-maker – and far more ambitious than the vanilla points offerings of British Airways or Lufthansa. It works by selling points at a profit to partners in its loyalty 'coalition'. Partners such as Woolworths, Hoyts, Rockpool, Airbnb and Uber buy Qantas Points to reward their own customers; Qantas made more money in 2017 selling points than selling international flights. It costs Qantas less to redeem them, so it makes money on every point; and points are typically redeemed after twenty-four months (if at all), so Qantas generates income on the cash held.

Some of the revenue comes from traditional retail channels. In 2011 Qantas bought an online retailer called Wishlist, which it turned into an online mall for spending and earning points on brands such as Apple or Adidas. But it's the new vertical businesses, and the income they generate, that are the bigger opportunity. In July 2011 the loyalty programme launched epiQure, a food and drink club that lets members buy the champagne served in first class and attend private dinners with accomplished chefs. The goal was to deepen customer engagement and build a more loyal community. Two years later it launched a cash card to help travellers spend while overseas; and in December 2014 it launched Qantas Golf Club, whose members earn points on their games and have access to tournaments, events and golfing holidays (potentially winning a million air miles for a hole in one).

Qantas Insurance, launched in partnership with health insurer nib, shows the potential of building businesses in sectors unrelated to airlines. Announced in November 2015, Qantas Insurance was a first step into Australia's A$19 billion private health insurance market, initially targeting a 2 to 3 per cent share; nib would provide the insurance, risk assessment and underwriting, and Qantas Loyalty would provide its marketing, data and customer-retention expertise. It would also keep improving the product by agile iteration: sixty people on Brian Funston's team are working on constant improvements to the insurance offerings, about half of them developers. Customers can use wearable technology, for instance, to earn Qantas Points by tracking physical activity such as running or even walking the dog – a benefit suggested by hundreds of hours of ethnographic research with potential customers. In its first two years, customers had measured 225 billion steps, the equivalent of 180 million kilometres, and earned 200 million Qantas Points doing so – enough to book 27,000 economy flights from Sydney to Melbourne. In 2017, Qantas Insurance was Australia's fastest-growing private health insurance brand.

Yet it took a big conceptual leap for management to agree to build a health insurer inside their airline business. 'We ran a Shark Tank to get approval for Qantas Insurance,' Funston recalls. 'Two hours of Q and A [from airline bosses]. It was challenging – but their feedback was really helpful.' The leadership understood that, over time, financial services would offer a much more stable revenue model than the volatile airline business. Plus, there was already a large and engaged customer base that would need minimal marketing spend to reach. That would cut the cost of acquisition and make it less risky to try new products even if they failed.

Qantas's great insight was that its loyalty programme provided two great defendable assets: vast amounts of data about its customers' behaviour and interests; and their trust in a brand that they knew would look after them. 'Trust is something you can't build up overnight, so it gives us an opportunity to go after these other verticals,' explains Olivia Wirth, CEO of Qantas Loyalty and previously responsible for government relations and the Qantas brand itself. 'Brands now face the challenge of who owns the customer, and how they might be disintermediated by others. That's why our

loyalty programme is so critical – it forms a core pillar for our relationship with our customers.' Companies such as Facebook and
Google have a direct and data-rich relationship with consumers,
and can charge advertisers a premium to reach them. Qantas Loyalty has a similar advantage. 'And unlike the digital companies,'
Wirth says, 'we do have an actual experience – the experience of
the flight – which provides an opportunity to deepen that relationship and differentiate.

'This is an iconic Australian brand with almost a hundred years
of history, a household name that plays a special role in the mind of
Australians and one that they love and feel connected to, like their
family.'

Qantas has access to additional customer data that the digital
companies lack, which it uses to personalize offers. In 2014, it
launched a business called Red Planet to mine customer-loyalty
data so that the group and its outside partners can improve their
media-buying decisions, analytics and research. It claims to understand 'holistic behaviours by marrying what customers do online
with their offline activities'. The next year, Qantas bought a majority stake in Taylor Fry, an analytics and actuarial firm; and in 2016
it made a multimillion-dollar investment in Data Republic, which
lets large organizations (such as its coalition partners) exchange
data in a secure environment.

'We knew data and analytics would be at the core of making the
loyalty business grow,' Wirth says. 'With the shift to digital platforms, we can far better target information to our customers as
we know more about them' – whether through cookies on the
frequent-flyer page or monitoring their behaviour through the
wider web. Red Planet is used inside the business, but it also helps
partners such as Avis and American Express to lower their costs of
sale and boost customer acquisitions.

But the key beneficiary, of course, is Qantas itself. 'A few years
ago we took a step back and said, "If we really understood what
value there is in this wealth of information we hold about our

customers, what else could we do? Where do we have a right and permission to go into sectors and markets as extensions?"'

The coalition of business partners had already proved that members wanted to earn and redeem loyalty points when buying cinema tickets, restaurant meals or groceries – in other words, transactions that had nothing to do with flying. That led Qantas to partner with banks to offer points on credit-card spending, so that Woolworths customers paying with an ANZ credit card, for instance, can earn points twice. epiQure came out of its awareness of how much customers care about food and wine. This led to a partnership with Neil Perry, who curates its in-flight menus, so that members can earn and spend points in his Rockpool restaurants.

'Our thinking was,' Wirth says, 'how do we form a coalition of partners across the Australian economy, to make Qantas Points essentially a second currency?' Rather like Bitcoin during its rise, I suggest? She laughs. 'Absolutely!'

So when insurance emerged as an opportunity, it made sense to work with existing insurers such as nib and simply white-label and customize their policies. 'The health insurance business at its core is about the wellness of our customers, not only when they're flying but helping them be healthier in their lives,' Wirth says. 'The partnership approach offers a unique proposition in this market, rewarding you with points for looking after yourself.' And it seems to work. In a fickle sector, it quickly accounted for high growth and satisfaction rates, and its wellbeing programme has experienced strong customer engagement.

After health came life insurance. 'And you can make your own assumptions about where that's going next . . . It gives us flexibility for the future.'

Another growth area is Qantas Loyalty-based financial services, again through partnerships with the big banks. This has led to a new internal startup called Qantas Money, run by Brian Funston's team. Already 35 per cent of credit-card spend in Australia earns Qantas Points, thanks to agreements with the four main banks. In

2013 the company launched Qantas Cash, a multi-currency Master-card travel-money card that's had 720,000 activations and A$3.5 billion of funds loaded. (The team had the smart idea of incorporating a Cash chip in its latest frequent-flyer cards, so that members simply need to enable the option.) But now it's launching its own credit cards, in partnership with Citi – with Qantas controlling the experience and the offer. First was the Qantas platinum credit card in 2017, offering a high rate of points earned (and an 80,000-point sign-up bonus) and travel benefits such as lounge access. That was joined six months later by an Everyday card, offering fewer benefits (and a 40,000 initial bonus) for a lower annual fee, in order to cover both ends of the market. In its 2018 first-quarter results, the company said the credit-card business was growing at 5.3 per cent, compared with 0.05 per cent for the overall market.

In my quest for examples of bold digital transformation, I've struggled to find an incumbent business achieving faster economic returns from a strategy of what's often called 'adjacent growth' – building new business lines outside the core income stream (though admittedly airline-run health insurance and credit cards stretch the definition of 'adjacent'). What I learned from my meetings at Qantas is that it's a multidisciplinary process, requiring consistent leadership that recognizes the urgency of change, an authentic basis in the company's distinct culture, a diverse and motivated internal team that feels empowered, occasional external adult supervision in formulating processes, and an agile startup mindset that tolerates (even encourages) experimentation that may just fail.

As the CEO leading the change, Alan Joyce has experienced disrupting his own business before. In 2003, three years after he joined Qantas, Dublin-raised Joyce was put in charge of launching its own low-cost airline, Jetstar. At the time, Virgin Australia was undercutting Qantas fares and taking a large dent out of revenues. The company's response was to risk cannibalizing its profits further, by positioning Jetstar as a cheaper domestic carrier offering 'all day, every day, low fares'. Although it competed with Qantas's full-service offerings, Jetstar was deliberately run from Melbourne rather than Sydney, and was managed largely independently of its parent. And it succeeded, later internationalizing as the Jetstar Group – which in 2018 announced underlying profits of A$461 million.

According to Tom von Oertzen, senior partner in the Boston Consulting Group's Sydney office and an aviation specialist involved in Jetstar's launch, 'There are always antibodies flying around when you try something new inside an established company, and legacy thinking would have killed Jetstar. Alan did a very good job of standing that business up and making sure it was separate and pure enough as a competitive airline. That was the big first bold move, and it's delivered: Qantas is the only carrier in the world that's now running the most successful local low-cost airline in-house. They've also learned how to play the risk–reward trade-off effectively and not get spooked by failures – Jetstar Hong Kong, for instance, didn't work, but that was OK.' Formed as a joint venture with China Eastern Airlines, it failed to obtain a licence and ceased operations in 2015.

Joyce was promoted to group CEO in 2008. 'With the Jetstar experience behind him, he felt he had a speedboat that was racing quickly and nimbly to make changes whereas the parent group was not moving very fast,' von Oertzen says. Joyce redesigned head office, went through multiple rounds of management culls, and changed the company culture. His strategy was to create business units where teams had end-to-end control, to create a culture of collaboration and foster constructive debate, and to ensure that when a decision was taken as a group, everyone stood behind it. 'The previous management style was command-and-control. Alan encourages his people to stick their neck out and take a risk. When the then head of loyalty, Lesley Grant, said she wanted to double that business, he said go for it.'

Von Oertzen's team at BCG's Digital Ventures (BCGDV) unit has been instrumental in helping Qantas Loyalty launch its new businesses. 'BCG Digital Ventures brought in global talent – MIT people, Silicon Valley people,' Brian Funston says. 'A lot was "test and learn". What we're doing is permutation number forty of the process. Some things just failed.' Olivia Wirth adds: 'They bring in different thinking, and help us disrupt ourselves.'

'I'm challenging their thinking, helping them quantify and articulate their strategies,' Tom von Oertzen says. The idea for insurance came through an innovation sprint process involving a hybrid BCGDV team that looked at twelve markets where Qantas might build disruptive businesses. 'We didn't know we'd go into insurance. There was a lot of soul-searching – how broadly the brand can be stretched is an ongoing discussion within Qantas. Plenty of people there still want to see it as an airline . . .' Some elements of airline culture have helped, he says: Qantas is used to making relatively big investments in new planes, so capital-light investments like insurance proved attractive. 'And the business has absorbed this idea of getting better by 1 per cent every day. You feel their constant drive to improve, using the data they've got, refining the purchasing funnel, improving the wellness app. Compared to other airlines Qantas is light years ahead in how it's thinking about the future shape of its business.'

Qantas also brought in Accenture consultants to help with strategy and execution. When in 2014 Qantas Loyalty decided to create the Qantas Golf Club, there was pressure to launch within four months, to tie in with the end of the Australian PGA Championship. Accenture turned to agile-development processes to build a website and booking system, working with developers over eight two- and three-week sprints. It also used the software-engineering approach known as DevOps, which unifies development and operations in a way that saves time in writing, testing and implementing code. The deadline was met; more than 12,000 members joined the Qantas Golf Club on its first day.

This diversity of external as well as internal talent has been central to the corporate transformation. 'We absolutely needed to bring in a different skill set based on new ways of working,' Olivia Wirth tells me. 'These new businesses are very much focused on design thinking, a completely agile workforce, heavy on technology and development, as essentially these are digital businesses that demand a capacity to reiterate very quickly. That's one of our competitive advantages – customer experience has always been front of mind, whether on flights or in the lounges, so it's been so critical to carry that expectation through to the digital asset.'

Qantas Insurance and Qantas Money each employs around sixty, half of them developers, plus up to 350 contractors according to project demands (sales, finance and marketing people work across both). But it's competing with banks and tech companies for talent, so Qantas has had to think laterally in order to attract developers and data scientists. It has been partnering with universities to find tech workers with non-traditional backgrounds before rival firms find them, and also identifying potential hires from within its own startup programme.

Qantas launched its startup accelerator in March 2017 in partnership with Slingshot, which brings corporate sponsors together with early- and mid-stage tech businesses. Companies selected for the twelve-week AVRO programme – named after the Avro 504K, Qantas's first aircraft – received up to A$150,000 in funding plus access to Qantas mentors, the group's data and anonymized customer insights, and potential future funding and airline contracts. Successful applicants for the 2017 cohort included Pawshake ('loving and trustworthy pet-minding services'), Aeroster ('makes it easy for pilots and cabin crew to view and share their rosters') and BoozeBud ('an alcohol discovery and delivery platform'). Applications for 2018, before the programme was shut down at the end of that year, were open to teams tackling challenges such as 'creating seamless journeys' ('revolutionize the travel experience from inspiration to destination'), 'care beyond the air' ('enrich customers' lives and our communities physically, socially and financially') and 'innovating without limits' ('uncover the next breakthrough business that we just need to know about').

A lot of corporate accelerators, Wirth suggests, have public relations as their goal. AVRO, she says, had buy-in 'from the CEO down' to solve genuine customer and operational issues. For instance, one in three customers, Qantas discovered, has a pet. So it invested in Mad Paws, an Airbnb for pets. Beyond any potential financial returns, the investment gives dog-owning customers one extra reason to book a Qantas plane ticket.

Qantas has typically been early in adapting new ideas, if rarely first (though it did invent the inflatable escape slide, back in 1965). It's not quite the oldest surviving airline: though it dates back to 16 November 1920, KLM and Avianca were established the previous year. It sometimes claims to have launched the world's first business-class service in 1979 on its 747s, but British Caledonian's Executive cabin was introduced in April 1978, and Pan Am's Clipper Class and British Airways' Club Class beat it by a few months. And though Qantas Frequent Flyer dates from January 1987 – with a grandfather clock among the early redemption prizes – the modern frequent-flyer programme dates from 1972, when Western Direct Marketing created a simple incentive scheme for United Airlines, and seven years later Texas International Airlines built a frequent-flyer programme that matched 'rewards' to miles flown.

But what's set apart Qantas's approach to loyalty – one that Credit Suisse Group estimates has built a niche business worth A$4 billion – has been its data-led, customer-focused, brand-consistent expansion in adaptable, pragmatic ways. But don't call it innovation – it's a word Olivia Wirth recoils from. 'It's so overused, so politicized, it's become meaningless. It's really about how you adapt to a continually changing world. How do you compete, how do you win, how do you stay alive? How do you get ahead of where the market's moving and monetize?' When the fuel price can vary by hundreds of millions of dollars in any one year, cost-cutting can't be a sustainable answer. 'You have to challenge people to find something different.'

So what can other industries learn from Qantas's loyalty-led upgrade? 'At the core for us was a solid and simple understanding that there wasn't going to be any innovation that wasn't attached to the customer,' Wirth says. By obsessively collecting and parsing customer data, for instance, Qantas has discovered insights that have prompted new revenue-generating products. Meanwhile its data-science teams also learned to track the movements on the tarmac of every plane, tug, catering truck, bag and spare part – all data points that can help drive efficiencies.

This is not the role an 'innovation team' can fulfil, Wirth says – it has to be part of a company's core identity, and with the support of the boss and the board. 'For Qantas, innovation has been a matter of survival. Think about how this business was created: two individuals [Paul McGinness and Hudson Fysh] came back from [the First World] war wanting to transport mail from one remote part of the country to another. They had big ambitions for what this incredible mail company was going to be. You've got to try some stuff and realize sometimes it's going to fail. At various times we've owned cruise ships and hotels, we've manufactured aircraft and engines – there's been loads of trial and error along the way. But this mindset – of try and fail and try again – has to be absolutely embedded in the culture, and driven from the top.'

I ask her what would be an extension too far. 'Well, obviously it has to be in line with the brand,' she replies. 'It's intrinsically linked to Australia, so a lot of the propositions we're currently looking at are very much Australia-based. It's premium. There's trust and safety: we fly aircraft! So when we stare into a new vertical opportunity, we have a lot of discussion around risks and trust. We also work out what the boundaries are from our customers by doing a lot of ethnographic research.'

I suggest some potential brand extensions that could build on Qantas Loyalty's knowledge of its customers. Would, say, a dating service be plausible? Wirth laughs. 'That's not on the radar. Although we do have a new technology on our 787 that lets passengers message each other, and a journalist thought it was hilarious and called it Tinder in the air. It is not Tinder in the air!'

What about . . . becoming a bank? Brian Funston quickly shakes his head. 'We see the value in the customer relationship,' he says. 'A bank has other strengths, such as compliance. Where's the most compelling offer we can give our customers? We go and ask them.'

What advice would Funston give other businesses looking to boost their agility and optimize their ability to build new value? 'Go expose yourself to people who are doing it by visiting, talking, seeing it,' he replies. 'We went to Silicon Valley, Israel, all the startup accelerators such as Y Combinator, Techstars, Dodgers in LA, Stanford. You speak to the corporates. You see, wow, the capabilities of the people, the speed of the business.' But the motivation for change must start within your leadership team, he says. 'You need entrepreneurial people. Don't wait for someone to ask you to launch something – it has to come from within. Putting Qantas Points on a pre-paid travel card as Qantas Cash came from within this team. We thought, "It's a no-brainer, let's just start." Qantas is getting better at removing impediments. It supports great ideas that people want to do.'

And the biggest threat to Qantas's innovation efforts? Amazon, Google, Expedia, he says – natively digital businesses that are awash in customer data, able to move fast, and don't see why they shouldn't disintermediate the airlines. 'It keeps you honest, though,' Funston says. 'You're up against some big guns, so you need to know where your advantage will be maintained.'

Or, as Alan Joyce put it in the Qantas 2016 Annual Review, 'Smartphones, 24/7 connectivity and new business models like Uber and Airbnb have given people much greater choice and access to services, information and entertainment. And big data – used securely and sensitively – gives companies the opportunity to understand their customers and respond to them in a much more personal and tailored way.' The challenge for an airline, he added, was to uncover its own competitive advantages that would let it 'disrupt rather than be disrupted'. And trust and loyalty, built up over a century, was as good a starting point as any.

Action Points

I'm from the media industry, and for years I've crafted words and pictures designed for consumption on beautiful, shiny paper. Clearly that's a challenging business model in an age when screens dominate our audience's engagement, cover price finds it hard to compete with free, and advertisers increasingly demand the ultra-personalized targeting that a perfectly printed Condé Nast advertising page can't quite match. From the start at *WIRED*, I knew that we'd have to identify discrete, authentic revenue models that would protect our finances while enhancing and staying true to the editorial brand.

So we launched an ambitious conference business, which allowed us to bring together our community for networking, education and fun: from *WIRED* Money to *WIRED* Health, we programmed high-quality speaker schedules in magical venues, and drew revenue from sponsorship and ticket sales. We also realized that many of our business readers needed to understand how the startups were thinking, so we launched a separate business which we called *WIRED* Consulting to match-make and leverage our network. It wasn't strategy consulting as much as connection-building. An Australian insurer paid us a monthly retainer to be introduced to blockchain entrepreneurs or health-startup founders who could answer their questions. A bank in Germany paid us to programme a client event for them. We were clear that we wouldn't compromise our editorial independence. But there was no rule against reframing how we made money from a quality magazine.

You don't need a fleet of aircraft to bring agile thinking to your organization. Just think how lucky you are not to have to confront such huge sunk costs and fuel-price volatility. So you have no excuse to ignore the lessons of Qantas's transformation:

1. Define the fundamental values and ethos of your organization which mustn't be compromised whatever present and future business challenges you need to confront.

2. Understand what your customers want: ask them, test them, use ethnography, but always begin with their needs.

3. Define your unfair advantage. It may be trust, or a particular expertise. What could there be along your company's entire value chain that could be exploited in new ways that benefit customers? How can you build new business lines that profit from these moats?

4. Study agile software-development methods and consider how your team may use them to prototype, test, iterate and release new products in short time frames. And remember: agile isn't only about software development; it's about a mindset.

5. An imperative for change must be driven authentically from the top. Paradoxically, the leadership needs to empower the wider team to express and

explore their own ideas. The era of hierarchically driven decision-making is over.

6. Look outwards and partner. Qantas Loyalty membership jumped only after it built a partnership coalition so that points could be earned and redeemed in partners' retail stores, banks and other third-party businesses.

7. Build a diversity of viewpoints, backgrounds and talents. New ideas emerge when opinions collide. This may require working with outside agencies or consultancies to embed processes that are foreign to your organization.

8. Ring-fence new experiments so that they are not suffocated at birth by the dominant company culture. Had Jetstar been headquartered in Sydney alongside its corporate parent, rather than in Melbourne, it may have been inhibited in defining its own competitive advantage.

9. Where's the data you're able to access but are not using? How can you turn that data into an unfair advantage?

10. If you were to disrupt your business in the face of outside challenges, what kind of business could it become?

13.

BUILD AN ECOSYSTEM

The phone giant kept alive by 460 startups

Along Wool Road, in north Beijing's Haidian District, is a bright, wide technology showroom that at first glance you might mistake for an Apple Store. Familiar-looking ultra-light 'Notebook Air' laptops and stunning bezel-free 'Mi phones' (not to be confused with iPhones) are displayed on long pale-wood benches; T-shirted staff offer to help you sync with 'Mi TV' smart displays or 'Mi Cloud' remote storage (as opposed to Apple's iTV and iCloud). When I first visited in 2015, looking to buy a tablet, I had to choose between pink/green/yellow/blue/white 'MiPad' options – not to be confused with the pink/green/yellow/blue/white choices for Apple's then low-cost iPhone line.

The airy minimalism of the store's design leaves no doubt as to which California company inspired it; but amid a neat wall display of phone covers and chargers, a giant red 'Mi' sign indicates that it actually belongs to an assembled-in-China technology company, Xiaomi (*'shao-o-me'*), whose CEO and founder, Lei Jun, acknowledges being 'greatly influenced' at college by reading about Steve Jobs. Indeed, when Lei announced the Mi 4 phone on stage in July 2014, he declared that Xiaomi had approached the iPhone's manufacturers to see how they might contribute. If the Apple influence wasn't clear enough, he then rather unwisely reinforced copycat suspicions by introducing Xiaomi's new fitness band while wearing Jobs's jeans-and-black-top uniform, and even using Jobs's catchphrase 'One more thing . . .' Could passing-off ever have been more blatant?

But this is not a story about yet another Chinese interloper cloning Apple's intellectual property and creative originality (even

262

though Jony Ive, Apple's chief design officer, did use *Vanity Fair's* New Establishment Summit in San Francisco three months later to accuse Xiaomi of downright 'theft'). It is, instead, a tale of how Lei Jun built a company that debuted on the Hong Kong stock market in July 2018 at a $54 billion valuation – briefly it was the world's most valuable tech startup – by creating not just a smartphone business, but a new kind of internet-enabled ecosystem. In nine years, Xiaomi has built a customer base of more than 200 million monthly active users for its MIUI Android-based operating system, entered seventy markets as diverse as India and Indonesia, and challenged Western assumptions about how Chinese tech companies think.

I'd grown tired of hearing the outdated cliché that Chinese startups were simply copycats of the West's. I knew from my travels in Shenzhen and Shanghai that the extraordinary product innovation coming out of China, from DJI's drones to Tencent's WeChat, was on a scale bigger than anything I'd seen in Silicon Valley. But could China innovate where business models are concerned, and teach the West something fresh about generating profit from scale? That's the question that took me to Xiaomi, a company whose high-quality devices may well be loss-leaders in the cut-throat Chinese smartphone market, but whose 'ecosystem' model, I discovered, is a phenomenal and original way to build growth.

'We're a very different Chinese company: we spare no costs in ensuring the high quality of each and every Mi product,' Lei Jun tells me. He stays firmly on message when talking to a British journalist. He answers pre-submitted questions through a translator, and won't make the mistake again of attempting to speak English in public: when he did so at a phone launch in New Delhi in April 2015, his awkward 'Are you OK?' to the crowd was later parodied in a thousand internet remixes and raps. He's a rock star to Xiaomi fans and a business hero to his World Economic Forum audiences, but he seems less interested in purveying his own personality than in blandly burnishing the brand. 'I believe Xiaomi will provide the impetus to raise the quality bar of all China-made products,' he says in one typically unchallenging answer, 'and will eventually help to lead to a perception that China is no longer about cheap manufacturing and copycats.'

Lei was born in Xiantao, Hubei, a wealthy region in east-central China, in December 1969 and studied computer science at Wuhan University. While a student, he read *Fire in the Valley*, Paul Freiberger and Michael Swaine's book about the birth of the computer industry. Fascinated by references to Steve Jobs, he decided 'to establish a company that was first class', as he later told the *New York Times*.

But Lei wants you to know that, unlike Apple, Xiaomi isn't a smartphone-and-computer business at all. Instead, he wants it to be seen as 'an internet company' that happens to use smartphones to build its customer base for upselling all sorts of other internet-connected products and services. Still, it has achieved extraordinary success in selling phones. The company's Twitter archive is a chronicle of growth: on 18 December 2011 it reported selling 100,000 phones in three hours; on 24 April 2012, 150,000 were sold in fifteen minutes; and by 20 September that year it took just four minutes to sell 300,000. In 2014, Xiaomi became China's biggest phone-maker, selling 61 million units, up from 18.7 million the previous year. That growth continued into the first half of 2015, when it sold 34.7 million, although it then ceded local dominance to Huawei and became more cautious about releasing sales numbers. Yet it bounced back in 2018, selling 32 million smartphones just in the second quarter.

The best way to understand Xiaomi, Lei insists, is to see it as democratizing access to smart, connected devices in the emerging Internet of Things. 'We put an emphasis on high-quality products that help to create a connected lifestyle for everyone as we move into a new era of technological innovation,' he explains. 'This doesn't only mean smartphones, tablets, TVs, routers – we invest in startups that form what we call an ecosystem. We have hundreds of products that come together to create a lifestyle for our consumers.'

These startups make products, from battery chargers to wearables to air and water purifiers, that are sold in the stores and on Mi.com, a web domain that cost Xiaomi $3.6 million in April 2015. As the company expands aggressively overseas, Xiaomi figured that 'Mi' would be easier for international customers to pronounce.

Lei also wants to explode the myth that Chinese technology companies simply copy from the West. Over the years, he says, Xiaomi's mission has evolved into changing the world's view of Chinese products. 'There's a lot of innovation happening in China that even the West hasn't caught up with,' he reflects. 'Look at WeChat: people think of it as a messaging app, but it's grown to become a platform that incorporates gaming, payments, internet services, etc. The same goes for Xiaomi. We have a business model that's unique: we're a smartphone company, but we are also an e-commerce company – Mi.com is the third-largest e-commerce site in China – and an internet services company, which even publishes games.

'Our motto is: Less is more. By focusing on making a small number of products, we can be the best at what we do. But when less is more, it means you need other companies to help you do more things. Therefore we invest in other companies and form an ecosystem to create more products.'

That ecosystem has extraordinary scale. According to Lei Jun's investment fund, Shunwei Capital, by mid-2017 Xiaomi had sold 55 million Mi battery chargers, 23 million fitness trackers, 5.5 million power extension cords, 3.3 million cameras, and was China's biggest seller of air purifiers. Between Shunwei, Xiaomi and Lei Jun personally, *Forbes* calculated that there have been at least 460 investments made in internet tech companies to build the Mi ecosystem. Before its listing, the company limited the financial data it disclosed, but in December 2016, at the China Mobile Worldwide Partner Conference, Lei stated that annual revenue from the ecosystem was

RMB 15 billion ($2.4 billion). At least four of those startups have become billion-dollar 'unicorns' in their own right, such as Huami, which has sold 45 million smart wearables, and Ninebot, which makes motorized scooters and bought the US company Segway.

Now Xiaomi says it will invest $1 billion in building a similar network of partners in India, its second-biggest market. It's also busy building 2,000 branded Mi Home Stores around the world. For Lei Jun, the journey has barely begun.

A stray dog adopted from a nearby building site excitedly greets visitors to Xiaomi's main headquarters on Maofang Road in Beijing. Corridor walls are covered with vast French Impressionist prints; Xiaomi's mascot, a bunny called Mitu, stares ubiquitously out from office shelves and employee desks. The desks are busily occupied at eight p.m. this Wednesday evening in October 2015: Xiaomi is, a spokeswoman explains, a 'nine-nine-six company', meaning that staff are expected to work from at least nine a.m. to nine p.m. six days a week.

The fans, too, appear mission-driven: wall posters advertise 'MiPop' parties where brand loyalists can meet and dance on-stage with senior company executives who may be wearing rock-star wigs. Display cabinets showcase home-made gifts sent in by these fans: Lei Jun action figures; branded sneakers; phone cases made out of carefully patterned millet seeds. Millet is a literal translation of Xiaomi's name in Mandarin, though in China a more subtle etymology resonates: in 1946, Mao Zedong predicted in a famous speech that his underdog Communists, armed only with 'millet and rifles', would defeat the better-resourced Nationalists' aircraft and tanks. Lei has also suggested that Mi stands for 'mobile internet', as well as his company's 'mission impossible' in taking on the incumbents by boldly inventing a new operating system and new quality expectations in phones.

'Ten years ago, I came to the conclusion that mobile internet is the future,' he says. 'I'm crazy about smartphones. When the very first iPhone and Android smartphones were released, I decided that I would make an Android smartphone.' But unlike those operating systems already on the market, this one – MIUI – would be open to its users to suggest and vote on improvements that would be incorporated in weekly updates. As he put it in a speech marking Xiaomi's fifth birthday, 'We treat our customers as our friends, and take into consideration all their valuable feedback to produce and upgrade our products . . . We believe our users, we listen and make friends with them.'

In 1992, a year after graduating, Lei joined a software company called Kingsoft, rising quickly through the ranks to become president and CEO six years later. He stayed until it listed on the Hong Kong stock exchange in 2007; he had, meanwhile, launched Joyo.com, an online bookshop, which Amazon bought for $75 million in 2004. On leaving Kingsoft, he became one of China's dominant angel investors, backing standout companies such as YY, a video-based social network, and Vancl.com, a clothes retailer. And then, in April 2010, he decided to launch Xiaomi and gathered seven other co-founders.

'Before I met Lei Jun I hadn't heard of him,' recalls Liu De, Xiaomi's head of ecosystem products, then a thirty-seven-year-old industrial design teacher whose wife had been college roommates with the wife of another co-founder, Hong Feng. 'The co-founders of Xiaomi were strangers who'd come from places such as Google, Motorola and Kingsoft. When Lei Jun first met me, he talked about the potential of smartphones and asked if I'd join him to create a new company. I rejected him. And then I spent a month thinking about the really big opportunity.'

Liu De, now in his mid-forties, is sitting in black T-shirt and jeans in an office surrounded by his Mi air purifier, 60-inch MiTV screen, Mi Smart weighing scales and Yeelight smart lightbulbs (all sold by Xiaomi). Liu's seventy-person department is responsible for the accessories sold at Mi.com and in the showcase Mi Home Stores across the world. Some of the most popular items when I visit include the phone-controlled Yi action camera (on Amazon at £44); the Mi Band wristband (a million a month sold on average, at RMB 79 or £8.20); the 10,400mAh Mi Power Bank (a battery charger – more than 10 million sold, at RMB 69 or £7.15); the Mi Air Purifier (RMB 899 or £93); the 60-inch TV (RMB 4,999 or £517); even the Mi Bunny Smartwatch (RMB 599 or £62). Yet Xiaomi makes only smartphones and tablets, TVs and set-top boxes, and routers; everything else, from the smart blood pressure monitor (made by California's iHealth Labs) to Yunmi Technology's water purifier, is produced by independent third-party companies in which Xiaomi has invested typically between $100,000 and $500,000.

'We have six hundred items for sale,' Liu tells me – mobile-phone accessories, smart wearables, internet-connected appliances, lifestyle gadgets such as scooters. 'We've reviewed six hundred startups in the last two years, and invested in fifty-four of them. We help them to define their product, adjust their company strategy to join the Xiaomi platform, and then we use the advantages we have to help them, from sales channel to supply chain, branding to financing. They're like our special forces, and we are the chief of command.'

What's surprising is that it's a team of twenty engineers, not finance people, who make the investment decisions. And they act quickly – 'usually within one meeting,' Liu tells me. 'We respond much faster than traditional investors, once the team has a deep understanding of the company. It's a totally new model for high-tech innovation. Most venture capitalists and investors tend to have experience in software and internet companies, not hardware, so a lot of the famous VCs rely on Xiaomi's judgement and follow up on our investments.'

But, I ask, why not acquire the talent to build the products in-house, as is common practice in the West? Xiaomi is, after all, an accomplished manufacturing business. 'First of all, small companies move much faster than we could,' Liu replies. 'We don't want to become a huge company as that will diminish our efficiency. We'd have twice as many staff and would struggle to get any decisions made. Plus, we feel the startups should remain independent so they can iterate faster. You have to stay nimble and adapt to change quickly.'

By partnering with startups that live or die according to how well they monitor fast-changing demand on the streets, Liu believes, Xiaomi minimizes its own risk of losing touch. He mentions how America's AT&T, after eighty years of dominance in technology innovation, ceded its crown to IBM, which developed the mainframe computer in the 1960s and 1970s; and how, twenty years later, IBM was overtaken by Microsoft. Ten years after that, he says, Google overtook Microsoft; and it took just four years for Facebook to become dominant. 'Internet companies are growing extremely fast right now. Traditional companies are like a tree, taking time to grow – but when they fall, they fall very fast.' Xiaomi's approach is akin to planting a bamboo forest, he tells me. 'Have you ever seen a bamboo forest die off? No, new baby bamboo is always growing fast to replenish it. So by investing in these portfolio companies, we're creating our own baby bamboo. We're building an ecosystem.'

It's the health of this ecosystem, rather than short-term financial returns, that determines Liu's investment strategy. 'We don't care about a company's valuation when we want to invest, only whether it has the best product and team. Our team of twenty engineers will join the companies' boards, but never as an opposition vote. We respect the founders and their dreams.' Still, it doesn't hurt for the startups to gain access to 200 million active monthly users: within a year of Xiaomi's investment, Zimi, the power-bank startup, had become the world's largest, and the Mi Band manufacturer Huami sold 10 million units in just six months.

Xiaomi is making a big decade-long bet on connected devices. The Internet of Things, Liu believes, will be an even bigger market than smartphones and the mobile internet. 'Everything we use in daily life – wearables, watches, weighing scales, home appliances – will be connected over the next ten years, and your smartphone will be the connector,' he reasons. 'We need to grab this opportunity. The ecosystem is our bet on the future.' It's a bold strategy that to some Western venture capitalists would seem contrarian. After all, the hype for early wearable tracking bands, for instance, was not matched by consumer interest, and Jawbone, a wearables startup once valued at a billion dollars, went out of business. Yet Xiaomi is in a strong position to dominate the market once demand picks up. It controls the operating system and the on- and offline distribution channels. It also wields influence over hundreds of independent startups in which it has made only modest financial investments.

Three days before my visit, Xiaomi announced the Ninebot Mini, a 16km/h self-balancing scooter made by one of its portfolio companies. It would soon become a commercial hit and a significant revenue generator. Louie Gao, Ninebot's CEO and founder, tells me that Xiaomi is 'much more involved than with a typical investor relationship – they'll give feedback, help iterate the design of the product, make introductions to supply partners, offer sales channels . . . Compared with doing it ourselves, that could mean a five-fold difference in sales volumes.' I'm told Lei Jun personally gave feedback about the Mini's appearance – that it was Lei who suggested knee-high handles to make riding more stable, so the team tweaked the existing design.

Xiaomi's team also helped Ninebot in its acquisition of Segway in 2015. The purchase brought Ninebot not only the original maker of self-balancing two-wheeled 'personal transporters', but also a treasure trove of intellectual property. 'Segway didn't manage to sustain its early hype,' Gao says, 'but with Ninebot, people will see our next products and think, "Wow, that's really cool, and at an appealing price." And after personal transportation, we're now looking at service robots. We're leading the research efforts. We have a lot of patents.'

The challenge in China, Gao reflects, is meeting demand once the fickle market has become excited. 'There's a saying in China that with hardware, slow is actually fast. If you take your time to iterate, when [your product] finally explodes on to the market you can meet that demand and scale much faster – unlike the Kickstarter model, where delays cause the hype to die. And with Xiaomi, pre-registration numbers for the Ninebot Mini were beyond our expectations. So our challenge is to make sure customers get their products on time.'

The ultimate determinant of success for a Chinese internet business, Hugo Barra explains, lies in 'having a ton of users', even if they're not initially bringing a company any significant revenue. It's an approach that some Western companies would have benefited from adopting: where eBay charged fees to sellers, Alibaba in China made transactions free in order to build volume fast – and then used its scale to develop dominant and profitable products such as Alipay, now a financial services giant, whereas eBay revenue has faced pressure.

Barra, forty-two, a former Google executive now at Facebook, was Xiaomi's international vice-president from 2013 to 2017, responsible for leading its global expansion. 'The only thing Xiaomi really cares about with all the products it sells today is the mobile internet platform,' he explains. 'The phones are simply the distribution vehicle for the platform.' The company's priority isn't selling phones, but maximizing user numbers. From there it can then expand: build a games-publishing business, a content business in movies and music and news, a mobile virtual network, a finance business . . . 'These users are coming from the traffic on the platform. People think Xiaomi is a smartphone company. It's actually an internet company.'

This, Barra says, is why Liu De's ecosystem is such a crucial innovation in a world of commodified smartphones. 'From an internet-thinking perspective, simply having smartphones that are superior to all the other smartphones out there may not be enough.

You need to sell cooler products and have a lot of them coming at all times, so people keep coming back to your website, your store. This ecosystem of smart devices is an important element of Xiaomi's user acquisition and retention strategy.'

Furthermore, if you're running one of Xiaomi's ecosystem start-ups, and your livelihood depends on the success of the product you're building, you're going to work much more passionately on ensuring the market wants what you're building. This boosts the likelihood that the startups will create an exceptional product. It all comes back, Barra notes, to Xiaomi's 'internet' way of thinking – 'acquiring users with amazing products, keeping them loyal, increasing their engagement, and monetizing them transactionally over time'.

Some Western companies, Barra says, have similarly mastered internet thinking (which he defines as 'platform followed by monetization'): he mentions Uber, and Google's Android team, from which he joined Xiaomi in October 2013. 'But there's something pretty unique about China. Guys like [Alibaba's] Jack Ma, [Tencent's] Pony Ma and Lei Jun have boundless thinking – it's unbelievable how they can execute an idea and make it enormous in a couple of weeks.' Barra predicts that China, with its vast manufacturing capability, will become the leader in consumer electronics not just in terms of execution but also innovation. Just give the ecosystem a few years.

'There are two things that are vital if you want to apply internet thinking to consumer products: focus and scale,' he reflects. 'Xiaomi only makes one model of any product, so even with high research costs the unit cost is much smaller than other people's. And because its scale is so big, cost per unit produced goes down over time.' Additionally, the loyal 'community' of Mi customers delivers huge benefits. 'They invest huge amounts of time volunteering [to test and promote products], and they produce some of the best content. You can't replace the community with any marketing strategy in the world.'

★

Xiaomi's chat boards have around 40 million members, of which a million or so 'Mi fans' are active on any one day. It's been Li Ming's job as head of community to keep the fans happy and ensure they're listened to: as employee number nine (he's proud of his early heritage), he's led a team of twenty in moderating forums, running fan events and collecting their feedback. Each year Xiaomi invites fans to cult-like MiPop 'popcorn parties' in twenty or thirty cities across the country where three or four hundred of them come together to dance and receive early access to unreleased products. 'We see them not as customers, but as friends, from the bottom of our hearts,' says Li, thirty-six – also wearing the Jobsian black top and jeans. 'The events have become such a rich experience – you have games, awards to longstanding Mi fans, lucky draws, performances by Mi fans. Initially we held them in meeting rooms; now it's nightclubs, and we've even held one aboard a yacht.' Mi community members also self-organize six or seven hundred smaller events a year in 120 cities without Xiaomi's involvement.

The buzz certainly helps shift product: when Xiaomi celebrated its fifth birthday on 6 April 2015 with a Mi Fan Festival, it used the promotional push to set a world record by selling 2,112,010 phones online in twenty-four hours. But just as valuable, says Li, is the two-way communication through chat forums and social platforms such as Weibo and WeChat. 'On social media a company can shout about its new products, but you have no idea whether someone's a Xiaomi user unless he actively posts on your Facebook page. But the Mi community is a club: a home where you find a sense of belonging. That explains why Mi fans are so willing to spend time making gifts for us. The value is limitless.'

And that results in customer loyalty – 'stickiness', as Li puts it. 'Traditional companies just want to sell product; we want to inter-act with users and gain their feedback. When you have a community, you easily build word of mouth, a key tenet of Xiaomi's operations. You can find out what users want, solve their problems directly on the spot.' Feedback is used to update the MIUI operating system each week; it also offers market insights as to local demand. 'We launched the Mi 4i phone in India as a device for the non-Chinese market – but after lots of Chinese users said they wanted it, we came up with the Mi 4c for China. We take their feedback seriously.'

I point out that the approach is not unique to Xiaomi: OnePlus, another Chinese handset maker, also involves its community in product iteration and in sharing launch invitations through fans' social channels. 'They probably took a few tips from our book,' Li responds dismissively. 'Chinese smartphone companies have all been trying to copy Xiaomi's community engagement style, but it's very difficult for them to do it successfully. It's not something you do by hiring a few employees; it's a culture that emanates from Lei Jun and goes all the way down the company.'

What about Xiaomi's famously effective flash sales, through which it built buzz by limiting new phones' availability? Li insists that 'scarcity marketing' has never been deliberately created, pointing out that consumer electronics aren't like wine, where the longer you keep phones the more precious they become; instead, there's depreciation on any inventory stored in your warehouse. 'Nobody would employ hunger marketing when sitting on huge stocks. The reason people have this idea about Xiaomi is because, as a small company, we could only do limited manufacturing, so some people couldn't get their hands on our phones. Even when we grew bigger, we couldn't match demand.' So when it has stock, it wants to shift it quickly. So quickly that, during one sale, in September 2014, it sold 100,000 phones in 4.2 seconds.

One night during the First World War, Arthur Tansley had a dream in which he found himself among savages in a sub-tropical country. Tansley had become separated from his friends in the dream and was surrounded by spear-wielding natives when he saw his wife approaching him, dressed entirely in white. At some stage he fired his rifle. What exactly happened next was unclear, but on waking he couldn't help wondering: had his dream represented a deep, suppressed desire to shoot and kill his wife?

Tansley, an accomplished Cambridge University botanist then working at the Ministry of Munitions, became fascinated by what his dream meant, and moved after the war to Vienna to undergo analysis by Sigmund Freud himself. His growing fascination with psychoanalysis, combined with his knowledge of botany, led him to formulate one of those provocative new ideas that come along only where disciplines collide. If, as Freud argued, the human brain was part of an interconnected system through which energy flowed, the same might be true for nature as a whole. Plants, Tansley reasoned, were part of a self-regulating system in which they interacted with climates, air, soil and animal and human activities, as if in a unified machine. In a 1935 paper he used a new word to describe this 'recognisable, self-contained entity': it was, he wrote, an 'ecosystem'.

Tansley's linguistic creation has become as much an internet-company buzzword as 'platform' and 'monetization'. A tech company claiming to have an 'ecosystem' business model is signalling both that it is building scale that extends beyond its own resources, and also that it is the gatekeeper to what could potentially be monopoly spoils. In the prospectus for its 2014 initial public offering, the Chinese e-commerce company Alibaba used the word 'ecosystem' more than 160 times to describe why it was valuable. Apple's App Store is built on a 'developer ecosystem', just as digital-currency startups claim to be gateways to the 'blockchain ecosystem'. Xiaomi is far from the first tech company to nurture an ecosystem of outside suppliers as a path to profit; in their different approaches, eBay, Tencent and Amazon have all shown the way.

But it's not only tech companies that can benefit from building business ecosystems around networks of symbiotic relationships. These ecosystems might unite diverse types of mature companies with startups, suppliers and distributors for mutual gain; they might involve informal alliances or more structured forms of interdependence. Typically these collaborations create incremental value for all parties as, for instance, when Procter & Gamble uses an 'open innovation' platform such as InnoCentive to invite start-ups to co-create new products, or a musician uses the website Patreon to find fans willing to donate money.

Here are three very different approaches that suggest how widely the ecosystem model can be applied to help awaken a legacy business: a maturing food-manufacturing company that's staying relevant by building an ecosystem around healthy eating; a 3D-printing pioneer that invests in solving customers' problems in fresh and comprehensive ways; and a vast industrial-legacy business that has used a crowdfunding platform to source valuable customer research.

Shinho is China's biggest manufacturer of organic soy sauce, and the country's second-biggest producer of soy sauce in general. Since Sun Deshan launched the business in 1992, Shinho has grown to 7,000 employees, eleven factories and eleven brands from soybean paste to honey. But trust in Chinese agricultural supply chains remains low, amid frequent scandals involving contaminated or dangerously mislabelled food. Even the government has said that four-fifths of groundwater that's used to grow crops is contaminated. The publicity-shy Sun family wanted to build more trust around China's food supply chain. So they decided to create a movement to boost awareness of optimal farming practices.

They've done this by building an ecosystem designed to improve food quality and supply-chain transparency. In October 2014 in Shanghai, brother and sister Anmao and Harn Sun opened the first of what they intend to be a national chain of Hunter Gatherer restaurants, China's first farm-to-table destinations which show where the food originated, and with grocery stores attached. To source organic food, the family that owns Shinho invested in two 60-hectare Sunrise Harvest farms in Shandong and Shanghai. Then in 2015 they backed a farm-to-door online farmers' market called Yimishiji; and in 2018 there followed a chefs' school to nurture a sustainability-driven approach to cooking. None of these initiatives is publicly linked to Shinho. But collectively they're intended in part to boost demand for the premium foods that Shinho sells – while also being profitable businesses in their own right.

Shinho is also investing in startups that are rethinking the way food is sourced and distributed. It has a startup accelerator and investment fund called Bits x Bites, which gives early-stage companies 120 days of training, access to a co-working space and a kitchen lab, and investment from a $30 million fund. Beneficiaries include Tropic Biosciences, a gene editing company; Jerusalem-based Future Meat Technologies, which produces meat by culturing animal cells; and Bugsolutely, which plans to make silkworm-based snacks for Chinese consumers.

'It's about the Shinho group's long-term vision,' explains Matilda Ho, who set up and runs Bits x Bites and Yimishiji from Shanghai and helped launch the restaurant chain while in a former role at IDEO. 'We have the aspiration to transform from a food company into a food-tech company.'

Some of the investments are intended to make the parent company more responsive to future opportunities. Bits x Bites put money into a blockchain company to understand how it could help Shinho's internal sales platform; it's been tracking individual bottles with QR codes. 'In ten years we won't be a condiments company,' Ho says. 'We'll have billions of data sets, and knowledge of machine learning and blockchain that goes beyond our competitors'. Eventually we want to benchmark against all the other internet companies.'

EOS is three years older than Shinho. Based in a forest in Krailling, outside Munich in Germany, it's a pioneer in the additive-manufacturing (or 3D-printing) process known as laser sintering. EOS makes up to 1,000 machines a year (starting price: €100,000) to enable manufacturers to custom-print parts out of polyamide, stainless steel, titanium, aluminium, cobalt, chrome, nickel alloy, bronze, polystyrene, gold and silver. Yet as a family-owned company that's thirty years old and has more than 1,200 staff, EOS (short for Electro Optical Systems) knows that its greatest risk lies in failing to move at the speed of customers' changing demands.

When I visit I'm taken past a hall full of giant white additive-manufacturing machines and a gallery of the breathtakingly complicated yet elegant products they make: a hollow Formula 1 brake pedal; a permeable skull implant; tooling to make plastic children's cups; bespoke surgical instruments for brain surgery. EOS is at the forefront of enabling the future 'digital factory' that will output pretty much anything that can be designed on a computer. Yet prospective customers often see the technology as not mature enough for their own needs, and they may lack the knowledge (and the talent) to adapt their processes to additive manufacturing. So EOS is creating an ecosystem of partners, start-ups and its own new businesses in order to make its target customers more likely to buy.

EOS is building internal new business units to pursue some obvious opportunities. There's Additive Minds, a consultancy that works (for a fee) with clients to educate them and help implement additive manufacturing in their factories, selling more machines in the process. A newer business unit called AMCM (Additive Manufacturing Customized Machines) works with industrial clients to adapt machines according to their needs. There are businesses that develop new metals and other materials to broaden the range of ways clients can work with EOS machines. And it has also launched an ambitious and wide-ranging investment fund that is financed out of the core EOS balance sheet.

AM Ventures is a corporate VC with a difference. Its goal is to promote growth in the sector in order, ultimately, to sell more machines and more of the powder that's the raw ingredient of additive manufacturing. Claiming to be the world's leading investor in the field of industrial 3D-printing, AM Ventures funds companies developing new materials, hardware, post-processing technology, software and automation. It typically invests at an early stage, from €50,000 to €1 million, and since 2015 has done that eighteen times

with companies such as Munich-based DyeMansion, which provides precision colouring and finish to 3D-printed polymer parts,
and 3YOURMIND, in Berlin, which scans uploaded designs to
assess whether or not they are printable and at what cost.

'Our goal is to grow the demand for additive manufacturing,'
explains Edmar Allitsch, who chairs the EOS board and runs the
thirteen-person venture fund. It's investing on average in one
startup a month, offering mentorship, software advice and access to
customers. 'I don't see myself as a venture capitalist, more as a business angel,' Allitsch says. 'We only invest in companies which help
us to accelerate additive manufacturing, and which we can help.'
The fund has made the parent company much more open to new
technologies, he says, which previously might have been dismissed
as competitive. But it doesn't want to integrate the startups inside
the parent. 'We want to keep them as entrepreneurs,' he says. 'We
give them advice but don't push them. We don't come with corporate thinking.' There's another benefit, too: the investments have
been bringing in a financial return of around 40 per cent a year.

And sometimes a corporate can leverage an existing third-party
ecosystem rather than build its own. GE Appliances, a $6 billion
manufacturer based in Kentucky, had for years been sitting on
internal research which suggested that prospective customers for
its fridges wanted them to make a porous form of ice that was
chewable. Each year the research department's enthusiasm ran up
against the resistance of the sales team, which didn't want to confuse the market with a novelty feature and risk its revenue targets.
So chewable ice remained just an idea.

Then in the summer of 2015 a GE Appliances engineer submitted
the idea, via its FirstBuild subsidiary, to the crowdfunding platform
Indiegogo, which has brought in 10 million backers to support
more than a million entrepreneurs since 2008. Rather than simply
freeze water into cubes, the Opal Nugget Ice Maker would scrape
flakes away from the inside of a chilled stainless-steel cylinder and
extrude chewable ice nuggets. More than 6,000 backers pledged

cash to the project, which raised $2,768,650 – seventeen times more than its funding target. The GE Appliances sales team suddenly took notice.

'For twenty years they were sitting on this research that people like chewable ice, yet every year they looked at the downside risk as opposed to the upside potential,' Slava Rubin, Indiegogo co-founder, tells me. 'All they wanted to do was prove people wanted chewable ice, so they created a one-off countertop device, not even a fridge. And it became the biggest press story for the entire year for all of GE Appliances. Customers would walk in to stores and ask for the refrigerator with chewable ice. And they'd say, "We don't make a refrigerator with chewable ice" – until the CEO said, "We should have a refrigerator with chewable ice, because the customers have been demanding it."'

By 2018, Xiaomi's investments in companies such as iCHUNMi (smart kitchen appliances), Roborock (AI robot vacuum cleaners) and XGIMI (home cinema projectors) were paying off, as was its investment in its own research and development: it had been granted almost 6,000 patents, and its ecosystem approach was drawing customers at scale to its operating system. It was describing itself as the world's third-largest smartphone seller, and the top smartphone vendor in India. In his February 2018 letter to his 18,000 employees, Lei Jun said they had just undergone a 'leapfrog year'. 'In October 2017, we exceeded the revenue goal of RMB 100 billion [$16 billion] set at the beginning of the year,' he wrote. 'I checked – and found out that to achieve this milestone, Apple took 20 years, Facebook took 12 years, Google took nine years, Alibaba took 17 years, Tencent took 17 years, Huawei took 21 years. Xiaomi has taken only slightly over seven years.' Even with the overall smartphone market declining, he added, Xiaomi maintained a year-on-year growth of 96.9 per cent.

How had Xiaomi achieved this turnaround? Not simply through technical advances that improved its phones, such as developing its own Surge S1 chipset. Xiaomi had succeeded by building an eco-system: one that transfers market-demand risk to hundreds of small startups in which it tactically invests; that slashes costs by minimiz-ing inventory and optimizing supply chains in fresh ways; that turns customers into 'fans' who co-design and then evangelize about products; and that, by selling high-quality devices at prices so low as to obliterate margins while profiting from services, content and accessories, is radically innovating at the top of its market.

And there's still plenty of upside. Xiaomi made more than $1 bil-lion profit in 2017, according to Cynthia Zhang, founder of the private-equity firm FutureX Capital – and that was from just a few business lines. 'Xiaomi's hardware doesn't contribute much to its profits right now, but its platform and internet services are still growing very rapidly,' Zhang told the China Money Podcast in April 2018. 'It could make money from games, e-commerce and data. It has more data on users than any other app, as they are using its phones, PCs, TVs, air purifiers and many other items. I see Xiaomi still having huge potential on the revenue side.'

As Lei told the media, 'In the next five years, we will invest in a hundred companies in India. We will replicate the most successful ecosystem business model of China in India. We will have all types of services and products and integrate them. That is the Xiaomi business model.'

Lei, who is married with two daughters, once gave a talk entitled 'What is the future of Xiaomi?' One day, he explained, Xiaomi would be the manufacturing equivalent of Sony in 1970s Japan, and of Samsung in 1990s Korea. 'In ten years' time, China will lead vari-ous fields in the world. We don't just want to produce good products, we all want the whole world to know who we are.'

Meanwhile, he is determined to rewrite the dominant Western story that Xiaomi sits in the shadow of Apple – a story that frames Lei himself as a copycat. The 'one more thing' line was a joke, a spokeswoman insists. 'The Steve Jobs thing is really just surface impression,' says Liu De. The issue has clearly frustrated Lei.

'Mr Jobs was a great man,' he posted on Xiaomi's website in October 2013. 'He did brilliant things, he changed the world, and was a huge inspiration to Xiaomi. But to use him as a point of comparison for myself is completely inappropriate.'

I ask him to explain the reality of his personal relationship with Jobs and Apple. 'I truly respect Steve Jobs for what he achieved with Apple,' he replies through his translator. 'But Xiaomi is an extremely different company. We are very open and we place a lot of emphasis on engaging our users, our Mi fans, incorporating their feedback into weekly software updates and throwing parties with them. We also believe strongly in bringing innovation to everyone, which is why we are very conscious about pricing our products close to cost.'

After all, China is very different from California. 'The role of China in the world is going to be much better understood in the next couple of years,' Hugo Barra predicts. 'It's going to be all about entrepreneurship, focus and scale. The world has a lesson or two to learn from China's internet way of thinking.'

Get ready to copy China.

Action Points

You don't need to be a billionaire running a $54 billion tech giant to adopt some of the lessons of Xiaomi's success. Start with the notion that smart, ambitious outside collaborations can bring outsize mutual benefits.

1. Consider how you might build new symbiotic relationships with suppliers, partners and other third parties. What are the core benefits that you can offer your collaborators? What benefits will you expect in return? And how extensive could such an ecosystem ultimately be?

2. If you are operating in a highly competitive, price-sensitive market, calculate whether you can reduce your headline prices to below those of competitors while leveraging other core strengths to lock in customers and drive revenues from ancillary products or services.

3. How can you turn your customers into brand advocates? For Xiaomi, this has long been a key marketing strategy – but one built on a genuine desire to keep customers (or 'users') happy. As Lei Jun puts it, 'As long as we continue delivering products that are innovative, powerful, with high quality and great design, and with an honest price tag, we can win the lasting trust of our users. And winning the lasting trust of our users is the most important thing to us.'

4. If you work with or invest in startups as a corporate, keep them as independent as possible. 'We don't want companies relying on us to manage their business, as we've got too much to do,' Edmar Allitsch of AM Ventures advises. They need to develop their own culture, even if that risks their failure. Ultimately, they need to fight to compete in the wider market.

5. Fast decision-making is key when working with startups. 'We lost a couple of good deals because it took us three months to make a decision,' says Matilda Ho of Bits x Bites. Processes inside a corporate must be rebalanced to match the speed of the market.

6. Before you start, you need to be comfortable
with risk. Slava Rubin of Indiegogo, which is
increasingly working with corporate clients to
test products on the platform, advises not to start
experimenting with something important to you.
'First use the muscle to see if your organization is
ready,' he suggests. 'Start with lower-return and
lower-risk products.'

14

LEVERAGE EMERGING TECH

Interactive saucepans and blockchain phones

In a converted barn on the rolling eastern slopes of a Napa Valley vineyard, six Michelin-star chefs are busy fricasséeing, blanching, simmering, sautéeing and grilling your future home-cooked dinner. Overlooking a lake on 51 hectares of land, where Cabernet Sauvignon, Merlot, Chardonnay, Petit Verdot and Malbec grapes are soaking up the northern Californian sun, these chefs, mostly trained at Thomas Keller restaurants, industriously weigh, trim and prep before measuring exactly how many seconds of heat their recipes need, and at precisely what temperatures. Because each time they perfect a shrimp tikka masala or a broccolini with chorizo and almonds, these measurements will let you replicate their precise flavours and textures in the comfort of your own kitchen. All you need is their internet-enabled saucepan.

The chefs work for a forty-five-person food startup called Hestan Smart Cooking (HSC), whose mission is to empower anyone to prepare a Michelin-quality meal at home in minutes. You simply follow their recipes using an iPad app that, as you advance, sends precise instructions by Bluetooth to your connected saucepan. The saucepan, manufactured with a heat sensor inside the metal, automatically cooks to the exact temperatures required using electrical induction from a nearby hot-plate. The process is called 'guided cooking', and it's further proof of the internet's power to disrupt every industry it touches – even the analogue world of pots and pans. Suddenly an aluminium-pan manufacturer can become a tech company with new internet-era business models.

Vincent Cheng was quick to sense the opportunity. Cheng, based in Hong Kong, was working in the family cookware business, Meyer Industries Limited, when in 2015 he became convinced that the analogue hardware it was making – pans – might become uncompetitive as digital devices took over the kitchen. He knew that, just as cars and thermostats and door locks had been transformed by connectivity, so would kitchen utensils be. He wasn't entirely sure how a 'smart' saucepan would work, but he was frustrated that his industry wasn't even trying to find out. 'In the cookware industry, "innovation" often consists of a new colour every year, or a new manufacturing process every ten years,' Cheng says. Such complacency carried risks for the family business, which had a lot more to lose than most: Meyer is the single biggest manufacturer of cookware in the US market, and the second-biggest in the entire world. It makes more than 42 million pans a year under sub-brands such as Circulon, Anolon, Farberware and SilverStone.

'I knew that for us to survive in this new smart-cooking arena, against not only major-appliance players but also startups, we'd have to be as nimble as a tech company,' Cheng tells me. So the thirty-six-year-old, who had always been a huge fan of companies that seamlessly integrate hardware and software 'to deliver great user experiences', suggested to his father Stanley, who had built Meyer into a multibillion-dollar operation, that they launch an internal, fully funded startup aiming to disrupt the traditional cooking industry. That's why HSC is staffed not by cookware people but by former Amazon engineers and Michelin-starred chefs who collaborate to create what they call 'guided cooking systems' – a combination of sensor-enabled cookware, heat sources and a cooking app packed with recipes. And Meyer just leaves them to experiment.

It takes bold company leadership to invest substantial sums in exploring how an emerging technology might some day transform, or even invalidate, today's core business. Initially the technology might more easily be rejected as a fad, a gimmick, a likely candidate for the 'trough of disillusionment' – the disappointment-defined falling curve identified by consulting firm Gartner in its 'hype cycle' of emerging tech. Certainly there are no short-term returns in committing resources to researching nascent tools with uncertain long-term financial potential. Yet failing to embrace what could be a significant technology-led shift – from desktop to mobile, say, or from diesel- to battery-powered – can be equally dangerous.

There's a hall of shame filled with once-complacent tech company execs who destroyed billions in valuation by casually dismissing the new. A week after Steve Jobs announced a device called the iPhone in January 2007, Microsoft's CEO Steve Ballmer mocked it live on CNBC television: 'Five hundred dollars? Fully subsidized, with a plan? That is the most expensive phone in the world, and it doesn't appeal to business customers because it doesn't have a keyboard, which makes it not a very good email machine . . .' Oops. Or, in December 2010, weeks after a DVD rental service called Netflix launched its international video-streaming service, Jeff Bewkes, head of media giant Time Warner, was ridiculing its aspirations in the *New York Times*: 'It's a little bit like, is the Albanian army going to take over the world? I don't think so . . .' Time Warner sold itself to AT&T in 2018 for roughly half the then valuation of Netflix.

A genuinely innovative organization will at the very least master an emerging technology and experiment with its potential to refine business models, customer offerings and strategies. There are no guarantees of success, and it's as easy to invest too early as too late. But there's a definite risk of being brutally overtaken, whether you're a phone manufacturer that fails to explore what blockchain might mean to networked communications, or an industrial manufacturer that ignores how autonomous transport might affect your global distribution channels. Or, indeed, a saucepan company that neglects to account for the sensor-enabled internet of physical devices.

Back in the Napa Valley barn – which is more a luxury low-built apartment, with a row of French windows looking out past vines towards the lake – I'm shown how to prepare crispy-skin Atlantic salmon to restaurant quality in fifteen minutes, searing it at 450°F for ninety seconds before the temperature quickly drops to 351°F. I know this because the 28cm three-layer stainless-steel pan sends its exact temperature to be displayed on the iPad, which in turn instructs the 1,600-Watt portable induction heater to reach the required heat through each recipe step. The pan-heater-app combination, called the Hestan Cue, currently retails at $499.95, a price which limits its mass adoption, but HSC is partnering with its own sister company Hestan Commercial as well as kitchen-equipment manufacturers such as GE Appliances (as seen in chapter 13) to integrate its system in their cooktops. At the Smart Kitchen Summit in Seattle last October – yes, there is a global series of conventions devoted to smart cooking – HSC promoted its system as available to select manufacturers.

The salmon is delicious, and cooked to perfection. I send my compliments to myself (and to the app-guided hardware).

HSC is an unusual company, a startup within a global corporation that's part science research lab, part media business, part user-experience academy, part hardware manufacturer, part software developer. Philip Tessier, who worked for eleven years with Thomas Keller, the renowned American chef and restaurateur, and was runner-up at the 2015 Bocuse d'Or (the world's ultimate gastronomic competition), built the cooking team that devises recipes here alongside a video crew, designers, firmware engineers and marketers. HSC lacked electronics engineering talent, so it bought a Kickstarter company called Meld in Seattle, where there are now around twenty people; a handful also work in Vallejo, California, on operations and project management. The whole team is led by Christoph Milz, a German-born former chef with a tightly cropped beard and a friendly grin.

'The user interface of the oven is flawed,' Milz says as he leads me through the barn's Culinary Science Department, where a periodic-table wall-chart overlooks a row of stand-alone ovens, iPads, pans, a colourimeter (to measure the precise colour of a light source), a viscometer (for a fluid's viscosity), temperature probes, and books with titles such as *Physics for Scientists and Engineers, Finite Mathematics* and *Hervé This's Molecular Gastronomy.* 'You set "medium" on the typical countertop and the temperature is not even confirmed,' Milz continues, his expression disbelieving, 'yet with sous-vide a chef can set the water temperature to one-tenth of one degree. How is that?' Here, the team has developed an algorithmic model to predict when a steak becomes medium rare without using probes, with the sensor ensuring there are no surprises. Plus, there's no need to stand by the pan when the algorithm can monitor it automatically. 'We think of it as "kitchen-as-a-service",' he says.

Milz grew up in southern Germany near Lake Constance, and became a chef at the age of fifteen after graduating from Germany's Realschule school system. He found himself the private chef to the German Minister of Defence during the Yugoslav Wars, an invisible presence amid politicians' backroom deals on fighter jets, but at twenty-one decided to resume his studies at Witten/Herdecke, a private German university with a holistic arts-and-science approach. He studied molecular medicine and became obsessed with the potential of science-lab tools to help in the kitchen. So he approached PolyScience, a specialist in temperature-control equipment for scientists, to build a culinary division that would introduce sous-vide cooking to restaurants and homes. There was just one problem: soon, agile Kickstarter startups were threatening to take the sous-vide market.

When Milz co-founded Hestan Smart Cooking in 2015, having been hired by Stanley Cheng as a consultant the previous year, he scoured Kickstarter to supplement the team. Meld, a team of ex-Amazon and Pinterest engineers, had produced a smart retro-fitted stove knob that wirelessly connected with a temperature sensor attached to cookware, automatically adjusting the gas or electricity levels as needed. Their Kickstarter campaign raised $209,688 of an initial $50,000 goal – all of which was refunded when Hestan bought the company that September. 'They thought software may be eating the world, but that soon we'll all be eating software,' Milz recalls.

As Milz is recounting the story in the barn, Stanley walks in holding a leather two-bottle wine carrier. He lives in an ornate Italianate villa, complete with replica Venus de Milo, a short stroll uphill along the vine rows which produce 70,000 bottles a year here. Cheng's wines tend to be well-reviewed: leading critic Robert Parker gave his 2014 Cabernet Sauvignon a 96-point rating. The White House served the 2012 Chardonnay at a welcome dinner for Chinese premier Xi Jinping.

After greeting the team, Cheng uncorks a Grenache and begins to tell his story. He was born in 1947 in Hong Kong, the fifth of seven children. His father had a factory in Kwun Tong making aluminium flashlights, cabinet hinges and ashtrays, but it was while studying business and mechanical engineering in Oregon that Stanley saw a bigger opportunity. Non-stick Teflon-coated pans were starting to be widely marketed in the US; he knew then that Meyer should move into aluminium non-stick cookware.

Cheng set up the factory, bought the production equipment and hired the Hong Kong team; then in 1972 he went on the road to sell his first pans. He launched a US company in Milwaukee in 1981 and immigrated with the family in 1992, buying what became Hestan Vineyards five years later. Hestan is named after Stanley and his wife Helen.

Meyer has always seen itself as an innovator, he explains: it has more than eighty patents and keeps evolving. It has built factories from Thailand to Italy, and has moved into making appliances for high-end restaurants and outdoor cookers for the patio. It also recently launched a titanium-based line of cookware called Nano-Bond, which it markets as '400 per cent harder' than stainless steel and resistant to scratches after years of use.

Yet now, he recognizes, cookware is being commodified. And many of the retail outlets where Meyer promotes its brand are closing. 'I'm an engineer,' he says. 'I like to use technology to solve problems.' So when his son Vincent proposed building HSC as a separate, nimble, tech-focused company with its own culture, processes and business models, Stanley knew he had to listen. 'The fact that Vincent doesn't watch TV tells me that the world has changed,' he tells me.

Vincent knows it's early days for the smart kitchen, but he's cool with experimenting, and has so far persuaded Stanley to ring-fence the startup from the mother ship. 'Food is going to be cooked, one way or another, and whatever form that takes in the future, we want to insert ourselves in the middle and help people feed themselves in a way that brings them joy,' Vincent says. 'Neither of us is married to the idea of being just a cookware company.'

And yet this is not some indulgent wild experiment. It has to make money for Meyer. 'I may be an innovator, but I'm a businessman,' Stanley says. 'This may be a passion but it's not a game. We're very serious about it. Our competition is not sitting still. But smart cooking is a marathon, not a sprint. Consumers don't yet know they need guided cooking. It's like that time before they knew they needed GPS for navigation and were still happy using paper maps.'

The technology is working; all that's needed now is strong word-of-mouth marketing as well as a sustainable business model. Christoph Milz sees HSC as a potential subscription business: its long-term value will lie in the relationship with the home cook, who perhaps pays a monthly fee for access to hundreds of guided recipes. The hardware itself might even be offered at below cost. Nimble tech startups can take such bold decisions, and iterate fast as market realities change.

I ask Stanley how big HSC could be. 'I believe it can be a billion-dollar business – or it can be zero,' he says. 'It's easier to fail than to succeed. But think about it. It's crazy to cook when the only options are "high", "medium" and "low", where you have no control. The ability to absolutely control temperature is so important in cooking – and consumers will know that they need it.'

It was over the reindeer burgers that I met Svein Flatebø. We were in Oslo's Grand Hotel, at a formal buffet reception for the *Aftenposten* newspaper's technology festival, and with guests speaking only Norwegian I was the awkward foreigner straining self-consciously for a friendly face. 'Hello there,' Flatebø, red-cheeked and avuncular, said, offering a firm handshake. He'd noticed me lingering. Then he introduced himself in a manner destined to accentuate my loneliness: 'I'm in fertilizers.'

Fertilizers? How on earth was I going to make small-talk about fertilizers?

It all began in 1903, Flatebø explained, when a Christiania-born physicist named Kristian Birkeland discovered how to extract nitrogen from the air to produce fertilizer. I listened politely, picking purposefully at some salmon roe. Birkeland's discovery had proved the most valuable patent in Norway's history, Flatebø continued, helping avert famine across Europe, and giving birth to a company, Yara International, which today sells to 150 countries and helps feed 300 million people. Yet Yara had a problem: it was the world's leading nitrogen-based fertilizer business, but it struggled to find enough drivers to deliver the 40,000 truckloads a year from the factory at Herøya to the ports in Brevik and Larvik. And not only was the road journey expensive, it hardly embraced the company's sustainability goals. That's why the autonomous, electric, emission-free cargo ship, Flatebø said, was such a step forward.

Autonomous . . . electric . . . I was back in the conversation. Yes, Flatebø responded, sensing my sudden excitement: Yara's board directors had agreed to invest $40 million to build the world's first autonomous battery-powered cargo ship. And it's funny, but since head office announced the project in May 2017, the phone hadn't stopped ringing with other Norwegian companies keen to use autonomous electric ships to traverse fjords and coastal waters with their own heavy cargoes. Maybe it's more interesting than we thought.

I gently pointed out to Flatebø that autonomous transport was such a hot investment space that his fertilizer business potentially had a rather big opportunity on its hands. Had he heard of Alphabet's Waymo (see chapter 5), valued by Morgan Stanley at up to $175 billion? Or Otto, a barely seven-month-old autonomous-truck company acquired by Uber at a reported $680 million? Or Cruise Automation, bought by General Motors in 2016 and now valued in the tens of billions? And that's just land-based autonomy. With most global trade carried on the seas, how vast a business opportunity would maritime autonomy be? Flatebø smiled and shrugged, and suggested that maybe I'd like to meet Petter Østbø and tell him why he was sitting on a battery-powered goldmine.

Østbø is responsible for twenty-eight production plants. A calmly spoken thirty-eight-year-old, he's the grandson of a former Yara plant manager, an economist by education, and a McKinsey veteran by training and temperament. 'McKinsey gives you a toolset and a mindset,' he explains when I visit Yara HQ in Oslo to meet him. 'You learn about taking accountability: if the plane is late, it's *your* responsibility for not taking an earlier plane.'

The autonomous ship wasn't Østbø's idea: credit belongs to Bjørn Tore Orvik, a finance and logistics manager in Yara's Porsgrunn factory, who considers himself less an innovator than a 'concept developer'. Orvik had been thinking about how renewable technologies might cut Yara's carbon footprint; Østbø took the idea to the CEO, Svein Tore Holsether, who nodded his approval within a couple of minutes.

Holsether had become CEO in September 2015, determined to end a command-and-control culture and instead empower all staff to be more active problem-solvers. He launched an online 'idea bank' to encourage staff to propose concrete improvements in their departments; he promoted Østbø the next year and encouraged him to spend half his time visiting plants to 'drive culture change'. This involves what sounds a very McKinseyish 'four-dimensional change matrix' involving setting KPIs (key performance indicators) and 'role modelling' (which appears to mean managers setting an example).

Holsether had been inspired by the money manager Larry Fink of BlackRock, whose annual letter to CEOs had argued that businesses are increasingly expected to serve a social purpose as well as deliver financial performance. Yara, a 16,000-person, $11.4-billion-revenue company that sold 27 million tonnes of fertilizer in 2017, was already aligned with that thinking; its declared mission, after all, is to 'responsibly feed the world and protect the planet'. But Holsether wanted to go further, promoting what he called 'innovation with a purpose' throughout the company as a way to support the United Nations' sustainable-development goals, while opening up future financial opportunities. And Orvik's shipping idea was right in that sweet spot. He's now managing the project.

'It is a bit strange that it takes a fertilizer company to be the first here,' Østbø reflects. 'This is a very conservative business. But we needed a culture change if we were going to continue to be successful.'

The *Yara Birkeland* is a key symbol of that culture shift. The 79.5-metre-long ship, named after Kristian Birkeland, is under construction in a Romanian yard belonging to the Norwegian shipbuilder Vard. It's a project built on collaboration. The Norwegian government, which has a fund to promote environmentally responsible energy, committed 133 million Norwegian kroner ($16 million); Marin Teknikk designed it; Kongsberg, a company that makes advanced cruise missiles, is working on sensors, electric drive, battery, propulsion control and other autonomous systems; Kalmar, which specializes in port loading equipment, is providing fully autonomous cargo handling at a new zero-emissions terminal in Porsgrunn. The ship is due to be delivered to Vard's Brevik yard in early 2020; she'll sail on southern routes between Herøya and Brevik (around 7 nautical miles) and between Herøya and Larvik (30 nautical miles). Initially a crew will need to be present, but the *Yara Birkeland* should be fully autonomous by 2022.

It's expensive to pack a cargo ship with batteries, proximity sensors, lidar, radar, infrared cameras and other advanced technologies – around three times the cost of a standard ship. That will be offset by eventual savings in wages and fuel. And of course Yara will cut local noise, traffic congestion and dust, making the roads safer and reducing greenhouse-gas emissions. The ship's batteries will be charged with clean Norwegian hydro power during loading and unloading, preventing what the company believes is 700 tonnes of carbon dioxide from entering the atmosphere every year. And it will remove 100 diesel trucks a day from the roads. Yara is also starting to think about longer-distance autonomous travel: it exports large quantities of fertilizer to the Baltics, which could be done by electric ships. And there have been conversations about an eventual transatlantic route to Brazil.

When launched, the ship will weigh 3,150 tonnes and carry around 120 shipping containers. A 6-metre-long, 2.4-tonne model was tested in September 2017 in a water tank in Trondheim; the resulting YouTube video prompted intense press interest, but PR was not the goal, Østbø insists. Still, it's helping attract a higher calibre of technical job applicants. 'The reputation for being innovative makes good business sense,' Østbø says. 'We had a lot of other companies contact us wanting to learn about autonomous shipping. Some wanted to see if this could be of value for their own shipping routes.'

Still, it's a project packed with risk. National and international regulations are in flux regarding autonomous ships; there's uncertainty over liability in an accident or shipwreck; and what if the navigation systems come under cyberattack? There are big technical questions still to resolve – Will the machine-learning algorithms be foolproof? Will batteries be reliable for longer journeys? – and one or two potentially troublesome social hurdles, not least the human crews' concern over their future livelihood.

The ambitious startups I work with tend to understand that bold risk-taking can bring outsized commercial rewards. If autonomous electric ships can deliver cost savings to the industry at scale, and if Yara's prototypes become a widely used model, I suggest to Østbø, couldn't this become a spin-off company with a value eventually exceeding that of the fertilizer business? Why doesn't Yara aim to build the platform on which the world's cargo shippers book their autonomous runs, or use its newfound expertise to build its own fleet-for-hire? Isn't there an opportunity here to be the Cruise Automation of the oceans?

That's not the goal, he tells me patiently, as if humouring an over-excited schoolboy. Yara has little interest in commercializing the intellectual property behind the development work it is leading and funding. 'You need to think of the capital you'd need to employ to make that happen,' he says. 'If you want a fleet of cargo ships, with built-in navigation, that's a big investment. We asked ourselves, do we want to branch out with an autonomous-ships business? And we said no.'

I feel impelled to play devil's advocate, but reply with a Silicon Valley stridency that I quickly realize must sound barbarically insolent to a Norwegian fertilizer executive: mightn't that prove an expensive mistake? Østbø remains unflustered. 'It's not the core of our future plans,' he responds calmly. 'If you want to be the platform owner, there needs to be a natural fit. For us to be a platform owner isn't natural; we wouldn't win.'

But he's giving away the IP that could power a nascent industry . . . 'To an extent, of course, yes,' he agrees, 'but we have other more core projects which have a much higher probability of having high value. For instance, we're looking for partners to build a solar-powered pilot plant for making fertilizer.'

I play my joker, and mention Nokia, the 1865-born Finnish serial innovator which prospered through transitions from making paper pulp to rubber boots to car tyres to feature phones . . . until it failed to acknowledge the impact of the newfangled smartphone. Mightn't autonomous ships be Yara's iPhone opportunity? 'It's conceivable,' Østbø replies patiently, 'but if you look at our portfolio of upcoming projects, this is not the most likely for our success. Other projects could be more valuable. Maybe this is the worst mistake ever,' he adds, 'but we don't think so.'

Cher Wang had a problem. HTC, her Taiwanese smartphone business that in 2011 had been number one in the American market – ahead even of Apple and Samsung – had been commodified. Its global market share had fallen below 1 per cent by spring 2018, year-on-year sales were down 68 per cent, and the latest declared quarterly loss was $337 million. Even after transferring 2,000 research staff to Google in a $1.1 billion deal, and letting 1,500 more employees go a few months later, the twenty-one-year-old company's very survival was in question. Once the innovator behind the first Windows and Android phones, and the widely acclaimed Google Pixel, HTC had ultimately failed to keep up.

Partly it was the competition. Huawei, Xiaomi, OnePlus and other emerging challengers were nimbler, more responsive to consumer needs, and certainly better at brand-building: becoming an invisible white-label manufacturer for third parties such as Microsoft and Google had sowed the seeds of later consumer disinterest, and HTC's own brand-marketing campaigns were often bizarre (its 2013 'Hipster Troll Carwash' commercial, claiming to explain what 'HTC' really stood for, was as awful as you might imagine). Its expansion into connected devices and wearables, from fitness trackers to cameras, failed as badly as its Facebook phone. Strategy was confused, software was often problematic, and rivals offered better specs. A share price that in April 2011 had reached 1,300 Taiwanese dollars was below 40 by September 2018.

But Wang, a youthful, curious and sport-loving sixty-year-old, who lives between Taipei and California, is not one to give up easily. The founder of two successful tech companies – the other, VIA Technologies, makes integrated circuits – she overcame a complicated start in life to define her own path. 'I had a tough time in childhood,' she recalls without rancour when we meet in her Taipei office. 'My family is quite difficult. I wanted to get out of Taiwan.'

Her father, Wang Yung-ching, was a former tea farmer and rice miller who in 1954 founded what became the plastics and petrochemicals conglomerate Formosa Plastics Group. At his death in 2008, aged ninety-one, he was listed by *Forbes* as the second-richest person in Taiwan, worth $6.8 billion. Cher was one of ten children from three women; he proved a less than supportive father, both emotionally and financially, and after his death the family fought over his legacy in a series of court disputes. Cher was sent at fifteen to California to study at the College Preparatory School in Oakland while living (as a committed Christian) with a Jewish host family; a year later her mother moved out to join her. Cher had planned to become a concert pianist and studied music at the University of California at Berkeley, but switched to economics after one semester when she realized she would never excel. She supported herself by buying and selling clothes, and then by buying medicines in the US to import at a margin to Taiwan.

After graduating, she joined the motherboard-manufacturing company First International Computer, co-founded by her sister Charlene. She hustled and proved a gifted saleswoman. Seeing that demand for motherboards was booming, she launched VIA Technologies in 1987. Ten years later she co-founded HTC. It was named not after hipster trolls but the small High Tech Computers it set out to make. And it innovated, consistently, releasing the first Window CE personal digital assistant in 1998, the first gesture-based smartphone in 2007, the first Google Android and WiMax 4G phones in 2008 and the first metal-body smartphone in 2013. In 2010, HTC sold 25 million handsets; the next year, when it overtook Nokia as the third-largest phone-maker behind Apple and Samsung, the markets valued the company at $35 billion. *Forbes* listed Wang with her husband Wen-Chi Chen as worth $8.8 billion. 'We weren't very marketing driven, but were making the best things for other people,' she says. And sooner or later, that would become a problem.

By 2014, HTC had fallen behind Apple, Samsung and LG in the US to just 6 per cent market share. Wang, as chairwoman, was brought back as CEO to replace her co-founder Peter Chou. She knew the company needed to find a hit beyond standard Android phones or it would not have a future. Her nephew Phil Chen, who had been in the business for five years, offered a potential opportunity: he had met Palmer Luckey, who had run a breakout Kickstarter campaign for an immersive virtual-reality headset called the Oculus Rift before Facebook bought his company for $3 billion. Chen was impressed and arranged for Wang to fly to Seattle to meet the games company Valve (see chapter 2), which had developed a VR platform called SteamVR. In March 2015, at Mobile World Congress in Barcelona, he announced that HTC would be making its own virtual-reality headset with Valve, called the HTC Vive. It seemed the company might be back in the game.

Chen, whose mother is Cher Wang's sister, grew up in a modest Taipei apartment with none of the benefits of his grandfather's wealth. He hated his 'colonial' American school, where he rebelled: he printed coded messages in the yearbook, and on the last day of school handed out decoders which revealed the messages as obscenities about his teachers. The school wanted to stop him graduating, but Chen, never an academic, had already decided to move to a community college to play basketball. That was itself a scandal for a family as prominent as Wang Yung-ching's.

At community college, Chen discovered his curiosity. He read as if liberated, from African-American literature to philosophy, and decided to become a physicist to understand the secrets of the universe, working at Stanford University's linear accelerator. His journey then took him to a post-graduate divinity degree at a seminary in Los Angeles and ordainment as a minister in the Korean Presbyterian Church. It was an aggressively missionary organization, and for two years Chen was on the road, building schools in Afghanistan and Ghana, and creating a non-profit, One Library Per Child, which digitized learning materials. That evolved into an e-reader company which was sold in 2007 to Barnes & Noble. Then, at twenty-eight, Chen joined his aunt Cher's phone business as HTC's chief content officer.

HTC initially marketed its VR product as the Re Vive – perhaps a nod to the huge expectations for it inside the company. Developed in what became HTC's Future Development Lab, the Vive was ambitious and technically advanced, offering high-resolution tracking through a head-mounted display at a price – initially $799 – designed to appeal to consumers. At launch it was the only VR headset offering motion controls and room-scale tracking out of the box, and critics were enthusiastic. Yet there was still only limited content available, and the price would take a while to fall to a level that might encourage wide adoption. The company did not issue sales numbers, but the Vive did not initially appear to change the game financially.

By the end of 2015, Chen was again restless. He left to become an investor with Horizons Ventures, the venture fund of Hong Kong's wealthiest man, Li Ka-shing, as well as running his own fund investing in virtual and augmented reality. He kept in touch with Wang, and in late 2017 mentioned an idea to her that he thought might be an HTC business opportunity. He'd met a Switzerland-based company called DFINITY that was using blockchain technology to build a decentralized cloud computer – a rival to Amazon's or Google's cloud services, but without a single central owner. Blockchains have become best known as secure, decentralized ways to record transactions of cryptocurrencies such as Bitcoin and Ether. But DFINITY's ambitions led Chen to believe that a 'crypto phone' – a smartphone that securely stored its owner's encrypted digital identity – could offer new and valuable ways for citizens to use blockchains to connect to, and profit from, the network.

Chen wasn't sure exactly what this would mean in practice. And blockchains were still a niche interest: according to his data, just 30 million people around the world had used a blockchain-based digital wallet to store or transact a cryptocurrency. But the philosopher and investor in him, processing the knowledge he'd accumulated building advanced devices, sensed a hugely disruptive opportunity. The internet had promised a more open culture of knowledge-sharing and collaboration. It had produced amazing peer-to-peer projects such as Wikipedia, the BitTorrent file-sharing protocol, and now Bitcoin. Yet the internet's open protocols had not prevented closed, profit-driven companies from capturing the majority of online engagement, and in particular the online personal data that Facebook and Google sell to their advertisers. If only ownership and control of that data could be restored to citizens, imagine the new value, wealth redistribution and creative expression that could be empowered by decentralized exchanges. The easiest way to let people participate in such exchanges, Chen figured, was the device already in their pocket: the smartphone, but one updated specifically for blockchains.

Most mainstream media coverage of blockchains tends to relate to the oscillating exchange values of cryptocurrencies, or the spurious, often fraudulent, claims made by entrepreneurs seeking to raise funds by selling crypto-coins, or 'tokens', to fund blockchain-linked projects. Such reports generally ignore the more fundamental reasons why so many investors and entrepreneurs are excited today by the technology.

A useful starting point is to consider recent internet history. Tim Berners-Lee, in creating the World Wide Web in 1989, enabled a brilliantly rich global information-sharing network built on open protocols and owned by nobody. And yet he neglected to encode a protocol to confirm an individual's identity, or the ownership and transfer of their assets, in a trusted, secure way. That allowed a bunch of private companies, in a wave known as Web 2.0, to build a social, participatory web which increasingly brought those companies vast profits from the personal data their networks were gathering. Network effects in particular – the tendency for a single company to dominate messaging, or photo-sharing, or social updates, the more people rely on them – led to a more centralized, closed web that offers users limited control over how their digital identity is commercialized.

It wasn't what Berners-Lee had planned, and he later complained that this centralization of the web 'failed instead of served humanity': from 'fake news' to Cambridge Analytica-style abuses of personal data, the web, dominated by unaccountable private monopolies such as Facebook and Google, had become what he called 'a large-scale emergent phenomenon which is anti-human'. That's where what's being called Web3 gives hope to the early web idealists. It's still being built, but it uses blockchains to decentralize the network and restore data ownership from the centralized apps (Facebook, et al.) to the individual. For the first time, there's an open protocol that securely validates your identity, and your assets, throughout the network, just as open protocols today ensure your emails reach the right address and your Netflix account streams the right movie.

To understand why this matters, it's worth reading the famous 2008 paper on cryptography written by a pseudonymous programmer (or programmers) called Satoshi Nakamoto. The paper, 'Bitcoin: A Peer-to-Peer Electronic Cash System', proposes an ingenious process to create a trusted digital currency that relies not on a central bank, but on a peer-to-peer network that uses a digital ledger to verify transactions. The ledger is maintained by the network's own computing power; share your computer-processing capacity to keep the ledger up-to-date and secure, and you can earn micropayments in the currency. It's a process known as 'mining'. A subsequent paper, by a then nineteen-year-old Russian-Canadian programmer called Vitalik Buterin, proposed a protocol called Ethereum on which apps could be built without needing a centralized app store to authorize their release. It's early days, but there are already hundreds of distributed apps (or 'DApps'): they include Filecoin, which lets anyone on the network rent out unused hard-drive storage space; WeiFund, which facilitates crowdfunding; and Etheria, a virtual Minecraft-like game world controlled by no single entity.

This is where Phil Chen saw an opportunity for his aunt's company. 'I have this crazy idea, just hear me out,' he said to Cher Wang in a phone call. Because HTC had such control over the hardware, right down to the chipset, he suggested, it could build the first phone designed specifically for the world of DApps. A secure offline part of the phone could serve as the digital 'wallet' to store an owner's identity and data; and the phone could support decentralized apps in a seamless user experience. She should get someone on to it.

'I didn't really understand what he was talking about at first, but I listened,' Wang recalls. 'I started learning from different blockchain-community people, who were super-enthusiastic and knowledgeable. How do you hide yourself online? How do you protect your information? Blockchain can do it.'

By spring 2018, HTC had decided to pursue the project as its opportunity to move beyond commodity hardware. Yet there was no obvious internal candidate to run it. Chen decided to quit his venture capital job and return to the company with a new job title: chief decentralized officer.

At a blockchain conference that May, Chen announced that HTC was working on a blockchain-powered smartphone called the Exodus. To some tech commentators, this was little more than bandwagon-jumping by a company already left for dead. Certainly Chen was adopting the revolutionary language typical of blockchain startups seeking dubious crowdfunding, enhanced by an ordained minister's messianic faith. The promise of the internet, he wrote in a paper, was that we would live in a world without borders; yet today, corporate sovereigns divided humanity into a handful of walled gardens. But we were 'at the end of the road for the Mobile Internet and now at the dawn of the Crypto Internet', with the Exodus as 'the agent of decentralization'. It was time finally to declare: 'Let my data go.'

I'd met Chen in February and May 2018 to track his thinking on the blockchain phone. In July I visit him again, at HTC's Taipei headquarters, to see how the actual product is taking shape. The building is a reminder of more confident days: designed with sustainability and health in mind, it uses natural air flow to keep cool, collects and purifies rainwater, and deploys solar roof panels to generate power. Staff can use a gym with professional trainers on the tenth floor and badminton and tennis courts on the seventeenth floor. The open white entrance hall is dominated by a giant poster for HTC's latest phone, the U12+, with its slogan: 'Live on the Edge'. The company's financial troubles, and its repeated headcount cuts, suggest that HTC has been living on the edge for a while.

Chen has around a dozen engineers working on his Exodus phone, plus two product managers, two marketing people and two social media assistants. 'I'm running it as a startup,' he explains in his glass-walled office dominated by a giant poster depicting the emerging crypto ecosystem. 'Agile development, iterative processes . . . It's the first time HTC has ever worked like this.'

He invites me to sit in on a meeting with the company's wider marketing and PR teams in which he explains blockchain and takes questions about the project. Using it will, he says, be like having your ID card on the phone with your biometric data secured. That might, for instance, help the unbanked obtain a loan. You'll control who is using your data and why. At some point, HTC would build a DApp store on which anyone could build a decentralized exchange. Longer term, owners of the phone could earn crypto-cash – call it 'HTC Coin' – by making their device's sensors and storage available to the network.

Here is a radical idea: using the phone to 'mine' for the network. Modern smartphones typically contain around fifteen built-in sensors, such as accelerometers, gyroscopes, cameras and barometers.

They also have unused storage and processing power. The data from your sensors, and your computing power and storage, could have a material value to third-party companies which might pay you in crypto-cash to access them. A company making centimetre-precise 3D maps, for instance, might give you a micropayment for making available your camera, gyro and accelerometer to provide detailed indoor and outdoor mapping. Earthquake researchers might pay to use your phone's accelerometer to monitor seismic movements. Car insurers might reward you for using your phone to monitor your driving; health insurers might give discounts for activity-sharing; media companies might rent your excess phone storage or bandwidth.

I ask what sort of sums phone owners could earn by such mining. 'Maybe five dollars a month,' Chen replies. But this is for later models. The first Exodus phone does not look any different from a standard high-end Android smartphone, bar a transparent plastic skin that exposes some of the sensors (partly a nod to data transparency). The real difference is at chip level, where users can store their private cryptographic keys securely. Later versions will have a separate small second screen linked to the secure wallet. 'The wallet metaphor is the wrong metaphor,' Chen says. 'In future, that's where you keep your data, your identity, your health data. You can decide who you exchange that data with in a private way. That's the disruptive idea.'

As with guided cooking at Meyer, and autonomous ships at Yara, it's too early to know if there will be any long-term material value created for HTC by its foray into blockchain phones. Handsets are a fickle and fiercely competitive market, and it may be too late to rescue HTC's declining brand. And yet, the Exodus project seems to be energizing the company internally and boosting morale. It's a signal that senior executives have not given up. By leveraging an emerging technology in an ambitious way, and planning for future iterations that require HTC to build a new kind of app store, even its own cryptocurrency, Cher Wang is confronting an internal culture that had become habituated to decline. This may be her last hope of reversing that.

The first Exodus phone launched at the end of 2018 (with pre-orders payable only in Bitcoin and Ethereum). I ask Wang how significant the blockchain phone will be for HTC. 'This is an investment for the long run,' she says. 'I don't think in the short run this phone will affect our business, but it's an important area to invest in. Let's see what the community wants. It's about educating people beyond the current blockchain community, the customers, about how to use blockchain. And we move from making the hardware to designing the whole experience, using AI, AR, 5G, VR, blockchain, to think about how the end user feels.' And that's why HTC is preparing to be a 'total experience' company rather than a phone-maker.

Later, away from his aunt, I ask Phil Chen whether he thinks HTC is serious about his project. 'If it works out, it will be the product that turns this company around,' he replies. 'The culture of the company has to change, but if it's able to achieve a key role in building this new internet, it will pivot from a hardware company to a software company.' Look at the top three or four blockchain apps out there today, he says – money exchanges, casinos, Ponzi schemes . . . 'Most people are in it to make money, not to build real technology. This, for us, is about the long run. The fact that a public company would commit to this – it's a big thing.'

Action Points

Exponential technologies, from artificial intelligence to quantum computing to autonomous transport, are clearly going to overturn a bunch of today's business models and create new winners. Yet that's not going to happen according to predictable timescales, or when you feel ready to exploit them. So how can you use such an emerging technology to your advantage, rather than be crushed by upstarts better placed to exploit them?

1. Amazon opened its first cashier-less store, Amazon Go, in its Seattle campus in December 2016, explaining that it would use computer vision, proximity sensors and various forms of AI to bill customers automatically for items they walked out with. Two years later, it was reportedly planning to open 3,000 of the stores across the US, thus transforming customer expectations of the near-future retail experience. Its slower retail competitors, once again, risked being left behind. So stay informed about tech that you're tempted to dismiss as speculative. Read widely (and *WIRED* is a good place to start). Attend events outside your comfort zone so you can understand how insiders understand the opportunities of connected devices, blockchains, machine learning, or whatever is next.

2. An early mover can secure intellectual property protection on specific-use cases for emerging technologies. That doesn't guarantee success, of course, but it can be a way to amortize the investment costs.

3. Don't get caught up in the buzzwords. Based on the realities of your own business, and its culture, encourage the leadership team to reflect openly on how specific new technologies might pose a threat to today's processes and products – and where they could build new value. At the very least, the

conversation will help define likely risks and potential strategic investments.

4. To encourage staff to adapt to new tech-led ways of doing business, send strong signals from the top. At Yara, Petter Østbø talks of 'role modelling' – letting staff see that he has mastered the basics of technologies such as artificial intelligence. 'I've just read ten books on AI, and taken courses on it, so at least I know what I'm talking about now,' he says. That lowers the chance of making a misjudged investment decision – and it's more likely to earn a team's confidence.

5. Physically distance an experimental tech-led project from the core business in order to protect its culture. Hestan Smart Cooking is not impeded by the conservatism of the parent company, and has developed its own distinctive culture. As a startup, it can move aggressively, go faster, and bring on outside investors if needed. Or as Cher Wang says about the Exodus team: 'The most important thing is let it breathe, let it be free, let it make decisions on its own.'

6. You need a compelling narrative to excite internal stakeholders, as well as customers, about the benefits of a new technology. 'You can have the best tech in the world,' Stanley Cheng says, 'but if you can't tell the story, you'll fail miserably.'

15

STRETCH THE BUSINESS MODEL

Counter-intuitive paths to profit

There's a strategy popular among startups whose business model is clearly failing: the *pivot*, a radical change of direction in an often existential search for product-market fit. Think of the agile basketball player who keeps one foot in place while repositioning to take a shot – achieving steadiness during a bold move towards a potentially liberating future, yet still acting within the formal rules of the game.

The team behind *Glitch*, a failing video game, realized in 2012 that viability might lie in releasing their internal collaboration tool as a standalone product called Slack: at a 2018 fundraising, Slack was valued at more than $7 billion. A podcast aggregator called Odeo had no chance when Apple's iTunes began offering podcasts in 2005; in a last throw of the dice, its founding team brainstormed and a short-messaging app called Twitter was born. Then there was the Finnish wood-pulp business formed in 1865 that pivoted so effectively and repeatedly that it became, at various times, a successful rubber boot company, a car tyre manufacturer, a home appliances business, and then the world's biggest producer of mobile feature phones. Alas, the company, called Nokia, then became so convinced of its own technical superiority that it failed to grasp why anyone in 2007 would want to buy an iPhone.

But for the most spectacularly successful pivot in modern business history, we must travel to a twenty-two-storey 1962 skyscraper in the Foreshore neighbourhood of Cape Town. Here, facing away from Table Mountain, is the headquarters of a century-old South African pro-nationalist newspaper publisher that was instrumental in promoting and sustaining the white-supremacist political system of apartheid. De Nationale Pers Beperkt ('The National Press Limited'), later rebranded as Naspers, was founded in 1915 to support Afrikaner nationalism and helped embed its race-based system in government. And yet in 2001, Naspers decided to bet $32 million to acquire 46.5 per cent of a loss-making Chinese messaging startup that, when it sold a tiny stake in March 2018, had become an investment valued at $164 billion. The startup was Tencent, creator of the hugely successful WeChat and QQ messaging services, and that single 512,000 per cent return enthroned Naspers as one of the world's greatest technology investors, and placed it among Africa's biggest companies. How did a declining incumbent print publisher stretch its ailing business model so radically yet so effectively?

Over the years I'd met Naspers executives at technology dinners and conferences, and I knew that Tencent was just one of its multi-billion-dollar investment success stories among a portfolio that included giants such as Russia's Mail.ru, India's Flipkart and Delivery Hero in Germany. And I was vaguely aware that Naspers wasn't a typical venture capital fund, given its print-publishing heritage and lack of external investment partners. But when it raised $10.6 billion in March 2018 by trimming its then Tencent stake from 33.3 to a still enormous 31.2 per cent, I needed to understand how it had so successfully reinvented itself to a degree that had eluded media companies around the world. What was it about Naspers' culture that had so profitably allowed it to overcome the decline both of the newspaper business and of apartheid as a political force?

As a starting point, I approach Bob van Dijk, who became CEO in April 2014 after a career as founder of an online derivatives trading business and then with eBay, McKinsey and the Norwegian media company Schibsted. The Tencent investment wasn't simply a random shot in the dark, van Dijk explains by phone from Amsterdam, where he is based: it needs to be understood in the context of a three-decade-long process of continual corporate self-reinvention. 'Thirty years ago we were a publisher for 90 per cent of our revenue, since when we've transformed to primarily a pay-TV business; then founded the first mobile telephony company in Africa; then in the last decade and a bit we have refocused ourselves as a consumer internet company,' he says. The common factor in these repeated evolutions has been 'a fairly radical culture focused on growth' – and on making necessarily risky bets on emerging technologies long before they have matured.

I must understand Naspers' decision to move into the pay-TV business in the 1980s, van Dijk suggests, in order to grasp its later willingness to invest in Chinese tech. Television had arrived only in 1976, when the government-controlled South African Broadcasting Corporation (SABC) was granted a monopoly. Soon it was drawing advertising spending away from newspapers. Naspers appointed a new managing director in 1984, a former political journalist and editor named Theunissen 'Ton' Vosloo, who recognized that its smaller newspapers in particular were suffering from the loss of ad revenue. Vosloo also knew that he would have to prepare the company for what he saw as the inevitable end of apartheid and white minority rule. Its publications' closeness to the ruling National Party would be a liability once apartheid was dismantled. As he told himself, 'We have to do something to get out of this bind.'

The opportunity presented itself just a few months after Vosloo became boss. A fax arrived in the middle of the night from a thirty-year-old MBA student at Columbia University in New York, and it contained an intriguing proposal. The student, Jacobus Petrus Bekker (who went by the name Koos), had been studying the American pay-TV channel Home Box Office (HBO) as part of his research at Columbia's business school. Bekker, an energetic and curious young man, was the son of cattle farmers who grew up an hour south of Johannesburg, and had studied law before working in an advertising agency. He'd moved to New York in 1981 with his wife, Karen Roos, who had a job as fashion editor at *Glamour* magazine, and he was considering joining HBO – indeed, it offered him a job working in affiliate relations in New York. HBO had been offering subscription television by cable since 1972, and Bekker wondered if the model, adapted for satellite broadcasting rather than cable, would work in South Africa, where he knew that terrestrial television was eating into print media's revenues.

He didn't know Vosloo, but Roos had worked at Naspers, and through an intermediary Bekker found a way to reach him. He had an idea that could benefit the business, he wrote in his fax, and he was prepared to fly to Cape Town at his own expense to present it. Vosloo, with nothing to lose, offered to convene the Naspers board, and Bekker, with zero media experience but the arrogance of youth, arrived with his analogue slide deck ready to project to half a dozen company directors. The fifth slide stuck, and for a moment there were restless murmurs around the table, with one director getting up to leave. But Bekker used scissors to eject the slide, and the presentation went on. It was an expensive and risky proposal, but Vosloo and the board were impressed. Why didn't Bekker return to South Africa, Vosloo suggested, and lead the project?

'I immediately knew what he was talking about, and I knew this would help us out of our bind,' Vosloo, now retired, recalls. 'Call it the luck of the journalist. I asked the board for 50 million rand [around $35 million] as the initial capital, and told them I was appointing this guy Bekker. That's where it started. That was our most important decision.'

Vosloo was an accomplished editor who had devoted his entire career to Naspers since joining *Die Oosterlig* (now *Die Burger Oos*) in 1956. Before being offered the MD's job, he'd helped launch two Sunday papers and one daily, and spent seven years editing the daily, *Beeld*. He'd grown up in Uitenhage in the Eastern Cape, raised by his mother after his father (and then his brother) died when he was young, and always had an entrepreneurial instinct: he had what he calls a 'fingertip feeling' for what would sell a newspaper, something the Germans have a word for – *Fingerspitzengefühl*. So he was always looking for the next opportunity. 'My leitmotif was a phrase I learned from one of the great English editors, Arthur Christiansen, who ran the *Daily Express* in the fifties: "Show me a contented editor and I'll show you a bad newspaper."' As MD, Vosloo adapted the phrase: 'Show me a contented MD and I'll show you a bad apple.'

M-Net, the region's first pay-TV system, launched with Bekker as CEO. In 1985, it applied for a broadcasting licence, but was blocked by SABC. Vosloo had to up his game. 'I went to the country's president at that time, P. W. Botha, who I knew from my political reporting days, and I put the fear of God into him,' he says. 'I said, "If you maintain a state monopoly on TV, which is eating our advertising income, all newspapers in this country will close, including those that support you." They appointed a commission of experts, and we won through.' M-Net faced two conditions: it couldn't broadcast news, and it had to share ownership with all the other South African publishers of daily newspapers.

Broadcasting began in September 1986, two years before Sky launched in Britain and just a few months after Canal+ went on air in France as the world's only other over-the-air pay-TV channel. Technically M-Net was advanced, but financially it began as a disaster: by March 1987, the monthly loss was 3.5 million rand on turnover of half a million. One of the partner newspaper groups declined to participate in further funding of the consortium, bankruptcy was looming, and more capital had to be raised. It also made mistakes: its handmade decoders were initially intended for entire apartment blocks, whose tenants simply could not agree collectively to subscribe; only when decoders suitable for individual apartments became available did it start to acquire customers, as subscribing became a householder's decision. By 1990, M-Net was turning a profit and was listed on the Johannesburg Stock Exchange. It began expanding across sub-Saharan Africa.

Vosloo then embarked on what he calls 'another groundbreaking adventure'. Around 1990, the pay-TV consortium with Vosloo as chair approached regulatory authorities for a licence to launch a mobile phone network. After considerable delay the licence was forth-coming, but again there was a condition attached: the government-owned telco must have a year's start on the consortium's venture. MTN became a hugely profitable business that expanded across Africa and the Middle East. But Bekker, who took over as Naspers MD in 1997, decided to prioritize the TV business and sold MTN in order to focus resources. He invested in web content under the Media24 brand from 1998, starting with the sites Pages24.com, News24.com, Fin24.com and the online bookseller Kalahari.net. Bekker also made a smart investment in his own future: refusing to draw a salary, he asked to be paid only in stock options. The decision was to make him a billionaire twice over.

Newspaper businesses often wield disproportionate political influ-ence over government policies and priorities. But rarely has a newspaper company been as single-mindedly effective at promot-ing, sustaining and justifying an extremist form of government as Naspers was in twentieth-century South Africa. This was its pur-pose from the very beginning, driven by James Barry Munnik Hertzog, a general on the losing Boer side in South Africa's brutal Anglo–Boer War between 1899 and 1902. In 1914 he formed a politi-cal party, the National Party, to promote the interests of the Afrikaans-speaking white minority after their defeat. It seemed natural the following year for Hertzog and some supporters to launch an Afrikaans-language newspaper, De (later Die) Burger, to spread the party's ideas and help turn Afrikaner nationalism into power. De Nationale Pers was founded in Cape Town in May 1915 as a holding company for the newspaper.

From that point the fortunes of the newspaper company and the National Party were intertwined. The first editor of Die Burger, an ordained Dutch Reformed Church minister called D. F. Malan, was elected to South Africa's whites-only parlia-ment in 1918. After the National Party took power in 1924, he became Minister of the Interior, Education and Public Health

– while retaining his editorship. Malan openly sympathized with Nazism and Hitler's Brownshirts, and when he became prime minister in 1948 he laid down the foundations of the apartheid system of legally enforced racial segregation. *Die Burger* remained the unofficial mouthpiece of the National Party and the defender of its apartheid policy until 1990, the year Nelson Mandela was released from prison.

'The initial nationalism was more an idealism to right the wrongs of what the British Empire did to the Afrikaners, but in the 1930s, when many Afrikaners studied in Germany, that more romantic nationalism turned into an ugly national socialism,' according to Lizette Rabe, a media historian and former Naspers editor who on the company's centenary compiled the definitive book on its history, *'N Konstante Revolusie: Naspers, Media24 en Oorgange*. Its journalists in the early decades, she tells me, should be better understood as propagandists. 'The titles, whether newspapers with a distinct political view or magazines with a softer approach, were all in the brunt of mobilizing and empowering Afrikaners. The opposition party didn't stand a chance.'

Naspers refused to participate in the media hearings of the Truth and Reconciliation Commission, which sat from 1996 to investigate, record and in some cases grant amnesty for human rights violations committed under apartheid. Still, 127 Naspers journalists made submissions to the commission in their individual capacities to apologize for their role. 'I, like many others . . . did not properly inform readers of the injustices of apartheid,' each of them wrote in a statement. '[I] did not oppose these injustices vigorously enough and, where I had knowledge of these injustices, too readily accepted the National Party government's denials and reassurances. To all those who suffered as a result of this, I offer my sincerest apology and fully commit myself to preventing the past from being repeated.'

Finally, on 25 July 2015, during an event marking Naspers' centenary, the company issued a limited apology to the victims and survivors of apartheid. 'We acknowledge complicity in a morally indefensible political regime and the hurtful way in which this played out in our newsrooms and boardrooms,' Esmaré Weideman, CEO of Naspers' print-media unit, Media24, said. 'Tonight we officially want to ask for forgiveness.'

The apology had been more than three decades in the making, for some at Naspers had understood since the early 1980s that its political allegiance was unsustainable. In a 1981 column, Ton Vosloo had provoked outrage in government by writing that 'the day will come when the National Party government will sit around a table' with Mandela's African National Congress. As MD from 1984, he'd made it a priority for the group to break away from the National Party. 'We said, no, we're not prepared to be the organ of the party any more,' he tells me. 'I knew that change was going to come, and our newspapers were in the forefront of looking for this new deal for South Africa, breaking away from the past.'

Naspers' business-model reinvention can't be understood in isolation from what was also a radical shift in its politics. 'The group transformed itself from a government-supporting entity into an independent business in which the newspapers regained their editorial voice,' Vosloo says. 'This hasn't simply been about our transformation in a business sense.'

Koos Bekker, in wellington boots to protect against construction mud, leads me past what will be a luxury spa, a swimming-pool barn, thirty or so unfinished bedroom suites, an ambitiously large working cider mill, a visitor centre, and a remarkably detailed multilayered garden incorporating a Gertrude Jekyll-style cottage garden, a water garden, a restored Victorian greenhouse and a tiny two-storey thatched cottage which, he explains excitedly, housed eleven people at the start of the First World War.

Tomorrow he flies to China for a Tencent board meeting, but this bright Friday afternoon in November 2018 I catch him in south Somerset, on his 121-hectare Emily Estate, outside a small market town called Castle Cary. When the estate and its Grade II*-listed seventeenth-century mansion Hadspen House were sold in early 2014, media reports suggested breathlessly that Johnny Depp would be moving in. In fact Bekker and his wife Karen Roos outbid the Hollywood actor with the aim of turning the sprawling estate into an English version of Babylonstoren, the magestic hotel and restaurant they opened in 2010 in the wine country east of Cape Town, where they converted a working farm into a luxury destination with spa, pool and a critically acclaimed menu. Roos, former editor of *Elle Decoration* in South Africa, is overseeing the Somerset project, due to open in spring 2019; planning applications submitted to Somerset South District Council suggest that, alongside the hotel and spa, the historic park, gardens and farm shop will accommodate up to 100,000 visitors a year.

Bekker is a youthful sixty-five, curious, engaged and clearly excited to share discoveries he's made since acquiring the estate, such as a pile of anguished letters in the attic that reveal moments of wartime turmoil within the Hobhouse family who used to live here. He talks knowledgeably about the qualities of Georgian building design, the volcanic origins of the house's floor tiles, the unusual golden shimmer of the local Cary stone. It seems a shame to bring the conversation back to business.

How, I ask him over tea, did he come to make the world's most judicious tech investment? What even gave a South African newspaper company the courage to go to China in the first place?

To understand that, Bekker explains, you have to go back to M-Net's rapid growth in the early 1990s, which spurred the company to expand outside Africa. In 1992 the pay-TV consortium, together with the luxury group Richemont, bought a European pay-TV group called FilmNet, which was prominent in Scandinavia and the Benelux countries, and it then invested in Telepiù in Italy. And then in 1997 one of Europe's most aggressive media dealmakers, the Vivendi CEO Jean-Marie Messier, made an overgenerous offer to combine these European holdings with his own Canal+. 'He offered us $2.2 billion in cash and Canal+ shares,

317

which it wasn't worth, so we said thank you and took the money,' Bekker says with a mischievous grin. 'The window for pay-TV was closing, and yet we now had money in our pockets with nowhere to go. What could we do with it? The only thing happening then was the internet.'

Bekker started looking at internet opportunities in China, 'because over the past 3,000 years most of the time China was the world's biggest economy'. He sent teams to Beijing and Hong Kong, and became fascinated by the culture, obsessively reading Chinese fiction in translation and forming a particular attachment to the short-story writer Lu Xun. The teams made several investments, including in an internet service provider in Beijing; in a financial portal in Shanghai; in a sports portal that was at one stage one of China's biggest; and in an online books business. All of these investments failed; the internet service provider alone lost $46 million in eighteen months.

'They were all write-offs – we lost all our money,' Bekker says with a shrug. 'We had a long and honourable tradition of losing big money – in Brazil we lost $400 million in a magazine company.' As he sees my eyes widen, he laughs. 'You have to be prepared for losses. Because you can't predict the future.

'But in China that was the best thing that happened to us,' he continues. 'The most dangerous moment for a company is when things go well, as you develop this illusion of perfection. The most promising moments are when you've just failed.' He then paraphrases Shakespeare's Richard II: 'So we sat upon the floor and told sad stories about the death of kings. That saved our skins. It forced us to see that we'd been outcompeted by the Chinese, who worked harder and were better managers.' Their mistake, they realized, was an imperial mindset that had led them to impose Western executives to run things. In their arrogance they had failed to understand the local business culture. 'So we thought, why don't we do the complete opposite? Let's go find the most able Chinese management team, and instead of telling them what to do, what about shutting up and letting them run the show? That's when we invested in Tencent.'

The internet economy had crashed, and Bekker knew that this was the last investment Naspers could afford. As he admits, they had one more throw of the dice, and it was a risky throw: if they'd missed that one, for four or five years they wouldn't have been able to invest in anything.

When Bekker first met Pony Ma, the founder of Tencent, it had no revenues, its team of thirty didn't speak any English, and it was holed up in a drab building in Shenzhen. But its instant-messaging system, QQ, had almost 2 million users. Ma, the son of Shenzhen's harbour master, had set up the company with five engineering classmates from Shenzhen University, and they were clearly technically gifted. 'You had a sense of excitement about them,' Bekker recalls. 'They didn't start with a plan, but thought, "What can we do that's interesting to people? Once we have a big audience, we can offer them games. Next, we can monetize the games – charge two pennies for a golden sword."' He also noticed that they seemed to be having fun as they coded – a distinguishing feature of successful teams, according to Bekker. 'Henry Ford said that wealth, like happiness, cannot be attained by aiming at it directly, but is a consequence of providing a useful service,' he says. 'The same is true for internet value. If you take an MBA approach with fixed intentions, it's likely to be unsuccessful; the more successful entrepreneurs want to do something riskier that's useful or fun.'

That's why, for that $32 million, he acquired almost half of the company. I ask him whether he ever thought Tencent could become as big as it has. 'No,' he replies without hesitation. 'Neither did its managers. It's fundamentally unpredictable. Did any of your friends in 2003 predict that Twitter was needed? Regressing from picture messaging back to 140 characters? It made no sense.' Bekker smiles. 'In contrast I've seen so many things that ought to have worked but didn't. It's *hard* to predict the future. And a fixed set of beliefs is a toxic thing in business.'

Naspers had boldly overcome its fixed set of beliefs to productive effect as market and political realities shifted fundamentally over the twentieth century. Yet sometimes a conventional business model can be stretched beyond precedent to confer advantage from the very start of a company's journey. As Pony Ma discovered, a founding team with a contrarian approach can build a resilient and profitable business on a single creative idea.

If Naspers exemplifies the corporate world's most effective pivot, sometimes a company discovers an extraordinarily counter-intuitive yet profitable business model from launch. When Transport for London awarded the franchise in 2014 to operate its £15 billion Crossrail train project, the Elizabeth Line, I was intrigued that it selected the company that runs Hong Kong's public-transport network, MTR Corporation (originally known as Mass Transit Railway). MTR had already been involved in running the London Overground, and currently operates Stockholm's Metro and some other Swedish lines, the Melbourne metropolitan train network and Sydney Metro Northwest, as well as individual subway lines in Beijing, Hangzhou and Shenzhen in China. How, I wondered, had a passenger-train operator in a single Asian city become the go-to company to take on some of the world's most high-profile transport projects?

I learn the answer on the thirty-third floor of Tower 2 at Hong Kong's International Finance Centre, where MTR is based – and it comes down to a bold rejection of the industry's conventional business model of relying on state subsidies or high fares. MTR, which operates ninety-three Hong Kong metro stations and opened its first line in 1979, has used a brilliantly simple idea to keep fares low and profits high, while operating at 99.9 per cent reliability. When it plans a new metro station, it does a deal with real-estate developers to capture a share of the value of new offices, shopping malls and apartments that it lets them build above and around the station or depot. MTR is never the actual developer – that would be taking on risks it's not comfortable with. Instead, it acts as landowner and invites developers to tender for the construction, and in return extracts assets in kind, such as ownership of eighteen floors of the eighty-eight-storey tower I'm now in, directly above Hong Kong Station. It's such a contrarian strategy for a rail operator to capture some of the property-price inflation created by its projects, yet on reflection so obvious, that I can't understand why more cities are not doing it.

Across the table from me, Steve Yiu, MTR's principal adviser for property planning, is explaining how this ingenious 'rail plus property' (or 'R+P') model has turned MTR into a highly profitable $33 billion (HK$261 billion) business that's currently spending the equivalent of $800 million to replace ninety-three eight-car trains, $95 million on buying forty light-rail vehicles, and $420 million on upgrading signals along its 231km of tracks. Unlike most urban metro systems, from London to New York, Hong Kong's is financially secure, independent from government operational subsidy, constantly maintained and renewed, and as a consequence is highly efficient and breathtakingly reliable, yet with fares that average just one American dollar for a ride. That's what happens when a transport operator thinks entrepreneurially to capture development value that would normally be abandoned to the wider market.

Yiu, middle-aged, in a dark suit and glasses, points out of the window across Victoria Harbour towards a 118-storey tower, the International Commerce Centre, that rises above a development at Kowloon Station. The tower, Hong Kong's tallest building, is part of a station development completed in 2010 that includes two luxury hotels, 6,400 housing units, a convention centre and office and retail space in what in total will be 1,090,000 square metres of new buildings. MTR's side of the bargain is ownership of 81 per cent of the shopping mall, as a long-term investment. But there are wider public benefits from a project that gained approval back in 1994. It includes parks, children's playgrounds, landscaped gardens and covered walkways that connect homes and offices to the station, 'all coordinated and integrated seamlessly'. In what could have been a set of railway vents are the makings of a thriving new community.

Property development accounts for more than half of MTR's income, Yiu explains. But it offers other benefits that meet wider government goals – and the government remains the majority owner of shares in the privatized MTR. First, R+P brings an economic boost, increasing residential and office density in prime locations. Then there are social benefits in the integrated private and public spaces created above the stations, as well as environmental gains in hiding what would be ugly and noisy transport infrastructure. And of course there's the financial upside in that government does not need to subsidize what MTR calls 'transit-oriented development'. There are now property developments above forty-five MTR stations and depots.

Hong Kong's cramped geography clearly differentiates it from many similarly sized urban transport hubs. Just one out of 4.5 households owns a car, and public transport accounts for 90 per cent of trips, which makes an efficient and attractive metro service a government priority. And yet the simple idea of enabling MTR to capture some of the value of development above its sites could easily be adapted for other cities. For each new station, MTR teams produce the master design and gain planning approval, and then the company pays a 'land premium' to the government based on the undeveloped cost of the land. 'The land before the development might be worth HK$10 million [$1.3 million], but afterwards it's HK$10 billion [$1.3 billion],' says Yiu. MTR's engineering expertise ensures that the seamlessly integrated upper layers pose no structural risks to the station below, while offering the ventilation and access points that it needs. 'We've created the upside, yet there's no lost government revenue. Because it makes sense to build above the station. It's location, location, location!'

The resulting financial windfalls, plus its need to master every aspect of railway expansion, from design to operations, have given MTR an expertise that is not only securing international contracts such as London's Elizabeth Line; it has also led the company to create an MTR Academy in Hong Kong as a world-class training hub for railway professionals from overseas. MTR is only just starting to embed the R+P model outside Hong Kong, but the idea is starting to take root elsewhere. In Delhi and Hyderabad railway companies have been experimenting with real-estate development as they plan new metro lines, and New York's Metropolitan Transportation Authority has been working with developers to fund a train extension to the Hudson Yards project.

In the meantime, Steve Yiu wants to share his excitement about the biggest project in his inbox: a station development above LOHAS Park Station (standing for 'Lifestyle of Health and Sustainability') on the Tseung Kwan O Line that will incorporate fifty residential towers, a 45,000-square-metre shopping centre, two kindergartens, three primary schools, two secondary schools, all-weather walkways, homes for the elderly and disabled, and 19,000 square metres of parks. 'It's an entire township for 68,000 people above a railway depot and station,' he says. 'It's been called a "dream city".' And, when complete in eight years, everyone will win – the new residents, workers, government, passengers, developers . . . and a super-punctual train company that operates like no other.

A company's business-model pivot is likely to succeed only if it builds on existing internal strengths. Naspers' Chinese investments were no random, isolated adventure: in terms of company culture, they came out of its century-long history of entrepreneurial risk-taking. 'Seeing business opportunities, being entrepreneurial and innovative, has always been part of the Naspers DNA right from the start,' says Lizette Rabe, who knows Naspers from the inside as a former journalist at *Die Burger* and editor of *Sarie* magazine. 'The company has always innovated according to the technology of the time, whether it was importing the best gravure printing presses in the 1960s, so that their products could be the best in South Africa, or creating the first pay-TV decoder system. Each new technology wave brought another opportunity, and every time the company was ready to invest because it was cash-rich thanks to its previous investments.'

Bob van Dijk calls it 'frontier thinking' – a quest for growth in immature markets long before competitors are comfortable there. I suspect that's in part because the isolation that came with apartheid freed the company to define its own rules, and forced it to find new friends elsewhere. 'Maybe it's the roots of the company – we've invested where Western investors typically went in much later, such as Russia and Asia, made a bunch of mistakes, and found some things that were spectacular,' he says. 'It's always been about where's the next frontier?' That's not to say that each new frontier will deliver profits; but its contrarian approach makes Naspers comfortable with being early and bold in an industry whose very name, 'venture capital', implies a risky or daring journey.

Van Dijk identifies three particular factors that have enabled Naspers to transform its business effectively. First, it has a high appetite for risk – 'We do a lot that goes completely wrong, and we're very comfortable with that.' Second, the core company has kept small and nimble. 'The number of people with "Naspers" on their business card around the world is probably two hundred. So if we want to change direction, it's relatively easy to do it quickly.' And third, there's what he calls a refreshing lack of complacency: 'The moment you feel happy with where you are, that's the beginning of the end.'

Its 2018 annual report shows how effective those strategies have been. Naspers' internet investments brought in revenues of $15.9 billion over the previous year, of which trading profit was $3.1 billion. Tencent's revenues were up 56 per cent to $34 billion, Mail.ru's were $850 million, and Naspers sold its stake in Flipkart, the Indian e-commerce business, to Walmart for $2.2 billion. Its thriving international investment portfolio ranges from payment services to travel aggregation.

I ask van Dijk to explain the Naspers investment philosophy. 'We're keen observers of how technology can change people's lives for the better,' he says. 'We think, for example, that people buy more stuff than they need. Given increased constraints on our planet and increased awareness, people will need to buy and sell used goods. We call it the classifieds – we do it in forty countries.' Naspers is currently the world leader in classifieds.

Another sector where it's active in around forty markets is food delivery. 'People fix two to three meals a day for themselves, which takes a fair amount of time and isn't necessarily satisfying or healthy. Models like Deliveroo are changing the way people eat, and we're probably only 1 per cent there in terms of impact.' Naspers is, for instance, the largest investor in an Indian food-delivery startup called Swiggy, which runs its own kitchens and delivers nutritionally optimized meals efficiently in batches. The Swiggy founding team exhibits the qualities that van Dijk typically seeks in entrepreneurs: an irrational determination, an enormous passion, complete focus on wanting to build something lasting, and a certain level of humility. 'They're still completely obsessed with making a great product that people love, rather than making money or building a legacy.'

Van Dijk remains responsible for Naspers' traditional media business, including sixty newspapers and thirty magazines, but that now accounts for just '1 to 2 per cent' of revenues. He learned while working at the Norwegian media house Schibsted that innovators need to be prepared to cannibalize today's core revenue drivers in order to build the future. Schibsted, founded in 1839, deliberately accelerated the demise of its newspapers' own high-margin print classified business in the late 1990s by launching online classifieds under separate, independent brands, such as Le Bon Coin and FINN.no, in twenty-two countries from Sweden to Brazil. The counter-intuitive strategy worked: the highly profitable spin-off digital sites came to dominate almost all of their markets.

Van Dijk has some advice for leaders of other businesses who see change coming. 'Go radical and go fast,' he says. 'Marginalism is not appropriate if you want to stay ahead of technology. But to move aggressively and in a new direction, you need to be nimble. Once your corporate functions become too large, you get institutional resistance to change.' It's also important to look outwards. 'If you spend most of your time in internal meetings, worrying about the internal workings of the group, that's very risky. We in the Naspers leadership team think about our competitors, our customers, the world around us rather than our specific operations.'

In May 2014, the accomplished venture capitalist Michael Moritz, himself a former *Time* journalist but best known for his investments (such as Google, LinkedIn and PayPal) at Sequoia Capital, wrote a provocative essay on LinkedIn entitled 'What the *New York Times* could have been'. Between the early 1990s and mid-2000s, he pointed out, the management of the troubled *New York Times* had spent around $2 billion acquiring mostly traditional print assets that later melted down. Naspers under Bekker, by contrast, 'decided to ride, rather than fight, the technology tide', turning the South African media company into 'an online juggernaut' whose market value grew a hundredfold in twenty years. Bekker's defining move, Moritz wrote, 'was his decision to put online first by starting, investing in or buying companies that were born on the web'. The *Times* hierarchy, meanwhile, was still 'paying homage to the past'.

Back on the Emily Estate in south Somerset, before I bid Koos Bekker farewell I ask him if there are strategies he would recommend to other executives who are feeling the wind of change blowing through their business models. 'As I grow older, I get more cynical about strategy,' he replies. 'It's about execution. There's also an element of luck – but in order to be lucky, you have to try constantly and keep looking for opportunities. In e-commerce we started and failed a few times till we bought a business in Poland; we looked at two investments in social networks before Facebook was born, and didn't invest in either.' There was no 'grand theory', he insists, simply a realization that print had no future, that an ambitious business had to break out of South Africa, and that, sitting on a $2.2 billion windfall, it had to do something bold.

It was Bekker's good luck that the Chinese bet paid off: even today, Naspers' market capitalization is lower than the value of its Tencent shares alone – suggesting that the markets see all its other activities as worth less than zero.

And yet, he says, there's no room for complacency. 'Modernity is always one mile ahead, and today there's already a worm in your barrel of apples. The business we're in now, the manipulation of electronic signals, has had a good run for fifty or seventy years.' The digital wave, after it has transformed every industry, will give way to some new disruptive force, just as happened with the railroads, electricity and the internal combustion engine. Why should today's digital giants expect to survive? 'At some point every generation of technology gets exhausted,' Bekker reflects. 'Will it be by biological sciences next? It's hard to know.'

Bekker is a keen student of history, and media history tells him that the rise of radio, in the years after the First World War, was not driven by print companies, just as the internet's growth was not driven by television executives. 'It's quite likely that someone inside a university is today inventing something that will completely blow away the world of today's internet executives. Look at Rank Xerox or Kodak, at how Nokia was optimizing supply-chain management to save two cents off the screen cost, while the smartphone thing sideswiped them.'

He gets up to say goodbye, but not before sharing one final reflection. 'Once you think you know how things work,' he says, 'that's the moment you're in greatest danger.'

Action Points

Sometimes the internet simply doesn't want a legacy business model to survive. That can be awkward for media companies that remain wedded to printing presses, say, or insurers stuck in the era before ubiquitous data gave agile startups new competitive advantages. A centuries-old legacy insurer, for instance, may lack the ability to read fast-changing market signals as effectively as new players. Their financial key performance indicators, based on existing long-term plans, are not adapted to new market realities.

The Naspers experience suggests that, with bold management and a willingness to take risks, a traditional pre-internet business can indeed build valuable new digital business models. But it takes certain conditions to allow that to happen.

1. Bring in outsiders. Ton Vosloo, the lifelong newspaper man, could not have made Naspers a player in pay television without taking a chance on an impressive outsider with the confidence to restart from zero. When an organizational culture is built on certainty, it's time to import a fresh culture through tactical recruitment.

2. Uncover your immediate threats and keep searching for more. Complacency leads to self-deception, in Koos Bekker's thinking, and every organization is already being challenged by competitors they may not yet be aware of.

3. Condition the board to expect change. 'The Naspers board as a norm understands that the company will look very different five years from now,' Bob van Dijk says, 'so big decisions are fairly natural for

them. It has internalized the message that change is good and that the biggest risk of all is not to change direction when the world is changing.'

4. Don't make transformation someone else's problem. Appointing somebody to take care of innovation is 'the most naive possible way to try to bring about change', according to van Dijk. He recommends that leadership teams devote 95 per cent of their time 'not to the business you have today, but the one you think you can build'. That conscious decision to refocus is painfully difficult but ultimately what distinguishes those likely to survive.

5. Build protocols to overcome internal barriers to change. MTR has to manage the interests both of railway engineers and developers in planning each new station. It knows that typically railway companies fight against development above their stations because of engineering needs such as ventilation outlets. So it found a way to coordinate two internal teams – a property team and a railway team – so that they work closely on a shared agenda from the start of every project.

6. Move quickly and radically when you believe your current revenue models are doomed. A small management team enables faster decision-making. And pivot if you need to.

7. Listen openly. Had Ton Vosloo not been prepared to take a meeting with an ambitious New York MBA student, Naspers might today still be a newspaper business.

8. Be prepared to be humiliated. Naspers failed repeatedly – four times in China alone. But its leaders were prepared to accept that they had made mistakes, not least in appointing Western executives to run their local businesses. They also showed the resilience to stay in the game.

16.

EXPLOIT A CRISIS

India's bed-linen king embraces transparency

The crisis kicked off at 6.30 p.m. Mumbai time, when the coldly worded statement from US retail giant Target hit *Bloomberg News*. Hundreds of thousands of luxury Egyptian cotton 500-thread-count bedsheets and pillowcases sold by Target under its Fieldcrest brand were allegedly not, in fact, Egyptian at all. After an 'extensive investigation', the retailer claimed that a supplier, Welspun India, had without its knowledge 'substituted another type of non-Egyptian cotton when producing these sheets between August 2014 and July 2016'. Not only did Target allege that Welspun had violated its code of conduct and ethical standards, but, according to the retailer, it had misled its customers, who were now being systematically contacted and offered a full refund. As a result, Target's $90 million contract with Welspun India was being terminated with immediate effect.

It was Friday evening, so the stock market was closed, but when it reopened Welspun's share price collapsed from 105 rupees ($1.47) to just 47 rupees ($0.66). Little known under its own name, but a prolific manufacturer of stores' own-label sheets, towels and rugs, Welspun India at that time supplied eighteen of the world's top thirty retailers, and made one in every five towels sold in the US. As institutional shareholders rushed to dump the stock, market commentators were questioning the prospects of the thirty-one-year-old family business, which the previous year had reported $900 million revenue and $106 million profit, with a declared path to $2 billion revenue and zero debt by 2020. And the news was about to get worse.

Soon after, the retail chains Walmart and Bed Bath & Beyond announced that they too were dropping Welspun's Egyptian cotton products; within weeks, it was facing five class-action lawsuits. Arvind Sinha, president of the Textile Association of India, warned that the scandal threatened the country's very reputation as a quality textile manufacturing centre. As Dipali Goenka, Welspun India's CEO and joint managing director, now recalls, 'We felt we wouldn't survive.'

This is the story of how Welspun India not only survived the immediate crisis, but leveraged it to become a beacon of supply-chain transparency. By realigning its processes around traceability, and inviting the world's scrutiny, Welspun has counter-intuitively discovered a market advantage: it's begun appealing to a new generation of consumers who care intensely about provenance. And that's already opening up additional revenue streams. 'Innovation only comes out of some kind of challenge that comes your way,' Goenka tells me in the company's Mumbai head office. 'There's always an opportunity that you can make the most from. Our product is a commodity – I mean, it's a towel and a sheet. So the opportunity in challenging times is to think: what can you do differently?'

But there was only chaos in the office that third Friday evening of August 2016. 'It was like a ton of bricks had landed on me,' recalls Altaf Jiwani, the fifty-one-year-old chief financial officer, who had just returned from investor meetings in London. 'Suddenly all our institutional investors were calling me to find out what was going on. But we didn't know exactly what had happened. Plus, our relationship with Target had been good – their customers rated this product as 4 and 4.5 stars out of 5.'

Somewhere along its complex supply chain, which involved suppliers, middlemen and wholesalers, rogue cotton may have slipped through. Welspun operates two factories in Gujarat where 20,000 employees make sheets, towels and rugs. Each day the factories handle 400 tonnes of raw cotton, yarn or fabric. Target, it transpired, had visited one of the factories unannounced the previous month and asked plant managers to trace back the fibres that had gone into the Fieldcrest bed linen. Surprise factory visits are routine; in 2017, according to Jiwani, there were inspections on 250 days. Employees are asked about working conditions; environmental compliance is checked; nearby villagers are invited to share any concerns. But factory officials could not produce documents explaining the origins of the fibres in this particular Egyptian cotton sheet. And that raised concerns with Target's compliance department.

'Suddenly we were facing an earthquake,' Jiwani says. 'Honestly, none of us was prepared for this. Some people didn't leave the office for two days. The pressure kept mounting as it was no longer just a business issue – we were dealing with the retailers' legal teams. The situation evolved every minute.'

Dipali Goenka's husband Balkrishan Goenka, the company's founder and chairman, took charge and called a board meeting the next morning, followed by an investor conference call for nine a.m. on Monday to explain everything the company knew. The immediate priority was damage control. Balkrishan (known as BKG), who had just celebrated his fiftieth birthday, told Jiwani to release whatever funds were necessary to compensate aggrieved retail partners. Dipali flew immediately to the US to meet retailers and reassure them that Welspun would underwrite their costs – a decision that would eventually require tens of millions of dollars in refunds and discounts. Management hit the phones to tell banks and lenders what they knew. Their positive spin was that Egyptian cotton represented just 6 per cent of the company's business, and that the Walmart account, should it be cancelled, produced just 1.5 per cent of company revenue.

And then came the ambulance-chasers. Within days, the law firm Hagens Berman Sobol Shapiro filed a claim alleging that 'consumers who have purchased Welspun bed linens have overpaid for an inferior product'. Class-action lawsuits followed from Florida to Missouri, claiming damages for alleged unjust enrichment, negligent misrepresentation, fraudulent concealment and other egregious breaches of sheet-selling ethics. Welspun felt it was on strong ground, as there had been no safety, health or environmental concerns, and it had quickly offered to compensate consumers for the full retail price paid. Still, legal pressures, on top of critical media scrutiny, were adding to the stress at HQ as senior executives debated their time-critical options.

'We could have submitted and given up, and had a mass recall,' Jiwani tells me. 'But there was another stream of thought: how can we as a company take a holistic view and create a strength out of this crisis? Could we find a way to let the end consumer track each and every item? And could we use that approach to take first-mover advantage to generate a new stream of revenue? Then everything else started falling in place.'

Welspun is run from the sixth floor of a nondescript office building in Kamala Mills, near the base of a flyover in Mumbai's industrial district of Lower Parel. I arrived in an archetypally over-crammed commuter train that somehow I boarded at Vile Parle railway station near the airport; my pleasant surprise at finding space on a hard bench seat gave way to guilt when an elderly man on crutches said something accusatory to me in which I made out the word 'handicapped' (I had inadvertently found myself risking a fine in a 'handicapped-only' carriage, just next to a women-only carriage where two jewellery-sellers had hung a cascading display of earrings and bracelets from a strap-hanger, a charming local take on mobile commerce).

Welspun's corporate meeting room is dominated by his-and-hers double beds, one with pink-and-white-patterned matching duvet cover and pillowcases, the other a simple silver-blue design with four pillows and three plumped cushions. The beds face floor-to-ceiling shelves packed neatly with towels, sheets and duvet covers bearing brands such as 'Better Homes & Gardens', 'Crown and Ivy' and 'LuxiPure'. There are special displays of

Welspun's patented fabric technologies: HygroCotton, whose hollow-core yarn boosts towels' absorbency and helps cool sheets in summer and warm them in winter; Nanocore, which inhibits dust mites and other allergens; Drylon, which can be bleached and resists creases. Welspun has filed or received thirty global patents since it was founded in 1985, and calculates that 37 per cent of revenue derives from such 'innovative' lines developed by its research teams.

The scale of the operation is breathtaking. The two Gujarat factories, in Anjar and Vapi, can produce 90,000 tonnes of towels each year, 90 million metres of bedsheets and 10 million square feet of rugs and carpets. Ninety-four per cent is exported, to more than fifty countries, and by some measures Welspun is the world's largest home-textile player by sales. Although you may not know its name, you'll certainly know the brands under which it sub-licenses its products: Disney, Wimbledon, Royal Ascot. And, of course, the retail chains with which it partners to customize its product lines.

BKG was eighteen when he launched the company with his cousin, Rajesh R. Mandawewala, initially to manufacture polyester filament yarns. Eight years later it began to make towels, but by 1997, as the Welspun Group, it had diversified into a new sector: industrial pipes, which it now produces in factories in India, Saudi Arabia and the US. From there the group expanded into oil and gas exploration, and infrastructure: its work on the fourteen-lane Delhi–Meerut Expressway helped commuters cut a forty-five-minute journey to eight minutes when Prime Minister Narendra Modi opened it in May 2018. The 24,000-person business made BKG, who avoids publicity and calls himself 'a simple merchant on a global scale', a dollar billionaire, ranked eighty-third on the 2015 *Forbes* India Rich List with an estimated personal wealth of $1.37 billion. But he failed to make the list the following year: the Egyptian cotton scandal was estimated by *Forbes* to have cost him $600 million personally.

In an improvised war room at HQ, BKG knew instantly that the only survival strategy was to take full responsibility for the situation. 'The route we took was "go ahead and own it",' says Dipali Goenka, who speaks quietly and deliberately. She and BKG have two daughters, and in addition to heading the textiles business she oversees the group's philanthropic efforts, such as a Welspun-sponsored high school in Vidya Mandir, Anjar. 'We told our other customers we would take full responsibility for the issue. It could have been easy for us to disown it, but they respected us as we went personally to meet each and every one. We said we'd come back with a system that would change the whole paradigm.'

The board appointed the global accounting firm EY to examine its supply chain and clarify what had gone wrong. EY's team was experienced in ensuring traceability in the pharmaceutical and automobile industries, and had studied crises relating to the authenticity of sources in tuna and teak. But the cotton supply chain is far more complex than tuna's: Welspun identified seventeen distinct steps between the farm and the finished sheet, with eight steps in the spinning process alone. At each step, a middleman can in theory introduce ingredients that are not what they seem.

'We were depending on our vendors to buy not only cotton but fibres and yarn, and they in turn would depend on multiple vendors,' says Jiwani. The board immediately decided that Welspun needed to consolidate its entire manufacturing process in-house, vertically integrating under its own factory roofs every step from spinning to weaving. It would no longer buy yarn or fibres, procuring only the raw cotton externally. But there was a further challenge. Even if it sourced raw cotton in Egypt, there was a possibility that it had in fact been imported from neighbouring countries and mislabelled. How could Welspun know that its Egyptian cotton was actually grown in Egypt?

Egyptian cotton has unusually long fibres which typically ensure a lighter, finer, more durable fabric than other cotton. But Egypt's cotton production has been falling for more than a decade. In 2016–17, according to the US Department of Agriculture, Egyptian output was just 160,000 480-pound bales of cotton, down from 1.4 million bales in 2004–05. And that lack of output has affected supply-chain integrity. 'We have taken samples from all over the world and found that a big percentage of what is labelled "Egyptian cotton" is not,' Khaled Schuman, executive director of the Cotton Egypt Association, told the magazine *Home & Textiles Today* in March 2016. It was an ominous observation that foretold the scandal that was to hit one of the world's biggest cotton buyers just five months later.

In addition to EY, Welspun took informal advice from consultancies such as KPMG and PricewaterhouseCoopers. It also consulted a media agency, but decided that its communications should be aimed at retail customers and investors rather than the wider public. That strategy carried its own risks: the Monday evening after the Target statement, Welspun invited its bankers to a meeting to explain everything it knew. 'Next day the media reported "Bankers summon Welspun",' Jiwani tells me, exasperated. 'We voluntarily invited them!'

Dipali Goenka's US tour seemed to be reassuring retailers. Some decided to relabel the disputed items; some offered discounts; some withdrew them from sale. The offer to cover their full costs reinforced goodwill; the company believed that it could over time rebuild all its key relationships, if not the one with Target. It had also bought time, maybe a year, to show the retailers that it had confronted and eradicated the problem with what it promised would be an industry-leading solution.

For that, it turned to a forty-six-year industry veteran who knew more about cotton than anyone in its network. Anil Channa, sixty-nine, had retired as Welspun's executive director of operations, managing its textile production in Anjar, where annual fabric output was worth $600 million. A hardcore operations man, he'd also spent part of his career at the Indian Institute of Technology

Delhi, and still lectures to final-year students. Channa was brought back and asked to build the industry's most advanced system for authenticating and tracking cotton. He knew that would require a substantial investment in technology.

'We pack close to half a million pieces a day,' Channa explains over pizza around the meeting-room table. 'It's not manually possible to keep track of half a million pieces. That's more than 5,000 product lines. It's an enormous task!'

The company's rapid expansion had vastly expanded the supply chain without systematically capturing data at each stage. That was complicated by the intricate process of refining cotton: numerous bales get converted into a single bundle of fabric, but that fabric then gets turned into many sheets or towels, each of which needs to be traced. Channa saw a solution in RFID – the tiny radio-frequency identification tags that can be attached to a physical item (say, a public-transport smart card) and scanned throughout its life cycle to establish its authenticity. If cotton bales are tagged on the farm, that cotton can be tracked from farm to gin, from gin to yarn, from yarn to fabric, from fabric to stitching.

Thus was born Wel-Trak, a patented tracking system that automatically captures data using RFID/barcode at every step. Channa talks about Welspun's new 'global cotton integrity process': bales are tagged where they're grown, by certified cotton ginners; each bin in the warehouse is tracked; after cotton is stretched to become yarn, the yarn pallet is tagged; fabrics too are tagged on production and scanned each time they are bleached or dyed. A QR code is available as an option to be attached to the final product so the consumer can snap it with their phone camera to trace the item's entire manufacturing journey. 'This is now live,' Channa says proudly. 'We built it in just six months. And already some of our retailers are offering this. We've been offering them entire data dumps.'

His team worked with an external RFID specialist but built the real-time database software in-house. Channa won't share the total investment, but describes it as 'not humungous'. The main expense was connecting a network of scanners. Some lessons were learned by studying how the food industry tracks ingredient origins – but food, Channa says, typically passes through a far simpler supply chain. 'We've never come across an example where what you're tracking changes from agricultural product to manufacturing product to a consumer product. The form of our underlying product changes at every stage.'

Welspun also signed an exclusive five-year contract with Oritain Global, a New Zealand company that uses lab-based chemical analysis to identify the geographic origin of natural materials. Oritain had previously worked with food companies, a healthcare business and a merino-wool fashion brand to authenticate products using a form of chemical fingerprinting. Cotton has a distinct characteristic according to its growth region that's measurable in up to forty-five elements, and Oritain's tests in independent labs can identify the origins of the growth centre for Egyptian cotton, Australian cotton, or American Supima, a high-quality US-grown variety.

By now, the industry was becoming curious. 'We went to the Heimtextil trade fair in Frankfurt in January 2018, and I've never seen our stall so busy,' Channa remembers. 'Traceability was the buzzword of the whole fair.' One major retailer even sent three representatives to Welspun's stand unannounced to investigate the new approach.

The simplest option for Welspun once the scandal broke would have been to exit the luxury Egyptian cotton market altogether. After all, at just 6 per cent of revenue, it meant that 94 per cent derived from wholly uncontroversial product lines. But something interesting happened on the journey to full traceability: Welspun discovered that consumers more generally were demanding greater transparency about where their fabrics originated, and some were prepared to pay a premium to know.

The evidence was persuasive if anecdotal. In 2016, Fashion Revolution, a UK social enterprise, claimed to have reached 129 million impressions through 70,000 posts using the Twitter hashtag #whomademyclothes. A year later its campaign claimed 533 million impressions, with 2,000 clothing brands providing details of their workforce using #Imadeyourclothes. Social media was forcing unprecedented openness on an industry that in the past has been mired in scandals over poor working conditions, factory pollution, even child labour. Over that year, the number of brands Fashion Revolution found disclosing at least some supply-chain details had risen from 29 to 106. Campaign groups and blockchain startups were meanwhile promoting greater consumer awareness about supply-chain integrity. The Sustainable Apparel Coalition publicized poor workplace conditions in fashion manufacturing and the use of toxic chemicals; Sourcemap open-sourced supply-chain information for companies such as Eileen Fisher and Mars; a startup called Provenance worked with Unilever to track its tea sourcing using a blockchain; and the Blockchain Supply Chain Traceability Project, from the World Wide Fund for Nature (WWF), tracked Pacific tuna to highlight illegal fishing and slave labour.

An ethical-fashion movement was growing, and a number of fashion brands were already driving market advantage by making transparency a central part of their story. Everlane, a fast-growing San Francisco clothing startup, was publishing factory and ingredient-cost information for its products; Icebreaker, in New Zealand, put a 'Baa Code' on its merino jumpers for customers to scan and discover which sheep farm produced the wool. It also published a Transparency Report which disclosed every supplier and partner at each stage of the supply chain. Even multinational clothing companies such as Esprit and Gap were openly listing their Chinese suppliers alongside factory environmental records on a supply-chain map developed by the US Natural Resources Defense Council and the Beijing-based Institute of Public & Environmental Affairs.

The towel and bed-linen sector had been slow to adapt to this emerging consumer demand. Now Welspun found itself with a defensible market advantage. 'Wel-Trak in itself can become a big revenue stream for us,' Altaf Jiwani says. 'The trends we're observing in the US, where consumers are demanding specific fibres, make Wel-Trak the automatic choice. And we're the leader, the first to enter this market.'

He shows me a new private-label product for the US chain Kohl's, called SV. It has a Wel-Trak logo on the paper tag. 'This entire business, which was not one of our labels, is now available to us,' Jiwani says. 'That's our patented solution, which no other player can offer, so it's creating market entry for us.' Welspun realized that its verification model could in fact be applied to any kind of fibre. 'Organic fibre, for instance – how do you give assurance to the wealthier customer? They're looking for traceability. Which is now called Wel-Trak.'

Three retailers launched with Wel-Trak in autumn 2018, and Welspun ran an ad campaign in the US educating consumers about the brand. Anil Channa sees this as a smart investment in positioning the company as the default provider of farm-to-fabric data. 'A stage will come when regulators will demand this level of transparency in our industry, maybe in three or five years,' he says. 'Millennials will push them. It's already happening in food. And we need to cater for that.'

The company is also exploring how a blockchain might link farmers and factory. It has launched a project among Indian farmers with small-holdings who record on a blockchain where each batch of cotton is grown, how it is transported, where it goes next. 'It's a small experiment,' says Channa. 'But blockchain is where the world is heading.'

In the meantime, Channa tells me, the company is confident that it has cleaned up its supply chain. 'We sleep well as we're not scared that something can go wrong. It's absolutely authentic, we're vertically integrated now, and everything is tracked under Wel-Trak. Eventually the whole industry will follow.'

There's been a cultural shift within Welspun, too. 'The internal view now is that we need to pursue transparency in whatever we do and how we conduct ourselves,' says Keyur Parekh, whose business card calls him 'Vice President of Sheets'. 'It's not only about the product, but about waste – we've started doing product life-cycle analysis, mapping where we're consuming more energy, what's our impact on the environment. We're making sustainability as transparent as possible. And we're at the starting point.'

Slowly, markets are starting to notice. A Credit Suisse report in April 2018 noted that Welspun's share price would be hit by a revenue fall of 5 to 8 per cent in the financial year 2018, but a recovery in 2019 should bring '15 per cent revenue growth'. When I visit, the share price has edged up to 66 rupees; some analysts covering the company have a target price of 85. Welspun isn't yet negotiating to bring Target back: there are the class-action lawsuits to resolve first. But conversations with Target will begin 'very soon', Jiwani assures me.

I ask him if perhaps he may one day look back gratefully on the crisis. He laughs. 'You know, nobody wants this kind of crisis. But you're right, if it had not taken place, we wouldn't have focused on traceability. And the crisis helped us crash the timeline. In a normal course, this solution would have taken three years to launch. It got crashed into six months.' And, he adds, the business is definitely healthier than before the crisis. 'The moment retailers start looking at Wel-Trak for other fibres, it will open up opportunities we hadn't even thought of – in organic, Turkish, Supima cotton. More importantly, it's been patented. It's very difficult to copy.'

Dipali Goenka quietly reflects on how Welspun India has changed since August 2016. 'It's made us a stronger, more resilient company,' she says after a pause. 'Like a phoenix – from the ashes she rises. It's been tough. I didn't get much sleep . . . for two years. But it was the natural choice. The millennials are looking at the authenticity of the products they use, looking for a responsible company they want to buy from, looking at traceability. And we're the industry's torchbearer.'

Action Points

Two years after facing an existential crisis over its luxury-cotton supply chain, Welspun India emerged with renewed confidence and a growing market share (despite losing a major American customer), with its factories working at 100 per cent capacity. It has also positioned itself as a leader in the nascent market for transparently sourced textiles. Here are some ways management used the urgency of a crisis to build future-facing value:

1. Rapid decision-making. Welspun was quick to take responsibility for the problem, clear in offering to compensate customers fully, and firm in its early resolve to invest significant resources in rebuilding trust. Investors, bankers and retail partners were invited to meetings within days, even when there was limited information to share.

2. Think ambitiously. The challenge of authenticating Egyptian cotton was relatively straightforward to solve. But investing in technology to trace raw ingredients more generally through the manufacturing process required a more focused strategy. It would also have far wider potential applications.

3. Authenticity. The leadership understood that it would be judged on its commitment to making long-term changes, and not simply using marketing

tools to signal transformation. So it introduced multiple layers of verification to minimize any future chance of losing track of its raw materials. At the factories, a manager was assigned responsibility for both purchase and tracking of cotton. At head office, a team was put in charge of monitoring practices at manufacturing level. And a third level of defence was to engage with third parties, such as independent auditors, who were given the freedom to ask whatever probing questions they wanted.

4. Cultural alignment. A campaign to become the Indian textile industry's most transparent manufacturer would have failed without the company's leadership and board being absolutely behind it. Family-controlled businesses such as Welspun have an advantage: they can define internal expectations and values, with the board's support, that staff then rally behind. The Goenkas had always positioned Welspun India as taking a leadership role in the industry; that made it easier to stand publicly for higher standards of sourcing integrity.

5. Clear communication. Welspun knew that survival would depend on telling an honest story to consumers and retail partners, as well as acting with integrity. It prioritized transparency in explaining how its products are made and the seventeen-step process of fabric manufacture. As it soon learned, there are no longer any secrets in an age when activist consumer organizations are sharing vast databases of on-the-ground research.

6. Lean on influential friends. Welspun appointed a council made up of prominent industry experts in cotton, branding and supply chains, and brought them in to oversee the entire manufacturing and sourcing process. They were then asked to present their findings to retailers. It was another aspect of third-party validation that helped restore the industry's confidence.

LAST WORD

Reflecting on an innovation quest

When Thomas Buberl took over Europe's second-biggest insurance firm in September 2016, he declared one strategic priority: 'How do we transform our business?' AXA, then a 200-year-old, 165,000-person conglomerate based in Paris, had grown by acquisition over three decades from a small mutual insurer into a global player – a health-care provider, an investment manager and financial services giant. Insurance remained largely an opaquely priced grudge purchase to protect against uncertain risks, yet digitally engaged consumers increasingly expected a seamless online service priced personally as new sources of data quantified their individual risk. 'Today our competition is [the insurers] Allianz and Generali, but tomorrow it could be Google and Facebook,' Buberl told the *Financial Times*. His focus would therefore be 'on transforming the business model for a digital future'.

The challenges confronting Buberl, then forty-three, were not unlike those facing the leaders of any legacy business, whether in media, manufacturing or medical devices. A multilayered, top-down corporate structure, incentivized to meet the stock market's short-term revenue demands, typically struggles to move fast when emerging technologies transform economic realities and customer expectations. A company's history, brand recognition and credit-worthiness count for little if an agile, tech-focused startup can recognize and respond more quickly to this new customer demand. Buberl knew he was in a race against time to change AXA's culture if it were to remain competitive as new digital-only competitors grew their market share. To succeed, AXA would need to put the customer first as it embarked on its own digital journey.

Buberl, who had been running AXA's German business, signalled the urgency when he was applying for the top job. The business model, he wrote in a manifesto, must move 'from payer to partner' – accelerating business innovation, as he put it, to meet customers' rapidly evolving needs in the digital world, and not simply selling them policies but finding new ways to keep them healthy and safe. AXA would achieve this by 'improving the customer journey' through automating processes, making better use of data, and exploring new business models. But first Buberl needed to shock the system. He cut staff and slashed budgets at head office, gave more autonomy to local managers, and announced a five-year plan that would cut €2.1 billion in costs. The company would also allocate €200 million each year to 'innovation acquisitions' – buying tech companies in the hope of accelerating the transformation.

Can this strategy deliver results before the digitally native insurers eat AXA's lunch? It's early in the transformation process, but I'm curious to see what's happening inside AXA's headquarters. So I visit its offices on the Avenue Matignon in the 8th arrondissement of Paris, where symbols of Buberl's intentions are hard to miss. Above a courtyard in the reception area, prominent signs display the company's updated values: 'Customer First . . . Courage . . . Integrity . . . One AXA'. In the office where I meet Astrid Stange, the chief operating officer, a Facebook wall poster declares 'Move fast and break things'. This is not a mindset normally associated with an insurer – and that's the point.

Stange, a former Boston Consulting Group consultant whom Buberl promoted from within the German business, describes herself as 'a business enabler' who is helping the company figure out what 'customer first' means. She has a €3 billion budget and runs a team of 8,000, but before they can transform the business, she says, there needs to be a cultural change inside AXA. 'In five years' time, selling policies won't be what we do – customers never loved this product,' she tells me. 'Instead, they want safety, people taking care of them. So how do we find new business models and get our teams to move there?'

Much of that challenge falls to Guillaume Borie, AXA's thirty-two-year-old chief innovation officer. Borie oversees what he calls the company's 'innovation ecosystem'. This includes a unit called Kamet, which launches new digital insurance startups from offices in Paris, London and Tel Aviv (or, in Kamet's own buzzword-packed description, it's an 'insurtech startup studio building disruptive companies from the ground up'). Kamet companies have so far included a virtual fertility clinic, an app for car servicing, and an insurance robo-adviser. Borie also oversees a €450 million venture-capital fund, AXA Venture Partners, which invests up to €20 million in tech companies relevant to insurance and asset management. And he manages a €200 million annual budget to spend on 'innovation'. AXA recently bought Maestro Health, a US health benefits administration company, for a reported $155 million.

Borie talks a lot about building new services that will re-engage customers and about removing pain points in their interactions with AXA. He too says it will require a change in the company's culture to succeed, with staff needing to be more open to new ideas, and more empowered to take decisions. But his job title worries me. It takes me back to Innova-Con, the International Association of Innovation Professionals' conference in Washington DC, where my journey began and where – for all the heads of innovation in the room – I learned precious little about any actual corporate transformation they had achieved. Isn't 'chief innovation officer' the wrong title, I suggest to Borie, as it deflects responsibility for change from the rest of the company? He pauses, and after a moment replies, 'I agree – innovation is everyone's job.'

Therein lies the challenge. Innovation isn't about labs or acquisition funds or job titles or conference keynotes. It's about embedding a culture within an organization that enables internal teams to think and execute quickly and iteratively like the most effective startups. And I fear that AXA, for all Buberl's efforts, still has too many comfortably profitable old business lines, hierarchical management layers, historic legacy computing systems, shareholder expectations and assumed ways of doing things to be comfortable moving fast and breaking things.

After my visit, I speak to Jean-Charles Samuelian, co-founder and CEO of a fast-growing two-year-old French health insurance startup called Alan, which is taking direct aim at AXA with clear pricing, transparent reimbursement policies and a technology-first mindset. Alan has quickly built a reputation for creating compelling user experiences, and after raising $41 million in investment is about to grow from twenty-five staff to eighty in just a few months. A big 200-year-old company like AXA, Samuelian says, is in denial about the threat it faces from startups as it lacks the signals to perceive the dangers. 'Even if they sense that there's a market being built by new players, all their financial key performance indicators tend to remain the same, as they've already made long-term plans.'

I ask Samuelian what he would do if he were in Buberl's shoes. He laughs: 'I'm not sure I'd want that job.' But, he says, he would try to identify areas where AXA is most vulnerable to digital competitors at the edges, because changes in customer behaviour can become huge threats within just a few years. 'And I'd break my insurance organization, because at Alan we're not defined by all the arcane rules of the insurance business. We see ourselves as a product and tech business that happens to offer insurance, and four-fifths of our team come from outside the insurance world – with engineers from the Valley and from the best companies in France. The best software engineers in the world will never go to AXA.'

And that, essentially, is Buberl's challenge. Today, when a small, nimble team of exceptional software engineers can build products that quickly attract millions of customers, an incumbent needs to position itself as an agile tech company, no matter what industry it is in. Of the businesses I visited for this book, those best able to adapt to new digital realities seem to share a few common traits. Typically they empower small, self-determined internal teams to discover and then respond to evolving customer needs. They understand that their ability to recruit, motivate and retain world-class talent is their greatest asset. They remain curious and outward-looking, constantly questioning and learning, fighting arrogance or complacency. They test their assumptions and rely on feedback to iterate at every step. They prioritize customers' needs over their own internal goals. They look beyond today's business models and products in an effort to understand emerging market trends. They challenge hierarchical structures and bureaucratic thinking, which slow decisions and create aversion to risk. They are tolerant when bold initiatives fail, as long as lessons are learned. They tend to have ownership structures that protect them from short-term market demands. They don't see 'innovation' as the responsibility of a particular individual or team. They enable cross-disciplinary working and hybrid thinking. They have a strong sense of company purpose and an articulated set of values. And mostly, they nurture a culture that constantly incentivizes and rewards internal entrepreneurship.

These are attributes more commonly found in the most success-ful tech startups than in incumbent businesses. In 2014, Tony Fadell sold Nest Labs, his four-year-old company making internet-connected devices such as thermostats and smoke alarms, to Google for $3.2 billion. Part of that success came from his decision to embed a startup culture that he had found lacking in his previous roles at Apple.

Fadell is sometimes called the 'father of the iPod': after joining Apple in 2001 he designed the business plan, oversaw the hardware and software architecture, and led the teams that shipped eighteen generations of the iPod. In nine years at Apple he also played a leading role in developing and shipping the first three iterations of the iPhone. But Steve Jobs's centralized control often frustrated the talent, he told me when I interviewed him before the sale in 2014. At Apple, he said, teams rarely felt they had ownership of their project, even if they came up with the original idea. In meetings, Jobs would often put down people's suggestions and make them feel disempowered. Fadell was striving for the opposite at Nest.

At one stage, he said, he even had to go behind Jobs's back to do what he felt was the right thing for the iPod business: allow iPods to work with PCs as well as Macs. 'Steve said, "Over my dead body are you going to put the iPod on the PC" – he said it would kill Mac sales, that iPod was the only reason people were going to buy Macs. So I had a secret skunkworks team making the whole PC connectivity happen. He wouldn't allow it.' It took two years, but Fadell's defiance was vindicated: once the iPod worked with PCs, sales took off.

Defiance is a tough quality for a corporate environment to tolerate for long. Fadell left Google abruptly in 2016 amid internal complaints about his own leadership style. At the time, Fadell published a blog post explaining that his departure had been planned for some time, as he wanted 'the time and flexibility to pursue new opportunities to create and disrupt other industries'. But a culture that empowers staff certainly correlates strongly with innovation-led performance. Patrick and John Collison, brothers from Limerick in Ireland, set up a digital payments company, Stripe, in 2010 to help businesses overcome the frustrations of working with the big banks. From the start they made it a priority to attract and empower the best talent. They codified their values in an internal document shared with all recruits, known as 'Stripes', called 'A Quick Guide to Stripe's Culture'. Many of these values could benefit other types of business. To quote a few examples:

> Because Stripe is highly interdependent, really good Stripes have
> a strong sense of overall ownership of the whole company but
> are non-territorial regarding their nominal domains. There are no
> bonus points for building large teams.

> We expect a lot of autonomy from Stripes both in the work they
> do and in their own development. We believe in performance

management and feedback, but we're not rigid in terms of a career path and box checking. That said, don't confuse lack of top-down direction with lack of interest from the top: high performers are recognized, enabled, and rewarded.

We care about being right and it often takes reasoning from first principles to get there. Rigour doesn't mean not-invented-here syndrome. We're interested in the world around us and think that other companies, industries and academic fields have much to teach us. We actively hunt in other fields for inspiration and ideas that challenge our assumptions and that we could learn from.

Move with urgency and focus. We don't track hours and we don't care about unnecessary face-time. Stripes have great flexibility around when and where they work because they know best what's needed to get their job done.

The Collisons raised $245 million in funding in September 2018, on top of $440 million previously raised, at a $20 billion valuation. That's what happens when a financial services business doesn't think like a legacy bank.

There's one final quality I've observed in the smartest leaders who manage to achieve genuine innovation inside their organizations. They see themselves primarily as running technology companies, whatever the nature of their business. If you had made an investment in Apple or Google shares between 2010 and mid-2018, you would be sitting on a return of around 420 per cent. An investment in Amazon over that period would have brought 1,500 per cent, and in Netflix 2,400 per cent. But for a 2,500 per cent return, you would have had to take a bet on a pizza business. Domino's Pizza has proved the stand-out success of the US stock market over the past decade – and that, according to former CEO Patrick Doyle, comes down to being 'as much a tech company as we are a pizza company'.

Doyle took over in 2010, when the company had a reputation for unappetizing pizzas, poor customer service and a lacklustre brand. Doyle realized that delivery logistics were as important as the food, and invested heavily in software and analytics to digitize operations and customer service. He wanted to make it as easy as possible for customers to order, whether through the Domino's app, via Twitter or Siri, even by texting a pizza-slice emoji. They could customize a pizza online and then track each stage of its preparation and delivery. By 2015, a J.P. Morgan analyst was advising clients, 'We have found ourselves describing the "new" Domino's as a technology company disguised as a marketing company disguised as a pizza company, and recent years of dominant outperformance . . . probably bears that comment as true.'

At the same time, Domino's reinvigorated the brand by openly acknowledging its poor food quality and its intention to turn the business around. Doyle appeared in unusually transparent television ads in which he shared comments from customers denouncing 'the worst pizza I ever had' or a sauce that 'tastes like ketchup'. Customers, he declared, had to be at the centre of the business.

When I meet Andre Ten Wolde, Domino's chief operating officer in Europe, it's like talking to the excitable founder of a robotics startup. He explains his plans to launch drone delivery in Europe as well as to give customers the ability to order physical pizzas in virtual-reality settings. 'Everything starts with curiosity outside your hemisphere,' he says. He gives all staff a notebook that he calls the Bad Ideas Book, and rewards them for submitting ideas, even bad ones, that can improve the customer experience. He encourages local teams to prototype and experiment in public, just as software startups do. 'We show a pizza that doesn't yet exist to 10 per cent of website customers to see if they want it,' he says. 'If they order, we apologize that we don't have that and give them a free pizza instead. We test names and prices of pizzas in a similar way. I'm a really big fan of prototyping.' This data-led, customer-centric approach has delivered astounding results.

When Doyle became CEO, the share price was below $9; as I write, it is above $300.

I did not, on my travels, discover evidence that innovation can be reduced to a scientific formula. But I regularly found, in visiting established but troubled organizations, that human biases can be innovation's greatest inhibitors. As machine learning, nanotechnology, genomics, additive manufacturing and endless other emerging technologies threaten today's business models, the biggest risk is to assume time is on your side.

Occasionally during my quest, a conversation with a relaxed, even complacent, senior company executive would bring to mind a now notorious editorial published in the *New York Times* on 9 October 1903. The article, headlined 'Flying Machines Which Do Not Fly', was written after a reporter witnessed a failed attempt by aviation pioneer Samuel Pierpont Langley to create 'a powered, heavier-than-air machine that could achieve controlled, sustained flight with a pilot aboard'. Langley's aircraft, the *Aerodrome*, crashed as it attempted to fly over the Potomac River in Maryland – 'a ridiculous fiasco', the newspaper reported. 'It might be assumed that the flying machine which will really fly might be evolved by the combined and continuous efforts of mathematicians and mechanicians in from one million to ten million years,' it predicted '– provided, of course, we can meanwhile eliminate such little drawbacks and embarrassments as the existing relation between weight and strength in inorganic materials.'

That very day, Orville Wright, who just weeks later would successfully fly an aircraft with his brother Wilbur at Kitty Hawk in North Carolina, wrote in his diary: 'We started assembly today.'

ACKNOWLEDGEMENTS

I could not have told these stories without the thoughtfulness, generosity, smart thinking and kindness of so many people who offered suggestions, introductions, feedback and insights. I'm grateful to you all and take sole responsibility for any inadvertent bullshit that may have sullied these pages. I offer particular thanks to:

At Penguin Random House: Susanna Wadeson, Helena Gonda, Larry Finlay, Gail Rebuck, Patsy Irwin, Tim Bainbridge, Josh Benn, Joshua Crosley, Ella Horne, Emma Burton, Chloe Johnson-Hill, Helen Edwards, Bethan Moore, Daniel Balado, Vanessa Bird. I've learned so much about the craft of storytelling from working with an amazing team of professionals.

The terrific agents I have the good fortune to work with, including Adrian Sington at Kruger Cowne, who took a proposal and made it real; to my speaking agents who despatch me to places where compelling stories seem to lurk, not least Don Walker, Tatiana Duus and Emily Trievel of the Harry Walker Agency; Leo von Bülow-Quirk of VBQ Speakers; the teams at the London Speaker Bureau; Chartwell; Speakers Corner; JLA; Speakers Associates; Kruger Cowne; Leading Authorities; and more.

At Condé Nast: Jonathan Newhouse, Nicholas Coleridge and Albert Read gave me a dream opportunity to launch a UK version of the world's greatest magazine about technology and ideas. There are no greater practitioners of magazine craft and it was a privilege to work for them for eight years, expanding the brand into a healthy digital, events and consulting business. Condé Nast is a very special company driven by creative excellence and world-class talent in every department. I'm particularly grateful to my *WIRED* colleagues on the editorial and commercial teams. Some of these case studies are adapted from stories I originally wrote for *WIRED*, and for permission to include them I'm grateful to Harriet Wilson. WIRED © The Condé Nast Publications Ltd.

At the International Association of Innovation Professionals: Brett Trusko, Abram Walton, Kirsten Trusko, John Wolverton, Jon Monett, Magnus Penker

At Hotstar: Ajit Mohan, Varun Narang

At the National History Museum: Vince Smith, Piers Jones, Kate Fielding, Harriet Brooks, Helen Hardy, Nathan Good, Celena Bretton, Dave Thomas, Hannah-Fleur Fitz-Rankin, Simon Patterson

At the NRMA: Rohan Lund, Bernhard Conoplia, Sam Taranto, Peter Colacino, Rob Giltinan, Harris Hutkin, Nadia McCrohon, Peter Khoury, Melanie Kansil, Tony Tamine, Sophie Isaac

At Intercorp: Carlos Rodríguez-Pastor, Hernán Carranza, Jorge Yzusqui, Andrea Portugal, Aurelia Alvarado, César Andrade, Ricardo Terukina, Juan Pablo Florez, Giancarlo Secco, Gino Abram, Jonathan Golergant, Jorge O'Hara, Flor Calderón, Rafael Dasso, Alessandra Corrochano, Carlos Tori, Alfonso Diaz, Úrsula Gamio, Oscar Malaspina, Maria Paula Loayza, Eduardo Marisca, Maria Fernanda Gómez

At ARUP: Tristram Carfrae, Dinesh Patel, Sarah Glover, Chris Luebkeman, Aisha Babb, Amy Lewis, Fiona Cousins

ACKNOWLEDGEMENTS

At the McGee Group: Jim Mackey

At Supercell: Ilkka Paananen, Linda Åström, Tiina Oikarainen, Alexander Patouchas, Timur Haussila, Jonathan Dower

At Defense Digital Service: Chris Lynch, Tim Van Name, Nicole Camarillo, Hunter Price, Sharon Woods, Will Gamble, Paul Tagliamonte, Harlan Lieberman-Berg, Danielle Griffith, Reina Staley, Lisa Wiswell, Alex Romero, Patrick Stoddart, Jyn Erso Program members who remain unnamed

At OP: Tom Dahlström, Masa Peura, Samuli Saarni, Nina Vesaniemi, Sonja Heikkilä, Jarkko Kyttänen, Kristian Luoma, Riina Kruut, Tuomas Manninen, Meeri Haataja, Johanna Kaijansinkko

At Heywood Hill: Nicky Dunne, Andrew Turton, Laura Scully and team

At X: Astro Teller, Obi Felten, Kathy Hannun, Libby Leahy

At Hatch Labs: Dinesh Moorjani, Whitney Wolfe

At Arsenal Football Club: Hywel Sloman

At L Marks: Daniel Saunders, Jess McGahan

At The Bridge: Gabby Czertok

At Co:Cubed: Jeremy Basset; at Diageo, Camilla Goodwin, Ajay Arora and Daniel Hatton

In Dubai: Walid Tarabih, HE Omar Sultan AlOlama, Khalfan Juma Belhoul, Abdulaziz AlJaziri, Maryam Al Hammadi, Atraf Shehab, Noah Raford, Mohamed Bintaliah, Chetan Choudhury

In Estonia: Kaspar Korjus, Linnar Viik, Taavet Hinrikus, Sten-Kristian Saluveer, Arnaud Castaignet, Benjamin Bathke

At Autodesk: Andrew Anagnost, Jeff Kowalski, Erin Bradner, Mickey McManus, Tom Wujec, Maurice Conti, Andrew Hessel, Jon Pittman, Scott Sheppard, Callan Carpenter, Lining Yao, Jana Hildebrand

At Ule: Solina Chau, Wendy Yu, Samson Yeung, Ken Yeung, Chen Qing, Han Guo Min, Lou Wener, Kerry Liu, Simon Loong

At ABB: Guido Jouret, Rami-Johan Jokela, Otto Preiss, Peter Maritz, Blair Hickey, Kay Watanabe, Simone Arnitz, Ray Bertschler

At the Crick: David King, Robyn Gilmour

At the MIT Media Lab: Joi Ito, Nicholas Negroponte, Canan Dagdeviren, Fadel Adib, Kevin Esvelt, Caleb Harper, Alexandra Kahn

At the Downtown Project: Tony Hsieh, Michael Downs, Megan Fazio

At Qantas: Andrew McGinnes, Christine Musumeci, Jessica Richards, Lesley Grant, Olivia Wirth, Brian Funston

At BCG: Tom von Oertzen, Simon MacGibbon, Gustav Gotteberg

At Xiaomi: Lei Jun, Kaylene Hong, Liu De, Hugo Barra, Li Ming, Louie Gao

At Shinho: Matilda Ho

At EOS: Edmar Allitsch, Claudia Jordan

At Hestan Smart Cooking: Vincent Cheng, Stanley Cheng, Philip Tessier, Christoph Milz, the kitchen team

At Yara: Svein Flatebø, Bjørn Tore Orvik, Petter Østbø, Kristin Nordal

At HTC: Cher Wang, Phil Chen, Florence Wu, Edith Yeung, Chris McCann

At Naspers: Shamiela Letsoalo, Lizette Rabe, Koos Bekker, Ton Vosloo, Bob van Dijk, James Allen, Meyke de Vries, Karen Roos

At MTR: Steve Yiu, Jeremy Austin, Aylan Aliyeva

At Axa: Thomas Buberl, Emmanuel Touzeau, Astrid Stange, Guillaume Borie, Romain Champetier, Bernadette Cichostepski

At Welspun: Dipali Goenka, Altaf Jiwani, Anil Channa, Keyur Parekh, Jaswinder Manchanda, Apurva Sharma, Sunil Gate

At IDEO: Sandy Speicher, Whitney Mortimer, Alice Huang, Charles Hayes, Paul Bennett, Sephora Woldu, Ariel Pan, Lindsey Armeen, Katrin Klausecker

At Spotify: Daniel Ek

At Dropbox: Drew Houston

At WhatsApp: Jan Koum, Brian Acton, Neeraj Arora

And for all sorts of other help, suggestions and guidance: Rachel Botsman; Phoebe Hugh; Helmut Schönenberger; Kathryn Nave; Nathalie Kåvin at Schibsted; Dharmash Mistry; Amol Sarva; Eliza Dabney; Oliver Lewis; Eze Vidra; Catherine Tan; Christina

Bisgaard and Simon Haldrup at Danske Bank; Dimitris Kalavros-Gousiou; Steffi Czerny and the DLD team; Brent Hoberman, Jonnie Goodwin and the Founders Forum team; Yossi Vardi; Paddy Cosgrave and the Founders team; Chris Anderson, Bruno Giussani and the TED team; Mishika Kochar; Barbara Belvisi; Greg Brandeau; Rohan Silva and Karin Killander at Second Home; Slava Rubin; Antoine Blondeau; Jean-Charles Samuelian; Tony Fadell; Andre Ten Wolde

And not least to Sarah Harris, Claudia Rowan, Joe Rowan and Charlie Rowan. Thank you for everything.

I'm at davidrowan.com and on Twitter at @iRowan

INDEX

#Imadeyourclothes 340
#whomademyclothes 340

ABB Ability 217, 219
ABB Group 216–19, 220–1
Abu Dhabi 151
Abu Dhabi Innovation Index 159
Accenture 90, 254
Acton, Brian 33, 34
Adams, Tony 135
Additive Minds 278
Adib, Fadel 229
Adidas 248
Adly 131
A/D/O 236
Aeroster 255
Affordable Care Act (2013) 65
Afghanistan 68–9
Afkari 161
African National Congress 316
Aftenposten 292
AFWERX 5
a-ha moments 6
AI (artificial intelligence) 306, 308
    Autodesk 190–2
    IBM 204
    and new revenue models
        81, 102
    OP 100
    Rubikloud 211
    UAE 149–50, 152–5
Airbnb 12, 56, 256
    Burning Man 232, 233
    insurance 99
    Qantas Loyalty 248
Airbus 139, 194–5
Alan 349
aLavaderia 140

Alibaba 272
    base 214
    bug bounties 61
    'ecosystems' 275
    success of 216, 280
    transactions 216, 271
Alipay 271
AlJaziri, Abdulaziz 159
Allen, Thomas J. 226
Allen curve 226
Allianz and Generali 346
Allitsch, Edmar 279, 283
AlOlama, Omar Sultan 148,
    149, 150, 152–4
Alpha 121, 199
Alphabet 76, 104, 107, 112, 120, 293
AM Ventures 278–9, 283
Amazon 184, 268, 286, 289
    Amazon Go 307
    Amazon Prime 211
    Amazon Video 15
    book sales 94, 95, 96
    Burning Man 232
    cloud services 300
    companies bought by 237, 267
    as a customer-first
        operation 159
    distribution power 140–1
    Estonian companies 181
    investment in 352
    JEDI contract 74
    success of 258, 275, 352
    'two-pizza rule' 14, 26
    'working backward' process 15
ambitious thinking 343
AMCM (Additive Manufac-
    turing Customized
    Machines) 278

American Express 250
American Telephone &
    Telegraph Company 116
Amnesty International 163
Anagnost, Andrew 192–3, 194,
    202–4, 205
Android 34, 35, 267, 297–9
ANET 69
animation software 187–90
Anjar 335, 336, 337
Annus, Ruth 170
Anolon 286
ANZ 251
App Store 127, 128, 132, 170, 275
Apple 6, 73, 83, 264, 297
    App Store 128, 170, 275
    Cardify 128
    and HTC 298, 299
    iCloud 262
    investment in 352
    iPhone 88, 129, 153, 238–9,
        262–3, 267, 287, 309, 350
    iPods 350, 351
    iTunes 35, 309
    iTV 262
    Mac 351
    mouse design 20
    Wishlist 248
    and Xiaomi 280, 281–2
Apple Park, Cupertino 45
Applied Analysis 240
architecture
    Claridge's 43–8, 58
    Francis Crick Institute 222–6
    workspace architecture
        222–42
Army Cyber Command 68,
    74–5

Army Digital Service 70
Arriva Cuida 28
Arriva Cura 28
Arsenal Football Club 135–7, 146, 147
Arsenal Innovation Lab 136
Arthur D. Little 13, 129
Arup 45–51, 56–8, 226
Arup, Ove 45, 49, 51
Asimov, Isaac 12–13
Ask Jeeves 129
assumptions, challenging 205
AT&T 224, 269, 287
Atlantic Richfield 196
Atlantis 156
Australian PGA Championship 254
authenticity 343–4
AutoCAD 189, 196–8, 203
Autodesk 57, 187–205
    Applied Research Lab 199–201
    Autodesk Inventor 189
    Bio/Nano/Programmable Matter 201–2
    Life Sciences unit 202
autonomous electric ships 292–7, 305
autonomy 77
    ensuring from HQ 122
Avianca 256
Aviation Festival 245
Avis 250
Aviva 28
AXA 346–9
AXA Venture Partners 348

Baa Codes 340
Babbage, Charles 7
Babylonstoren 317
backgrounds, diversity of 261
Badeen, Jonathan 131, 132
Ballmer, Steve 287
Bank of America 30–1, 245
Barclays 222
Barlow, John Perry 176
Barnes & Noble 300
Barra, Hugo 271–2, 282
barriers, internal 59
BASF 217

Basset, Jeremy 139–41
bateriophage 201
battery-powered cargo ships 292–7, 305
BBC 153
BCG, Digital Ventures (BCGDV) 253–4
'beacons' 25–6, 41
Bed Bath & Beyond 332
bedlinen 331–45
Beeld 312
Beijing 45, 50, 262–3, 266, 316, 318, 320
Bekker, Jacobus Petrus (Koos) 311–12, 313, 314, 316, 317–19, 326–7, 328
Belhoul, Khalfan Juma 157–9
Bell, Cressida 96
Bell Labs 116, 123, 224–5
Bennett, Paul 161–2
The Berkeley, London 44
Berners-Lee, Tim 301–2
'Better Homes & Gardens' 334
Bewkes, Jeff 287
Beyoncé 111
Bezos, Jeff 14, 232
Bhowmick, Joyjit 180
Bill Gates School 32
Bird, Brad 229–30
Birkeland, Kristian 292, 294
Bishopsgate development, London 44
Bitcoin 177, 251, 300, 301, 302, 306
Bits x Bites 277, 283
BitTorrent 301
Björk 6
'Black Cab Stout' 92
BlackRock 294
Black Rock City 232–5, 237
Blatt, Greg 144
'blended learning' 20
Blockchain Supply Chain Traceability Project 340
blockchains 178, 180, 287, 300–2, 303–6, 340, 341
Blockfest 91
Bloomberg News 331
Blu Trumpet 127
Blue State Digital 236

Blush 128
BMW 92, 217
Bocuse d'Or 288
bookshop, Heywood Hill 94–8
Boom Beach 52, 55
bootcamps 5
Booz Allen Hamilton Innovation Center 4–5
BoozeBud 255
Borderless accounts 183
Borie, Guillaume 348
Boston Consulting Group 253, 347
Boswell Mitchell & Johnston 225
Botha, P. W. 313
Bradner, Erin 188–9
brand advocates 283
Brandeau, Greg 230–1
Brawl Stars 52, 54
Brexit 181
The Bridge 138
Brin, Sergey 103, 108, 111, 115, 116, 118, 120, 232
British Airways 137–8, 248, 256
British Caledonian 256
BroDown 127
Brownstein, John 226–7
Brunelleschi, Filippo 223
BskyB 37
Buberl, Thomas 346–7, 348, 349
Buddy Healthcare 90
Bugsolutely 277
The Builder 46
Bulb 236
Bumble 142–3
Burberry 140
Burj Khalifa 156
Burning Man 231–5, 236, 239
Business Insider, Ignition conference 133
business models 309–30
Buterin, Vitalik 178, 302
buzzwords 307

Camarillo, Nicole 74–5
Cambridge Analytica 302

Camden Council 225
Canal+ 313, 317
cancer 201, 202, 222, 224
Cancer Research UK 223
Cannes Lions 180
car rental
    National Roads and
        Motorists' Association
        (NRMA) 38
    OP Kausiauto 92
carbon-neutral liquid fuel
    103–6, 121–2
Cardify 126, 128, 131, 132
Carfrae, Tristram 45, 49–51
cargo ships, battery-powered
    292–7, 305
Carranza, Hernán 23, 24–5
Carter, Ash 62
Catmull, Ed 231
Cavendish, Andrew (11th
    Duke of Devonshire) 97
CCTV headquarters, Beijing
    45
Cerebellum Capital 107
CERN 56
Chanel 210–11
change, preparing for 328–9
Channa, Anil 337–9, 341
Chapman, Herbert 137
Charles, Prince 111
Chau, Solina 212
the Cheesegrater, London 44,
    46
Chen, Phil 299–301, 303–4, 305,
    306
Chen Qing 213–15
Cheng, Helen 290
Cheng, Stanley 286, 289,
    290–2, 308
Cheng, Vincent 286, 291
Chesky, Brian 56
China
    Naspers' investment in
        317–18, 323, 327, 330
    Ule 206–16
    Xiaomi 262–75, 280–2
China Eastern Airlines 253
China Mobile Worldwide
    Partner Conference 265
China Money Podcast 281

China Post 207–8, 210, 212,
    213–16, 219–20
Chou, Peter 299
Christensen, Clayton, The
    Innovator's Dilemma 10
Christiansen, Arthur 313
Chronicle 108
Churchill, Winston 43
Cima 27
Cimagine 138
Circulon 286
Cisco 217
Citi 252
Citysearch 129
Civil 3D 189
Claridge's, London 43–8, 58
Clash 54
Clash of Clans 52, 55
Clash Royale 52, 53, 54, 55
Clinton, Hillary 46
cloud computing 202–4
'cloud and crowd' 9
CNBC 287
Co:Cubed 140
co-working spaces 222–42
coalitions 261
Coca-Cola 138
Cole Jarman 225
collaborations 223, 282
Collison, John 351–2
Collison, Patrick 351–2
Comcast Ventures 135
COMDEX 197
communication
    clear 344
    internal 221
community managers 241–2
Condé Nast 259
Congregation Partners 236
The Connaught, London 44
Conoplia, Bernhard 37
ConsenSys 158
Conti, Maurice 199–201
cooking, guided 285–92
cope purpose, identifying
    101–2
'Corona' 92
Corrochano, Ale 27–8
Cortés, Hernán 192
cotton, Egyptian 333–45

Cotton Egypt Association 337
'creative destruction' 9
Credit Suisse Group 256, 342
Crick, Sir Francis 222, 225
crisis management 78
Crossrail 320, 323
Crowdfail 127
'Crown and Ivy' 334
Cruise Automation 293
crypto-cash 304
Crypto Internet 303
cryptocurrency 177–81, 183,
    300–2
cryptography 302
cryptophones 300–6
Cuautitlán Izcalli, Mexico 20
cultural alignment 344
culture
    building 184–5
    diversifying 102
currencies, crypto 177–81, 183,
    300–2
Cushman & Wakefield 235–6
customers
    customers' needs 40–2, 102,
        260, 350
    simplifying experience 185
cybersecurity laws 163
Czertok, Gabby 138, 146, 147

Dagdeviren, Canan 229
Dahlström, Tom 86–8, 94,
    100–1
Daily Express 313
Daily Mail 235
Daimler 139, 181
Dallas Morning News 143
Dandelion Energy 122–3
DApps 303, 304
Daptiv 73
DARPA (Defense Advanced
    Research Projects
    Agency) 12, 62
Dartmouth College 30
Darwin, Charles 12
Dasgupta, Rana 175
Dassault Systèmes 203
data 261
    data analytics 216–20
    data flow 208

Data Republic 250
De Nationale Pers 314
De Nationale Pers Beperkt
    (Naspers) 308–11, 312–20,
    323–7, 328–30
Debreu, Gérard 107
decision-making, speedy 147,
    283, 329, 343
Defense Digital Service
    (DDS) 62–79
Defense.gov 62
defiance 351
Del Monte 229
Deliveroo 325
Delivery Hero 310
Deloitte 169, 177, 182–3
Depp, Johnny 317
Design Graph 196
designathons 5
DeVaul, Rich 104, 123
Devonshire, 12th Duke of 95
DevOps 67–8, 254
DFINITY 300
Diageo 140
Dickerson, Mikey 65
Die Burger 314–15, 323
Die Burger Oos 312
Die Oosterlig 312
difference, points of 166–7
Digital Chocolate 55
digitizing businesses 220–1
Dijk, Bob van 310–11, 324,
    325–6, 328–9
Diller, Barry 128, 129–30, 132
DIMOC.mil 62
Dior 211
Disney 139, 230, 335
DJI 263
DLD Conference 35
Dodgers 258
DoDLive 62
Dole 2
Domino's Pizza 352–4
Dower, Jonathan 51–2, 53, 56
Downs, Michael 240
Downtown Project 237–41
Doyle, Patrick 352–3, 354
Draghi, Mario 178
Dreamcatcher 195–6
DriveNow 92, 93

drone-disabling tools 68, 78–9
Dropbox 35, 39, 64, 232
Drylon 335
DTP Companies 241
Dubai 148–67
Dubai Future Accelerators 155
Dubai Future Foundation
    156–7, 158, 166
Dubai Now 164–5
Dubai Police 155
Dunne, Nicky 95–8
dunnhumby 210, 213
DVIDS 62
DyeMansion 279

e-books 95
E. coli 201
e-commerce 206–16
e-Estonia 182, 184
e-residency 168–86
easyJet 139
eBay 216, 275, 310
    distribution power 140–1
    sellers' fees 271
    Skype 15, 182
    TOM Group 216
ecosystems 275–6, 278, 280–1,
    282
EDlooper 90
education
    Innova Schools 18–22, 32–3,
        40
    Peru 17–22, 31–3, 39–40
Egyptian cotton 338–45
Eileen Fisher 340
Einstein, Albert 4, 228
Eisaman, Matthew 104–5, 106
Ek, Daniel 11–12
Electronic Frontier
    Foundation 176
Electronics 8
Elizabeth II, Queen 43
Elizabeth Line 320, 323
Elle Decoration 317
Embarcadero, San Francisco
    187, 190–4, 199–201
Emerson, Ralph Waldo 29
Emirates airline 155
Emirates NBD 155
Emirates Stadium, London 135

Emirates Towers, Services I
    centre 148–9
Emmer Pfenninger 225
empowerment 58, 260–1
Energy & Environmental Science
    103
Enterprise Estonia 171
EOS (Electro Optical
    Systems) 277–9
epiQure 248, 251
Ernst & Young 235
Erso, Jyn 74
Esprit 340
estcoins 178–80, 186
Estonia 164, 168–86
Estonian Development
    Foundation 170
Estonian e-Governance
    Academy 172
Esvelt, Kevin 229
Ether 300
Ethereum 177, 178, 302, 306
Etheria 303
ethical fashion 340
ethical hackers 61–79
ethos, defining fundamental
    260
euro 178
euro estcoins 179
Europcar 92
European Central Bank 178
Evans, Gareth 245
Evening Standard 144–5
Everlane 340
Exodus phone 303–6, 308
Expedia 129, 258
experimentation 205
    experimental projects 308
EY 336, 337

Facebook 69, 118, 273, 299, 347
    advertising 99, 141
    customers' data 250, 301, 302
    customers' needs 211
    cybersecurity laws 163
    employee handbook 9
    Facebook groups 176, 184
    Facebook Messenger 33
    HTC Facebook phone 297
    insurance 346

Microsoft 136
  staff 14, 15, 271
  startup incubator 204
  success 269, 280
  WhatsApp 34–5
Factorli 239
Fadell, Tony 350–1
failure
  celebrating lessons learned
    from 122–3
  fear of 59
  post-mortems of 123
  preparing for 102
  and taking bold risks 122–3
fake news 302
Farberware 286
fashion industry, ethical 340
Fashion Revolution 340
FBI 72
fear of failure 59
Feld, Brad 65, 66
Felten, Obi 113–14, 115, 120, 123
Fieldcrest 331, 332
Filecoin 303
film industry 188–90, 193
FilmNet 317
Fin24.com 314
Financial Times 346
Fink, Larry 294
Finland 80–94, 98–101
FINN.no 325
First International Computer
  298
fit for purpose 78–9
Flatebø, Svein 292, 293
Flipkart 310, 324
Florida, Richard 238
Flying Kangaroo 243–59, 260
Foghorn project 105–6, 121–2
Forbes 265, 298
Forbes India Rich List 335
Ford, Henry 319
foresight function 59–60
forgiveness 186
Formosa Plastics Group 298
Fort Gordon, Georgia 75
Fortum 92 42 152
Foster, Richard N. 9
Founders Factory 139
Founders Forum 139

Foursquare 90
Fox Broadcasting 129
Foxtel 35, 37
Francis Crick Institute
  ('Crick') 222–6, 242
Franklin, Ben 7
Franklin, Rosalind 225
Freeman, Richard 227–8
Freiberger, Paul 264
Freud, Sigmund 275
Friis, Janus 182
Fritz, Robert 4
FTSE 100 companies 9
fuel, carbon-neutral liquid
  103–6, 121–2
Funderbeam 180
Funston, Brian 243–4, 245–7,
  249, 251, 254, 258
Fusion 360 189, 195
FutureCon 104
future investments 204
Future Meat Technologies
  277
FutureX Capital 281
Fysh, Hudson 257

Gamble, Will 71
Gao, Louie 270–1
Gap 340
Gartner 287
Gates, Bill 32
GE Appliances 279–80, 288
Gehry, Frank 130
General Electric 7, 130
General Motors 195, 293
Gertner, Jon 224
GitHub 69
Gladwell, Malcolm 149
Glaeser, Edward 238
Glamour 311
Glitch 309
Global Innovation Index 159
Global Innovation Institute 8
Global Innovation Manage-
  ment Institute 8
*Global Innovation Science
  Handbook* 2–3
Global Positioning System
  satellites 67–8
Glover, Sarah 47

Glowfrog 225
goals, identifying clear 147
Goenka, Balkrishan (BKG)
  333, 335–6, 344
Goenka, Dipali 332, 333, 336,
  337, 342–3, 344
Gold Spike 239
Goldman Sachs 129
Golergant, Jonathan 22
Google 29, 82, 141, 154, 184,
  326
  Android team 272
  Artificial Intelligence (AI)
    100
  Burning Man 234
  cloud services 300
  co-working spaces 236
  customer data 250, 258, 301,
    302
  European headquarters 222
  former staff 65, 232,
    267, 271
  Google Android 298
  Google Brain 108, 113
  Google Glass 111, 112, 115
  Google Pixel 297
  Google[x] 103–25, 201, 230
  HTC deal 297
  insurance 346
  investment in 352
  Nest Labs 350, 351
  objectives and key results
    tools 15
  search engine techniques
    34
  success of 269, 280
  transactions 170
  Zeitgeist (2013) 107
  Zeitgeist (2017) 52, 54
Gorrie, Dr John 4
Grant, Lesley 253
Grant Hotel, Oslo 292
Greene, Robert, *The 48 Laws
  of Power* 4
GRid70 236, 242
Guardian 15
guided cooking 285–92
Guitar Hero 228
Gujarat 332, 335
Gulczynski, Chris 131, 143

Ha, Ian 127–8
Haataja, Meeri 100
Hack the Air Force 63
Hack the Army 63
Hack the Pentagon 61–79
HackerOne 63
hackers, ethical 61–79
Hagens Berman Sobol
    Shapiro 333
Half-Life 54
Al Hammadi, Maryam 160
Hammersley, Ben 174
Han Guo Min 210
HanaHaus 242
Hangzhou 208, 211, 212–13,
    214
Hangzhou Daily 214
Hannun, Kathy 103–5, 106,
    109, 121–3
Hansson, Ardo 178–9
Harper, Caleb 229
Harper's Bazaar 142
Harvard University 18, 21, 32,
    226–7
Harvey, Larry 231–2, 233
Hatch Labs 130–5, 142
    Hatch Value System 141
    MatchBox (Tinder) 127, 128,
        131, 132–5, 143–4, 146
Haussila, Timur 55, 59
Hay Day 52, 55
healthcare
    Peru 28, 39, 41
    Pohjola Terveys 81–5
Heart Attack Grill 239
HeathCare.gov 65
Hedges, Matthew 163
Heikkilä, Sonja 92
Heimtextil (2018) 339
Helsinki 80–1, 83, 85, 98
Helsinki Mission 100
Hepburn, Katharine 43
Herd, Michael 142
Herman Miller 196
Heron Tower, London 46
Hertzog, James Barry
    Munnik 314
Hessel, Andrew 201, 202
Hestan Commercial 288
Hestan Cue 288

Hestan Smart Cooking (HSC)
    285, 286–92, 308
Hestan Vineyards 290
Hewlett-Packard 113
Heywood Hill bookshop
    94–8
Hinrikus, Taavet 181–3
Ho, Matilda 277, 283
HOK (Hellmuth, Obata +
    Kassabaum) 225
Hollein, Hans 29
Holsether, Svein Tore 293–4
Home Box Office (HBO)
    311–12
Home & Textiles Today 337
Hong Feng 267
Hong Kong 320–3
Horizons Ventures 212, 300
Hotstar 13–14
Houston, Drew 35
Hoyts 248
Hsieh, Tony 236–9, 240, 241
HTC 297–306, 308
    HTC Coin 304
    HTC Vive 299, 300
Huami 266, 269
Huang, Wei 227–8
Huawei 280, 297
Hugo, Victor 166
human rights 150, 154, 162–3
Human Rights Watch 154, 163
Humane Genomics 202
humiliation, preparing for 330
HygroCotton 335

I Like That 137
IAC/InterActiveCorp 128,
    129–35, 139, 141, 143–6
IAG 138
IAOIP (International
    Association of
    Innovation Professionals)
    1–3
IAOIP (International
    Association of
    Innovation Professionals)
    Academy 3
IBM 149, 172, 197, 204, 269
Icebreaker 340
Iceland 20, 138

iCHUNMi 280
ideas
    copying 147
    power of 167
IDEO 40, 64, 277
    Innova Schools 18, 19–20
    La Victoria Lab 23, 24, 40
    Palmwood 162
    Paul Bennett 161, 162
iHealth Labs 268
Ilves, Toomas Hendrik 171,
    180
Imperial College Business
    School 160–1
improvements, small 185
incentives, budgetary 221
The Incredibles 188
India 177, 332, 335, 341
Indian Institute of Technol-
    ogy Delhi 337–8
Indiegogo 279–80, 284
Industrial Light & Magic 188
influential friends, leaning on
    345
InfraWorks 189
initial coin offering (ICO) 178,
    179, 180, 181
Inkafarma 25, 28, 41
InnoCentive 276
InnoSurvey® 5
InnoSurvey™ 5
Innova Cercado school, Lima
    17–18
Innova-Con (2018) 1–8, 348
Innova Schools 18–23, 25, 32–3,
    40
Innovation Diploma Team
    160–1
Innovati°n360 5
Instagram 90, 240
Institute of Public &
    Environmental Affairs,
    Beijing 340
insurance 346–9
Intel 8
intellectual property
    protection 307
Interact 196
interactive saucepans 285–92
Interbank 25, 27

Interbank Tower 21, 25
Intercorp 18–33, 39–40, 41
International Association of
    Innovation Professionals
    (IAOIP), Innova-Con
    (2018) 1–8
International Commerce
    Centre, Hong Kong 321
International Finance Centre,
    Hong Kong 45, 320
*International Journal of
    Innovation Science* 2, 3, 6
International Organization
    for Standardization 3
International Society for
    Professional Innovation
    Management 8
International Spy Museum 1, 3
internet-enabled saucepans
    285–92
Internet of Things 99, 269–70
investments
    defining strategic 308
    external investments 205
iPads 285, 288
iPhones 88, 129, 153, 238–9,
    262, 267, 287, 309, 350
iPods 9, 350, 351
ISIS 61
Islamic fighters 175
ISO 279 3
Ito, Joi 228–9
iTunes 35, 309
Ivan the Terrible 172
Ive, Jony 263

James, Jerry 232
Jawbone 270
Jetstar 252–3, 261
Jetstar Group 253
Jetstar Hong Kong 253
Jiwani, Altaf 332, 333, 334, 336,
    337, 341, 342
JKMM Architects 89
JLab 147
Jobs, Steve 6, 73, 121, 273
    influence on Lei Jun 262,
        264, 281–2
    iPhone 287
    iPod 350–1

Pixar Animation Studios
    229–30, 231
    quotes by 7, 8, 77
Johannesburg Stock
    Exchange 313
John Lewis 137, 147
Johnson, Clarence 'Kelly'
    116–17
Joint Enterprise Defense
    Infrastructure (JEDI) 74,
    76
Jokela, Rami-Johan 218, 219
Jones, Benjamin 227
Jones, Felicity 74
Jones, Piers 15
Jouret, Guido 216–17, 218,
    219–21
Joyce, Alan 247, 248, 252, 253,
    258–9
Joyo.com 267
J.P. Morgan 353
Jumeirah Emirates Towers
    Boulevard 155
Jyn Erso initiative 74–5, 79

Käärmann, Kristo 182–3
KakaoTalk 33
Kalahari.net 314
Kalba Ring Road 154
Kaljulaid, Kersti 183
Kalmar 294
Kamala Mills, Mumbai 334
Kamet 348
Kansil, Melanie 38, 41
Kappa Kappa Gamma
    sorority 126–7
Karhinen, Reijo 83
Kayak 244
Keller, Thomas 285, 288
Kellogg Foundation 20
Kelly, Mervin 224–5
Kickstarter 233, 271, 288,
    289–90, 299
Kiev 177
Kik Interactive 33
kill metrics 105, 106, 121, 124
Kindle 228
King, David 222–4, 225, 226
Kings High School, Cincinnati
    72

Kingsoft 267
KLM 256
Knowledge and Human
    Development Authority
    159
Kodak 327
Kohane, Isaac 226–7
Kohl's 341
Kongsberg 294
Korean Presbyterian Church
    299–300
Korjus, Kaspar 168–72, 176,
    177–8, 179, 180, 183–4, 186
Korjus, Ruufus 176
Kotipizza 91
Kotka, Taavi 170
Koum, Jan 33–4
Kowalski, Jeff 189–90, 193–4,
    195, 196, 199, 201, 202, 205
KPIs (key performance
    indicators) 294
KPMG 337
Kremlin 174
Kuka robots 22, 113, 187
Kuopio 83
Kutcher, Ashton 181
Kyttänen, Jarkko 93, 94
Kyungjoon Lee 226–7

L Marks 137–8, 147
La Casita 27
La Victoria Lab 23–4, 28,
    40, 41
LaBentana 27–8
Laika 29
Langley, Samuel Pierpont 354
laser sintering 277–8
Lasseter, John 230
Lauver, Captain Steven 5
Le Bon Coin 325
le Carré, John 94–5
leaders 77
LeaderShape 115
leadership 166
LEGO 191
    LEGO Mindstorms 228
Lei Jun 262, 263–7, 270, 272,
    274, 280, 281–2, 283
lessons learned 122–3
Levy, Steven 115

LG 299
Li Ka-shing 212, 300
Li Ming 273, 274
Lima, Innova Cercado school 17–18
LINE 33
LinkedIn 326
listening 329
Litecoin 177
Liu, Kerry 211–12, 213
Liu De 267, 268–70, 271, 281
Liverpool Street railway station, London 44
Lloyd's of London 138
Loayza, Maria Paula 23, 27
Lockheed Martin, Skunk Works 116–17, 123
LOHAS Park Station 323
London Overground 320
Look@World 173
Loon 108, 112, 113, 119–20, 123
Looney Tunes 10
Loong, Simon 212–13
Loosemore, Tom 26
L'Oréal 139
Lu Jiajin 216
Lu Xun 318
Lucas, Edward 171
Lucas, George 188
Luckey, Palmer 299
Luebkeman, Chris 56–7, 59–60
Lufthansa 248
Lund, Rohan 35–6, 38, 39, 40, 41
Luoma, Kristian 90
'LuxiPure' 334
Lympo 181
Lynch, Chris 64–70, 72–4, 76–7, 78

M-Net 313, 317
Ma, Emily 109
Ma, Jack 272
Ma, Pony 272, 319, 320
MaaS 87, 92
Mabrook Ma Dabart ceremony 148
McGee Group 44–8
McGinness, Paul 257

McGrath, Rita Gunther 9
Mackey, Jim 43–8
McKillen, Paddy 44, 45
McKinsey 13, 293–4, 310
McManus, Mickey 190–1
Macron, Emmanuel 171
Macworld convention 129
Mad Paws 256
Maduro, Nicolás 179
Maestro Health 348
Mail.ru 310, 324
Mainspring 129
Makani 115
Malan, D. F. 314–15
Malaspina, Oscar 28–9
Malthus, Thomas, *An Essay on the Principle of Population* 12
Manchester United 136
Mandawewala, Rajesh R. 335
Mandela, Nelson 315, 316
Manifesto for Agile Software Development 245–6
Manly Fast Ferry 38
Manninen, Tuomas 98–9
Mansoor, Ahmed 163
Mao Zedong 266
Marin Software Partners 197
Marina Bay, Singapore 50
Marinchip Systems 197
Marisca, Eduardo 25–6
Mars 340
Mars (planet) 151
Marx, Karl 96
Mascot 243
Masdar 151
Mass Transit Railway 320
Massachusetts Institute of Technology (MIT) 204, 226, 228
Mastercard 252
Match Group 135, 141, 142–5
MatchBox 126–7, 131, 132–5
see also Tinder
Match.com 128, 132, 133, 146
Mateen, Alexa 132
Mateen, Justin 131–2, 141–2
Mattis, James 76
Maya 187–9
Maybourne Hotel Group 44

Mayfair, London 94
Mayfield Mall, Mountain View 113
Mayo Clinic 23
measurement, creating culture of 166
Media Lab 228–9
Media24 314, 316
Medical Research Council 223
Medium 178
Meetic 128
Meijer 236
Meld 288, 289
Mercedes-Benz 138
Mercury 27
Mercy Health 236
Merkel, Angela 171
Messi, Lionel 7
Messier, Jean-Marie 317
Metropolitan Transportation Authority, New York 323
Meyer Industries Limited 286, 290–1, 305
Mi 262–75, 280–2, 283
Mi.com 265, 267
Mi Fan Festival 273
Mi Home Stores 266, 267
Michelin stars 285
Mick, Sarah 143
Microsoft 118, 136, 287, 297
   Bill Gates School 32
   Chris Lynch 73
   iPhones 287
   Microsoft Kinect motion sensor 81
   research unit 204
   Skype 15
   success of 269
   Window CE personal digital assistant 298
   Windows 198, 297
Millennium Bridge, London 45
Millennium Falcon 187
Mills, Richard 226–7
Milne, Oswald 43
Milz, Christoph 288–9, 290, 291
MINI 236
mining 302–3, 304

MiPop 'popcorn parties' 266, 273, 282
MIRS (Military Entrance Processing Command Integrated Resource System) 70–2
mistakes, learning from 186
MIT 21
Mitford, Nancy 95
Mitu 266
MIUI operating system 263, 267, 274
mobile phones
crypto phones 300–6
HTC 297–306
iPhone 88, 129, 153, 238–9, 262–3, 267, 287, 309, 350
Xiaomi 262–75, 280, 297
Mobile World Congress 299
Modi, Narendra 335
Mohammed bin Rashid Al Maktoum, Sheikh 148–50, 151, 152, 156, 160
Mohammed bin Rashid Centre for Accelerated Research 157
Mohammed bin Rashid Centre for Government Innovation 151, 155
Mohammed bin Rashid Government Excellence Award 160
Mohammed bin Rashid Space Centre 151
Mohammed bin Rashid Space Settlement Challenge 157
Mohan, Ajit 13, 14
Monett, Jon 3
Monotype 140
Moody's 248
moonshots 103–25, 230
Moore, Gordon 8
Moore's Law 8, 39, 196, 207
Moorjani, Dinesh 128–31, 132, 133, 134–5, 141
Morgan Stanley 293
Moritz, Michael 326
Mothership 181
motivation 122
Motorola 267

Move.mil 76
MTN 314
MTR Academy 323
MTR Corporation 320–3, 329
Mumbai 332, 334
Muñoz, Joe 131
Museum of the Future, Dubai 156, 166
Musk, Elon 6, 29, 192, 234
MVVs (mission, vision, values) 5
my AFN 62

Nakamoto, Satoshi 302
Nakasone, General Paul 68
NanoBond 290
Nanocore 335
Narang, Varun 14
narratives, compelling 308
NASA 7, 229
Naspers 308–11, 312–20, 323–7, 328–30
National Party 311, 314–15, 316
National Roads and Motorists' Association (NRMA) 35–9, 40, 41–2
NATO 68–9
Natural History Museum, London 14–15
needs, customers' 40–2, 102, 260, 350
Negroponte, Nicholas 228
NEi Software 196
Nest (National Endowment for Science, Technology and the Arts) 160–1
Nest Labs 350–1
Net Promoter Scores 39, 84
Netfabb 195
Netflix 64, 170, 211, 287, 302, 352
Netscape Navigator 70
Nevada desert 232–5
New Enterprise Associates 122
New Establishment Summit 263
New York Fashion Week 111
New York Stock Exchange 145

New York Times 78, 354
Bumble 143
Google Glass 111
Joi Ito 228
Lei Jun 264
Michael Moritz 326
Netflix 287
Rich DeVaul 104
Steve Jobs 229
New York University 24
News24.com 314
NeXT 230
nib 248
Nielsen 210, 213
Nine Entertainment 38
Ninebot 266
Ninebot Mini 270–1
Nissan 92
Nobar 180–1
Nobel Prize 7, 116
Nokia 90, 98, 327
competitiveness of 6, 88, 296–7, 298, 309
digital health 217
Northwestern University, Illinois 227
'not-invented-here' culture 221, 352
Novartis 123
Nurse, Sir Paul 224, 225

Obama, Barack 65, 66
Oculus Rift 299
Odeo 309
OECD countries 181
Oechsle 25
Oerlikon, Switzerland 216–17
Oertzen, Tom von 253, 254
O'Hara, Jorge 28
OkCupid 128
Olapic 140
Olympics Aquatic Centre, Beijing 50
Omo 140
Omo Express 140
One Hyde Park, Kensington, London 46
One Library Per Child 300
OnePlus 274, 297
122 Leadenhall Street, London 44

The Onion 10–11
OP Financial Group 81–94,
    98–101
  New Businesses 89, 92–3
  OP Lab 90
  Personal Finance Manager
    app 99
  'smart cast' 81, 100
OP Kausiauto 92
OP Kevytyrittäjä 91
OP Kulku 92
OP Matka 93
Opal Nugget Ice Maker
    279–80
OPKassa 87
Orange 236, 242
Orbital Insight 220
Øresund Bridge 45
organic cotton 341, 342
Organisation for Economic
    Co-operation and
    Development 17
Organovo 201
Orgoo 131
Oritain Global 339
Orvik, Bjørn Tore 293, 294
Østbø, Petter 293–4, 295,
    296–7, 308
Osuuskassojen Keskuslain-
    arahasto 81
Otto 293
Oulu 83, 91, 98
outsiders, bringing in 328

Paananen, Ilkka 52–3, 54, 55, 56,
    59
Page, Larry 108, 115–16, 118,
    120, 232
Pages24.com 314
Palantir 64
Palmwood 162
Palo Alto Research Center
    (PARC) 103, 104–5, 116
Palovakuutus-Osakeyhtiö
    Pohjola 81
Pambakian, Rosette 144
Pan Am 256
paperwork 147
Paramount Pictures 129
Parekh, Keyur 342

Park, Todd 66
Parker, Robert 290
partnerships 261
  importance of 123
Patel, Dinesh 45–6, 48, 58
Patouchas, Alexander 55
Patreon 276
Patterson, Simon 15
Pawshake 255
Payment Highway 87
PayPal 171, 181, 326
Peninsula Curling Rink 113
Penker, Magnus 5
  *The Complete Guide to
    Business Innovation* 5
Pentagon 61–79
performance indicators 166
permissionless innovation
    228
Perry, Neil 251
Peru 17–33
  education 17–22, 31–3, 39–40
  finance 23–8
  healthcare 28, 39, 41
Perú Champs foundation 21
Perú Pasión 31
petro 179
Peura, Masa 89–90, 91–2
Phi-X174 bateriophage 201
phones 9
  crypto phones 300–6
  HTC 297–306
  iPhone 88, 129, 153, 238–9,
    262–3, 267, 287, 309, 350
  Xiaomi 262–75, 280, 297
Pier 9, Embarcadero, San
    Francisco 187, 190–4,
    199–201
Pink, Daniel, *Drive* 58
Pinterest 289
Pipedrive 181
Pivo 91
Pixar Animation Studios
    229–31
Plattner, Hasso 242
Playtech 181
PlentyOfFish 128
PLOS ONE 226–7
PLP Architecture 226
Plug and Play 90, 139

Pohjola 81, 86
Pohjola Hospital, Helsinki
    80–1, 83, 85
Pohjola Terveys 82–5
Pokémon Go 9
Pokorny Lichtarchitektur 225
PolyScience 289
Porat, Ruth 120
Portugal, Andrea 21
Postal Savings Bank of China
    208, 209, 212, 214, 216
'potential game-changers' 11
Prager, André 119
Preiss, Otto 221
Premier League 135, 136
prices, reducing headline 283
PricewaterhouseCoopers 337
Princeton University 32
processes, improving on 123
Procter & Gamble 20, 57, 276
Project Wing 108, 112–14,
    119–20
prototypes 102, 166, 205
Provenance 340
psychological safety 122
PubMed 227
Purdue University 157

Qantas 243–59, 260
  AVRO 255–6
  Frequent Flyer 256
  Qantas Loyalty Ventures
    244–5, 246–54, 257–8, 261
  Qantas Cash 252, 258
  Qantas Golf Club 248, 254
  Qantas Insurance 246, 247,
    248–9, 254, 255
  Qantas Money 246, 251–2, 255
QQ 310, 319
QR codes 338
Quality of Life Plus 3
Queensland and Northern
    Territory Aerial Services
    244
questions, refining 124

R3 91
Rabe, Lizette 315, 323–4
Rad, Sean 131–2, 141, 142, 143,
    144, 145

Raford, Noah 166
Ragged Edge 236
Rank Xerox 327
Ratatouille 229
Raye 7 90
real-estate, Finland 94
Rebel Alliance (DDS) 62–79
recruitment 77, 122
    tactical 328
Red 187
Red Planet 250
REEF Associates 225
research 167
resilience 330
responsibility, taking 343
Revit 189
RFID 338–9
Richemont 317
Riddle, Mike 196–7, 198
Ries, Eric 91, 245
ring-fencing 261
risk 307
    being comfortable with
      284
    taking bold risks 122
Rive, Lyndon 234
Roborock 280
robot-human collaboration
    188–90, 193
RoC 238
Rockpool 248
Rodríguez-Pastor, Carlos
    (CRP) 18, 19, 24–5, 26, 27,
    29–33, 40
Rodríguez-Pastor Mendoza,
    Carlos 30–1
Rõivas, Taavi 181
role modelling 308
roll-outs, speedy 147
Rolling Stone 132
Romero, Alex 61–3
Roos, Karen 311, 317
Royal Ascot 335
Royal London Hospital,
    London 222
Royal Warrant 94
Rubikloud 211–13
Rubin, Slava 280, 284
Russia 172, 174
Rutgers University 157

S&P 500 companies 9
Saarni, Samuli 82–3, 84–5, 101
St Bartholomew's Hospital,
    London 222
Samsung 131, 281, 297, 298, 299
    Samsung Electronics
      North America 129
Samuelian, Jean-Charles 349
San Felipe Neri, Los Olivos 19
San Francisco 187, 190–4, 199,
    231
San Miguel Industrias 22
Sandboxes 4
Sandia National Laboratories
    3
Sanoma 93
Santos, Renato P. dos 181
SAP 236, 242
Sarie 323
saucepans, interactive 285–92
Saunasaari, Helsinki 52
Saunders, Daniel 138, 146
Savoy Hotel, London 44
Schibsted 310, 325
Schmidt, Eric 76, 232
schools
    Cuautitlán Izcalli, Mexico
      20
    Innova Cercado, Lima
      17–18
    San Felipe Neri, Los Olivos
      19
Schuman, Khaled 337
Science 227
Searls, Doc 232
Second Avenue Subway, New
    York 45
Second Home 235–6
Segway 266, 270
Seoul 177
Sequoia Capital 326
Seven West Media 35
Shabib, Amal bin 148, 150
The Shard, London 45
Shaw, George Bernard 11
Shaw, William 96–7
Shehab, Atraf 164, 165, 167
Shell Oil 217
Shinho 276–7
Shining Path 24

Shipfunk 91
Shitter 127–8
Shunwei Capital 265
Sikkut, Siim 170, 180
Silicon Valley 118, 122, 136, 166,
    263
    Burning Man 234–5
    innovation and 7
    Singularity University 152,
      191–2, 215
    startups in 90, 117
    tours of 3, 10
Silver Lake Partners 15
SilverStone 286
Singer's Sewing Center 113
Singularity University 152,
    191–2, 215
Sinha, Arvind 332
Siri 164, 353
Skolkovo Innovation Centre
    161
Skunk Works 116–17, 123
Sky 313
Skype 15, 182
Skyscanner 244
Skywalker, Luke 75
Slack 309
Slingshot 255
Sloman, Hywel 135–7
Slush 92
Smart Kitchen Summit 288
Smash Land 51–2, 53
Snapchat 33, 138
social media 9, 340
    see also Facebook; Twitter;
    etc
Sofia eConsulting 181
soft skills, value of 221
software 187–205
software-development
    methods 260
SolarCity 234
Solman, Hywel 147
Solutions Studios 4
Sony 228, 281
Sourcemap 340
South Africa 308–16, 323–4, 327
South African Broadcasting
    Corporation (SABC)
    311, 312

South by Southwest (SXSW) 10–11
Southern Methodist University, Dallas 126–7
SpaceX 192
Speicher, Sandy 20
Spotify 11, 12, 38, 39
Sprint 236
staff, empowering 58
Staley, Reina 66, 70, 77–8
Stange, Astrid 347–8
Star India 13
Star Wars 61, 64, 69–70, 74, 188
Starship Technologies 181
startups
    acquisitions of 205
    customers' needs 33, 35, 39
    working with 145–6, 283
State Farm 236
Steam 54
SteamVR 299
Steelcase 236
Stoddart, Patrick 70, 71
stories
    compelling 185
    powerful storytelling 204–5
strengths, identifying 102
Stripe 351–2
Sun, Anmao 276–7
Sun, Harn 276–7
Sun Deshan 276
Sun Microsystems 232
Sunrise Harvest 276
Supercell 52–4, 55–6, 58, 59
Supermercados Peruanos 31
Supima cotton 339, 342
Susman, Galyn 231
Sustainable Apparel Coalition 340
Suunto 100
Swaine, Michael 264
Sweden 172, 325
Swiggy 325
Sydney International Airport 243
Sydney Metro Northwest 320
Sydney Opera House 45
Symbian 34
symbiotic relationships 282

Tagliamonte, Paul 67, 68
TaKaDu 219
talent 145–6, 167
    diversity of 261
Tallinn 168–86
Tamine, Tony 37
Tampere 83
Tang, David 97
Tansley, Arthur 274–5
Taobao 206, 209
Tarabih, Walid 155–6
Target 139, 331, 332–3, 337, 342
targets
    granular targets 166
    target-setting 166
Tatooine 75, 76
Taxify 181
Taylor Fry 250
teams, impact of small 78
TechCrunch Disrupt NYC 132
Technogym 139
technologies
    emerging 307
    exciting people about 308
    investing in 204
Techstars 139, 258
Ted Baker 137
TED Talks 118–19, 192, 199
Teknikk, Marin 294
Telefónica 121, 123, 199
telephones 9
    crypto phones 300–6
    HTC 297–306
    iPhone 88, 129, 153, 238–9, 262–3, 267, 287, 309, 350
    Xiaomi 262–75, 280, 297
Telepiù 317
TeliaSonera 171
Teller, Astro (Brin) 103, 106–10, 111–12, 113, 117–19, 120–1
Teller, Edward 107
Tencent 272, 275
    Naspers' investment in 310–11, 316, 319–20, 324, 327
    success of 280, 324
    Supercell 52
    WeChat 33, 207, 263, 265, 273, 310

10X 116
'tequila moments' 25
Tesco 211
Tesla 86–7, 92, 154, 232, 238, 239
Tessier, Philip 288
Texas International Airlines 256
Textile Association of India 332
third-party validation 345
threats, uncovering 328
3D-printing
    AM Ventures 278–9
    Autodesk 190, 193, 194–6, 201, 202, 203
    buildings 156, 166
    laser sintering 277
    synthetic Phi-X174 bacterio-phage 201
Three Horizons Model 192–3, 194
3YOURMIND 279
Thrun, Sebastian 107, 116
Ticketmaster 129
Tiigrihüpe (Tiger Leap) project 173
time-scales 78
Time Warner 287
Tinder (ex-MatchBox) 126–7, 128, 131, 132–5, 139, 141–6, 258
TIPS 3
Toffler, Alvin 205
TOM Group 212, 215–16
Tomorrow Labs 90
Tossed 147
towels 331–45
Toy Story 2 230–1
Toyota 189
TransAmerica Building 191
Transferwise 181, 182–3
transformation 329
transparency 59, 344
Transport for London 320
Travelodge 38
Treaty of Westphalia (1648) 175
TripAdvisor 129
Tropic Biosciences 277

Trump, Donald 46
Trusko, Brett 1–3, 7–8
Trusko, Kirsten 3
trust 59
  enhancing customers' 102
  winning 283
Truth and Reconciliation
  Commission 315
Tseung Kwan O Line 323
Tunki 27
'tunking' 23
Turing Award 116
Turkish cotton 342
Turku 83
Turner, Fred 234–5
Turner Broadcasting 138
20th Century Fox 129
21st Century Fox 13
Twitter 128, 136, 264, 309, 319,
  340, 353

UAE 148–67
UAE Hackathon 161
UAE Innovation Month 161
UAE Vision 2021 151, 165
Uber 154, 216, 232, 248, 272,
  293
Ule 207–16
Under Armour 195
unfair advantages 260, 261
Unilever 340
  New Business Unit 139–40
  Unilever Foundry 140
  Unilever Ventures 140
United Airlines 256
United States Air Force 5
United States Congress 71
  House Armed Services
    Committee 76
United States Department of
  Agriculture 337
United States Department of
  Defense (DoD) 12, 61–79
United States Department of
  Justice 63
United States Department of
  Veterans Affairs 65–7
United States Digital Service
  (USDS) 65–6, 72
United States Marines 61

United States Natural
  Resources Defense
  Council 340
Universidad Tecnológica del
  Perú (UTP) 21–2
University of California,
  Berkeley 18, 21, 30
University of Cambridge 151,
  160–1
University of Liverpool 157
Unix 116
Unmortgage 236
USA Broadcasting 129
Uzzi, Brian 227

validation, third-party 345
values
  defining fundamental 260
  identifying 101–2
Valve 54–5, 299
Van Name, Tim 76, 78
Vancl.com 267
Vanity Fair 263
Vapi 335
Vard 294
Vegas 236–41
VegasTechFund 239
Venezuela 175, 179, 184
Venter, Craig 149
Veriff 181
Verily 108
Vesaniemi, Nina 80–1, 85
VIA Technologies 298
Victoria & Albert Museum,
  London 46
Vidya Mandir, Anjar 336
viewpoints, diversity of 261
Viik, Linnar 172–3, 174, 175–6,
  185–6
Villa Bonne Nouvelle 236
Vimeo 129
Virgin Australia 252
Virgin Hyperloop One 158
virtual reality 299, 300
visions, big 166
visual effects software 187–90
Vitatech Electromagnetics 225
Vivendi 317
Vogue 111
Volkswagen 235

von Fürstenberg, Diane 111
Vosloo, Theunissen 'Ton' 311,
  312–13, 316, 328
VTF Capital 239

Walker, John 197–8
Wallace, Alfred 12
Walmart 209, 324, 332, 333
Walton, Abram 6–7
Wang, Charlene 298
Wang, Cher 297–9, 300, 303,
  305–6, 308
Wang, Tricia 40
Wang Yang 216
Wang Yung-ching 298, 299
Wanxiang 208
Wanxiang Innova City 208
Warren County Juvenile
  Detention Center 72
Waterstones 95
Watson 149
Watson, James 225
Waymo 108, 112, 123, 293
Web 2.0 301–2
Web 3 302
WeChat 33, 207, 263, 265, 273,
  310
Weibo 273
Weideman, Esmaré 316
WeiFund 303
Wel-Trak 338–9, 341, 342
WeLab 212–13
Welspun Group 335
Welspun India 331–45
Welch, Jack 10, 130
WeLend 212–13
Wellcome Foundation 223
Wells Fargo 30
Weltanschauung 135–6
Wen-Chi Chen 299
Wener, Lou 206–7, 208–9, 210
Western Direct Marketing 256
Western Electric 116
WhatsApp 33–5, 39, 42, 163
White House 72, 290
Wikipedia 301
Wilkins, Maurice 225
William Morris Agency 129
WiMax 4G phones 298
Wimbledon 335

INDEX

Windward 220

Wing 108, 112–14, 119–20

wins, small 79

WIRED 6, 9–10, 152, 228, 239, 307

   Estonia 174

   Google 115

   revenue models 259–60

   WIRED Consulting 259

   WIRED Health 259

   WIRED Money 259

Wirth, Olivia 249–51, 254–5, 256–8

Wishlist 248

Wiswell, Lisa 62–3

Within Technologies 196, 205

Wolde, Andre Ten 353

Wolfe, Whitney 126–7, 128, 132, 141–2

Wolverine 236

Wolverton, John 3–4

Woods, Sharon 71–2

Woolworths 248, 251

WoraPay 137

workspace architecture 222–42

World Economic Forum 165, 263

World Government Summit 149, 159

World Wide Fund for Nature (WWF) 340

World Wide Web 301–2

Wren, Christopher 223

Wright, Orville 354

Wright, Wilbur 354

Wuchty, Stefan 227

Wujec, Tom 199

X (Google [X]) 103–25, 201, 230

   Dandelion 122–3

   Foghorn project 105–6, 121–2

   Rapid Evaluation 104–6, 114

X-Road 173, 185

Xerox 103, 116

XGIMI 280

Xi Jinping 290

Xiabao 206

Xiaomi 262–75, 280–2, 283, 297

Xtreme Labs 130

Y Combinator 258

Yahoo! 7 35

Yahoo! Shopping 34

Yandex 139

Yaocun 210

Yara Birkeland 294–5

Yara International 292, 293, 294–7, 305, 308

Yaraslav the Wise 172

Yeung, Ken 215, 216

Yeung, Samson 209, 210, 215

Yimishiji 276–7

Yiu, Steve 321, 322, 323

York, Duke of 171

Youth Hub 155

YouTube 50, 108

Yunmi Technology 268

YY 267

Yzusqui, Jorge 19, 20–1, 22

Zappos 237, 238

Zarechnev, Arseniy 181

Zeitgeist festival

   2013 107

   2017 52, 54

Zendesk 61

Zennström, Niklas 182

Zhang, Cynthia 281

Zhejiang province, China 214

Zimi 269

Zuckerberg, Mark 126, 232

ABOUT THE AUTHOR

David Rowan was founding editor-in-chief of *WIRED*'s UK edition and technology columnist for *The Times, GQ, Condé Nast Traveller* and the *Sunday Times*. He travels excessively to meet crazy-driven startup entrepreneurs who are reinventing every industry in fascinating ways. Fortune 100 companies regularly hire him to explain how these startups plan to kill their businesses, and he invests these speaking fees holistically in startups that plan to kill the corporates' businesses. David founded Voyagers.io to build meaningful community through magical travel adventures. And he's still searching for the future.